Reproducing the British Caribbean

Reproducing the British Caribbean

Sex, Gender, and Population Politics after Slavery

JUANITA DE BARROS

The University of North Carolina Press *Chapel Hill*

All rights reserved. Set in Quadraat by codeMantra.
Manufactured in the United States of America.

Portions of this work appeared previously in somewhat different form in
Juanita De Barros, "'A Laudable Experiment': Infant Welfare Work and Medical
Intermediaries in Early Twentieth-Century Barbados," in *Public Health in the British
Empire: Intermediaries, Subordinates, and the Practice of Public Health, 1850–1960*, ed. Ryan
Johnson and Amna Khalid (New York: Routledge, 2012), 100–117, and Juanita
De Barros, "Improving the Standards of Motherhood," in *Health and Medicine in
the Circum-Caribbean, 1800–1968*, ed. Juanita De Barros, Steven Palmer, and David
Wright (New York: Routledge, 2009), 98–120. Reproduced with permission.

The paper in this book meets the guidelines for permanence and durability of the
Committee on Production Guidelines for Book Longevity of the Council on Library
Resources. The University of North Carolina Press has been a member of the Green
Press Initiative since 2003.

Library of Congress Cataloging-in-Publication Data
De Barros, Juanita.
Reproducing the British Caribbean : sex, gender, and population politics after
slavery / Juanita De Barros. — 1 Edition.
pages cm
Includes bibliographical references and index.
ISBN 978-1-4696-1605-6 (pbk : alk. paper) — ISBN 978-1-4696-1606-3 (ebook)
1. Caribbean Area—Economic policy. 2. Caribbean Area—Social policy.
3. Caribbean Area—Population. I. Title.
HC155.5.A5D43 2014
304.6'320972909171241—dc23
2013051115

18 17 16 15 14   5 4 3 2 1

FOR THE PAST AND THE PRESENT

In memory of Gwen De Barros and for Katherine, Martin, and Winfried

Contents

Illustrations and Tables

Acknowledgments

I have many people to thank for their help with this book. I must start with David Trotman, my former Ph.D. supervisor, and Woodville Marshall, professor emeritus at the University of the West Indies and someone who introduced me to Barbados. Both have been generous colleagues and tough readers who provided advice and encouragement at crucial stages of this project. I have also been very fortunate in finding an international group of Caribbean historians whose intellectual enthusiasm and dedication to our field and our craft both inspires and energizes me. At various stages of this project, they have provided the detailed comments and hard but necessary questions I needed. In no particular order, I want to thank Michele Johnson, Leonard Smith, Jacques Dumont, Anne Macpherson, Diana Paton, Audra Diptee, Laurie Jacklin, Tara Inniss, Denise Challenger, Rita Pemberton, Gad Heuman, Keith Laurence, Pedro Welch, and Lara Putnam. I have presented sections of this work at a number of conferences, workshops, and other venues over the years, and I benefited greatly from the comments and questions offered. These include meetings of the Association of Caribbean Historians, the Latin American Studies Association, the Canadian Association of Medical History, the Canadian Association of Latin American and Caribbean Studies, the Society for Caribbean Studies, and the Southern Historical Association, as well as several workshops I attended in the United Kingdom in 2008–9 and invited talks at McMaster University, the University of Michigan, York University, the University of Toronto, and Tulane University. I want to express my appreciation especially to David Arnold, Margaret Jones, Sarah Hodges, Sean Lang, Amna Khalid, Ryan Johnson, Rosanne Adderley, Darlene Clark Hine, and Julius Scott III. Other colleagues who have helped me think through particularly challenging methodical or interpretative problems through well-timed comments or by providing hard-to-get sources include Letizia Gramaglia, Sister Noel Menezes, Adele Perry, Roberta Kilkenny, Claire Millington, Frederick Smith, Alissa Trotz, Harvey Neptune, Samuel Roberts Jr., Aviston Downes, Henrice Altink, Nancy Christie, Nigel Westmaas, Stuart McCook,

Anne Rubenstein, and Elinor Melville. Elinor passed away a few years ago, but I still value the example of careful scholarship, good humor, and dedicated mentorship that she set for me. I have also benefited enormously from the help and encouragement of a wonderful group of historians of medicine, especially Steven Palmer, Anne-Emanuelle Birn, David Wright, and Deborah Neill. I also appreciate the ongoing support and encouragement offered by Franklin Knight, Bridget Brereton, Bobby Hill, Nigel Bolland, and historians whom I first met while I was a graduate student at York University and who continue to be part of my intellectual life, including Paul Lovejoy and Sean Stilwell. I should also thank my colleagues at Western Michigan University, where I first started to work on this project, as well as those at the Department of History at McMaster University, where I have been happily teaching since 2004. I should note especially the helpful comments offered by Megan Armstrong, Tracy McDonald, Stephen Heathorn, John Weaver, Bonny Ibhawoh, and Karen Balcom as well as the support of the three departmental chairs while I was working on this book, Virginia Aksan, Ken Cruikshank, and Pamela Swett. Staff in the history department and the library have been extremely helpful and patient, especially Wendy Benedetti, Debbie Loban, Olga Perkovic, and Kim Picket. I have also been lucky to work with some excellent graduate and undergraduate students at McMaster; our seminar discussions have helped me work through some particularly vexing problems.

A number of grants and fellowships helped fund my trips to archives in Britain, the Caribbean, and the United States and also paid for the invaluable research assistance without which I could not have completed this book. The Social Sciences and Humanities Research Council of Canada provided two substantial grants that funded much of this research, as did a number of smaller grants from the Arts Research Board at McMaster University and York University. Over the years, I have also benefited from financial support from the Wood Institute (in Philadelphia), the Wellcome Trust, the Rockefeller Foundation Archives, and the Du Bois, Mandela, and Rodney Fellowship at the Center for African American Studies at the University of Michigan. These funds helped pay for research trips to the United States, Trinidad, Jamaica, Britain, Barbados, and Guyana, where I was fortunate to find helpful and patient archival and library staff who helped me find crucial sources. This funding (and that provided by the work-study program at McMaster University) also enabled me to employ research assistants whose help has been invaluable. They include especially Ateeka Khan, Laurie Jacklin, John Rankin,

Amanda Vyce, Emily Lukaweski, Hannah Elias, Rachel Cordiner, and Jennifer Squibb.

This work has also been strengthened by the valuable comments and editorial assistance at the University of North Carolina Press offered by the anonymous reviewers, the editorial staff, and senior editor Elaine Maisner. It also benefited from suggestions provided by the anonymous reviewers at Routledge, where some of this material was first published. I am grateful to Taylor and Francis for allowing me to reprint this material.

Finally, I want to thank my family and friends who remind me that there is much more to life than work, as engaging and stimulating as it can be. Karen Green, Anne Simard, and Lynda Shorten have been true, unwavering friends who, along with my other good friends in Hamilton, Toronto, Boston, and elsewhere, have kept me balanced. Most of all, I want to thank my family. My mother died while I was working on this project, but her grace, courage, and wonderful dogged stubbornness will always inspire me. I should also thank my brother and sister, Martin and Katherine, along with their partners and children; my wonderful Auntie Val; and my English cousins whose hospitality makes visiting England such a pleasure. But first and last, I thank Winfried, whose love, patience, humor, and creativity keep me grounded and make me happier than I ever could have imagined.

Reproducing the British Caribbean

Introduction

In 1893, in St. George parish, Barbados, Catherine Barrow gave birth in a mule pen. A homeless woman without friends or family to house her, she stayed in this inhospitable setting for fourteen days. During this time, Barrow received visits from parish authorities and daily rations of rice and milk. As Barrow's opinions were not recorded in the written sources, we can only surmise what she thought of these arrangements. But T. Law Gaskin, a physician and the temporary poor law inspector for Barbados in the early 1890s, did register his views, and they were decidedly mixed. Gaskin was not quite sure what to think. He believed simple compassion demanded that poor women like Barrow have safe places to give birth, and he used her case to push for the establishment of such facilities throughout Barbados. But he worried about the implications of this munificence and was reluctant to be seen rewarding these women for their "immoral" behavior. Finally, he fretted about Barbados's reputation. Gaskin worried that Barrow's story would be discovered by self-righteous Englishmen anxious to find some new moral cause with which to bludgeon Barbados's planters.

Why did Catherine Barrow deliver her child in a stable, and why did colonial officials in British colonies like Barbados care? After the end of slavery in 1834, imperial politicians and philanthropists sitting in London and officials in Britain's Caribbean colonies, as well as doctors, ministers, newspaper editors, and indeed much of the literate classes, were passionately interested in questions around sex and reproduction. In the late nineteenth and early twentieth centuries, colonial governments in Barbados, Jamaica, and Guyana, the main focus of this book, devised new methods for counting births and deaths, crafted regulations governing midwives, trained and hired Afro– and Indo–West Indian women as midwives and health visitors, and built infant welfare clinics that were to be the locus of colonial reproduction policies. These were all part of an attempt to ensure the size and health of British Caribbean populations, one of the goals of the "great experiment" of slave emancipation. But these efforts also reflected concerns expressed in other places in the late nineteenth and early twentieth centuries, notably anxieties about shrinking and "unfit" populations, the "discovery" of mothers and children as worthy subjects of official concern and beneficence, and the emergence of tropical medicine.[1]

In the British Caribbean, ideas about the best ways to deal with the population crisis of the late nineteenth and early twentieth centuries were disseminated and implemented by an ethnically diverse group of officials, physicians, infant welfare workers, and philanthropists who communicated with one another and their counterparts in Europe and the United States. They drew on the intellectual trends that shaped much of the thinking about the health and size of populations and the health of infants and their mothers in this period. Despite the very real differences among the colonies of the British Caribbean, the social and economic commonalities emerging from a shared history of colonialism and slavery ensured similar approaches to the demographic anxieties of the period.

Two historical moments frame my discussion of these issues in the British Caribbean: the end of slavery in 1834/1838 and the series of violent labor protests that swept through this part of the world between 1934 and 1938 and signaled the emergence of the nationalist movements that would start to press for independence in the decades after World War II. In the first half of the nineteenth century, slavery was seen as an obstacle to population growth, and contemporaries judged the success of emancipation on its ability to halt the downward trend. Perceptions of the sexual and domestic practices of African-descended men and women in the Caribbean as uncivilized and immoral informed this interpretation. Although similar condemnations have been hurled regularly at poor men and women, in former slave societies ideas about race played an important role. A kind of racial inheritance and the legacy of slavery itself were seen as condemning black men and women especially to sexual profligacy and neglect of their children, behavior that was believed to doom their infants to early death and Caribbean populations as a whole to degeneration and decline. One hundred years later, commentators on the riots of the 1930s expressed some of the same concerns, but by this point, worries about a surfeit of people mobilized them. Apprehensions about the impact of a "population surplus" were expressed in Barbados in the late nineteenth and early twentieth centuries, but by the 1930s this Barbadian problem seemed to have become a regional one, in which older, racialized views about sex, health, and reproduction intersected with those focusing on the economic and social costs of "overpopulation."[2]

In the intervening years, former slaves, former masters, imperial officials, and newly arrived indentured laborers from South Asia and elsewhere struggled to assert their social, cultural, and political ideas about the shape these free societies should take. For former slaves, access to land, their role on the estates, and the ways they raised their families, celebrated, socialized, and loved brought them into conflict with planters, colonial authorities, missionaries, and other representatives of European and Euro-American "respectability." They cultivated and maintained networks of friends and relatives and developed friendly societies, churches and other self-help initiatives, and by the early twentieth century, labor organizations, all of which provided some certainty to a mostly unenfranchised population in a time of economic hardship. During the period covered by this book, these territories were administered by a mixture of appointed officials and politicians elected under an extremely restrictive franchise that, until the 1940s, limited the vote to men who possessed a minimum amount of property. Propertied women received the vote in Jamaica in 1919; those in Trinidad and Tobago, in the mid-1920s.[3] Before the 1860s, places like Barbados and Jamaica had nominally representative forms of government, but except for Barbados, in most colonies these were replaced by the even less representative crown colony system in the 1860s and 1870s. Gordon K. Lewis has characterized Guyana's crown colony government as "semi-representative," a term he applied to Jamaica's after the 1880s when an elected element was reintroduced.[4] As Patrick Bryan noted, however, this change merely "allowed oligarchs to be elected rather than nominated."[5] At the time of the protests in the 1930s, the electorate remained tiny, comprising 3.3 percent of the total population in Barbados, for example, and 6.6 percent in Trinidad.[6] Within this limited sphere, men and women in the British Caribbean and indeed in the region as a whole attempted to exert pressure on political officials.[7] Nonelite men and women protested to advance their political and social goals, and members of the mostly nonwhite creole middle and professional class used their access to the worlds of formal politics and their cultural capital to do likewise. The emergence of this class was a product of colonial and imperial education systems, diversifying colonial economies, and a growing colonial bureaucracy. Indeed, this last was part of the response by colonial governments to help ensure that the laboring population was big enough and sufficiently healthy to produce the agricultural staples seen as constituting the region's raison d'être, at least in the eyes of planters and Europeans. Some of the products may have changed—bananas became a major Jamaican export, and Trinidad began producing cocoa and developed a petroleum industry—but the demands for labor did not cease.

In the British Caribbean, as in many places in the late nineteenth and early twentieth centuries, concerns about the health and size of populations elicited a combination of personal and political responses. For individuals, the sickness and death of family members and friends, especially of infants, was a personal tragedy. Employers of labor, colonial and imperial officials, physicians, and middle-class and elite philanthropists may have understood this, but they also saw high rates of mortality and particularly infant mortality as an economic and social crisis. Their responses to the British Caribbean population crisis of the late nineteenth and early twentieth centuries involved a mixture of state- and volunteer-supported infant and maternal welfare initiatives and attempts to eradicate diseases seen as especially threatening to the vitality and survival of populations: malaria, hookworm, and venereal diseases. For many members of the foreign and local educated and elite classes, much of the fault lay with poor and mostly nonwhite men and women; they were represented as uncivilized and incapable of following the contemporary sanitary and medical rules seen as preventing illness and death, especially among the young. The Guyanese physician A. J. Craigen spoke for many of his contemporaries when he argued that the rate of infant mortality in Guyana could never fall as low as in places like New Zealand and Australia, which he described as "more temperate and healthy localities" inhabited by "more intelligent and educated people."[8] A member of the educated "colored" elite in Guyana and the man responsible for initiating many infant and maternal welfare measures in this colony, Craigen indicated something of the diverse influences that shaped colonial policies in this part of the world.

Exchanges about these issues freely crossed colonial and imperial boundaries. Communicating with imperial officials in London and with other members of their class throughout the wider Caribbean region ensured that West Indians knew about the kinds of medical and social welfare policies in their sister colonies and in Britain as well as elsewhere in the hemisphere. The arrival of the Americans in the 1910s under the auspices of the Rockefeller Foundation's International Health Commission contributed to this process. As in many colonies, white, British women were on the front lines of these initiatives; a combination of class and ethnicity made them indispensable, at least in the eyes of colonial and imperial officials. But Caribbean women, many of them part of influential colonial families, were at the heart of the infant and maternal welfare projects that aimed to ensure population growth. Impelled by contemporary ideas about the educational and nurturing role that women of their class should play, these colonial women energetically attempted to "raise the standard of motherhood" and thereby advance "civilization" in their islands. Many were white, from elite families of British origin, and from the traditional privileged "colored" class. But increasing numbers were from the black and brown educated and middle classes. Perceptions of the responsibilities and expertise imposed by class and gender underlay their actions, but some black women were also motivated by a desire to "uplift the race." The economic, political, and social diversity of the region and the often acrimonious interactions among diverse groups with competing agendas meant these initiatives could have unpredictable and inconsistent results. But always, policies about reproduction and infant and maternal welfare were subject to pressures exerted by poor and mostly nonwhite Caribbean women.

Similar economic, social, and political structures and a shared history of colonialism meant that these developments occurred in many places in the British Caribbean. This book addresses regional patterns but focuses on three colonies that, taken together, indicate the diverse colonial responses to the population questions of the late nineteenth and early twentieth centuries. In Jamaica, Barbados, and Guyana, imperial demands and colonial goals were mutually constitutive, mediated by Caribbean and British men and women and shaped by distinct political-economic factors. Jamaica's size and economic importance had long earned it imperial attention. It is the third largest island in the Caribbean and the largest in the British Caribbean, and certainly the most populous, and had been an English possession since the mid-seventeenth century. During its height as a sugar-producing island, Jamaica was perhaps Britain's most important colony in this part of the world. It was a major producer of sugar and coffee, the nominal home of scores of absentee planters who made England their effective home, and the target of abolitionist and missionary interests. Taken together, these factors combined to ensure that, to a great extent, representations of Jamaica largely dominated British views of the Caribbean during the period of slavery and into the postemancipation period when the decline of its plantation sector and the emergence of peasant agriculture convinced many in the metropole that emancipation had failed. In the early twentieth century, efforts to revitalize the colonial economy and concerns about the effects of high mortality rates and emigration convinced middle-class and more elite Jamaican men and women, in conjunction with colonial and imperial officials and foreign philanthropists, to launch a series of initiatives geared toward producing a healthy population.

Despite Jamaica's prominence in the eyes of imperial officials, Guyana served as the incubator for many of the state-run public health and social welfare policies that emerged in this part of the world in the late nineteenth and early twentieth centuries. Chronic concerns about the size of its population and consequently its ability to produce the tropical staples on which the health of the economy relied underlay these initiatives. One of only two mainland colonies in the British Caribbean region, Guyana lies on the coast of South America, the only English-speaking territory on the continent.[9] Britain acquired this low-lying coastal territory during the late eighteenth- and early nineteenth-century Napoleonic Wars, and this timing made it a late-developing slave colony for the British and one where planters regularly complained about labor shortages. Most of its sugar estates stretched along a narrow coastal strip or inland up a few major rivers, and in the postslavery period, Guyana's jungled interior became the site of timber and mining production and the destination of many former slaves. After the end of slavery, Guyana's planters, like those in other parts of the British Caribbean, including Jamaica, began importing foreign workers. In the case of Guyana, this was done on a massive scale; planters imported several hundred thousand workers from Asia, Madeira, and West Africa to make up for a perceived labor deficit and to supplement the former slaves who stubbornly insisted on using their freedom to pursue nonplantation livelihoods. Consequently, in the postslavery period, Guyana had one of the most diverse populations in the region. By 1891, for example, South Asians made up around 37 percent of the overall population, a percentage that rose to a little over 40 percent by 1911.[10] The same groups emigrated to other colonies in this period, especially Trinidad, which received the second largest number of South Asian immigrants in the region. Fewer went to Jamaica, where South Asians comprised 1.58 percent in 1891 and a little over 2 percent in 1911.[11] In all these colonies, planters and officials regarded them as a crucial labor source and as necessary to "save" the plantations.

Barbados offers a stark contrast to these colonies and was the source of very different population "anxieties." It was the most populous of the "small islands." With 182,000 souls in 1891, it had significantly more people than Antigua and St. Kitts (with populations of 35,119 and 30,876, respectively) but many fewer than Jamaica (639,491), Trinidad (200,028) and Guyana (270,865).[12] Barbados was geographically compact and densely populated, attributes that convinced imperial and colonial observers that it was overcrowded. Barbados was also one of Britain's oldest colonial possessions, famously nicknamed Little England. It had been colonized by England in the early seventeenth century and, unusually for the Caribbean, did not change hands, remaining a British colony for its entire colonial history.[13] Its economy and landscape were dominated by plantation-produced sugar during the period of slavery and well into the postemancipation years. Unlike Jamaica, Guyana, and Trinidad, most of its inhabitants had been born in the island. In 1891, for example, locals made up 98 percent of the island's population, a figure to which the census's compiler pointed with great pride.[14] Most Barbadians were of African descent (both black and of mixed African and European ancestry, an important socioeconomic distinction during the period covered in this book), but the island was also home to proportionately more whites than both Guyana and Jamaica in the postslavery years. In 1891, approximately 8 percent of its population was defined as white in the census reports, compared with around 2 percent in Jamaica in 1891 and 1.64 percent in Guyana.[15] In Barbados, these numbers fell steadily after the end of slavery, a development that was especially pronounced among the "poor whites," descendants of English, Scottish, and Irish indentured servants who arrived in the seventeenth century. To colonial officials, their decline suggested that the population problems of the day were not restricted to poor Afro-Barbadians, whose behavior was commonly blamed for illness and high rates of death, especially infant mortality. But the response of Barbadian government officials to health problems generally, especially infant mortality, also unsettled ideas about whiteness and civilization, at least from an imperial perspective: In a period when civilization was increasingly identified with developing a "modern" public health infrastructure and protecting infant life, the slow development of infant and maternal welfare initiatives in Barbados made imperial authorities look askance at this Little England.

Concerns about the size and health of populations were expressed widely in the period covered in this book. To varying degrees, government officials and men and women of the middle and professional classes in Europe, the United States, the independent nations of South and Central America, British settler colonies like Australia and Canada, and European colonies in Africa, Asia, and the Caribbean expressed anxiety about the effects of falling birthrates, rising rates of infant mortality, and population "degeneration." Healthy populations were seen as markers of national wealth, a point the British physician and sanitarian Benjamin Richardson emphasized when he coined the phrase "National Health is National Wealth" as the motto for the *Journal of Public Health and Sanitary Review*.[16] As the Argentine Juan Bautista Alberdi famously chimed in from across the ocean, "'To govern is to populate.'"[17] Historians have pointed to worries about the impact of impoverished immigrants and poor urban conditions on population vitality in places such as the United States and Argentina. In France and Britain, losses due to war and the poor performance of recruits influenced thinking (the Franco-Prussian War of 1870–71 for the French and the Boer War, 1899–1902, for the British).[18] Eugenics or the "'science of improving the stock,'" in the words of Francis Galton, helped shape contemporary thinking about these issues.[19] Some advocates wanted to selectively discourage or prevent the "unfit" from reproducing by means such as sterilization and euthanasia, while others wanted to encourage the "fit" to have children and thereby improve "the race," and still others concentrated on improving the lives of children already in existence.[20]

Impoverished men and women were blamed for these problems. Poverty contributed to the poor conditions that condemned many to sickly lives and early death, but they were also represented as at least partially culpable, doomed by ignorance about modern sanitation and hygiene. Poor women in particular found themselves condemned as ignorant and indifferent mothers whose poor mothering skills were seen as contributing to infant mortality. In the colonial world and postslave territories, ideas about race influenced these representations. The cultural practices, social arrangements, and behavior of nonwhite men and women were seen as uncivilized, immoral, potentially deadly, and indicating a profound inferiority to Europeans and Euro-Americans based on biological race. In the slave-owning territories of the Americas, these views provided a justification for slavery and, after its end, part of the lament of its apologists. The discourse of the "bad mother," for example, which targeted poor, marginalized women in numerous societies, including in Europe, took on a particularly toxic element in slave and postslave societies, where it provided part of the racist, ideological apparatus that underlay this system of labor control. It can also be seen as part of the "extinctionist" literature that in the postslavery United States held that former slaves were doomed without white guidance.[21] In colonized territories in Africa, Asia, and the Caribbean, similar representations constituted part of the rationale for colonial control. In the late nineteenth century, "science" was used to give credence to views of innate, biological differences among different groups of humans and their associated social and cultural traits. It was part of the ideological apparatus of the time.[22]

In the nineteenth-century British Caribbean, imperial and colonial officials, planters, and some missionaries associated these representations with assessments of emancipation. Despite the initial optimism with which the end of slavery was greeted, by the 1850s and 1860s, many had come to see it as a failed experiment. In doing so, they echoed planters' negative views of former slaves and of emancipation itself. During the period of slavery, planters and their fellow travelers had regularly expressed negrophobic views and condemned people of African descent as intellectually inferior and morally weak. In the postslavery period, growing disenchantment with emancipation led to what Catherine Hall has described as an "increasing turn to the language of race to explain and justify the inequalities and persistent differences between peoples" in the postemancipation period.[23] Constrained by the economic and political realities of the period, former slaves made decisions about their domestic lives and their livelihoods that saw them condemned by planters and officials. By not working when and where planters dictated and, as Thomas Holt has argued, by "defin[ing] the content of their freedom in apparent opposition to market forces," they were seen as a "different kind of human being," as "wayward children" and "fit subjects for a 'benevolent despotism.'"[24]

Reproduction was also used as a measure of emancipation's success. Worries about shrinking populations and assumptions that slavery itself was the cause underlay much of the rhetoric of British antislavery forces.[25] In the eyes of colonial officials, the two were intimately entangled. Population decline after the end of slavery seemed to suggest that former slaves were not ready for the responsibilities of freedom, unable to take the measures needed to safeguard their own health and that of their families. To planters in the Caribbean as well as to politicians in Britain, the mid-nineteenth-century cholera epidemics in the British Caribbean and the deaths and sickness that resulted were the inevitable result. It was a "political disease," one that seemed to symbolize the failure of emancipation and demonstrate the need for measures to ensure population growth.[26] The epidemics seemed to show that former slaves were "unsanitary subjects" rather than "sanitary citizens." As free people, they were believed incapable of employing the modern and rational medical and sanitary measures required to keep them and their families healthy.[27]

The emergence of tropical medicine as an area of medical research and practice focusing on diseases seen as specific to tropical places intensified this rhetoric. As Alexandra Stern has argued, despite differences in approach and effect, tropical medicine and the "race betterment" movement emerged "during a reconstellation of the diagnostic, therapeutic, and heuristic role of medicine in modern society," and they were united by their "shared vocabulary of racial degeneracy and fitness."[28] Michael Worboys has described tropical medicine as "one of the most powerful tools of empire," and scholars have demonstrated the efforts of imperial officials, researchers, and physicians to keep Europeans and Euro-Americans in their colonies healthy, their continued presence and survival believed necessary for military and economic reasons and for civilization. In the early twentieth century, tropical medicine experts and imperial governments increasingly turned their attention to the colonial peoples who worked in key economic areas such as plantations and mines and implemented a range of public health and medical measures designed to ensure their survival as healthy and (re)productive men and women.[29] Europeans had long feared the tropics as unhealthy, the site of enervating heat and deadly fevers that sickened and killed whites and weakened "natives," and David Arnold has argued that tropical medicine researchers "helped give scientific specificity" to these anxieties.[30] But they did not eradicate them or the demographic and "racial anxieties" with which they were associated.[31] Tropical medicine was also part of the "civilizing mission" and the effort to remake colonial subjects into modern, sanitary "probationary citizen-subjects," to use Warwick Anderson's phrase.[32] This imperial project and the effort to spread the purportedly civilizing and modernizing benefits of modern health and medicine were multinational, involving European nations such as Britain, France, and Germany and the United States under the auspices of military intervention and the Rockefeller Foundation through its International Health Commission.[33]

The colonies and independent nations of the Caribbean were subjects of these imperial medical projects, orchestrated by European governments in France, Britain, and the Netherlands and by the Americans. As this book shows, the British Caribbean was part of the world of British and American tropical medical research, the destination of medical expeditions, and the recipient of imperial attention for many of the same reasons as other parts of the empire.[34] In these colonies, as Steven Palmer has argued, the presence of the Rockefeller Foundation presaged the start of a larger U.S. role in the region, a kind of passing on of "the torch of empire."[35] Here, as in other places, much of this work was undertaken by members of the locally born educated classes, who used them to advance their own interests and help define their own identities.[36]

A combination of state and volunteer efforts geared toward educating poor women in hygienic child rearing and domestic management were part of the project to improve the size and health of populations in Europe, in its colonies, and in the Americas, including the British Caribbean. Most involved midwifery training and included educational initiatives in the form of home visiting undertaken by volunteer and paid female health workers, but public and private institutions providing child care and medical services were also educational sites, including crèches, baby clinics, and hospital maternity wards. In some places, facilities were established to provide pasteurized or breast milk for infants, reflecting the emphasis on the importance of "proper" feeding for infant health. The influence of religious organizations varied; it was stronger in Latin American countries and France and less of a factor in the United States, for example.[37] Many of the early initiatives were located in urban areas; this was the case for the United States and Argentina as well as in British colonies in the Caribbean and Asia. The extent of state involvement differed, but overall it tended to grow as the twentieth century progressed and gained strength especially in the interwar period. Regional and international gatherings held in Europe and the Americas in the first two decades of the twentieth century—such as the 1909 International Sanitary Convention, the 1913 conferences in London and Brussels, and the 1916 Pan American Child Congress—advanced these efforts, as did the social and labor initiatives of the League of Nations.[38] As this book shows, developments in the British Caribbean tended to follow this trajectory.

Women were at the center of maternal education and infant welfare initiatives. Historians have used the term "maternalist" to characterize some of these volunteer and state efforts by middle-class and elite women that were influenced by their belief that "women's superior moral and motherly capacities" qualified them to "represent and protect" poor women and children.[39] These initiatives could be politically empowering for those dispensing the aid and education, leading to involvement in other kinds of social welfare activities and interventions generally in the public realm, including struggles for the vote in Britain, for example.[40] For nonwhite women and white creoles in places like the Caribbean and Latin America, maternalist activities helped distinguish them from the "uncivilized" poor while also helping "uplift" or "civilize" them.[41] In societies where the former shared an ethnic affinity with the poor and where biological race was seen as entangled with the purportedly uncivilized behavior of nonwhite groups, the stakes were especially high. This was the case in the United States, as Glenda Elizabeth Gilmore has shown in her work on African American women's activism in early twentieth-century North Carolina, but it was just as significant in colonial societies, particularly those recently emerged from slavery, such as in the Caribbean.[42] The presence of metropolitan white women in colonial societies who, either voluntarily or for salaries, had the task of "making mothers" highlighted these tensions. In Britain's colonies, white British women were believed necessary to solve a range of social problems that were attributed to the behavior of colonial people, including infant mortality.[43] They arrived in the colonies imbued with an acceptance of European cultural and social superiority and a belief that contemporary European ideas about caring for infants were superior to those held by the "natives." As Barbara Ramusack has noted, they were "cultural missionaries," certain that colonial women would benefit from European "models, principles, and techniques."[44] Some of their number included nurses employed by the Colonial Nursing Association, whose members played an important role in the early twentieth-century British Caribbean, where they trained local women as nurses and midwives.[45] Dispensing a kind of "maternal imperialism," they were part of the imperial ideological and administrative system.[46]

Among the purportedly unhealthy and dangerous practices of nonwhite groups that these cultural missionaries targeted were those involving sex. Europeans and Euro-Americans regularly represented the sexual practices of nonwhite and colonial peoples as immoral and dangerous. Practices such as prostitution, child marriage, and various kinds of "deviant sex" were believed to define the colonized and to demonstrate their "need of the civilizing hand of colonialism."[47] As Pamela Scully has argued, sexuality was a "key site of colonial anxieties," especially in postslavery societies such as South Africa (and the Caribbean), where ensuring that former slaves adhered to particular kinds of "sexual and moral practices" was part of the grounds on which emancipation was judged.[48] Regulating sex helped clarify and determine colonial categories, distinguishing the civilized from the uncivilized, black from white, men from women. Antiprostitution campaigns in the British imperial world and places of U.S. military occupation reflected moral and medical worries about sexual practices. In the Caribbean, examples include the British Contagious Diseases Acts and the venereal disease campaigns by the newly arrived Americans in Puerto Rico and the Dominican Republic. By attacking prostitution, officials hoped to limit the spread of sexually transmitted diseases, which were seen as weakening a nation's fighting strength. In this respect, venereal diseases were strategically significant in much the same way as were "tropical diseases." Indeed, Briggs has argued for a "similarity in structure between the imperial logic of tropical medicine and that of venereal diseases."[49] In the postslavery British Caribbean as in other places, marriage, or rather its absence, was also a source of anxiety. Sexual relationships outside the bounds of legal marriage were seen as uncivilized and unrespectable, but also as dangerous. Brian Moore and Michele Johnson have argued that sex and marriage were "at the very heart of the agenda of the British civilizing mission," a point that scholars have made for other colonial areas as well.[50] Formal marriage was seen as necessary to ensure that children were raised to productive adulthood, and unmarried parents were believed to produce offspring doomed to early death or condemned to become part of a sickly, criminal residuum. In an era when the reproduction of healthy, productive populations was seen as crucial for the health of colonial economies and as a marker of civilization, the stakes were high.

In the colonial world, non-European and nonwhite men and women helped construct these discourses about civilization. As physicians, social workers, clergymen, teachers, and bureaucrats, they preached sermons, wrote newspaper articles, crafted reports, and generally weighed in on contemporary concerns about the health and size of populations. They contributed to what Cooper and Stoler have described as "self-conscious projects of collecting and organizing knowledge."[51] In the British imperial world, including the Caribbean, this took the form of annual reports, government investigations, and increasingly systematic population counts, all of which reflected the "triumphant empiricism" that was part of the apparatus of colonial control and rational modernity.[52] As Benedict Anderson has noted, it was also part of the construction of the "grammar of the colonial state."[53] Census reports and other kinds of statistical accumulations shaped ideas and policies about colonial populations. The massive West India Royal Commission (the Moyne Commission) investigation into the labor protests that shook the British Caribbean is a dramatic example of this kind of "triumphant empiricism." The commission reflected the interest of the British government in crafting a more socially interventionist role for itself in the British Caribbean in an attempt to validate its continuing presence in this part of the world. But in doing so, it looked to the past as much as it did to the future. The British commissioners and many of the British and Caribbean witnesses described the region's populations as unhealthy and as facing high levels of infant mortality, views that had not changed much since early in the century. The British men and women who sat on the commission appealed to long-standing ideas about race, gender, and class to make sense of the population problems they saw. By the 1930s, however, the context was one of overcrowding and surplus populations rather than one of population decline. Like much of the "third world" after World War II, in the 1930s the colonies of the British Caribbean were seen as facing the challenge of coping with overpopulation. In formerly colonized territories in Africa, Asia, and the Caribbean, officials and others worried about the social, economic, and political costs of uncontrolled population growth.[54] The Moyne Commission, though, did not reflect solely the British perspective. Caribbean people helped shape the discourse of population and reproduction in their home territories and the social welfare and health policies that resulted, contributing to this reflection on the past and the future of the Caribbean and drawing from the political and intellectual ferment of this turbulent decade.

This book examines ideas about reproduction and the size and health of Caribbean populations in the British Caribbean from the early nineteenth century to the 1930s. The first chapter explores the debates about population growth in Britain's Caribbean colonies both before and immediately after the end of slavery. It shows their relationship to assessments of the emancipation "experiment" as well as to some of the major crises of the early postslavery period, including the cholera epidemics of the 1850s.

The second chapter focuses on the late nineteenth- and early twentieth-century discussion about the health and size of populations, much of which was centered on the problem of infant mortality. Influenced by ideas in Britain about health and population fitness and by the reports of colonial physicians in the Caribbean itself, officials on both sides of the Atlantic concluded that this problem was particularly prevalent among the majority African-descended population. They pointed to what they saw as the many moral failings of this group, including the nature of their intimate domestic practices. Low rates of marriage and high rates of illegitimate births were held partly responsible for infant mortality. Implementing a range of new ideas about medicine and public health constituted one attempt to deal with this problem. Immigration, especially from India, represented the other key strategy. Both were designed to ensure the population growth needed to sustain the colonial economies.

Chapters 3 and 4 explore the introduction of infant and maternal welfare measures that constituted another element of the Caribbean response to concerns about population health and size. Midwife training programs were introduced first in Jamaica, followed by Guyana and Barbados, part of the effort to replace the "traditional" midwives blamed for infant deaths with "respectable" native women. Gender and racial ideologies meant that white, British women were recruited to train these midwives, who were charged with instructing their largely nonwhite, impoverished clientele in modern, hygienic methods of child rearing. Middle-class women of African descent and members of the traditional elites dominated the volunteer-run baby-saving leagues that also emerged in this period to offer child-rearing advice to poor, mostly nonwhite women. These initiatives served the interests of the colonial state, but they also offered Caribbean women opportunities to realize some of their own personal and professional goals. These chapters emphasize the tensions that resulted when the varying agendas of these different groups came into conflict.

The fifth chapter looks at the influence of the ideas and institutions of tropical medicine on perceptions of Caribbean populations. Although British and American tropical medicine researchers were involved in the investigations conducted in the British Caribbean, they worked closely with colonial physicians, many of them members of the expanding and ethnically diverse Caribbean middle and professional classes. Indeed, for men from these groups, the population problems of their colonies constituted a crisis. As had been the case in the nineteenth century, immigration and implementing the sanitary and other rules of tropical medicine and hygiene were seen as the main solutions. An increasingly interventionist group of imperial officials who saw the health of colonial populations as worthy targets of imperial trusteeship and the arrival of the Americans under the auspices of the Rockefeller Foundation brought Caribbean health into an international arena.

The Conclusion explores the extent to which many of these ideas and approaches continued to be expressed in the 1930s in the context of the Moyne Commission hearings. In doing so, it emphasizes the role of Caribbean men and women in shaping the commission's views and making their own demands.

CHAPTER ONE

Slavery, Emancipation, and Reproducing the Race

Whatever then may be said for West Indian slavery,
this damning thing must be said against it, that *the slaves were dying of it.*

—Charles Buxton, *Slavery and Freedom in the British West Indies*, 1860

IN 1860, A LITTLE MORE THAN twenty-five years after the end of slavery in the British Caribbean, Charles Buxton published a passionate defense of emancipation. The son of Thomas Fowell Buxton, a leading antislavery activist in Great Britain, the younger Buxton summarized some of the reasons his father's generation of abolitionists had advanced to support emancipation. It was brutal and immoral as well as being an inefficient use of labor. It was also a killer. To abolitionists, the demographic consequences of slavery were clear and inexorable and could only be reversed if the system was brought to a speedy end. From the perspective of 1860, it was apparent to Charles Buxton that the growing awareness of slavery's demographic cost had convinced the British Parliament to pass legislation ending slavery; the "population returns" constituted a "death-blow."[1]

For Charles Buxton, emancipation was a moral, economic, and most of all, demographic success.[2] To many of his contemporaries, population growth in the Caribbean after slavery's end was a measure of the "mighty experiment." Ironically, Buxton published his assessment at the very moment when growing numbers of Britons were condemning emancipation as a failure. As former slaves demonstrated their willingness to construct their lives in opposition to British-defined ideas, imperial officials and the British public expressed growing disenchantment with the results of emancipation.[3] Much of this disillusionment was rooted in the gap between the goals of British policy makers and those of Caribbean men and women. Former slaves had their own ideas about what freedom would bring. They wanted control over their working lives, access to land, fair wages and working conditions, freedom of movement, and reunification of the families that slavery had torn apart. Imperial officials had their own goals, the most pressing of which was ensuring economic viability and social stability. To them, the survival of plantations worked by reliable workers was the key to achieving both.[4]

Imperial officials' increasingly negative views about the results of emancipation were also tied to assessments of population growth, which was to be one of freedom's great accomplishments. The initial optimistic assessments that the end of slavery would naturally result in population growth were replaced gradually with much gloomier views. The high death rates consequent upon the mid-nineteenth-century cholera epidemics helped crystallize these views. To many imperial officials and representatives of the colonial elites, former slaves were unable to cope with the challenges of freedom, and their "savage" responses to the epidemics condemned them and their families to premature death. This view of former slaves was part of a hardening racialized rhetoric in this period that represented people of African descent as immoral and undisciplined and incapable of freedom.

Slave Populations

As the quotation by Charles Buxton that introduced this chapter demonstrates, questions about population size lay at the heart of the abolition debates that roiled Britain in the first half of the nineteenth century.[5] In marshaling their arguments against the slave trade and slavery, British abolitionists pointed to the immorality and inefficiency of this labor control system. Written and oral accounts by missionaries and by slaves themselves testified to its brutality and corrupting effects on masters and slaves alike. Adam Smith's arguments had served to convince many that slave labor was less productive and more expensive than that of free workers.[6] But demographic arguments were central to the case against slavery. In the early nineteenth century, in their efforts to convince the British government to pass legislation ending British involvement in the transatlantic slave trade, abolitionists and like-minded government ministers drew on contemporary ideas that populations "naturally" grew and represented the British Caribbean as reflecting this "normal" pattern. This argument had the merit of undermining concerns about the impact of ending the slave trade.[7] The abolitionist and member of the British House of Lords Lord Grenville, for example, calculated that Jamaica's "excess of deaths over births" had declined consistently over the past century and that therefore its population was able to reproduce without the slave trade.[8] As the future prime minister Lord Howick (later Earl Grey) argued, "nature" in the Caribbean would as elsewhere "accomplish her own ends, and . . . the population would maintain itself."[9]

The passage of legislation ending Britain's involvement in the transatlantic slave trade led to the creation of the "population returns" lauded by Charles Buxton. These were a series of reports detailing the number of slaves in each colony as well as births, deaths, sales, and manumissions. After the end of the slave trade, abolitionists pushed for legislation compelling planters to register their slaves and record all population movements. James Stephen, the undersecretary of state for the colonies and a longtime abolitionist, crafted an order-in-council for Trinidad that required planters to provide yearly enumerations of their slaves as well as any changes in their status. Its slaves were registered in 1813; two years later, a similar order-in-council was put in place for St. Lucia.[10] As both islands were crown colonies, the British government could implement policies more directly than was possible for self-governing colonies such as Jamaica and Barbados with their planter-dominated elected legislatures. The assemblies of these two islands passed registration acts in 1816, and the other colonies followed in 1817, although a few laggards delayed until the 1820s.[11]

The returns revealed that overall and in most colonies slave populations declined after 1807.[12] They fell most significantly in late-developing sugar colonies such as Trinidad, St. Lucia, Demerara-Essequibo, and Berbice, somewhat less so in Jamaica. The decline was smaller in long-established sugar-producing colonies, and especially in colonies not devoted to plantation agriculture, such as the Bahamas. Only in Barbados did the number of slaves grow, a development that most historians have attributed to its stage of development as a plantation colony.[13] The population decrease presented an interpretative challenge for abolitionists who had predicted that populations would grow naturally without the slave trade, but they quickly adjusted. They argued that in fact slavery itself prevented the natural growth of the population in opposition to the "law of nature" and used the data to make a case for more humane treatment of slaves and the end of slavery itself.[14] The growth of some slave populations made the population returns less than entirely satisfactory from a propaganda perspective, but abolitionists were adamant about the impact of slavery on population growth.[15] As the abolitionist James Stephen declared, the argument that slavery was "'unfriendly to the multiplication of our species [could not] admit of a doubt.'"[16]

The "amelioration" laws passed in the 1820s were intended to encourage planters to treat slaves more humanely in the hope that the populations would increase.[17] These acts aimed to ameliorate the worst abuses of slavery and prepare slaves for eventual freedom. They encouraged slave marriages and religious instruction, facilitated slave self-purchase, and imposed limits on the imposition of corporal punishment.[18] Although a product of the 1820s, they built on earlier pro-natalist measures. From the late eighteenth and early nineteenth centuries, some planters had attempted to encourage population growth by offering new mothers cash or other rewards, including lighter work duties; others freed women who had borne a certain number of living children from performing onerous physical labor. Doing so was an acknowledgment of the deleterious impact of slavery on the health of mothers, a point that even the proslavery writer Edward Long acknowledged. He observed that the workload of pregnant women had a direct impact on the survival of their infants.[19] Planters also built additional slave hospitals (or "hot-houses") and lying-in facilities and hired more European physicians. A number of Caribbean governments rewarded planters and overseers whose slaves reproduced themselves.[20] All wanted to ensure that more children were born and that they survived to adulthood.

Imperial officials hoped that the legal end of slavery itself on August 1, 1834, would accomplish this aim while also ensuring that the population continued to work on the estates.[21] The Abolition Act gave former slave owners financial compensation for the loss of "their" laborers in the amount of £20 million. Under the apprenticeship system that was to be the transition from slavery to freedom, former slaves older than six years were to provide unpaid labor for their former owners and receive food, clothing, shelter, and medical care. Apprentices were allowed to work during their "free" time for wages, which they could use to buy their freedom early if they chose. Children under six were freed outright, with the proviso that they could be indentured until they turned twenty-one if their mothers were unable to care for them. One hundred special magistrates were hired to oversee the system.[22] The apprenticeship ended two years early, in 1838, following a series of reports of poor treatment of apprentices and conflicts between masters and apprentices, and a renewed abolitionist campaign calling for immediate freedom.

Ironically, given emancipation's goal of ensuring population growth especially through the survival of more infants and children, some aspects of the apprenticeship system were decidedly unhealthy. A number of the pro-natalist policies introduced earlier in the century were abandoned during this period. Some planters withdrew the "indulgences" from their female apprentices that they had provided for pregnant and postpartum women during slavery and stopped providing free medical care for young children.[23] James Thome and Horace Kimball, the American abolitionists who visited Barbados, Jamaica, and Antigua in 1837, declared that the treatment of free children in Jamaica especially was "often very deplorable." Masters did not provide for children, and the parents were unable to. Thome and Kimball maintained that conditions for pregnant and postpartum women had actually deteriorated from what they had been during slavery.[24] Many planters also refused to provide food for the free children of their apprentices. In places like Jamaica, apprentices had access to land where they could grow their own food and provide for their children. In Barbados, where most ex-slaves did not have this, the situation was very different and far more dangerous for children who did not receive food from planters.[25] The Barbadian planter William Sharpe observed that parents removed their children from the estates and gave them to relatives rather than seeing them bound to the plantations. He believed that many ended up dying "from want of care," something he attributed to what he saw as their parents' irresponsible behavior.[26] The Jamaican apprentices cited by the British abolitionists Joseph Sturge and Thomas Harvey had a somewhat different view. They criticized planters' withdrawal of the slavery-era "privileges" that had enabled parents to look after their children.[27] As the apprentices on Oxford Estate noted, "The free children receive[d] nothing from the estate," a point Sturge and Harvey repeated for Barbados.[28]

Sturge and Harvey's book was part of the growing opposition to the apprenticeship system.[29] The anti-apprenticeship campaigners in Britain may have been certain that they bore much of the responsibility for the system's early end in 1838, but the resistance of apprentices also played a role.[30] The governor of Barbados, Sir Murray McGreggor, pushed the colony's planter-controlled assembly to approve its early end to preempt further abolitionist protests and potentially unfavorable (for planters, at any rate) measures by the British government. Legislatures in the rest of the region quickly passed similar measures.[31]

The Mighty Experiment

The "mighty experiment" of slave emancipation began in 1838 with the end of the apprenticeship system.[32] British officials hoped that emancipation would show the merits of free labor over coercion and demonstrate that slaves could be transformed into disciplined, hard-working laborers with consumer desires that only wage labor could supply. These aims, noted the secretary of state for the colonies, Lord John Russell, reflected the "religious and benevolent views of the nation at large" as well as more pragmatic concerns. Russell emphasized the importance of economic matters; the colonies should continue to produce the crops "for which the climate [was] adapted" and purchase British manufactured goods. But he also wanted to see whether Caribbean populations would grow once slavery had ended. He hoped that the former slaves who had been "kept down by legal oppression and licentious morals, consequent on a state of slavery" would "advance in numbers under the institution of marriage, and in the enjoyment of property." He was optimistic about the long term: The "increase in numbers, if accompanied by education and civilised habits [would] lead to increase in industry and be productive of wealth."[33]

Russell made these comments in a letter to Guyana's governor in the early 1840s, part of an extensive exchange of letters and reports between imperial and colonial officials in the early postemancipation years assessing the results of emancipation. Drawing on regular reports from governors and the stipendiary (special) magistrates appointed during the apprenticeship system, Russell and other officials monitored the operation of the mighty experiment. As Russell's comments suggest, officials were keen to ascertain whether former slaves continued to work on the estates and to assess the well-being of the plantations, which were seen as a crucial determinant of colonial economic health.[34] Thriving estates producing agricultural products for export, especially sugar, were seen as crucial for the colonial economies. But plantations were also perceived to serve a civilizing mission. To Colonial Office officials as well as to many abolitionists, plantations were necessary to prevent the freed populations from "reverting" to "barbarism."[35]

Imperial officials as well as planters saw inexpensive, reliable laborers as the best means to achieve these goals. But the actions of ex-slaves themselves—the "flight from the estates"—undermined this.[36] In the immediate aftermath of emancipation, many free people reduced the amount of time they gave to the estates. Instead, and where possible, they devoted their energies to cultivating their own plots of land, pursuing other livelihood options, and caring for their families.[37] Nineteenth-century population theorists such as Edward Gibbon Wakefield and Herman Mcrivale helped shape the thinking of imperial officials about these developments, already worried as they were that available arable land would convince former slaves to abandon plantation work or at least limit their commitment to it. Wakefield maintained that populations would inevitably disperse in frontier or underpopulated areas, something that would imperil the profitable production of colonial goods as well as undermine civilization as the scattered population would return to their previously "savage" ways. The solution as Wakefield saw it was to artificially create land scarcity by establishing prices that would limit access to it.[38] In a series of lectures published in 1841, Herman Merivale, the Oxford lecturer and soon-to-be "resident expert on emigration" in the Colonial Office, also pondered the impact of land availability on labor supplies.[39] Merivale argued that shortages of labor would occur more readily in larger islands such as Jamaica that had considerable amounts of available land; Trinidad and Guyana, both with relatively small populations, were also believed vulnerable. Densely populated islands like Barbados, St. Kitts, and Antigua, on the other hand, were perceived as relatively immune to this pattern due to a deficit of available, cultivable land.[40] As the British travel writer James Anthony Froude observed in his 1888 publication, Barbados had "plenty of labour always," its (black) "population being so dense, and the place itself being so small, the squatting system could not be tried."[41] Following Wakefieldian logic, planters and the governments they dominated tried to create shortages of land by imposing restrictions on its sale. They limited access to crown land by setting high prices and large minimum amounts that could be purchased, policies designed to place these lands beyond the means of former slaves. Planter-dominated colonial governments passed a variety of laws designed to buttress these efforts to control labor. Legislation attempting to impose long labor contracts on former slaves and to compel them to work for cash wages, ideally on the estates, were part of this. In some areas, planters tried to limit access to rented land on plantations to laborers working on the estate. Labor control laws varied from colony to colony, but they all reflected a desire to ensure that former slaves continued to labor for the plantations.[42]

Despite these policies, former slaves in some colonies were able to realize their wishes to become small-scale agriculturists.[43] In colonies such as Jamaica, Trinidad, and Guyana, they took advantage of available land to establish villages and smallholdings. Squatting on abandoned estates or crown land, joining forces to purchase land, or turning to missionaries for their assistance provided the means to do so. The numbers were significant; Woodville Marshall has estimated that perhaps half or even two-thirds of former slaves had moved off the estates in these colonies.[44]

The number of peasant agriculturalists and smallholders who cultivated crops for subsistence as well as for the internal and external markets grew significantly in Jamaica especially; by 1845, 21 percent of Jamaica's former apprentices had become peasant agriculturalists.[45] But a similar development occurred in Trinidad and Guyana. By the mid-1840s, the number of Afro-Guyanese who lived in villages and small settlements was 44,456, a significant proportion of a population that in 1844 had totaled a little more than 98,000 souls. In comparison, there were fewer than 20,000 on the estates.[46] In this colony, however, a combination of environmental, economic, and political factors contributed to the "decline" of the peasant sector. These included the costly dykes and drains required to make the low-lying coastal lands arable, the economic crisis of the late nineteenth century, and antipeasant laws passed by a planter-dominated colonial government.[47] In places like Barbados, Antigua, St. Kitts, and Nevis, on the other hand, the more complete monopolization of local oligarchies over land limited these kinds of nonplantation economic activities, with the result that many former slaves became wage workers on the estates, albeit with access to plots of land for houses and provision grounds.[48]

The imperial investigations conducted in the early 1840s to assess the consequences of emancipation reveal imperial interest in these developments. Officials wanted to know if former slaves were healthy and becoming "civilized" and if the plantations were functioning and had enough workers.[49] The members of the 1842 parliamentary committee were generally pleased with the effects of emancipation, at least in terms of its civilizing mission. They concluded that the "great act of emancipating the slaves" had led to "the most favourable and gratifying results" in terms of the "character and condition of the Negro Population." The former slaves displayed "an increased and increasing desire for religious and general instruction; a growing disposition to take upon themselves the obligation of marriage, and to fulfill the duties of domestic life; improved morals; rapid advance in civilization, and increased sense of the value of property and independent station."[50]

Given the composition of the committee, this conclusion is not surprising. Two of its members, Lords Stanley and Grey (Viscount Howick), had supported emancipation and disagreed with "racist" interpretations of slaves' actions and maintained that they "shared basic, innate traits of other human beings."[51] But the committee members also echoed some of the positive conclusions offered by some of the missionaries and abolitionists who testified. The long-serving Jamaica-based missionary

William Knibb declared that the "moral and religious habits of the population had improved" with the end of slavery, and the abolitionist John Scoble answered in the affirmative when asked whether conditions had improved for laborers with the end of slavery.[52] Jamaica's governor, C. T. Metcalfe, tended to agree. He observed that the "peasantry" was "thriving" and that marriage was more common and the "morals" of the population "much improved."[53]

British abolitionists and missionaries made similar points in their published accounts of the now-free Caribbean. Sturge and Harvey and James Phillippo all praised the initial, positive results of the "great experiment," arguing that former slaves had improved morally and were "progressing." Phillippo, a British missionary who came to Jamaica in the early 1820s, contrasted free Jamaica with the state of the island during the period of slavery, when "licentiousness" was common. Now, marriages occurred "almost daily," and the numbers of those living in "concubinage" had fallen.[54]

Official views were more equivocal on the question of labor. Metcalfe noted that "in general" landowners had "reason" to complain about a lack of reliable labor and its negative effect on property.[55] The committee members pointed to considerable economic "distress," especially in Jamaica, Trinidad, and Guyana. In these colonies, sugar production had fallen, a development that was disastrous for planters, leading to bankruptcy for many. The commissioners argued that a labor shortage lay at the root of this problem, what they referred to as a "diminished supply of labour." They blamed a number of factors, including the unwillingness of former slaves to provide cheap, "steady and continuous" labor for planters and their decision to work on their provision grounds and in other, nonplantation occupations. The commissioners contrasted these places with the "smaller and more populous Islands" where distress was much less pronounced. The solution, as they saw it, was to import more laborers.[56]

Demographic questions, specifically those concerning reproduction, were intimately connected with perceptions of the labor supply. Indeed, emancipation was judged on its ability to solve the population problem.[57] Metcalfe observed that the labor shortage was due to the population's ability to "support themselves without labouring in the service of others" but that "the actual want of population" was also a factor.[58] Colonial Office officials queried governors and planters about the impact of emancipation on the size of the population, specifically whether it was "increasing by natural causes."[59] That it would do so was one of the assumptions underlying emancipation. As one resident of Antigua had observed in 1838, he "expect[ed] the population to increase" with freedom.[60] Despite his confidence, assessments of the extent of population growth varied significantly. In Barbados, the acting police magistrate for St. Andrew parish, James Bascom, observed that the "season" had caused "alarming" mortality among the laboring population, especially the children.[61] On the other hand, in Berbice, Guyana, according to a stipendiary magistrate, W. J. Brittain, mortality was less than it had been during slavery, and children were the recipients of "greatly increased care . . . from their mothers." However, he believed that "correct statistical returns . . . [could] alone ascertain the present rate of their mortality."[62]

In the absence of "correct statistical returns," assessments of the extent to which the free populations were or were not growing rested on assumptions. In the early days of freedom, many missionaries concluded that the former slave population was growing, but they attributed this trend to the dual process of Christianization and civilization. In their view, a more civilized and Christianized population would inevitably increase. Knibb was not alone in his conclusion that the population was growing mostly in places "where the influence of Christianity [was] felt."[63] For their part, many planters noted that mortality rates had risen after the end of slavery, something they blamed on the refusal of "lazy" former slaves to purchase medical care. During slavery and the apprenticeship period, planters had provided medical care, such as it was. Plantations had hospitals and received regular visits from physicians under contracts to provide medical attendance. This ended after 1838, leaving former slaves responsible for paying for their own health care, something most could not afford. Planters and physicians tended to see their inability to purchase medical care as proof of the population's laziness. In the eyes of planters and other apologists for slavery, "laziness" referred to the stubborn determination of former slaves to attempt to control their working lives. By refusing to work on the estates for the wages and conditions offered by planters rather than on their own plots of land or in other nonplantation livelihoods, former slaves found themselves condemned as lazy.[64] Some planters argued that the "reluctance" of former slaves to work on the estates and to purchase medical care could lead to premature death, especially among the very young.[65] But the consequences were potentially even more dire. One planter who testified before the 1842 parliamentary select committee agreed completely when asked whether the refusal of former slaves in Jamaica to employ physicians and the latter's consequent mass exodus from the colony threatened "civilization" in the island.[66]

In an effort to obtain information about the extent of population growth, Lord Stanley called for the West Indian governments to follow Jamaica's lead in taking a census of their populations.[67] The conclusions were mixed. The earl of Elgin, James Bruce, who had replaced Metcalfe as Jamaica's governor, was disappointed with the results of his colony's census, concluding that it did not indicate that the population had grown and that the results themselves were likely unreliable.[68] Elgin was probably right. Scattered populations and often-inaccessible villages prevented easy or reliable population counts, as did the resistance of former slaves. In Dominica, for example, large numbers of former slaves objected to the census, which many believed was an attempt to reestablish slavery; they attacked and threatened the census takers, with an obvious impact on the accuracy of the population count.[69] Most governors, however, were more positive. C. E. Grey, the governor of the Windward Islands (which at that time included Barbados, Grenada and Cariacou, St. Vincent, St. Lucia, and Tobago) described the population as "fast increasing."[70] The Leeward Islands' governor, Charles Fitzroy, was similarly optimistic about the growth of Antigua's population, declaring that there "[could] be no reasonable doubt that a material increase ha[d] taken place since the abolition of slavery."[71] The administrator of Montserrat, Edward Baynes, was just as bullish. The census proved his belief that the island's population had grown "rapidly" since the end of slavery, an increase that did not surprise him, given the "known destructive influences of slavery so hostile to human life."[72] In Guyana as well, the "Creole population [was] on a steady increase."[73] Diseases that had commonly killed children during slavery were "hardly known," and children were "watched, and nursed and cleaned, perhaps as well as in the most favoured parts of Europe."[74] The benevolent Caribbean environment was seen as contributing to this trend. In Barbados, as Governor Grey noted, the climate was "as favourable to human life as in England."[75] Even Guyana, tormented as it was by yellow fever and malaria, was seen in this fashion. As Governor Henry Light declared, "Everything tend[ed] to increase the population by ordinary means; nature [was] bountiful in the increase, and secure[d] food for that increase."[76]

By the late 1840s and 1850s, however, negative views were increasingly common. Barely four years after his optimistic missive lauding the new order, Light was much gloomier. A work stoppage by plantation workers in 1848 seemed to represent all that had gone wrong in the colony. In his eyes, a credulous, indolent population had been convinced by outside "agitators" to stop work in the hopes of receiving higher wages. Previous to this, rising wages saw the creoles refuse work regularly, choosing instead "irregular habits," namely shooting, fishing, and "wandering." The beset planters, vulnerable to the "caprice of the Negro," faced ruin.[77] As Light noted, his views had changed. He no longer believed that any good would come of allowing former slaves to purchase estates; indeed, this development did not lead to the "civilization, advancement or industry of the purchasers." To Light, the behavior of former slaves had changed for the worse. They were "less respectful," and he noted that he had been forced to employ police to protect himself and others from the "jeering and impertinent remarks of the loungers" near the capital city of Georgetown.[78]

Planters had always been suspicious of freedom's promises, but the decline in the sugar industry in much of the British Caribbean, along with accounts of former slaves' unwillingness to work on plantations and their purportedly worsening characters, saw planters' views given more credence. The expansion of sugar production in places such as Mauritius and Cuba contributed to a general decline in sugar prices.[79] In the British Caribbean, sugar production had fallen in the immediate aftermath of emancipation, but the decision of the ruling Whigs in Britain under Russell to gradually reduce the duties paid to British West Indian sugar producers saw it drop even further, triggering an economic crisis in the region that lasted until the mid-1850s and in some islands until the end of the century. The decline was not universal and was much worse in Jamaica than in Barbados and Guyana.[80] Overall, the fall in sugar prices combined with depression in Europe had an immediate impact on these Caribbean colonies. Many planters found themselves unable to obtain credit and ended up selling their now bankrupt plantations.[81] A British government investigation in 1847–48 that heard testimony from British Caribbean planters and merchants as well as from newly impoverished members of the British Parliament recounted stories of bankruptcies and economic loss.[82]

These developments contributed to the growing sense among many Britons that emancipation had "failed." Overall, free workers seemed unable to produce sugar as cheaply as tied ones and were unwilling to work regularly on the estates. British newspapers published numerous editorials on the subject, and William Wilberforce's son Samuel described the "'vast social experiment'" as having become the "'fearful experiment.'"[83] These views of emancipation and its associated economic and social consequences were tied to ideas about race. Many Britons, including abolitionists, did not regard blacks as entirely equal with whites. Equality, it was argued, would come with time as former slaves "improved" and became "civilized."[84] But the economic crisis after the end of slavery and the decision of former slaves to construct their lives as they saw fit in response to their own goals and the economic imperatives of the global sugar market saw them condemned as lazy and uncivilized. It also contributed to the emergence of what Thomas Holt has described as a "virulent official racism" that "helped give shape and focus to the racial thought of the larger public."[85]

The writings of Thomas Carlyle provide an example of this development. Catherine Hall has argued that his "Occasional Discourse on the Negro [Nigger] Question" indicated "a marked shift in the discursive terrain" from the 1840s, an "increasing turn to the language of race to explain and justify the inequalities and persistent differences between peoples."[86] To Holt, Carlyle's writings "popularized" ideas about the purported innate laziness of blacks and the necessity that they be forced to work, views that became increasingly accepted.[87] But to a significant extent they also reflected current thinking. Holt has pointed to the "basic complementarity" of Carlyle's work with "official discourse" and has argued that the confidential observations of Henry Taylor written in 1846 echoed those of his friend and fellow writer Carlyle.[88] Taylor, a long-standing Colonial Office official, supported the conclusions of Jamaican planters that exslaves needed to be controlled and required the "discipline" of "wage labor" and used racist language to make his case.[89] In a magazine article first published in 1849, Carlyle employed the trope of the bountiful Caribbean environment to support his view. He argued that the environment allowed purportedly lazy former slaves to survive comfortably with apparently little effort. Referring to the 1848 strike by Guyanese plantation workers that had so exercised Light, Carlyle noted that the "Black man" refused to work while the "white man could not" and the "cane-crop . . . [stood] rotting."[90]

Cholera and the Failure of Emancipation

The 1865 Morant Bay uprising in Jamaica crystallized these views of race and emancipation. This massive and violent protest emerged out of the frustrations of former slaves with a freedom that seemed more of an illusion with each passing year. The colonial government repressed the rebellion brutally, killing more than 400 people. The governor of the day,

Edward Eyre, managed to convince Jamaica's elected assembly to change the constitution and end self-government. Colonial Office officials had wanted something of the sort for some time, and similar steps would soon be taken throughout most of the region.[91] To imperial officials and British observers, the events in Jamaica seemed to demonstrate the "failure" of emancipation and former slaves' purported lack of fitness for freedom. By refusing to work in the manner prescribed by planters and imperial officials, ex-slaves had shown that they were unfit to rule themselves.[92]

But in the eyes of imperial officials, this was not the first time that former slaves had failed such a test. Their response to the cholera epidemics of the 1850s was another such moment. Part of a series of global pandemics that hit Asia, Europe, and the Americas in the nineteenth century, the outbreaks in the British Caribbean were seen as highlighting the failure of emancipation. Imperial observers and West Indian planters blamed former slaves' purportedly undisciplined and immoral behavior for the high levels of sickness and death that marked the epidemics' course in the Caribbean. Without the constraints of slavery, they were seen as reverting to barbarism and threatening not only their own survival but that of European civilization in the islands.

Cholera has been characterized as the "shock-horror disease of the nineteenth century." Caused by *Vibrio cholerae*, cholera, even today, appears suddenly and can kill quickly. Sufferers experience severe vomiting and diarrhea and painful cramps before lapsing into comas and finally succumbing to death. Today, antibiotics and rehydration therapy are used, methods that were not available in the nineteenth century. For the most part, nineteenth-century victims were treated with bleeding, purgatives, and prayers, this last encouraged by the dramatic nature of the disease.[93] Prayers may or may not have helped, but bleeding and bloodletting certainly did not, merely speeding up the course of the disease.[94] Nineteenth-century responses were also characterized by a search for culprits. Cholera's propensity for attacking the poor and socially marginalized, many of whom suffered from the unsanitary living conditions and malnutrition that contributed to the disease's spread, encouraged observers to blame the victims. They were seen as condemned by their own social and cultural behavior.[95] All of these patterns were apparent in the Caribbean epidemics.

Cholera arrived in the Caribbean in the 1830s, returning in 1850 and again in the 1860s. Cuba was the only Caribbean territory attacked by the disease in the 1830s; it arrived there in 1833. The outbreak between 1850 and 1855 was notable for its geographic scope and the sheer number of lives lost.[96] It hit Cuba in 1850 and then Jamaica shortly afterward. In the next few years, it attacked other Caribbean territories, including Guyana, Barbados, and St. Lucia.[97] One of the British doctors sent to the Caribbean to report on the disease, Hector Gavin, estimated that between 1849 and 1854, cholera killed some 88,000 people in the various territories of the British Caribbean.[98] Estimates put the number of deaths in Jamaica at between 40,000 and 50,000, or between 10 and 13 percent of the population. In Barbados, some 20,000 to 25,000 died, or around 15 percent of the population.[99]

Hector Gavin, along with Gavin Milroy and James Laidlaw, was dispatched to the region as part of the British government's response to the epidemic. They were to provide local authorities with "advice and assistance" about implementing the various "precautionary measures" that had proven effective in England.[100] All three had dealt with cholera elsewhere. Milroy and Gavin had worked as medical superintending inspectors with the English General Board of Health during the cholera epidemic in London in 1848–49, and Laidlaw was experienced in dealing with cholera in "tropical climates."[101] The secretary of state for the colonies, Earl Grey, was clear about their responsibilities. They were not to treat the victims. Doing so was in fact pointless in Grey's view. He noted that the English Board of Health had concluded that "medical treatment [was] of comparably little service" once cholera "had declared itself in an aggravated form." Instead, the trio should concentrate on helping prevent the disease from spreading.[102] For whatever it was worth, however, Grey sent the colonial governors the medical advice provided by the English General Board of Health. Sufferers should be sent to bed and kept warm. Sweating was encouraged, so hot poultices should be applied to victims, who were also to be given laudanum mixed with rum or brandy. Physicians were reminded that cholera was not contagious and that the "true danger" lay in "continuing to live in infected districts, in close, damp, and filthy dwellings."[103]

Their education and experiences in Britain doubtless encouraged Milroy, Gavin, and Laidlaw to pay particular attention to this last point. Like other physicians of their generation, they worried about the deadly emanations from miasmas and blamed filth and poor sanitation for causing disease. They saw ample proof of these problems in the Caribbean. Although an editorial in the *Jamaica Physical Journal* from 1834 praised Kingston as the healthiest spot in Jamaica, Gavin Milroy described the city in far less complimentary terms.[104] Streets and private yards were frequently garbage-strewn, home to pigs who freely rooted though the rubbish and sometimes the excrement that was deposited nearby. The homes of the poor were tiny, crowded, and airless, and rich and poor alike lacked reliable access to clean water.[105] Impoverished West Indians were also malnourished. In Barbados, for example, Governor William Colebrooke noted that inadequate food supplies made people vulnerable to cholera, an observation which might have been made of many parts of the region in the 1850s.[106] The climate and geography of the Caribbean added another element: Torrential rains could turn unpaved dry streets into rivers of mud and filth. In Georgetown, the capital city of Guyana, which was below sea level, rains and high tides often led to flooding. Collectively, Gavin, Milroy, and Laidlaw recommended that the colonial governments introduce the kinds of public health and sanitary measures implemented in the mother country.[107] The 1850s saw the passage of a number of sanitary regulations, many of which were modeled on those in effect in England.[108] However, these measures were generally ineffective, and for the most part, little serious improvement in sanitary conditions was seen before the early twentieth century.[109]

The poverty and hunger experienced by Afro–West Indians contributed to cholera's ferocity, but in the eyes of British doctors, planters, and officials on both sides of the Atlantic, so did the perceived moral failings of former slaves themselves. Their purportedly lazy, feckless, and savage natures made them unwilling to employ European-trained physicians, the last defense against disease and the feared collapse of European civilization in the Caribbean. Planters had complained about the decline in the number of physicians in this part of the world since the early 1840s and had predicted any number of dire consequences. They were right about the fall in the number of formally trained physicians; contemporary sources note that the number of practicing physicians fell in the region once planters terminated their contracts with these men after the end of slavery. The 200 physicians present in Jamaica in 1833 had fallen to 90 by 1850 and to some 67 by 1861. Most of those remaining were based in urban areas, beyond the reach of most of the population.[110] Gavin Milroy observed that many parishes in Jamaica did not have physicians and that the epidemic itself had killed some of those few remaining.[111] Hector Gavin noted a similar deficit in Guyana, where a combination of long distances, poor roads, and inhospitable climate presented obstacles to those physicians who had remained.[112] In this much smaller colony, there were 38 physicians in 1851, 15 of whom were based in urban areas (11 in the capital city of Georgetown and 4 in the much smaller New Amsterdam).[113] This number seems to have fallen from perhaps 45 European medical practitioners in the 1820s.[114]

For Grey, cholera's true consequences could be seen in Jamaica. Following its outbreak, he corresponded with planters and others in the colony about the impact of the disease. Their accounts only seemed to confirm some of his long-standing views about the future of this part of the world after the end of slavery. For Grey, one of the epidemic's most serious consequences was its effect on the labor supply. It aggravated the labor shortages resulting from emancipation. Grey acknowledged that immigration would help matters, but he was convinced that the solution lay in using the "proper inducements" to convince the existing population to become more productive. Grey regretted that emancipation itself had not included some kind of mechanism to accomplish this, an omission he characterized as a "great and unfortunate error."[115] He had advocated the imposition of taxes on land at the time of emancipation, something he believed would encourage former slaves to work by limiting their access to land; the cholera epidemic only seemed to have strengthened his certainty on this matter.[116] Unless the main agricultural crops continued to be produced, "the most civilized" members of Jamaica's population would leave, with serious consequences for the colony's future and that of its recently freed people.[117]

Grey believed that the reluctance of former slaves to work regularly on the sugar estates reflected a principle of human nature. As they had access to plots of land of their own, they could refuse to work on the estates. In a similar situation, an Englishman would do much the same. Grey argued that "to men, whatever may be their colour, their country, or their rank, idleness [was] ever a source of corruption" and the "negroes [were] no exception to the rule." Such "idleness," however, had serious consequences; it retarded the "advancement in civilization and morality." Despite his appeal to this law of "human nature," Grey suggested that history had made Jamaicans (and, by extension, all Afro–West Indians) a special kind of human. They were motivated by "animal instincts." These ensured that they worked enough to meet "their immediate physical wants," but they did not understand the importance of meeting more elevated needs, such as "education, religious instruction, and the procuring of medical advice for themselves and their children." The cholera epidemic was proof. As he and his colonial informants argued, the refusal of former slaves to pay physicians for medical care contributed to the high mortality rates. Repeating points that planters had been making since the 1840s, Grey argued that former slaves did not understand the necessity of paying for their own health care because it had been provided for them for free during the period of slavery. Their inability to shake off the shackles of history contributed to the slow population growth in Jamaica, a place where, Grey asserted in an echo of Carlylean logic, the "necessities of life" were in "extreme abundance."[118]

For officials like Grey and for the British physicians dispatched to the Caribbean, idleness had calamitous consequences. Milroy agreed with Hector Gavin's conclusion that unemployment that led to "destitution and misery" significantly contributed to the high mortality rates from cholera. Rather than blaming this on the state of the sugar industry or decisions of planters, however, Hector Gavin pointed to former slaves. He believed that in Barbados, the population did not work due to "disinclination" and a "feeling of degradation in labor." This led in quick succession to "idleness, . . . profligacy, poverty and destitution" and, from these, "death." Milroy declared that the same pattern could be seen in Jamaica's towns.[119]

In his report on cholera in Jamaica, Gavin Milroy repeated many of these points. But his writings also resonated with the racist sentiments that were becoming so prevalent in official and popular discourse about the Caribbean and that echoed the views of the old planter class. Accounts from Jamaican planters, ministers, and physicians convinced him that former slaves were indifferent to "their own lives" and "utter[ly] unconcerned" with those of their friends and relatives. The "dreadful exhibition of heartlessness during the cholera" epidemic proved this.[120] Milroy claimed that family members "cruelly neglected" their sick relatives, aggravating their sufferings and even hastening their deaths by burying them before their lives had ended.[121] He described black Jamaicans as a "semibarbarous people" who were callously indifferent to human life.[122] White Jamaicans told Milroy of their shock at the "barbarism" and declared that the epidemic's death toll demonstrated their "sordid, unwholesome, and vicious habits."[123] Milroy concluded that the combination of poor sanitary conditions and the "depraved habits" and general "recklessness of life" of former slaves inevitably led to high mortality rates.[124] Despite these views, in reality a scarcity of European-trained physicians, the sheer cost of medical care, and perhaps a rational assessment of its ineffectiveness in the face of cholera and other diseases were likely at the root of this neglect to obtain medical care. Understandable fear at a terrible disease also may have motivated many. A Jamaican physician, for example, observed that the "'confusion, panic, and terror'" was unimaginable to those who had not witnessed it. Milroy himself described carts so filled with coffins that they could scarcely move and cemeteries where "graves could not be dug quickly enough."[125]

The willingness of planters and others to interpret this behavior as a moral failing on the part of laborers indicates its discursive power. It reflected the contemporary association between biological race and medical and sanitary behavior that, according to Europeans and Euro-Americans, contributed to poor health and early death. But these representations of former slaves resonated with a wider, anti-emancipation discourse that condemned them as barbaric and lazy and as prone to "reverting" to barbarism without the "civilizing" effect of planter (white) control. Slavery or at least European control was seen as protecting them from premature death. Examples of these views can be seen in the "extinctionist" literature produced by southern U.S. physicians after the end of slavery that described former slaves as susceptible to illness and liable to early death under freedom.[126] To one British commentator, the purported degeneration of African Americans under freedom was part of a universal pattern.[127] During the cholera epidemic in the British Caribbean, these discourses intersected with long-standing views of former slaves' perceived unwillingness to work. Slavery's defenders had long argued that Africans and people of African descent in the Caribbean required compulsion to work, an argument that was repeated in the decades after 1838. Witnesses testifying before the 1842 parliamentary committee described former slaves in this fashion and declared that this behavior would lead to death and calamity. To Grey, Milroy, and Gavin, these predictions seemed to have come true: In refusing to work, former slaves were unable to pay for medical care, the last defense against the devastating effects of cholera.

To Grey and the British health inspectors, taxes were the solution. Taxes had been used as a tool of social policy for some years with the goal of "encouraging" former slaves to work on the estates, and these Britons used the cholera epidemics to make the same case.[128] They argued that the sums realized would pay for hospitals, dispensaries, and the like. Several previous attempts had been made to do something of this kind but with varying degrees of success. An attempt to establish a dispensary system in Jamaica in 1845 failed due to the inadequate number of doctors and the inability (or unwillingness, as whites saw it) of poor Jamaicans to pay the annual fees.[129] However, some urban physicians managed to operate dispensaries that provided medical care at the cost of one shilling a month. The poor could use this system if they found officials willing to verify their poverty.[130] Guyana's attempt at an estate-based dispensary system was a little more successful. On some estates, planters deducted a small amount each month to pay for a "medical attendant" who could use the existing estate hospitals to see patients.[131] In the aftermath of the cholera epidemic, Grey, Gavin, and Milroy suggested schemes for both colonies that would see local assessments imposed to pay for dispensaries. In both colonies, politicians initially balked at these measures. In Jamaica, the legislature rejected a bill to "establish dispensaries and 'efficient medical relief in the rural districts.'"[132] In Guyana, after some delay and following the arrival of cholera in Barbados in 1854, "experimental" legislation was passed that empowered the governor to establish dispensaries in any villages where he thought them necessary.[133]

These "medical" taxes were intended to realize ideological goals. Like the various fees imposed on nonestate livelihoods, such as huckstering, they were to encourage former slaves to work for cash wages, ideally on the estates. As Hector Gavin noted, taxes would encourage the population to work and discourage "idleness and savage[ry]," something he believed was especially important in Guyana, where large numbers of the population were "retrograding into a barbarous condition of existence."[134] A "medical tax" would also ensure the continued presence of physicians in the colonies. Milroy believed that their presence might have prevented some of the sickness and death resulting from the cholera epidemic. Physicians alone had the necessary medical knowledge to predict and prevent such calamities. They could also register deaths, oversee censuses, and prepare medical reports.[135] Physicians could also play a civilizing role. Given the recent "intellectual and moral" regression of the former slaves, physicians could exert influence on the "wretched condition of the homes of the people" and their "debased domestic habits," achieving results that educators and clergymen could not.[136] Gavin believed that physician-run dispensaries could also help curtail the "excessive infantine mortality which prevail[ed] among the black population." For example, dispensaries could uncover instances of "criminal neglect" and "criminal abortion," which he believed was common. All in all, such a scheme would lead to an "improvement in the physical condition of the population, [and] especially in their social position, and in their perception of moral obligations."[137]

Taxing ex-slaves to pay for a physician-based medical system was also supposed to free former slaves from their "dangerous" reliance on other, less civilized health care providers. In Guyana, for example, many villagers relied on Portuguese shop owners who, according to the governor, were as "ignorant as their customers of the value and properties of their own drugs."[138] But it would also liberate them from reliance on obeahmen and -women. Obeah (and myalism in Jamaica) refers to African-derived religious/medical practices developed by enslaved peoples in the British Caribbean, involving the use of herbs and rituals. Although some contemporary sources described obeah as witchcraft and myalism as relatively less harmful, a kind of "anti-obeah,"[139] both were condemned as barbaric and as forms of quackery; indeed, the terms were often used interchangeably. Milroy, like other commentators, linked the growing presence of obeah and myalism in Jamaica to what he saw as the increasing "ignorance and barbarism" of Jamaica's black masses.[140] Although he suggested that the black masses turned to such individuals because of the physician "shortage," he also implied that they did so willingly. They would not visit European-trained physicians when ill and instead would "apply to ignorant imposters of their own colour" who "often blended the practice of superstitious rites with their mischievous prescriptions."[141]

Counting Former Slaves

Gavin Milroy observed that by the time of the cholera epidemic, the "best informed" believed that Jamaica's population had not been growing "for many years" and that it may even have been decreasing. He believed that the fault lay not with the birthrate but, rather, with high mortality rates, particularly among the very young.[142] The period in which he and other postslavery commentators were writing saw increasingly systematic attempts to move away from such anecdotal accounts and to collect regular, accurate population data. This information provided the basis for conclusions about the size and health of colonial populations and the justification for public health measures aimed at ensuring population growth.

British colonies had been required to provide annual statistical reports from the early nineteenth century, but these became more detailed and complete as the century progressed. This was part of the increasing effort by officials to monitor and classify colonial populations and especially to determine important matters such as their health and numbers. These reports included information about the military and civil establishments, lists of the year's laws and proclamations, returns dealing with financial matters, and population returns based on the most recent census.[143]

Collecting such information increasingly came to be seen as one of the main tasks of a state.[144] With the exception of Jamaica, British Caribbean governments began holding more or less regular decennial censuses from 1851. Jamaica joined the rest in 1861.[145] From 1871, the Colonial Office encouraged colonial governments to hold "simultaneous" censuses and, in 1911, asked governors for "as much uniformity as possible."[146] For the most part, the colonies of the British Caribbean followed these recommendations. Two major exceptions were in 1901 and 1931, when economic crises discouraged many colonies from holding censuses.[147]

These censuses were seen as indicators of rationality and modernity, assessments of their increasing reliability seen as moving in tandem with the "civilization" of the Caribbean. The first census in the 1840s attracted a considerable amount of criticism. The then-governor of Jamaica considered it unreliable, as did other contemporaries. The Canadian-born *New York Times* journalist William Sewell did not trust it.[148] He was the author of a series of articles about the economic consequences of emancipation, a kind of primer for Americans concerned about what freedom might hold.[149] But later censuses also came in for condemnation. The Jamaican governor believed that the 1861 census was not entirely reliable, but he had high hopes for the one in 1871.[150] The colony's first registrar general, S. P. Smeeton, dashed these, blaming a popular "repugnance" toward the census and unspecified "hindrances." By 1881, however, he was more optimistic. He rejoiced that an "increased intelligence and a wider understanding of the purpose of the undertaking" had resulted in a more accurate count.[151] Smeeton's views reflected those of other members of the political and economic elites who regularly condemned former slaves (and African-descended peoples more generally) as irrational and unintelligent. But comments by Barbados's governor indicate the contingent nature of the early census data. In his response to the 1871 census, Rawson W. Rawson noted that the numbers of the various "complexions" were an approximation. They depended "to some degree on personal judgment of the enumerators" and "somewhat" on the "views" of the individuals being counted.[152]

Despite these concerns about accuracy, contemporaries used the numbers to draw conclusions about the state of postslavery populations. Sewell, for example, cited the recent censuses and the slave registration reports as the basis for his conclusions that the populations of Antigua, St. Kitts, and Jamaica had fallen since the end of slavery.[153] Like other contemporary observers, he blamed "vices engendered by slavery" and "immorality of the grossest kind" for halting the "natural growth" of the African-descended population. Just as Milroy and Gavin had a few years earlier, Sewell also blamed a shortage of physicians for this trend, especially in rural areas.[154] In making this point, he was also echoing conclusions of Edward Eyre, the acting governor of Antigua at the time of his visit. Eyre blamed Antigua's population decline and the high rates of mortality, especially among the very young, on the absence of "proper medical care."[155]

The argument that vice, parental neglect, and the general moral failings of former slaves contributed to population decline was expressed in post–Morant Bay Jamaica. In 1867, the governor of Jamaica, John Peter Grant, asked members of the clergy, local officials, and planters to comment on the state of the colony's population, particularly whether it was growing. Although the aftermath of the Morant Bay uprising likely contributed to this concern, Sewell's claims a few years earlier about population decline may also have played a role.[156] His informants made many of the points expressed during the cholera epidemics. They all agreed that the population would increase if parents cared for their children and if they saw physicians when they were ill. Observers attributed what they saw as ex-slaves' unwillingness to do so to their purported reluctance to work.[157] Grant concluded that the population seemed to be increasing but that population growth was limited by the "ignorance and vicious habits of the people," a high infant mortality rate, parental neglect, and a lack of medical care by physicians.[158] Eradicating these factors would take time, but the government could play a role, specifically by legislating that parents support their children and that children care for their elderly parents. (He blamed the abandonment of dependents for "pauperism" and believed that it contributed "to the rate of death throughout the island.") Grant also intended to introduce a system to register births and deaths on the grounds that this could "check" the death rate among infants to the extent that it was "caused wilfully or by culpable neglect on the part of parents."[159]

As Grant's comments suggest, the collection of vital statistics was a crucial step in the process of assessing the size of local populations, the number of births and deaths, and the causes of death and the ages at which it occurred. Between the late 1840s and the late 1870s, most British Caribbean colonies passed registration laws.[160] Barbados was an exception, and its officials repeatedly complained about the absence of a "proper system" of registering births and deaths. They noted that this impeded efforts to accurately assess the size of the population overall and that of the colony's white minority in particular.[161] By 1891, legislation providing for the registration of births was in place, but that allowing for death registration did not appear until well into the twentieth century. In its absence, church ministers were the main source of information; they relayed the numbers of burials to Barbados's registrar.[162] Barbadian officials blamed poverty, noting that the colony could not afford the expense. But physicians in other British Caribbean colonies were horrified.[163] During a Caribbean medical conference in 1913, the medical officer of health for Kingston, Jamaica, Angus MacDonald, expressed sympathy for Barbados's public health inspector, John Hutson, and suggested that the delegates pass a resolution calling on the Barbadian government to set up a system for registering deaths. He declared that it was "simply deplorable to think that there was no system of registration in a British colony." Hutson refused, noting that such an approach would not be "wise" and that it would be best to "leave it to public opinion."[164]

The debates and exchanges examined in this chapter demonstrate the varying ends to which ideas about the size of Caribbean populations were made to serve in the nineteenth century. Questions about the reproduction of the enslaved populations in this part of the world were central in the abolition debates and provided much of the justification for the end of the slave trade and slavery itself. The initial euphoria with which emancipation was greeted in Britain colored views of population growth; with the end of slavery, the population must surely be increasing. With the economic crisis of the late 1840s and a growing official unhappiness with the choices that free men and women in the Caribbean were making came a hardening of racial views. People of African descent were seen as uncivilized and as profoundly inferior to white Europeans. Officials and others in Britain saw Jamaica's Morant Bay uprising as evidence of this, but the cholera epidemics of the 1850s helped shape their ideas. They also pointed to what was seen as an inevitable consequence of such purported barbarity, rising mortality rates. Believed to be victimized by their own laziness and savagery, former slaves were seen as unable to take the simple steps needed to ensure their own survival and population growth. West Indian planters had long expressed such views—they were part of the proslavery ideological apparatus—but they were increasingly accepted by other groups. As the nineteenth century progressed, imperial officials and others continued to worry about population growth in the Caribbean. As the next chapter shows, by the late nineteenth and early twentieth centuries, concerns about infant mortality increasingly came to dominate these discussions. The ability of infants to survive and become productive adults became a central concern of imperial policy.

CHAPTER TWO

Population Anxieties and Infant Mortality

In the course of time we may hope to see the black population,
which was kept down by legal oppression and licentious morals,
consequent on a state of slavery, advance in numbers under the
institution of marriage, and in the enjoyment of property.

—Lord John Russell, February 15, 1840

It may be inferred that the population of which Lord John Russell
wrote has not advanced in numbers: it may even be feared that the
numbers have actually decreased.

—British Guiana governor James Swettenham
to Joseph Chamberlain, January 5, 1903

IN HIS 1903 LETTER TO JOSEPH CHAMBERLAIN, the governor of Guyana, James Swettenham, described a colony facing a population crisis. As he told the British secretary of state, the black population had increased by barely 22,000 souls since the end of slavery, and the total number may even have been falling. Immigration from Asia only served to disguise this fact. Most worrying of all to this colonial official, deaths among black infants far outnumbered those of other groups. Guyanese planters and officials had long complained of labor shortages in this colony, which adopted the model of slave-worked plantations later than most other British Caribbean territories. For them, as for planters and officials throughout the region, adequate numbers of laborers meant economic survival. Concerns about shrinking populations due to high death rates, especially among the very young, were widely expressed in this period, shaped by the combined forces of science and ideology. Newer medical ideas about disease causation and infant health and older stereotypes about indifferent parents provided a ready explanation. But in colonial and former slave societies such as those in the Caribbean, negative representations of nonwhite people were also significant. In colonies where most men and women lived in poverty, ex-slaves were seen as careless parents whose indifference was believed to condemn their children to early death. Former slaves were also regarded as promiscuous; their "reluctance" to sanctify reproduction with legal marriage was seen as indicating their immorality and as contributing to population decline. Planters, colonial officials, and foreign and creole physicians disseminated these ideas, relaying them to an imperial bureaucracy newly interested in the health of colonial populations. In Guyana, Jamaica, and Barbados, investigations into the causes of infant mortality held in the early twentieth century summed up colonial ideas about infant mortality and the need for healthy populations, part of the background to the infant and maternal welfare initiatives introduced in the early twentieth century and addressed in subsequent chapters.

Population Anxieties

The transition to freedom in the British Caribbean coincided with what Randall Packard has called a "revolution in medicine and public health."[1] It profoundly affected the lives of former slaves and other, newly arrived groups and influenced the ways in which physicians and colonial officials represented them.

This medical and public health "revolution" of the latter part of the nineteenth century emerged from various developments in science and scientific technology that allowed researchers to determine the causes of a number of deadly diseases. The impact of this work and acceptance of the "germ theory" was felt only gradually, and long-standing ideas about the causes of disease, such as the effects of the local environment (miasmas), remained influential.[2] The response of British doctors such as Gavin Milroy to the mid-nineteenth-century cholera epidemics in the British Caribbean is an example of the explanatory power of these concepts. In the late nineteenth century, researchers applied them to deadly and debilitating diseases associated with "warm climates," such as sleeping sickness, malaria, yellow fever, and ankylostomiasis (hookworm disease). These were seen as threatening European health and "native" productivity. Identifying these diseases and their causes resulted in public health policies targeting the environmental conditions that allowed them to flourish.[3]

Tropical medicine, as this branch of research became known, was part of "empire building and empire maintenance."[4] In colonial Africa, India, and the Caribbean and in areas of U.S. imperial activity (such as Panama, the Philippines, and Cuba), governments invested considerable resources in attacking these diseases and the conditions that gave rise to them.[5] In the British empire, the Colonial Office under Joseph Chamberlain (1895–1903) played a key role in institutionalizing tropical medicine as part of a wider effort to make colonies more profitable.[6] Schools of tropical medicine in London and Liverpool were established, and colonial physicians were encouraged to attend, something that was soon made mandatory.[7] The British government also developed increasingly formal mechanisms to ensure that its officials had access to expert advice on colonial health. Chamberlain enlisted Patrick Manson as the "medical researcher" to the Colonial Office, a position the "father of tropical medicine" held until 1911.[8] And in 1909, the British government established a medical committee comprised of tropical medicine experts to advise the Colonial Office about medical and sanitary matters in Africa; by 1922, its formal purview included the British Caribbean.[9]

These scientific and institutional developments affected responses to poor health in the colonial world, but so did ideas about race and class. White Europeans and Euro-Americans saw nonwhite colonial populations as morally and intellectually inferior and associated their behavior with the spread of disease. But they also saw impoverished members of their own societies in a similar fashion. In Britain, late nineteenth-century concerns about population health tended to focus on the urban poor, regarded as a degenerate "residuum" who drained the country's resources and whose presence was seen as threatening the survival of the "race."[10] Public health and sanitary improvements were believed to undermine "Darwinian laws of nature" and to allow more of the "'unfit'" to survive and reproduce.[11] Military losses during the Boer War and high rates of rejection among recruits seemed to justify these worries.[12] The British government responded to this "national deterioration discussion" by establishing the Interdepartmental Committee on Physical Deterioration in the early twentieth century. The committee concluded that the behavior of the very poor made them, and especially their children, prone to ill health. In particular, the committee members pointed to what they saw as the poor's "'laziness, want of thrift, ignorance of household management, and particularly the choice and preparation of food, filth, indifference to parental obligations, [and] drunkenness.'"[13] Insert the contemporary terms for any number of nonwhite groups in the Caribbean or other colonial or postslavery society, and the sentence would apply to any of these places. For officials and physicians in the British Caribbean worried about population decline, these combined ideas about class, culture, and biological race offered a ready and persuasive explanation.

Sugar and Caribbean Labor

The Caribbean and British professionals, officials, and employers of labor in the British Caribbean who were educated in the United Kingdom were familiar with current ideas about health and fit populations. Time spent in Britain and extensive communication networks that allowed island residents and Britons to regularly exchange views about the pressing question of population growth facilitated this. In the late nineteenth and early twentieth centuries, concerns about labor and the economy lay at the center of these discussions.

Much of this worry about population size focused on the health of the plantations and especially the sugar industry. By the middle years of the 1850s, sugar prices had recovered somewhat from the effects of the gradual reduction in sugar duties instituted in 1846. In Barbados especially, sugar exports increased steadily in this decade.[14] An international economic depression in the 1870s contributed to another fall in prices, and the "sugar bounty depression" that occurred soon afterward only made matters worse. The decision of some European governments in the 1880s to support an expansion of the beet sugar industry with massive subsidies led to a dramatic fall in the price of sugar, initiating the bounty depression in the British Caribbean. Its effects were felt throughout the region, especially in the 1890s. The price for sugar on the international market did not fully recover until World War I, but the end of the bounties in 1902 and the increasing importance of the United States and Canada as markets for Caribbean sugar helped somewhat. Despite these developments, the sugar industry continued to be significant until the late nineteenth century and later in places such as Trinidad, Guyana, Barbados, St. Kitts, Nevis, and Antigua. Indeed, sugar and its related products constituted more than 90 percent of the latter four colonies' exports. In Guyana they played a similar role until the last two decades of the nineteenth century, comprising around 90 percent of the colony's total exports and slightly less toward the end of the century and into the next. They remained steady and very important export items until the 1920s.[15] Sugar production fell dramatically in Jamaica, but agricultural production continued, albeit in a different form. Instead, peasants and smallholders on this island grew subsistence (or "provision") crops, as they did in other colonies. But they also cultivated crops for export, including coffee and especially bananas.[16] From the late nineteenth century, the banana industry became increasingly important in Jamaica as the U.S. company United Fruit moved in at the expense of the Afro-creole peasants, and by the turn of the century, bananas had well overtaken sugar as an export item.[17]

The introduction of new and more efficient sugar production techniques was part of the effort to produce sugar more profitably.[18] But cheap, adequate, reliable labor supplies were seen as the main solution to the postemancipation sugar crisis. In 1840, Jamaica's Governor Metcalfe identified what would become the two main methods of solving the postslavery "crisis" in plantation production, population growth and immigration. He argued that an "increase in numbers" could solve the problem, but that this would take time. "Extensive immigration" was another possibility, and Europe, Asia, and North America were potential sources.[19] Even before slavery ended, planters from the British Caribbean had begun to search the globe for workers in an effort to solve the labor crisis they were certain would follow emancipation. Between the end of slavery and the end of the nineteenth century, almost 40,000 Africans went to the British Caribbean, along with some 41,000 Europeans (many from Portuguese Madeira) and almost 19,000 Chinese. But migration from South Asia was by far the most significant numerically: Between 1834 and 1920, 429,454 South Asians traveled to the British Caribbean; 238,861 to Guyana; 149,623 to Trinidad; and 38,595 to Jamaica.[20] Their numbers began to fall from the 1880s and dropped even further after the turn of the century.[21] Planters continued to call for more imports into the twentieth century on the grounds that there were insufficient supplies of local cheap labor to profitably produce the sugar, bananas, and cocoa needed to sustain the colonial economies.[22] The system of indentured immigration from South Asia was supposed to be temporary, bringing workers to the Caribbean to labor on the sugar estates for a fixed number of years before returning home, but around 70 percent remained, adding a permanent new presence to these colonies.[23]

Planters also looked to neighboring islands for laborers in the postemancipation period. Low wages and limited land for cultivation encouraged Barbadians, Antiguans, and residents of other "small islands" where planters had more completely dominated landownership to travel to Guyana and

Trinidad.[24] In total, a little over 21,000 Barbadians emigrated between 1861 and 1881.[25] Planters and colonial governments in these islands watched the exodus with dismay and ensured the passage of legislation discouraging would-be migrants.[26] British Caribbean people emigrated farther afield as well. Construction of the Panama Canal, first by the French in the 1880s and then by the Americans in the early twentieth century, drew tens of thousands.[27] Sugar plantations in Cuba and fruit production in Central America were also attractive to would-be migrants, as was the U.S. mainland.[28]

As Jamaica's Metcalfe argued in 1840, reproduction was also seen as a solution to the postslavery demographic crisis. The official reports that appeared with greater regularity as the nineteenth century progressed demonstrated the nature of the problem that needed to be solved. By the late nineteenth century, the increasing availability of demographic data allowed officials and physicians to draw conclusions about the size of the laboring population. The official reports showed that overall, populations were increasing. (See Table 1.) In Jamaica, immigration and especially an excess of births over deaths contributed to this pattern.[29] Guyana's population, on the other hand, would not have grown at all without immigrants, at least before the 1920s, something that colonial officials were well aware of.[30] Above all, the reports also showed high mortality rates generally in the region, especially among the very young.

The response of colonial officials in Barbados about that colony's postemancipation population "crisis" reflected a mixture of relief, alarm, and racial anxiety. To planters, a large population in an island with few options for mass landownership ensured the presence of the large numbers of cheap workers believed necessary for the profitable production of sugar. But some officials and commentators worried that this large population could undermine political stability and precipitate a "Malthusian" population crisis; indeed, in the early 1830s, a Barbadian newspaper predicted just such a development and called for the "excess" population to be sent to the United States.[31] The official policy on emigration fluctuated in response to these concerns. In the early postemancipation period, the Barbadian government attempted to restrict emigration by passing a series of anti-emigration measures, such as the 1838 "bastardy" law that penalized parents who left the colony and "abandoned" their children.[32] Some objected to emigration because of its perceived impact on population fitness. Writing in 1891, for example, the author of the census report, C. J. Lawance, argued that the current system of migration led to the exodus of the more "productive" groups and to an increase in the

Table 1. *Census Results for the British Caribbean, 1841 to 1931*

COLONY	1841–44	1851	1861	1871	1881	1891
Barbados	122,198	135,939	152,727	162,042	171,860	182,867
Guyana	98,133	125,692	148,026	193,491	244,478	270,865
Belize	(10,000)	—	25,635	24,710	27,452	31,471
Jamaica	377,433	—	441,255	506,154	580,804	639,491
Antigua	36,687	37,757	37,125	35,157	34,964	36,819
Montserrat	7,365	7,053	7,645	8,893	10,083	11,762
St. Kitts–Nevis	32,748	20,741	34,125	42,576	44,220	47,662
Virgin Islands	6,689	—	—	6,651	5,287	4,639
Trinidad and Tobago	73,023	82,978	99,848	126,692	171,179	218,381
Dominica	22,469	—	25,065	27,178	28,211	26,841
Grenada	28,923	32,671	31,900	37,684	42,403	53,209
St. Lucia	21,001	24,318	26,674	31,610	38,551	42,220
St. Vincent	27,248	30,128	31,755	35,755	40,548	41,054
Total BWI	863,917	—	—	123,8326	1,440,040	1,607,218

numbers of the "infirm" and "the comparatively non-productive sections of the population," points that his successors would repeat into the 1920s and 1930s.[33]

Environmental and political crises convinced others of the need for emigration, and the Darwinian concepts of population struggle and survival provided a framework to express these anxieties. In the early 1860s, in the face of drought and food shortages so severe that many Barbadians had to steal food to survive, colonial authorities reduced the restrictions on emigration.[34] The 1871 census convinced Governor Rawson W. Rawson that "pestilence or emigration" were the likely results if another drought or two occurred. He wanted to see a "well-regulated emigration" system rather than a "free-for-all" exodus, which he believed would harm the economy.[35] The violent disturbances of 1876 (the Federation Riots) were also seen as demonstrating the risks of overpopulation.[36] The commissioners investigating the colonial poor laws drew a similar conclusion, arguing that the population "redundancy" contributed to the "widespread poverty" afflicting the island. In their eyes, the colony was "teeming" with people, "swarm[ing] with human beings like a bee-hive or ant-hill."[37] Calls for emigration as a solution to the population crisis continued as the century progressed and as the fortunes of the sugar industry declined further. Lawance described "densely peopled" Barbados as the site of a Darwinian

1901	1911	1921	1931
—	172,237	156,774	—
—	289,140	288,541	302,585
37,479	40,458	45,317	51,347
—	831,383	858,118	—
34,971	32,269	29,767	—
12,215	12,196	12,120	—
46,446	42,303	38,214	—
4,908	5,562	5,082	—
273,899	333,552	365,913	412,789
28,894	33,863	37,059	—
63,483	66,750	66,302	—
49,883	48,637	51,505	—
—	41,877	44,447	47,961
—	1,951,327	1,999,159	—

Source: Roberts, *Population of Jamaica*, 330–32. For some census years, Roberts recalculated the totals to take account of problems with the original figures. For Guyana, for example, he excluded the indigenous population from his calculation, arguing that the population numbers for this group were never accurate. The compilers for the Guyanese census reports often noted that they could not identify the number of aboriginals in the colony.

struggle, a place where a "[keen] struggle for existence" was part of daily life. In such a context, population growth was a "calamity."[38] In the annual report for 1899, the colonial secretary, Ralph Williams, described Barbados as a place where a surfeit of people and a scarcity of resources meant that the "weakest" would inevitably "go to the wall."[39] Both men believed that emigration was the solution. The "abundant population," Williams argued, "must somehow find an outlet."[40]

Both black and white Barbadians emigrated, but to colonial officials, the exodus of "poor whites" was the source of racial anxieties. This group comprised the majority of Barbados's white population, and during slavery white men in particular had served an important strategic purpose through their role in the militia. With emancipation, they were no longer needed for this role, and their poverty meant they could not afford to buy land. The result was considerable economic hardship.[41] Colonial officials encouraged them to emigrate to other islands or to North America, a policy that may have reflected a similar desire seen in other colonial settings to rid colonies of "nonproductive men" who could threaten "the image of a healthy, empowered, and 'vigorous' race" and "colonial prestige."[42] Indeed, this group stood out as among the only whites in Barbados seriously affected by the cholera epidemics of the 1850s. According to Rawson, they "suffered severely."[43] If this was the reason behind their emigration, it seemed to have been successful. In 1871, Rawson was able to observe that the poor whites were "gradually disappearing as a class."[44] Census reports noted the steady fall in the number of Barbadians identified as white, from 11.7 percent in 1851 to 6.7 percent in 1921.[45] But to one official, the shrinking number of whites reflected the kinds of concerns expressed about the reproduction of the "better classes" heard in contemporary Britain, leavened by a particularly colonial apprehension. Lawance speculated that the "habit of self-denial by persons in the higher walks of life"—and hence their likely decision to postpone starting families—contributed to the falling number of whites. In contrast, the "large mass of the lower orders of Society" was probably immune to such a "prudential motive." He also saw whites as unfit for the tropics and suspected that the "law of natural selection" would eventually result in the replacement of Europeans by a "hardier race" able to survive in the colony.[46] This old climatic understanding of race combined with a Darwinian view that only the fittest would flourish seemed to predict an end to Europeans in the Caribbean.

Throughout much of the British Caribbean in this period, government reports and censuses pointed to another demographic trend that was seen as constituting a crisis, infant mortality. These figures were not collected systematically until the early twentieth century, but they began to appear in some official sources from the 1880s.[47] Most would have agreed with the statement by Barbados's chairman of the central poor law board, H. Pilgrim, that a "healthy and long-lived working population" was necessary for a colony's success and that infant mortality threatened this.[48] In underpopulated Guyana, these views were expressed strongly. In the 1890s, a group of Guyanese physicians began to advocate for policies encouraging population growth by reproduction.

The Scottish-born physician Robert Grieve essayed one of the first forays into the discussion. The former naval surgeon arrived in Guyana in the 1880s and helped create the institutional structures that facilitated these debates in this colony. Grieve headed the Berbice Lunatic Asylum before becoming Guyana's surgeon general in 1885, a position he held until 1894. He also helped revitalize the Guyanese branch of the British Medical Association, one of the oldest such groups in the British Caribbean but inactive since its official establishment in 1883. In 1886, the branch began holding regular meetings at which members could present the results of their medical research and advocate for professional causes. Grieve was president of the branch from 1888 to 1894 and a regular contributor to

Guyana's two main medical publications, the *Berbice Asylum Journal*, which he edited and mostly wrote, and its successor publication, the *British Guiana Medical Annual*, which began publishing intermittently from 1890.[49]

The first reports issued by the colonial registrar general convinced Grieve that Guyana's rate of infant mortality was unusually high, which he found surprising for a place that he did not see as especially lethal. At 203 deaths of children under one year per 1,000 births, the rate was double that of England as a whole and much higher than in English cities.[50] He believed that most of these deaths could be prevented if more care was paid to eradicating "filth" and ensuring that infants had access to clean air and adequate food.[51] He held parents responsible, arguing that their ignorance, "carelessness, and indifference" were potentially deadly.[52] Grieve also believed they were lazy. Their "dislike of hard work" contributed to the poverty that condemned their infants to early death.[53] These interpretations of infant mortality were expressed in other places, including contemporary Britain, but in a postslavery colony such as Guyana, they resonated with race-based interpretations of emancipation.

Creole physicians also contributed to the growing discussion about infant mortality in these colonies and, for the most part, echoed dominant contemporary interpretations about its causes. Scottish physicians like Grieve had a long history in the British Caribbean, where they worked on the sugar estates during the period of slavery, but many white (and some colored) creoles also practiced medicine in these colonies.[54] They set up private practices and worked in the government medical services established in most of the region by the late nineteenth century. In Guyana, two white creole physicians played important roles in addressing the combined subjects of infant health and reproduction, Joseph Edward (J. E.) Godfrey and William de Weever (W. de W.) Wishart. Godfrey first worked as a government medical officer before becoming the surgeon general (1904 to 1914).[55] He was also the president of the local branch of the British Medical Association in the late 1890s, and both positions gave him considerable influence. Wishart was the first medical officer of health for Georgetown and would become a relentless advocate for infant and maternal welfare reforms in the first three decades of the twentieth century.[56] Wishart, Godfrey, and colonial physicians used the *British Guiana Medical Annual* and the local medical association to explore this problem and suggest solutions. They saw themselves as standing on the shoulders of earlier physicians, especially Grieve, and repeated their arguments about the environmental and social factors leading to infant mortality, notably congestion, poor air, poor food, and parental ignorance.[57] Like his British counterparts, Wishart believed that these problems were particularly prevalent among poor mothers, whom he saw as dangerously ignorant about child rearing.[58] Godfrey saw education as the solution and argued that physicians in particular had a "duty" to address the problem of infant mortality and should "preach to the Public" about their failings in this respect.[59] He believed that the methods used in Britain, such as milk depots and "practical lessons" for poor mothers, should be introduced in Guyana, as they would help reduce the extent of "improper feeding" and "maternal ignorance," seen as the main causes of infant death.[60] Doubtless aware of late nineteenth-century studies pointing to the health risks for infants who consumed contaminated milk, physicians like Godfrey encouraged mothers to breast-feed, rather than giving their infants indigestible mixtures of starch (arrowroot, rice, corn, flour, or cassava), water, and sugar known as "paps."[61]

To Godfrey, infant mortality was primarily a problem of "the Black race." He observed that its incidence was much higher among Afro-Guyanese than South Asians, 238 per 1,000 and 171 per 1,000, respectively, something he attributed to what he saw as South Asians' tendency to follow contemporary sanitary "rules" for ensuring infant survival.[62] He argued that South Asian women were more likely to breast-feed their infants or to feed them "pure milk" and to ensure they had "pure air." Occupation had something to do with this; many South Asians kept cows to provide milk for sale and personal consumption, and Godfrey believed this enabled them to feed their infants "properly."[63] A mixture of older miasmic ideas (pure air) and newer ones about the importance of clean, hygienic milk for infant health informed his thinking, but it also resonated with representations of former slaves as irrational "sanitary subjects." Former slaves had been condemned during the cholera epidemic of the 1850s for their "purported indifference" to their health and that of their families, and similar views were expressed in the 1896 British government investigation into the British Caribbean economy, part of the imperial response to the late nineteenth-century economic crisis. The commission heard from colonial physicians and Britons and West Indians involved in the sugar industry who described Afro-Caribbean men and women as incapable of looking after their own health and as bad parents. A British sugar merchant whose firm owned property in Guyana, Quintin Hogg, described former slaves as generally incapable of obeying simple sanitary laws, something he maintained contributed to their high rates of sickness.[64] Trinidad's surgeon general, F. Lovell, blamed both "neglect" and "poor feeding" for the high mortality among black infants, and the district medical officer, S. A. De Wolf, pointed to their parents' "ignorance and carelessness."[65] In contrast, some planters held that South Asians were kinder and more "careful" parents.[66]

In the late 1890s, a Guyana-based clergyman, Rev. J. G. Pearson, published two articles in a local publication that starkly set out this contrast. Pearson used the racist language of the old, embittered planter class to describe former slaves as well as a gendered view of emancipation. Africans, he argued, were "barbarians" without "history and tradition," and slaves were fortunate in being brought to the Caribbean, where they benefited from the influence of the "white man."[67] But after the end of slavery, Pearson maintained, former slaves refused to work, lapsing into "apathetic indifference to the claims of manhood" and reverting to barbarism. What he saw as a failure of manhood had deadly results; men who refused to work put their children at "risk of passive infanticide."[68] In contrast, and despite his use of ethnic stereotypes (parsimonious, crafty, and philosophical are just a few), Pearson described the "East Indian" and "his" wife as good parents who raised their son to prosperous and reproductive manhood.[69] But by the early twentieth century, as increasing numbers of former indentured South Asians left the estates and their controlling influence for life in villages and towns, they began to present a similar problem. A government medical officer in Guyana noted that once they were no longer "under the control of the Estates' authorities, their mode of life [was] not conducive to the nurturing of healthy infants."[70]

The hysteria over the sale of "impure" milk by South Asian milk vendors in Guyana in the early twentieth century can be seen as one example of this tendency to characterize free populations as dangers to themselves and their offspring. The revolutions in public health and medical science that saw municipal governments increase oversight and regulation of urban consumer items such as milk combined to target the milk industry as a source of danger and "free" South Asian milk sellers as its purveyor. Newspapers published stories and editorials to this effect, and colonial physicians provided the scientific proof. The future surgeon general, K. S. Wise, and a colonial physician and bacteriologist, E. P. Minett, argued that the production and storage of milk in unsanitary conditions and its sale by "a people who [had] no idea of even the rudiments of hygiene" resulted in the sale of milk "unfit for human food, especially for infants."[71]

Although some Afro-creoles sold milk, much of the "moral panic" surrounding its sale in the early twentieth century targeted South Asians.[72]

These colonial concerns about population health and reproduction came together in Swettenham's 1903 letter to Joseph Chamberlain that opened this chapter.[73] Swettenham pointed to a shrinking population and high rates of illegitimate births and infant mortality among the African-descended population as developments that made him fear for the future and that proved that the earlier optimism about emancipation's results had not been realized. The failure of the Afro-Guyanese population to grow had an impact on the indentureship system, notably whether it should be "encouraged or discouraged."[74]

Swettenham was describing a Guyanese problem, and he drew heavily from the reports of his own surgeon general, Joseph Godfrey. But his letter arrived in a Colonial Office ready to interpret the Guyanese data as part of a regional trend. Two Jamaican governors (Sydney Oliver and Henry Blake) had relayed similar concerns to Chamberlain, as had the governor of Barbados, Frederick Hodgson.[75] This flurry of correspondence convinced one Colonial Office official that the "black population [was] not advancing" and may even have been "retrogressing morally." If this was the case, the situation was "very serious, not merely from a purely religious point of view . . . but from the social & political point of view, as the terms of personal responsibility and the family life [were] the basis of sound and healthy national life."[76]

Imperial officials called for colonial officials to investigate not only the extent of infant mortality but also the incidence of crime and illegitimacy and the degree of social responsibility to family and country.[77]

Investigating Infant Mortality

These exchanges inaugurated an era of increasingly systematic efforts in the British Caribbean to collect information about the intertwined problems of population growth, infant health, and reproduction. It also reflected the increasingly paternalistic approach that the British government took to imperial affairs in this period and the extent to which health and reproduction were made to serve this end.[78] A few British Caribbean governments had collected infant mortality statistics before 1900, but the practice became ubiquitous after 1903.[79] Colonial concerns about health and population decline not only in the British Caribbean but elsewhere in the empire encouraged the Colonial Office to prod Caribbean governments to collect this information, as did the findings of Britain's own Interdepartmental Committee on Physical Deterioration.[80] Some of the British actors may have changed—Chamberlain left his position in fall 1903, and Liberals replaced the Unionist-Conservative coalition in 1905—but concerns about health and degeneration continued to be expressed.[81] Shortly after the 1903 exchanges between Swettenham and Joseph Chamberlain's Colonial Office, the governments of Guyana, Jamaica, and Barbados initiated extensive investigations into colonial population problems. These inquiries brought together colonial officials, physicians, and members of the traditional elites and the emerging colonial middle class.

Imperial officials saw the Guyanese interest in population health and infant mortality as an opportunity. When Frederick Hodgson arrived in Guyana as governor in 1904 after several years in Barbados, one of his first acts was to send a copy of Godfrey's most recent report as surgeon general to the Colonial Office. The report bluntly described the high rates of infant mortality in the colony. Godfrey believed that his report played a key role in the 1905 infant mortality investigation, and he was probably correct.[82] It caught the attention of Colonial Office officials, including Secretary of State Alfred Lyttleton, who encouraged the governor to investigate the situation.[83] Colonial Office officials subsequently noted that Guyana could be a "lesson for the rest of the West Indies" in dealing with the problem of infant mortality and that they should offer as much assistance as possible.[84]

The Guyanese commission into infant and general mortality represented a cross section of the colonial professional and political classes. It included Godfrey, Wishart, and Luke Mullock (L. M.) Hill, the town superintendent for Georgetown who had taken a particular interest in sanitary matters for some time. For years, he had acted as a kind of de facto chief sanitary inspector and medical officer of health combined. Colonial government representatives for Georgetown were also included, as were several municipal politicians.[85] Those who testified or who provided written reports included ministers, physicians, sanitary inspectors, and municipal and colonial officials. Some of the commissioners and witnesses were from Britain, but others were Guyanese of British, Portuguese, or African descent.

In assessing the causes of infant mortality, the commissioners drew on a combination of old and new medical ideas as well as contemporary views that highlighted the significance of poverty.[86] They repeated points that Godfrey and Wishart had been making since the late 1890s

and those expressed in the more or less contemporaneous British investigation into "physical deterioration." They concluded that poor sanitation and malnutrition contributed to infant deaths, the latter caused by
maternal "neglect of breast-feeding" in favor of "starchy and other indigestible foods." They also pointed to some of the newer medical findings
about the role of disease in this respect, notably "heredity syphilis" and
the "physical degeneration of the mother" caused by malaria.[87] Poverty
also contributed to infant mortality, something that they saw as cut-
ting across ethnic lines. Poverty-stricken Afro-, Indo-, and Portuguese-
Guyanese all experienced the poor living conditions that caused infant
mortality.[88]

The presence of the Portuguese in Guyana and the readiness with
which they found themselves described in sanitarian terms points to the
porous nature of the categories used to represent the causes of infant
mortality and population decline. As did "poor whites" in Barbados, the
Portuguese in Guyana occupied an ambiguous social position. Imported
to work on the sugar estates after the end of slavery, by the early twentieth
century many had moved into the petty retail sector in the colony's towns
and villages. Some became wealthy merchants and members of the middle and professional classes, using their economic and cultural capital to
enter the political realm. But significant numbers remained poor. Like
their black neighbors in Georgetown's poor districts, they lived in ram-
shackle homes in unsanitary areas. The commissioners condemned both
groups as ignorant about the "primary principles of sanitary living" and
noted that both experienced the highest rates of mortality in the city, infantile and otherwise.[89] One of the physicians who testified at the inquiry,
W. F. Law, incited a controversy when his comment that the "lowest class
of Portuguese in the city [were] about the dirtiest in their habits" was reprinted in the *Daily Chronicle* newspaper.[90]

The Wages of Sin

The commissioners and witnesses to the Guyanese investigation into
the causes of infant mortality pointed to a range of factors they believed
responsible, from urban poverty and poor sanitary conditions to "tropical" diseases such as malaria. They also saw this population problem as
profoundly entangled with moral questions. Specifically, they maintained
that "illegitimate" infants were more likely to die young, condemned to
an early death by their "careless" and "indifferent" parents.

The perceived moral and social costs of illegitimacy and concubinage were objects of concern in a number of countries and colonies where they were seen as a social and moral evil or as upsetting colonial hierarchies, blurring crucial differences.[91] In Britain, "powerful social mores," legislation, and policies "stigmatized" illegitimacy and other unrespectable sexual practices.[92] In the late eighteenth and early nineteenth centuries, religious leaders responded to rapidly rising rates of illegitimacy and extramarital sex by encouraging members of the British working classes to marry and live more "respectable" domestic lives.[93] In the British Caribbean, low rates of marriage and high rates of illegitimacy were also subjects of moral concern, but they were tied to assessments about the success or failure of emancipation. During the period of slavery, abolitionists and missionaries had encouraged slaves to marry, seeing this ritual as synonymous with Christianity and salvation and as contributing to population growth.[94] Higman has argued that planters accepted a relationship between marriage or "faithful cohabitation" and fertility levels, but the same can be said for abolitionists. Planters and abolitionists blamed "'promiscuity' and 'vice'" for slaves' failure to reproduce, but whereas planters tended to attribute this to slaves' "debauched" nature, abolitionists held the slave system itself responsible for slaves' "immoral" behavior.[95] Clergymen believed that sex outside the bonds of marriage weakened civilization and inhibited population growth.[96] Missionaries saw formal marriage as synonymous with Christianity and salvation, and consequently they were among the most enthusiastic advocates of slave marriage.[97] Enslaved men and women could marry, but they faced significant obstacles, including the necessity that they obtain their owners' permission and the likelihood that they could be sold away from their spouses.[98] With the passage of amelioration legislation in the 1820s, abolitionists hoped that slave marriage would become more frequent, and they anticipated that the end of slavery would lead to an increase in the incidence of marriage.[99] The willingness of former slaves to marry and form such families became the standard against which their advance in civilization was measured. Initial reports that the incidence of marriage had increased after the end of slavery were soon replaced by claims that former slaves continued to "live in sin." The refusal of many black men and women to marry formally and their decision to live in alternate domestic arrangements were represented as evidence of their debauched and uncivilized nature. The Guyanese planter Barton Premium spoke for many when he described the reluctance of former slaves to marry as evidence of their having become "more wicked than they were ten years ago."[100] Social and political elites throughout the British Caribbean maintained that the low incidence of marriage among Afro-creoles proved that they were uncivilized and unfit for freedom.[101] Many agreed with Jamaica's Governor A. Musgrave that the low incidence of marriage in late nineteenth-century Jamaica reflected the poor moral state of the population.[102]

When officials and missionaries referred to marriage, they were referring to a particular religious (Christian) and legal ritual, one recognized by the state and mainstream Christian groups as sanctifying sexual relations between men and women and providing a context for reproducing the population. For a variety of economic, social, and cultural reasons, rates of formal marriage in the British Caribbean have tended to be low. Some scholars have blamed the hold of the past for this pattern, notably African kinship patterns and the legacy of plantation slavery.[103] Others have pointed to more prosaic factors such as the price of a marriage license and the cost of meeting the social expectations attendant upon marriage, notably entertaining friends and family during the celebration itself and setting up a household. The economic demands of the period also played an important role. High rates of migration, especially relevant for Barbados and Jamaica in this period, as well as internal migration, that saw men and women leave their homes to work in cities or the mining and timber sectors in places like Guyana and Belize presented significant obstacles for anyone who wanted to create and maintain permanent domestic relationships, regardless of their form and legality. As Christine Barrow has argued for postemancipation Barbados, "Colonial conjugal ideas of romantic, monogamous, enduring marriage and co-residence along with full-time wife/motherhood and familial patriarchy" were at the very least "impractical" for most people.[104]

Much of the discourse around marriage and illegitimacy in the postemancipation British Caribbean focused on former slaves; in the eyes of imperial and colonial officials, low rates of formal marriage among this group were among the most disappointing results of emancipation. But officials also worried about marriage and sexual relationships among the predominantly Hindu and Muslim South Asian population. Rates of formal, Christian marriage were extremely low, and non-Christian rites were not recognized unless participants took the extra step of appearing before a government official to have the marriage registered, something that most seemed not to have done.[105] The importation of significantly fewer women than men was believed to lead to immoral and violent sexual behavior.[106]

Women were described as exploiting their scarcity by moving from man to man, and their purportedly immoral behavior provoked what officials saw as inevitable male violence.[107] The rash of "wife murders" in Guyana was seen as the natural result.[108]

To colonial officials in the British Caribbean, marriage was necessary to nurture the successful reproduction of the population. Unmarried women and men were seen as incapable of successfully raising the next generation of (re)productive adults. When Guyana's Governor James Longden declared that former slaves were "indifferent to the welfare of their children," he meant unmarried parents.[109] To Jamaica's first registrar general, S. P. Smeeton, the fact that almost 60 percent of all births were "illegitimate" was a "sad state of things." To officials like Smeeton, the consequences were potentially dire. The children of unmarried parents were seen as likely candidates for a poor, criminal class, a "residuum." Smeeton believed that legally sanctioned families had a "cohesive force" and produced "law-abiding and thrifty members of a progressive community." On the other hand, the products of nonlegal unions became either "burdens upon or outlaws against, the better portions of the people."[110] The members of the Barbados Poor Law Commission in 1874–75 echoed these points, declaring that illegitimacy led to poverty and that the children of "temporary connections" were "neglected and ill cared for," ending up sickly, ignorant, and criminal.[111] The temporary poor law inspector in early twentieth-century Barbados, J. Briggs Clarke, declared that "bastardy and concubinage" "furnishe[d] the almshouse with most of the children which the Ratepayers [had] to support in these institutions." He argued that frequently "two or three broods of children [were] propagated by the same father, each set left in its turn to fight out its own salvation with the result that if the mothers [were] not able to support them, these children drift[ed] on the poor rates."[112]

The "Darwinian" views expressed by this Barbadian official reflected a long-standing tendency to denigrate Caribbean mating patterns and to see them as responsible for a range of social ills rather than highlighting, for example, the economic crisis of the day. In his testimony before the late nineteenth-century West India commission struck to investigate this very matter, Rev. Henry Clarke, who had been in Jamaica since 1847, argued that illegitimate status determined the future life chances of children. These children were likely to die young and thus contributed to the high rate of infant mortality. Those who survived did so without the benefit of "parental training or control except what [was] evil." They ended up unemployed and were probably responsible for the "praedial larceny which [was] so loudly complained of throughout the island."[113] As Clarke's comments suggest, illegitimacy was seen as doing much worse than producing a criminal residuum. It also led to infant mortality and consequently threatened the survival of the population. This view was expressed regularly by colonial officials in the late nineteenth and early twentieth centuries. Smeeton declared that the "baneful touch of illegitimacy" could be felt in Jamaica's high levels of infant mortality. In such families, he argued, affection and loyalty were absent, something that may well have contributed to indifferent efforts to keep infants alive.[114]

Despite these condemnations, there was still some debate about the meaning of illegitimacy. By "illegitimate," most officials, physicians, planters, and other contributors to colonial writings on this subject meant children born outside formal marriage. Some attempted a slightly more nuanced view, such as the commissioners investigating infant mortality in Guyana. They distinguished "concubinage of the West Indian type" from "promiscuous and temporary sexual relationships" and argued that the former did not contribute to infant mortality, whereas the latter did.[115] But this ambiguity was not reflected in official accounts, which tended to use illegitimacy as an all-encompassing category that included all children born to unmarried mothers. This approach led to the kind of conclusions expressed by Jamaica's Smeeton. Starting in 1900, he began publishing the deaths of "legitimate" and "illegitimate" children to show, as he noted, "the extent to which Illegitimacy appear[ed] to be inimical to Infant Life."[116] For Smeeton, illegitimacy was a single, unqualified category. David Balfour, who took over as registrar general in 1908, did not follow Smeeton's lead. As did other colonial officials, Balfour condemned illegitimacy. But he suggested that tracking the numbers of deaths of children considered illegitimate did not reveal much more than was already known about the factors determining infant health. He argued that most illegitimate children were born to "the poorest and most ignorant mothers, and in most unsanitary surroundings." Married parents were, for the most part, wealthier and better educated. Balfour maintained that poor, unmarried mothers did not "deliberately [neglect]" their children and did not regard them as burdens "simply because they [were] illegitimate."[117]

Balfour's argument that illegitimate children suffered mostly from the effects of poverty and his suggestion that social class heavily influenced infant survival were commonly expressed. For many, illegitimacy pointed to a constellation of social factors that, taken together, were believed detrimental to infant health. The economic crisis of the late nineteenth century convinced many men to leave their home islands to look for work and compelled many mothers to work outside the home, factors blamed for poor infant health. Some working mothers, in turn, left their children in the care of others who could be neglectful. The mothers themselves were unable to nurse their children during the day, and many could not afford to buy milk as a healthy substitute. For colonial officials and physicians such as Guyana's Robert Grieve, the relationship between illegitimacy and infant mortality was clear. It was also universal. Grieve believed that this pattern held in England as well as in tropical colonies like Guyana. The children of unmarried parents were seen as facing a struggle to survive.[118]

To some Caribbean observers, however, the apparent relationship between infant mortality and illegitimacy pointed in a more ominous direction; infant deaths were a criminal matter. The late nineteenth-century police magistrate in Guyana, Henry Kirke, described the "lingering death by starvation and neglect" that was the lot of illegitimate children as a kind of "infanticide," but he noted that it was not the "deliberate slaying of infants by violence."[119] In late nineteenth- and early twentieth-century Jamaica, however, officials, physicians, and other commentators associated infant mortality with infanticide. Charles Mosse, Jamaica's superintending medical officer in the late nineteenth century, believed that "indifference and neglect" were partly responsible for the deaths of infants and young children, but that the "desire to be relieved of" illegitimate children was likely also responsible.[120] To Mosse, this was a criminal and moral matter, but it was also an economic one. He believed that "in a country of so sparse a labouring population," the "money loss resulting from premature and avoidable mortality" should be a source of "deep concern to and elicit the helpful sympathy of the philanthropic members of a community which includes many thoughtful and cultured minds."[121] Mosse's comments were part of a wider "moral panic" in late nineteenth- and early twentieth-century Jamaica about the extent of infanticide. Letters to the editor, editorials, and trial accounts of women accused of killing their children all contributed to this.[122] An editorial in the Gleaner from the late nineteenth century agreed with the view of a local physician who argued that infant deaths were due to "unqualified midwives," "unconsciousness ignorance," and a "lack of precaution," but that a "large percentage" were the "result of criminal neglect or worse."[123]

In postslavery colonies such as those in the Caribbean, these interpretations intersected with perceptions of race and gender. Black men were seen as sexually voracious, a proclivity believed to strip them of any sense of parental responsibility, a point made by several of the physicians who testified at the 1896 royal commission. W. G. Branch, for example, argued that the purported excessive sexual appetites of black men and their innate lack of parental affection made them neglectful fathers; not knowing the identities of their children made them indifferent to their survival.[124] A. E. Edwards, a district medical officer in Antigua, acknowledged that poverty doubtless compelled many men to migrate to places like Trinidad or South America for work, but he also saw this exodus as a willful act motivated by a desire to escape familial responsibilities.[125] The commissioners to Guyana's 1905 investigation into mortality argued that men's "lack of strong parental feelings" and "legal responsibility" to their offspring impoverished mothers and doomed their infants to early death. Women, too, were condemned, or at least those "of the lowest class of women."[126] Some of the harshest rhetoric came from members of the clergy. As Rev. W. B. Ritchie of the Church of Scotland (probably) thundered, "*The wages of sin [were] death.*"[127]

These views about the medical and moral consequences of illegitimacy were expressed by some Afro-creoles, particularly members of the clergy. As did their white counterparts, they saw sex and marriage as serious matters and believed that violating sacred laws had profound consequences. In making this point, men such as Guyana's Rev. F. C. (Fitzgerald Charles) Glasgow used the moral language of the day. In his testimony before the 1905 mortality commission, this Congregationalist minister blamed infant mortality on "loose, careless, and improper moral habits" and the "careless exposure of infants by thoughtless women."[128] An adherence to the "respectable" values of sex and gender seemed to limit Glasgow's sympathy.

Similar views were expressed in Jamaica, where they, too, were part of the discussion about marriage and illegitimacy. In this colony, a number of individuals and groups lobbied for marriage and against informal unions, including Smeeton and the Society for the Promotion of Social Purity, which was formed to address the "evils arising from the widespread neglect of marriage."[129] Their pressure doubtless encouraged the governor, Augustus Lawson Hemming, to establish an inquiry into the operation of the marriage laws in 1903, but regional and imperial developments also played a role.[130] This discussion occurred while Guyanese officials were addressing this issue and Colonial Office officials were encouraging Caribbean governments to investigate what they saw as the combined problems of illegitimacy and infant mortality. The Jamaican commission itself sat in December 1903, less than a year after Swettenham relayed his concerns to the Colonial Office. Hemming's earlier experiences in Guyana as the governor of that colony, where he would have heard physicians and others discuss the intertwined problems of infant mortality and population size, likely also played a role in the Jamaican developments.[131]

Whereas Guyana's inquiry a year later focused mostly on infant mortality, that held in Jamaica concentrated on investigating the laws regulating marriage and legitimacy, identifying the causes of concubinage and illegitimacy, and suggesting solutions. Their conclusions indicated the moral concerns of those involved and their desire to purify Jamaican society. The commission was led by clergymen and colonial officials such as Smeeton. The commissioners blamed a combination of social and economic factors, including poor, overcrowded housing; the inability or unwillingness of men to support their families; absence of recreational facilities; and the general low "moral tone" of the population. They also blamed history or, rather, the experience of slavery, when legal, Christian marriage was discouraged and local whites set poor examples of connubial bliss. The commissioners believed that with time, education, and religious training, more members of the "race" would attain a higher level of "development" and that Jamaica would enter "an era in which its spiritual, moral, and mental development [would] be more rapid than hitherto."[132] To speed this along, they called for new rules facilitating marriage, including reducing the number of times the banns had to be published and the cost of the marriage license, and they recommended facilitating legal recognition of the paternity of illegitimate children.[133] The commissioners hoped that these measures would encourage marriage and discourage "vice and illegitimacy." But their goals were more ambitious than this. They also wanted a clearer moral order, one in which the differences between "marriage and concubinage, . . . legitimacy and illegitimacy, . . . and virtue and vice" would be accepted.[134]

But as was the case in Guyana, these moral goals were entangled with worries about reproduction, specifically the relationship between illegitimacy and infant mortality. As would their Guyanese counterparts some twelve months later, Jamaican commissioners pointed out the differences in mortality rates among infants under a year old born to unmarried parents in comparison to legitimate children. As evidence, they cited the 1902 report by the superintending medical officer (probably Charles Mosse) that pointed to a clear correlation between high rates of illegitimacy and infant mortality, which he blamed on the unwillingness or inability of unmarried mothers to care for their children. Indeed, Mosse emphasized women's responsibility in this respect. He predicted that the "lamentable sacrifice of infant life" would continue until the "rising members of the community, especially the female sex" were educated enough to realize that "this violation of the moral law [was] a heinous sin and crime."[135] For their part, the commissioners focused on the fathers; they proposed legislation that would name "putative" fathers of illegitimate offspring and hold them responsible.[136]

The moral and health costs of illegitimacy weighed on contemporaries, but so did the financial burden they were believed to pose. In British Caribbean colonies such as Jamaica, Barbados, and Guyana, poor relief systems funded by local taxes were responsible for maintaining the sick poor and the indigent, including women and their offspring. Modeled on the British poor law system, these Caribbean institutions provided "indoor" and "outdoor" relief to those deemed eligible.[137] Colonial bastardy laws were supposed to ensure that mothers and their children did not become "burdens" on the taxpayers and that they were maintained by their children's fathers. In places such as Jamaica and especially Barbados, with their high rates of migration, this possibility exercised local officials, as we have seen. Financial concerns and the gendered and racist perceptions of black men and women as sexually uncontrolled came together in the diatribe by Barbados's J. Briggs Clarke when he was the acting poor law inspector. He used this forum to express outrage that men who emigrated left behind families who ended up dependent on the poor laws. He objected when "honest and independent members of a community" had to "support and educate the bastards of improvident and worthless scoundrels."[138] And he vehemently condemned "the indiscriminate admission of lewd women" into the maternity ward in the almshouse in St. Michael's parish, the only such facility in the entire colony. Clarke maintained that these women saw the almshouse as a "convenient place in which to deposit the outcome of their promiscuous intercourse with incorrigible villains in the form of such men as seem[ed] to regard the poor rates as instituted for their especial benefit in this direction."[139]

Barbadian officials responded to concerns about illegitimacy and infant mortality by focusing on perceived problems with the "bastardy laws." John Hutson led the campaign. Like Wishart and Godfrey, he was a white creole who had studied medicine in the United Kingdom (Edinburgh). Hutson was Barbados's poor law and public health inspector until the mid-1920s and another relentless advocate of public health reform.[140] Like the commissioners in Jamaica, he saw amending the bastardy laws as part of the solution to high rates of infant mortality.[141] The exchanges between colonial officials in Guyana and imperial officials in London seemed to have encouraged some of Hutson's investigations into the problem of infant mortality, but they were also shaped by specifically Barbadian concerns. Hutson began tabulating infant mortality figures for Barbados in late 1903, several months after Colonial Office officials responded to Swettenham's dispatch with a call for information.[142] By the following year, he concluded that many of the commonly identified causes of infant mortality were present in Barbados, notably maternal neglect, "industrial conditions" that forced mothers to work and leave their babies at home, and improper feeding, which he attributed to poverty. He also argued that low marriage rates were a factor and that the colony's bastardy acts made the situation even worse by preventing impoverished women from easily obtaining financial support from their children's fathers.[143] Like Jamaica's Smeeton, Hutson called on colonial officials to gather statistics about the mortality rates of infants born to unmarried parents; he believed that doing so would prove his argument about the flawed bastardy laws.[144] His efforts paid off, and the colonial government amended the bastardy act to allow women access to the courts to obtain money from delinquent fathers. (Previously women had been forced to try to obtain it from the fathers themselves.)[145] The impact of this change is uncertain, however, given the requirement that women deposit a shilling to launch legal proceedings.[146]

For Hutson, the ineffective bastardy law provided a plausible explanation for what he and other officials saw as the puzzle of infant mortality in Barbados. They could not understand why it was so high compared with England, a place where, according to Hutson, the climate was "most trying to the extremes of life."[147] Others were just as confused. To the governor of Barbados, Gilbert Carter, "climatic conditions" in Barbados were "favourable to infant life."[148] Barbadians had long perceived their island as healthier than other places in the Caribbean. The authors of the 1874 poor law report explained the reluctance of Barbadians to emigrate by referring to the colony's "healthiness." Unlike other places in the region—with their "rank and uncleared vegetation," their "marshes and stagnant waters, with corresponding miasmatic exhalations"—Barbados was drier, less prone to flooding, and simply healthier.[149] The experiences of Barbadian migrants in places like Guyana and Central America, with their jungles and fevers, doubtless contributed to this view even once the language of miasmas was no longer employed. The regular recuperative visits to Barbados by stricken missionaries and officials based in less salubrious colonies like Guyana were probably also significant in this respect.

The conclusion by Barbados's chief justice William Herbert (W. H.) Greaves that infant mortality was a crime rather than a public health problem suggests a willful blindness on the part of local elites about the conditions in which the vast majority of their countrymen and -women lived. The Barbadian-born Greaves had not realized that the rate of infant mortality in Barbados was higher than elsewhere in the region. He was especially surprised to discover this because, as he noted, as attorney general he should have been made aware of all investigations in Barbados into suspicious deaths. He assumed that infant mortality fell into this category.[150] Greaves's surprise at Hutson's infant mortality figures saw him contact the governor and colonial officials to try to track down the origin of the numbers.[151] The absence of a system to register deaths and identify their causes presented an obstacle, but one that the elected House of Assembly seemed to have no interest in changing, leaving officials to rely on clergy tabulations of burials. Based on this calculation, in 1904 around 43 percent of all burials were for infants under the age of one year, a figure that convinced the colonial secretary, S. W. Knaggs, that in fact there was "excessive infant mortality in Barbados."[152]

Just as they had with Guyana, imperial officials pushed the Barbadian governor to identify the steps he would take to deal with the problem of infant mortality.[153] The governor called on parish poor law officials to weigh in on this matter. Their conclusions surprised at least two officials. The inquiry convinced Knaggs that instances of deliberate abuse were relatively rare and that most parents "treat[ed] their children with kindness and consideration" to the extent that "their means and circumstances" allowed.[154] This was a considerable change, given that he had earlier interpreted infant mortality as a criminal matter. In accordance with these views, he had previously pushed for a law against cruelty to children; one was passed in 1904 following "the lines of the English legislation on the subject."[155] The investigation also changed Greaves's mind. It showed him that poverty rather than "willful neglect" caused most infant deaths.[156]

Despite these sympathetic utterances and the suggested solutions, perceptions of the relationship between behavior, culture, and biological race convinced some officials that infant mortality was inevitable. Indeed, some even speculated on its utility. The parochial poor law officials who had been surveyed concluded that "poverty, ignorance and vice" were to blame for infant mortality, something they believed would probably not change until the "masses" were taught the "responsibilities and duties which they owe[d] towards their children."[157] Knaggs did not think improvement in the rates of infant mortality could come quickly. He argued that as more than 200 years of "evolution" had left the "West Indian negro" with "as little idea or power of self-control as he possessed in his native Africa," "years of gradual and patient teaching" were needed before change would be seen.[158] Governor Carter agreed. In his eyes, the large number of infant deaths in Barbados was "not exceptional." He declared that in every tropical colony in which he had worked, he had seen the same pattern; he considered it inevitable in places where, as he noted, "large numbers of coloured people [were] herded together, and [could] not be got to pay attention to Sanitary matters."[159] These officials also suggested that the overcrowded nature of Barbados presented additional obstacles to reducing the rate of infant mortality. Knaggs suggested that high rates of infant mortality were inevitable in Barbados due to the colony's overcrowded state.[160] Given this, Herbert Greaves speculated that infant mortality might even have served some kind of evolutionary purpose. He noted that the government was obliged to attempt to "preserve" the lives of infants, but that high mortality rates among this group were "a case of the survival of the fittest" and represented a "safety valve" for Barbados.[161] Colonial Office officials themselves pondered this, suggesting that Barbados's "surplus population" might lead to a "tendency" to "hold infant life cheap" and to a reluctance to take steps for its "preservation," as "would be the case where the population [was] too small for the country."[162]

These comments point to the different ways that contemporaries interpreted population growth and infant mortality in the late nineteenth- and early twentieth-century Caribbean. Reproduction was at once a medical, moral, and economic issue. Contemporary population anxieties and the emergence of tropical medicine influenced these concerns and suggested solutions, but so did colonial views of race, gender, and class. These ideas had very real consequences, as the next two chapters demonstrate. They significantly shaped the infant welfare policies established in Guyana,

Jamaica, and Barbados in the first two decades of the twentieth century. Much of the discussion about reproduction and population was carried out among officials in London and the Caribbean who exchanged ideas and tried to see their goals realized with varying degrees of success. Women and their reproductive behavior were their main targets. But as the next chapter shows, Caribbean women had their own ideas about these matters.

CHAPTER THREE

Grannies, Midwives, and Colonial Encounters

COMMENTATORS IN POSTSLAVERY SOCIETIES tended to represent midwives as a cross between Dickensian, gin-swilling slatterns and savage, uncivilized black women. In the postslavery British Caribbean, these old- and new-world tropes found form in the image of the "granny" midwife, whom Violet Nurse, an English matron, described as exercising a "sinister influence in advising the mothers in the use of bush medicines."[1] In the nineteenth- and early twentieth-century British Caribbean, "bush medicine" referred to a popular medical tradition that was often associated with obeah. In describing the grannies as practitioners of bush medicine, Nurse was adding a Caribbean twist to the timeworn characterization of traditional midwives as ignorant and superstitious women whose lack of skill and medical knowledge was seen as sentencing newborns and their mothers to death. Formally trained medical workers such as Nurse blamed traditional midwives, most of whom were of African or South Asian descent, for infant deaths and implicitly held them responsible for the population decline that worried colonial officials. They were also seen as uncivilized and potentially dangerous figures who may even have used such "devilish" practices as obeah.

In late nineteenth- and early twentieth-century Jamaica, Guyana, and Barbados, officials saw replacing the grannies with formally trained and certified midwives as key to solving the population problem discussed in the last chapter. Their efforts to do so highlighted some of the race and class tensions in these societies. White, British-born women like Nurse and Caribbean-based physicians from various ethnic and racial backgrounds defended professional boundaries designed to ensure that only formally trained midwives from "respectable" backgrounds could minister to new mothers and instruct them in modern methods of child rearing. But the poor, mostly nonwhite women who were the targets of the various infant and maternal welfare initiatives that emerged in the early twentieth century also played an important role in the development of Caribbean midwife training. They used the trained midwives and the maternity hospitals established in this period, sometimes too enthusiastically, in the opinion of the colonial officials who condemned them for taking advantage of these facilities. But these women also continued to rely on granny midwives. Their reasons varied, but in doing so they ensured that the grannies did not vanish from the Caribbean landscape, as much as physicians and matrons like Nurse hoped they would. Their presence and the everyday realities of life in these islands forced officials and physicians to make room for them in the regulated world of colonial midwifery. This reflected a pragmatic assessment that the goals of ensuring safe childbirths and disseminating modern child-rearing information could best be achieved if the grannies were subjected to some official oversight. But this policy also indicated that in making their own decisions about childbirth, constrained as these were by a range of economic and cultural imperatives, Caribbean women helped shape the options that were available to them.

"Filthy and Ignorant"

In the late nineteenth and early twentieth centuries, traditional midwives were widely condemned. One Briton living in Guyana in the 1880s described them as drunken and "innate[ly] savage" and either so "sottish[ly] indifferen[t] to the feelings of other people" or so "maddened" with drink that they "committed acts of brutality."[2] Although hyperbolic, these comments highlight common discursive patterns in the representation of black midwives in slave and postslave societies. In her work on the relationship between physicians and African midwives in the Cape Colony, Harriet Deacon has argued that a "neat combination of the European image of the 'untrained' midwife as a dirty, ignorant, drunk and gossipy old woman" intersected with racist colonial views of black women.[3] Scholars have argued that such representations indicate the professional tensions in the nineteenth and early twentieth centuries that accompanied the gradual entrance of male physicians into the previously female-dominated world of childbirth.[4] But these images also resonate with cultural conflicts seen in many parts of the world in this period, something that in the colonial context was tied to the self-proclaimed civilizing mission of imperial authorities.[5] Untangling the discourses of race, gender, and class that underlay images of traditional midwives is especially challenging in postslavery societies. In the United States, the following quotations from two early twentieth-century physicians demonstrate the ways in which they could overlap. To these physicians, traditional midwives were "old, gin-fingering, guzzling [women] . . . with [their] mouth full of snuff, [their] fingers full of dirt, and [their] brains full of arrogance and superstition"; they were "'filthy and ignorant and not far removed from the jungles of Africa.'"[6] Remove the reference to Africa, and this observation could have been expressed in any number of locales in this period.

Common to most descriptions was the perception of traditional midwives as ignorant and superstitious women whose lack of skill menaced infants and mothers alike and who were dangerously ignorant about hygiene, medicine, and child rearing generally. Physicians represented midwives in especially harsh terms. They contrasted their own scientific and modern approach to childbirth with the superstitions used by midwives. In an observation that could be applied to many places, Sharla Fett has argued that in the United States during the period of slavery, words like "superstition" acted as a kind of "racial currency" and helped "maintain the boundaries central to middle- and upper-class identity." But the oppositions they implied (such as "progress and primitivism, reason and irrationality") "subsumed constructions of race and gender that closely linked 'women' and 'negroes' to 'superstition.'"[7]

Historians have emphasized the danger that childbirth posed to women in the period before the 1930s, regardless of who attended them. Prolonged labor could mean death or debility, and puerperal fever spread by physicians could also kill.[8] But in a period when ideas about the importance of sanitation and hygiene were gaining increasing acceptance, some traditional birthing practices were roundly condemned. There is some truth to these claims, as Irvine Loudon's work suggests. He examined maternal mortality statistics from several European and North American countries in the late nineteenth and early twentieth centuries and concluded that whereas formally trained midwives provided good care for mothers, their untrained counterparts often did not.[9] Other historians have argued that some birthing practices posed a real health hazard to mothers and their newborns. Sean Lang, for example, has pointed out that traditional birth attendants (dais) in colonial India used "a sharpened piece of bamboo or shell covered in cow dung" to cut the umbilical cord. Not surprisingly, such practices led to disease, such as tetanus and puerperal fever, both of which were "reportedly common in Indian birthing," according to Lang.[10] Both Lang and David Arnold have noted the frequency with which Indian women gave birth in dirty sheds and "squalid" outhouses.[11] Such practices doubtless contributed to the poor light in which Europeans saw the dais as well as to high rates of infant and maternal deaths. In light of these descriptions, Arnold's characterization of the dais' methods as "crude and often dangerous" and his reference to the "horrors [they] perpetrated" seems justified.[12]

In Britain and its colonies, midwifery training and regulation were seen as the best solution to the danger traditional midwives were believed to pose. But these efforts also acknowledged midwives' continuing relevance. In Great Britain, some hospitals began training midwives in the second half of the nineteenth century.[13] In 1902, the British government passed the Midwives Act with the aim of regulating midwifery; it provided for a Central Midwives' Board that certified both formally trained midwives and those qualified by long practice, the bona fides.[14] Although certifying these traditional birth attendants suggested an official willingness to incorporate them into the formal world of obstetrical work, this was not to be a permanent solution. By 1910, all certified midwives were to have undergone formal training, a provision that assumed the eventual disappearance of the bona fides.[15]

Scholars have identified similar tensions over the role of untrained midwives in the colonial world. Sean Lang has argued that in India, physicians were divided over whether to train the dais and thereby make them part of a "European-style maternity strategy" or to bypass them entirely in the hope that eventually they would "become redundant."[16] Both strategies were pursued. In 1866, Amristar was the site of the first attempt to train dais, but as Arnold has noted, the dais were "middle aged or elderly, illiterate, and understandably suspicious of attempts to coach them out of their old ways." Efforts to train more "respectable" women as midwives also had a limited impact, at least until the 1920s.[17] With the exception of South Africa, where from the early nineteenth century most of the women trained as midwives were white, midwifery training and regulation did not occur in Britain's African colonies until the 1910s and 1920s.[18] In Anglo-Egyptian Sudan, for example, the government medical department opened a midwifery school in 1919 with the goal of training "respectable" Sudanese women as midwives who would return to their home communities and eventually, it was hoped, replace the traditional midwives, or dayas. Attempts were also made to regulate the dayas themselves until they could be replaced.[19] As this chapter shows, midwifery training arrived earlier in the British Caribbean than it did in British-colonized Africa, but it reflected some of the same social tensions.

Granny Midwives in the Caribbean

In the nineteenth and early twentieth centuries, physicians in the British Caribbean characterized traditional midwives in much the same fashion as did their counterparts in the United States, Britain, Africa, and Asia. They condemned the grannies as unskilled and ignorant women who used superstitious childbirth practices that threatened the survival of mothers and their babies. This language offered them a discursive template, but British policies governing midwifery as well as the economic, social, and political realities of Caribbean life shaped the regulatory framework within which these ideas were expressed.

Popular medical practices were an important part of these realities. Reflecting the demographic and political history of this part of the world, these practices had their roots in Africa, South Asia, Europe, and the Americas. During the period of slavery and into the postemancipation years, "obeah" and "bush medicine" were terms used to characterize popular responses to sickness and childbirth. Obeah was a West African–derived religious and medical practice that David Trotman has described as an attempt to "put into practical and everyday use a knowledge of the natural world combined with manipulation of the supernatural world."[20] It offered assistance for the heartbroken and the aggrieved and anyone desiring justice in a world where formal authorities could not or would not help. But obeah was also a response to illness. The term "obeah" originated in Ibo words meaning "practitioner," or "herbalist" or "doctor."[21] Remembered African knowledge inspired obeah practitioners, but the landscape and the plant life of the new world also shaped their approach and pharmacology.

To Europeans, obeah was at once a form of quackery and a type of witchcraft and something they alternately mocked and reviled. In the first few decades after the end of slavery, contemporaries frequently, and disapprovingly, commented on former slaves' reliance on obeah and allied practices.[22] By the late nineteenth and early twentieth centuries, some commentators argued that the increasing civilization of the population and the passage of anti-obeah legislation (part of a larger attack on uncivilized cultural practices) was leading to the decline of obeah. Others, though, maintained that it continued to flourish into the twentieth century.[23] Obeah was seen as closely allied with bush medicine. Certainly, traditional healers, whether they were called obeahmen or -women or bush doctors, used local plants and made their own remedies to deal with a range of illnesses. Despite the expansion of governmental medical systems and the increasingly widespread use of formally trained health workers, traditional healers continued to play an important role well into the twentieth century. During her ethnographic work in Jamaica in the 1920s, Martha Beckwith noted that traditional healers used local plants and that the "folk" tended to accept the "obeahman's or revivalist's claim to special control over their mysteries."[24]

Obeah and bush medicine provided a discursive framework for representations of traditional midwifery in the nineteenth- and early twentieth-century Caribbean. To physicians and other commentators, midwives' use of herbs and their reliance on rituals while tending to women during childbirth and their advice that new mothers feed their infants "bush teas" was superstitious nonsense. But these practices were also seen as having a sinister element, as the quotation by Violet Nurse at the beginning of this chapter shows.[25]

During the period of slavery, male physicians conducted deliveries. However, overseeing childbirth was primarily the province of informally trained female birth attendants, most of whom were of African descent.[26] Enslaved female midwives were regularly condemned as superstitious, unskilled, incompetent, and a danger to maternal and infant health. The Jamaican planter Edward Long was not alone in his view that the "unskilfulness and absurd management of the Negro midwives" was responsible for the deaths of large numbers of infants and their mothers.[27] John Williamson, the Edinburgh-trained physician who practiced in Jamaica in the early nineteenth century, characterized these women as "barbarous," "ignorant and cruel in the extreme."[28] In the eyes of the English visitor to Jamaica Robert Renny, they were similar to their "fair sisters in Europe" in that they were "always illiterate, generally careless, and often intoxicated." According to Renny, they used unhygienic methods and left new mothers alone in "wretched huts" after childbirth, condemnations that echoed those expressed elsewhere in this period.[29] Significantly, these descriptions ignored the culpability of the planters who neglected to provide more salubrious accommodations for parturient women. One of the few accounts by a white woman in the British Caribbean about her encounters with slave midwives repeats some of the points made by these male commentators but with important differences. For men like Renny, Long, and Williamson, slave midwives were cruel and dangerous figures. But to Maria Nugent, the wife of Jamaica's governor in the early nineteenth century, they were more ludicrous than anything else. Nugent described Nurse Flora, the slave midwife present during her own labor, as eager to try out "various charms," much to the disapproval of Nugent and the white midwife also attending her. Rather than the deliberately malicious and cruel individual portrayed by Long and others, the slave midwife was represented by Nugent almost as a figure of fun.[30] Despite this difference, she remained an untrustworthy childbirth attendant.

In the postslavery period, informally trained midwives continued to monopolize childbirth. Male physicians saw relatively affluent women who were able to pay their fees. Those employed by poor law boards and government medical services tended some poor women of African, European, and South Asian descent, women whose access to doctors was facilitated by a combination of government and private philanthropic assistance. But most women continued to turn to informally trained midwives. The majority of these midwives were of African descent, but in places like Trinidad, Jamaica, and Guyana, where indentured South Asian agricultural workers had been imported to labor on the sugar estates after the end of slavery, women from this part of the world also worked as midwives.

In the postemancipation period, informally trained female birth attendants were described in much the same way as they had been during slavery. The comments by Jamaica's superintending medical officer, Charles Mosse, were typical. In his 1885 report, he blamed infant deaths on "the unskilful treatment of ignorant women who profess[ed] some knowledge of midwifery."[31] The poor law inspector in late nineteenth-century Barbados, Charles Hutson, described a case where a midwife identified the swollen face and extremities of a pregnant woman as evidence that she was carrying a girl rather than as an indication of a serious medical condition. The woman died from "puerperal convulsions," a result Hutson believed might have been avoided if a trained nurse had been present. To Hutson, this case was not unique. He concluded that a significant number of the 300-odd stillbirths in Barbados in 1896 could be blamed on "the gross ignorance, . . . culpable carelessness and neglect of the so-called 'midwives.'"[32] He called on the colony's parochial medical officers to report instances of malpractice by these midwives in the hope that sufficient data would push the colonial government to institute midwifery training.[33] However, if this woman was in fact suffering from puerperal convulsions, or toxemia, Hutson was too hard on the attending midwife. Although late nineteenth-century physicians called for "early diagnosis and treatment" of this condition, according to Irvine Loudon, there "was and still is very little that can be done to treat toxaemia apart from the early induction of labour and delivery," something that became more common later in the twentieth century.[34]

With the growing acceptance by physicians of the role of germs in spreading disease and the importance of cleanliness during medical procedures, physicians and increasing numbers of lay commentators castigated traditional midwives for their unsanitary practices. Loudon dates the "introduction of antisepsis and asepsis" in England and Wales to around 1890.[35] By the early twentieth century, the predominantly British-trained physicians in the British Caribbean complained that midwives were ignorant of these medical facts, acceptance of which was slowly becoming widespread among lay commentators as well. In Guyana, for example, members of the 1905 commission struck to investigate the causes behind high mortality rates declared that most midwives were ignorant of the "elementary principles of hygiene" and indifferent to "cleanliness" and that they spread infections to mothers and newborns.[36] These ideas about infection and antisepsis built on the trope of the "filthy" midwife.[37]

Giving Birth in the Caribbean

In the nineteenth- and early twentieth-century British Caribbean, most women gave birth at home, where, for the most part, they were tended by traditional midwives. The late nineteenth century saw the emergence of maternity wards in some colonies. They provided accommodation for women whose labor was complicated or unusually risky as well as for some poor women. One of their main functions, however, was to train midwives and ensure the production of a corps of trained, certified birth attendants who could help reduce colonial infant mortality rates. They were to play a role in helping reproduce the population.

By the late nineteenth century, British Caribbean colonies had hospitals and other smaller medical facilities in which the sick could receive care and a range of nonphysician medical workers could be trained. The midwifery hospitals and lying-in wards established in the late nineteenth and early twentieth centuries were part of this colonial, medical infrastructure and were also places of medical care and education. Most large

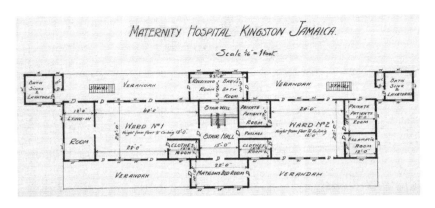

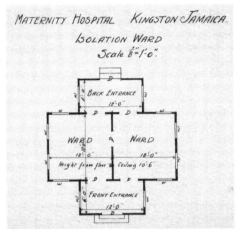

Maternity Hospital, Kingston, Jamaica ("Plans of Maternity Hospital, Kingston, Jamaica," CO 137/702, Jamaica no. 11323, CO no. 74, NA)

urban areas had public hospitals, with the exception of Bridgetown, Barbados, whose colonial hospital was privately run despite receiving government funding, and many plantations in Guyana, Jamaica, and Trinidad had small hospitals or dispensaries. Almshouses could also fulfill this function as well as their main task of housing the indigent poor—"the destitute old and idiot people," in the words of a local physician and occasional acting poor law inspector in Barbados, J. B. Clarke.[38]

By the late nineteenth and early twentieth centuries, the larger hospitals had become sites of medical education, training dispensers, nurses, and midwives. As the first and sometimes only source of medical care for poor men and women, some of these health workers themselves were to play an educational role, dispatching information about modern, hygienic illness prevention. District nurses were charged with this, as were midwives. Indeed, the latters' responsibility was especially great, given their perceived contribution to high rates of infant mortality. When Jamaica's superintending medical officer, Charles Mosse, noted in the mid-1880s that a significant proportion of that colony's deaths in childbirth were due to "unskilful treatment of ignorant women who profess[ed] some knowledge of midwifery," he was making a point with which few of his colleagues in Jamaica and other colonies would have disagreed.[39] The stakes were extraordinarily high, as the Scottish physician James Ogilvie reminded his political bosses. This former mayor of Kingston, Jamaica, and the medical officer for the city in the early twentieth century noted that infant mortality "affect[ed] the life and best interest of the community," and the "very existence of the race" depended on addressing it.[40]

The different colonies in the British Caribbean responded to this imperative in various ways, but all emphasized the importance of developing modern institutions to train midwives. In Jamaica, colonial authorities established a lying-in hospital in the late 1880s, timed to coincide with Queen Victoria's Golden Jubilee. Such a facility had been proposed a few years earlier, but worries about the cost delayed it. The imperial commemoration seemed to be the necessary motivation.[41] Mosse hoped it would lead to the replacement of the "ignorant old women" responsible for "much suffering and death" by "thoroughly educated and intelligent Midwives."[42] As we will see, the hospital did not lead to the eradication of the grannies. However, its modernity and tropical setting pleased visitors and locals. The hospital's long-serving director, Dr. Michael Grabham, regularly quoted the effusive praise that the "distinguished medical visitors" inscribed in the visitor's book.[43] One such visitor was the editor of the *British Medical Journal*, Ernest Hart. He toured the hospital in 1907 and was impressed with what he saw. It was a "charming little hospital" situated in a "garden ablaze with tropical flowers," with "open verandahs" that allowed the air to move freely inside.[44] Overall, he was "'delighted with [its] beauty, cleanliness, and good order.'"[45] It was also a modern facility, at least according to the *British Medical Journal's* Dr. J. A. Coutes. He toured it in 1901 and came away convinced that it was "thoroughly up to modern requirements."[46]

The establishment of such modern facilities was constrained by local factors, as the delays in Jamaica show, but regional influences were also significant. In Guyana and Barbados, financial and political considerations dictated that existing medical facilities provide the basis for midwifery training and lying-in facilities. In Guyana, a maternity ward was established in the Georgetown Public Hospital in 1888, and midwifery courses were offered beginning in the mid-1890s.[47] The maternity ward inspired both envy and admiration in Barbados's Charles Hutson. "What a blessing to Bridgetown would such a ward be and what a school for the training of midwives!!" he exclaimed in his annual report. Hutson wanted something similar for Barbados, and over the next decade and a half he and his successor, John Hutson, repeatedly called for such an initiative. But the board of the privately run hospital refused. In the late 1880s a small maternity ward had been established in the almshouse in St. Michael parish, and in 1902 it became the site of a midwife training course.[48]

Officials like Charles Hutson believed that maternity wards were necessary to train midwives. But they also provided a space for poor women to give birth. In late nineteenth-century Barbados, officials hoped that such facilities would help reduce the incidence of "vagrant midwifery," the term used to refer to those instances when women gave birth outdoors, in canefields or on the road. Poor law inspectors in Barbados kept track of these cases. Charles Hutson noted that in one six-month period in the early 1880s, around fourteen women gave birth in the street or in canefields. He described some of these cases as "really most painful," partially, it seems, for reasons of "decency." In some instances, women were subjected to a degree of "indecent exposure which to most . . . would be horribly revolting."[49]

These accounts reveal the attempts of colonial officials to reconcile conflicting imperatives. Charles Hutson saw his dilemma as trying to ensure that poor pregnant women who were, as he saw it, "great nuisances" should nevertheless have access to medical relief.[50] The 1893 case of Catherine Barrow, a homeless woman from St. George parish, brought these views into sharp focus. Without a home of her own and living in a parish where the local almshouse did not have hospital facilities or a maternity ward, Barrow ended up giving birth in a mule pen. Barrow stayed in the mule pen for two weeks while she recovered, apparently too weak to be moved. Both the local poor law inspector and the parochial medical officer visited her, ensuring that she received rice and milk daily and that she had a "well-sheltered" section of the pen. The acting poor law inspector, T. Law Gaskin, called this event "scandalous" and used it to draw attention to the need for parochial childbirth facilities. Gaskin, like Charles Hutson, was torn. Both men maintained that poor, parturient women should have access to lying-in facilities; simple compassion demanded no less. But both men saw women like Barrow as inconvenient "nuisances." Gaskin especially worried that "immoral" women would take advantage of governmental medical facilities. But like other members of

St. Michael's Almshouse, Barbados (CO 1069/243/71, NA)

the white elite in Barbados, Gaskin also fretted about the reputation of this self-proclaimed Little England, especially to British observers ready to bludgeon Barbados for its moral failings. Would "some Mr. Chester" publicize the fact that in Barbados, women were "confined in . . . mule pens"?[51]

Gaskin did not say much about Catherine Barrow beyond this, but her place in the larger social system of Barbados is apparent. She was poor, of course. And the willingness of local officials to allow her to give birth in a mule pen rather than, for example, seeing her housed in a private home or even in the almshouse itself despite the absence of hospital facilities suggests that she was likely black. Skin color and class tended to coincide in the postslavery British Caribbean, but the relationship was not entirely clear-cut, especially in Barbados with its "poor white" population. Although all impoverished, "deserving" Barbadians whose status was verified by poor law officials had access to parochial poor relief, impoverished whites seem to have received more assistance.[52] These policies may have reflected a compassion that fellow whites were believed to deserve, but they may also have resulted from an official desire to ensure that representations of white superiority were not undermined.[53]

Colonial lying-in facilities were intended to provide assistance for poor women from all ethnic groups. By the time that Catherine Barrow gave birth in a mule pen, the lying-in ward in the St. Michael parish almshouse had already been established; it was, as John Hutson noted years later, a "great boon to the poor."[54] Although the maternity facilities in the Georgetown Public Hospital and Jamaica's Victoria Jubilee Hospital made provision for private patients, officials in these places also emphasized the help they provided for the poor.[55] The Jamaican sources also indicate that most of these women were black. The visiting Ernest Hart described the patients at Jamaica's Victoria Maternity Hospital as comprising "every shade of colour," but he seemed to have exaggerated, at least according to the hospital's admission records.[56] They show the vast majority of patients to have been of African descent, mostly black, with smaller numbers of "mixed" women and a few South Asian and white women. The existing Barbadian sources are less informative, but the presence of poor black and white women in St. Michael parish, the location of the almshouse maternity ward, suggests that both groups could have used this facility. The multiethnic nature of Guyana was probably reflected in the composition of patients in the Georgetown Public Hospital.

These medical and educational spaces were sites of unusually intimate and diverse colonial encounters as men and women from numerous ethnic backgrounds came into contact. As the next chapter shows, the matrons were British (English, for the most part). Most of the male physicians were also of British ancestry, some born in Britain and others in the Caribbean, but in Guyana by the 1910s, the Georgetown Public Hospital also employed a handful of nonwhite physicians of African, mixed, and South Asian ancestry.[57] The sources do not indicate the ethnicity of the midwifery students, but the emphasis on training local women suggests they may have reflected the ethnic composition of the population as a whole, with a likely bias toward more "respectable" women. Whites were seen as respectable, but class and education could qualify people of African and mixed European and African descent for this designation. The presence of a "Spanish Arawak Indian woman" from one of the interior districts in the training program in Georgetown suggests that the efforts to recruit local women could see nonwhite women admitted to these programs. The surgeon general believed that she would be a "great assistance to her own people amongst whom she [would] practice."[58] Both Jamaica and Guyana had some South Asian midwives, as did Trinidad, but these women may not have attended the midwifery training schools.[59] The numbers were relatively small, though, as the comments of Guyana's governor from the 1920s indicate; he declared that he would like to see more South Asian midwives working among that population.[60]

Modern Western (British) ideas about infant welfare and hygienic birthing practices seemed to have dominated much of the professional interactions of these diverse groups, at least within the midwifery training facilities.[61] The midwifery programs did not obviously make space for traditional Afro- or Indo-Caribbean (or indigenous) ideas about appropriate childbirth methods.[62] During this time, students witnessed the kind of modern methods that Guyana's Allen James (A. J.) Craigen described as carried out in the maternity ward in the Georgetown Public Hospital. Its staff followed "strict up-to-date aseptic and antiseptic principles." Instruments, gowns, and sheets were sterilized, and a strict regime of hand-washing was followed; staff were instructed to soak their hands for a minimum of five minutes in an "antiseptic solution such as Lysol." Newborns' eyes were washed out with sublimate and received a drop of silver nitrate, with the result that, as Craigen noted with some pride, ophthalmia neonatorum was unheard of.[63] As well as learning about these methods, students attended lectures and demonstrations that imparted information about anatomy as well as how to conduct normal births and to recognize abnormal ones and deal with serious problems such as puerperal eclampsia. They were also taught the most up-to-date ideas about infant welfare.[64]

Competing Goals

In his 1898 talk about the infant mortality problem in Guyana, Joseph Godfrey declared that educating mothers in the "elementary principles essential to the proper rearing of infants" was the first step in reducing high rates of infant mortality among the "Black race." Only trained midwives could educate mothers and overcome the factors that led to these high death rates, namely "ignorance, prejudice, and superstition" and the "habits and customs handed down from generation to generation."[65] Colonial authorities hoped that the midwifery schools would see these trained midwives replace grannies and end their baneful influence over poor women. However, the competing agendas of formally trained midwives and poor women helped undermine these goals. The midwives may well have shared some of these medical and ideological aims, but they also wanted paid employment. And the mothers themselves? They wanted a safe childbirth but defined in their own terms.

Colonial officials intended the midwifery schools to produce midwives who could then be sent throughout the colonies to oversee childbirth and help reduce high rates of infant mortality. In the early years of the schools' existence, officials experimented with a number of methods to accomplish this, but they were inevitably disappointed, frustrated by uncooperative local authorities and midwives. In Jamaica, officials tried to choose students from as many different parishes as possible and to get prospective students to agree to live and work where they were sent and to offer their services to poor women at agreed-upon rates.[66] Some of the nurses seemed to have done just that, fanning out to the various districts to work.[67] But the reluctance of local authorities to subsidize their employment limited the extent of their cooperation. In the mid-1890s, a few parishes paid "small salaries" to qualified midwives, but by the early twentieth century, only one seemed to be doing so.[68] The medical director of the Victoria Hospital criticized parish officials for their neglect and gloomily wondered whether the hospital should close.[69] An editorial in the *Gleaner* echoed Grabham's concerns, arguing that subsidizing trained midwives was the only way to ensure that poor women had access to their services and that the midwives themselves could earn a living. Those few who already offered subsidies should augment them, as the current rate of £20 or so a year was far too low.[70]

The Guyanese government encountered similar obstacles in its efforts to scatter trained midwives around the colony.[71] A district midwife scheme had been suggested as early as 1893 but was not implemented until 1897 when Surgeon General David Palmer Ross prompted the colonial government to act by noting the high numbers of infant deaths in the colony. The colonial government offered financial incentives to certified midwives to work in villages and rural areas until their practices were established. The subsidies were then to be transferred to midwives in other underserved areas. The midwives were to provide free services for paupers and to charge poor women reduced fees, but they could also see private patients. The initial subsidy was relatively small, BG$5 a month, but rose to BG$8 in 1898.[72]

Less than a decade later, Godfrey as surgeon general concluded that this system had failed. The few trained midwives supported under the scheme did not see many patients, no more than twenty-two in any one year, and the midwives themselves were quickly fired or quit due to a shortage of work. Of the four appointed, only one lasted longer than two years, Mrs. S., who was appointed to Mahaicony district in 1903. Mrs. A. lasted eleven months; Mrs. M., just shy of two years. Another Mrs. A., this one appointed to Plaisance Village, quit after almost eight months, blaming competition from granny midwives for her decision. Specifically, she criticized the practice of certifying grannies to work as midwives. She claimed that a "large number of women well known in the district" had been given certificates, thereby "practically reducing her practice to nothing." Godfrey agreed. He maintained that certifying untrained but long-standing midwives, as was done in 1900 under the amended medical ordinance, created a glut of midwives with whom their trained counterparts could not compete. Under this legislation, anyone who could prove that she had practiced midwifery before 1900 could be certified. But he also blamed poor women. He argued that they were "steeped in the grossest ignorance and seem[ed] to prefer the ignorant and incompetent so-called midwives" over those who were "properly trained and qualified."[73]

Godfrey's plans to reorganize midwifery training aimed to solve these problems. He called for training schools to be established in the main public hospitals in the two major urban areas, Georgetown and New Amsterdam, and in the smaller town of Suddie. "Intelligent women" from throughout the colony would be encouraged to enroll under the assumption that once they completed the course, they would return to their home communities as trained midwives. Godfrey maintained that this approach was much better than dispatching strangers into the villages.[74] The first was established in Georgetown, and within the next few years, similar programs were established in the hospital maternity wards in New Amsterdam and Suddie.[75] The colonial government provided financial support, paying the fees and living expenses for midwifery students from rural areas who could not afford the costs themselves.[76] It also supplied employment subsidies for trained midwives to work in rural areas and in the more isolated parts of the colony's interior. The new scheme began in 1905; within four years, subsidized midwives were working in four "outlying" districts, and by 1913, they had been dispatched to another three.[77]

Officials in Barbados used similar methods, namely tuition assistance and employment subsidies, to encourage women to work in their home districts. And, as in the case of Guyana and Jamaica, midwives and local government authorities did not always cooperate. Hutson was intrigued by the actions of the Guyanese government in funding these initiatives, but as in Jamaica, this ended up as a parochial undertaking.[78] In Barbados's St. Thomas parish, authorities paid the £5 fee that the midwifery school in the St. Michael parish almshouse charged.[79] Officials in St. Philip, Christ Church, St. George, and St. Lucy seemed to have done likewise, whereas those in St. Joseph, St. John, and St. James did not. Poor law officials in the latter two declared that their parishes did not need midwives, and the authorities in St. Peter worried that midwives would not return once they had finished the course.[80] These officials may well have had a point. Many midwives refused to stay put. In Barbados, two of the first graduates of the midwifery training program in St. Michael parish returned to their own home parishes of St. Lucy and St. Thomas.[81] But most graduates remained in St. Michael, the colony's most populous parish and site of the capital, Bridgetown. Even students whose education was financed by their home parishes chose to remain in St. Michael. The parish of St. Thomas seemed to have been particularly unlucky in this respect. Having paid for and subsequently lost four nurses to the charms of other parishes, the St. Thomas authorities decided to force potential students to agree to work for the parish for five years or reimburse the £5 paid for their training.[82] By the late 1910s, not much seemed to have changed; Hutson observed with some disapproval that trained midwives tended to remain in St. Michael, providing services only to "better class patients."[83]

The census reports provide some support for Hutson's complaints and indicate the desire of midwives to practice in urban areas. In 1911, almost 72 percent of those women who identified themselves as midwives were based in Bridgetown or St. Michael; the percentage fell to 58 percent in 1921, but this parish still attracted a majority of midwives.[84] In Jamaica, the contrast was less stark; but Kingston clearly attracted significant numbers of midwives, and its appeal seemed to grow over time. In 1911, Kingston and the parish of St. Andrew were home to almost 20 percent of the self-declared midwives, a percentage that jumped to 40 by 1921.[85] Some midwives ended up leaving the country or found positions in colonial hospitals or as private nurses, much to the disappointment of officials. Grabham wanted to discourage trained midwives from pursuing such an independent course, but it is not clear what could have been done, apart from establishing a more extensive scheme to subsidize their employment.[86] Indeed, the 1901 *Gleaner* editorial noting the dearth of subsidized trained midwives called for just such a development, recommending that something analogous to the government scheme for district medical officers be developed for nurses.[87] Despite Grabham's unhappiness, the employment options available for trained midwives seemed to have encouraged women to apply for spots in the colonial training programs, something that officials in both Jamaica and Guyana observed.[88]

Trained midwives were not the only women whose goals could come into conflict with those of colonial officials. Poor mothers could be just as uncooperative, but in ways that point to some of the contradictions in how population policies were seen in colonial and postslavery societies. Physicians and officials encouraged women to use trained midwives rather than the grannies. Sources for the Victoria Jubilee Lying-in Hospital indicated that women were enthusiastic about the services it offered. Less than a decade after it opened, the hospital was regularly full, and by the late 1890s, it was occasionally unable to provide beds for all the women who wanted to be admitted.[89] But officials were torn over how to interpret this demand. On one hand, they were gratified at the public health victory it seemed to represent. Charles Mosse argued that the applications for admission showed the increasing "confidence" felt by those who had "experienced the liberal and successful help administered by the Institution."[90] Grabham agreed; he declared that more poor Jamaicans "recognized and appreciated" the services the hospital provided.[91] Indeed, even the "friends of midwives" were willing to send women to the hospital in the event of problems during childbirth.[92] The editor of the *Gleaner* supported Grabham's view, repeating the comments from his 1897 report in an editorial that same year.[93]

But this growing popularity was also seen as troublesome and troubling. The superintending medical officers for Jamaica in the late nineteenth and early twentieth centuries, Charles Mosse and John Errington Kerr, both expressed concerns. Mosse had practical worries, fretting that the clamor for admissions could "interfere" with the hospital's role as a training facility.[94] But Kerr's growing unhappiness with the increasing numbers was more ideological in nature and echoed long-standing negative views of Afro-creoles. Kerr claimed that the women waiting for admission at the hospital gate were noisy and attracted "a large crowd." In his words, his own "humanity" compelled him to allow them in, but Kerr clearly also disapproved of their actions and their motivation. Kerr believed that the women demanding admission behaved in such a fashion either "out of sheer ignorance" or from a desire to "avoid payment" and take advantage of the government largesse funding the hospital.[95] Kerr was not the only official who complained that pregnant, nonwhite women "took advantage" of government-financed childbirth facilities. In Barbados, Charles Hutson declared that pregnant women who "pretended" to be close to delivery were "constantly . . . impos[ing]" on the almshouse. Once they were admitted, they could luxuriate for months in the comforts it offered.[96] In making these points, Kerr and Hutson were drawing on the trope of the improvident poor who were represented as unwilling to pay for medical care and were at risk of "pauperization." These views were, and still are, expressed in many places. But in the late nineteenth- and early twentieth-century Caribbean, these perceptions intersected with views expressed about former slaves in the immediate postslavery period; as Chapter 1 showed, physicians, planters, and government officials regularly declared that former slaves expected free medical care and were too lazy to earn the money needed to pay for this and other necessities. Following slavery's end, planters and officials frequently argued that the purported laziness and improvidence of former slaves required that they be compelled to labor on the estates.

Officials made numerous attempts to solve the problem these women were believed to pose. In Barbados, a new policy was introduced in the late 1890s. Women who applied for "lying-in relief" were given an "order of admission" with instructions to use it only when they were in labor but no sooner. Any woman in the lying-in ward discovered to be "malingering" was immediately discharged unless a physician said otherwise.[97] Jamaican officials also attempted to discourage "malingerers." Although emergency cases were admitted to the Victoria Jubilee Lying-in Hospital, by the mid-1890s officials were attempting to restrict all other admissions while keeping in mind their goal of ensuring sufficient numbers of patients for the "purposes of training." New regulations authorized them to turn away patients if beds were not available, and paupers were to present certificates from poor law officials and district medical officers attesting to their financial and medical need or risk being denied entry.[98] Despite these rules, overcrowding continued. In 1903–4, thirty-two women were refused admission, and some of those allowed in ended up on the floor.[99]

Kerr's main goal was to ensure that the hospital could function as a training facility. To do that, he recommended that enough "material," that is, patients, be admitted.[100] In describing these women as "material," Kerr—like other physicians and government officials at the time—was stripping away their agency and rationality, even their humanity. But the women whom Kerr dismissed as material and Hutson as malingerers were rational individuals, making choices in a world of limited options. The women who demanded admission to the Victoria Jubilee Lying-in Hospital and the almshouse in St. Michael parish were determined and possibly desperate individuals. The economic hardships of this period, compounded by the exodus of many family members to look for work on other islands or even farther afield, were part of the reality of many women's lives. They had little money and not enough food, and they often lived in substandard housing. Indeed, the 1911 Jamaican census reported that close to 60 percent of all houses in Kingston were one-room shelters.[101] The maternity hospital offered beds, food, shelter, and the promise of safe childbirth. In the aftermath of the 1907 earthquake, which caused significant damage in Kingston, patients continued to press for admission to the facility despite the damages it had sustained. For months, patients were housed in tents on the hospital grounds.[102] Practical reasons clearly brought women to the doors of these facilities. However, a sense of ownership may also have played a role. In the case of Jamaica, as Ernest Hart noted, the Victoria Jubilee Lying-in Hospital had been built with money "raised in a great measure by small contributions from the people of Jamaica."[103] As was the case with medical facilities for the sick poor in other colonies, it was also supported by colonial funds, money raised by taxes paid by ordinary men and women.

Medical Rivalries

Poor women in Jamaica, Guyana, and Barbados turned to the growing numbers of trained midwives available as the twentieth century progressed. But they continued to use the grannies as well, their decisions influenced by a variety of factors. In doing so, they were condemned by physicians and the matrons who trained and supervised midwives. In characterizing the birthing methods of granny midwives as dangerous superstitions, these formally educated childbirth attendants drew on contemporary ideas about race and culture that represented nonwhites as primitive. However, professional tensions also played a role. To physicians and trained midwives, the grannies were rivals, and this factor as much as anything informed their perceptions of these traditional childbirth attendants.

Contemporaries complained that poor women continued to use granny midwives rather than the graduates of the colonial midwifery schools. More than ten years after the midwife training course had been established in the St. Michael parish almshouse, Barbados's John Hutson noted that many trained midwives could not find work in rural areas, something he blamed on women's determination to use the grannies.[104] Several years later, Hutson's temporary replacement, C. E. Gooding, made the same point, declaring that most poor women relied on "ignorant and often officious old 'grann[ies]'" with frequently dangerous results. He blamed this for the inability of trained midwives to find work in rural areas and called on parish authorities to subsidize their employment.[105]

As Jamaica's Kerr declared, many women "still prefer[ed] the old order of things."[106] But could poor women in the early twentieth century freely choose from among different kinds of birth attendants in the consumerist fashion suggested by Kerr? Such pronouncements downplayed the range of social and economic factors that constrained women's abilities to exercise their "preference," as did optimistic assessments such as that expressed by the head of Guyana's Baby Saving League shortly after its establishment. In stating that trained midwives had become the "guide, confidante, and trusted counselor of all races," this official, like Kerr, ignored the complicated reality of colonial life that limited the choices available to poor women.[107]

Cost was one factor. The sources do not indicate the fees that the grannies charged, but they may well have used a more informal payment structure than that available to government-subsidized midwives. Grannies and their patients might have bargained over the amount to be paid. They may also have accepted payment in forms other than cash. In contrast, formally trained midwives employed by the parishes (in Jamaica and Barbados) or subsidized by the colonial government (in Guyana) charged cash fees determined by government policies. Poor relief laws in Jamaica and Barbados and colonial legislation in Guyana stipulated the fees that midwives could impose for their services to poor women. Women who could produce certificates or "tickets" from one of a number of reputable individuals (such as physicians, clergymen, and poor law commissioners) were entitled to free care. Trained midwives were also constrained by the cost of their equipment. Early twentieth-century Guyanese regulations provide an indication of this. The rules stipulated that midwives were to carry syringes, catheters, scissors, thermometers, nail brushes, and liquid carbolic acid.[108] Their work just cost more to carry out.

Clearly, access to trained midwives also determined the extent to which poor women could use their services. Lying-in wards in colonial hospitals and almshouses had limited numbers of beds and could accommodate relatively few women at any one time. For example, the maternity ward at the public hospital in Georgetown could house fifteen patients, and Jamaica's Victoria Jubilee Lying-in Hospital accommodated perhaps sixteen.[109] Far fewer women in Barbados had access to trained midwives. The maternity ward in the St. Michael parish almshouse seemed to have had fewer beds than the Jamaican and Guyanese facilities and served far fewer women. Between 1902 and 1916, on average, ninety-one women gave birth each year in the St. Michael parish facility, a tiny proportion of the number of women giving birth in the colony, perhaps as little as 1 percent.[110] The training courses themselves did not seem to have produced enough trained midwives to serve the populations of these colonies, especially in the rural areas where most poor women could not pay for their services. In its first twelve years, the program in Barbados produced 117 graduates.[111] Jamaica's lying-in hospital trained over 225 women between 1892 and 1924, and Guyana's public hospitals trained 288 women between 1906 and 1920.[112]

The perceived foreignness of trained, certified midwives may have been another factor in poor women's decision making. Despite the emphasis on recruiting and training local midwives, the sources imply that these formally educated birth attendants were socially and culturally distant from the poor women to whom they sold their services. Trained midwives were distinguished by their "respectability." In the postslavery British Caribbean, this term described men and women seen as manifesting a number of social and cultural characteristics, including Christianity, temperance, and chastity or monogamy. It was also used to refer to individuals whose culture was seen as distant from the African or South Asian practices that were the subject of increasing official/elite condemnation in this period.[113] Their literacy skills may well have added to this distance. Midwifery schools demanded that students have reading and writing skills; once they began practicing, trained midwives also needed to be able to write up their case notes. Literacy rates in the early twentieth-century British Caribbean were relatively high. In early twentieth-century Jamaica, for example, around 60 percent of men and women could read and write, as could close to 50 percent of men and women in Guyana.[114] But a substantial minority could not read and write in English, including the vast majority of South Asians in Guyana, something that may well have been seen as increasing the cultural distance between trained midwives and their poor clients.[115] Trained midwives' advocacy of "elite" birthing and child-rearing techniques also served to distinguish them from traditional midwives and their poor clientele. The certificates they were granted upon graduation testified to this. In Guyana, their mandatory "midwife bags" and uniforms, as well as their government-issued sign plates, only contributed to their foreign appearance.[116]

In contrast, granny midwives were well known in the communities in which they practiced and likely used birthing methods that were familiar to their predominantly African- and South Asian–descended clientele. The author of the 1915 report of Guyana's Baby Saving League made just this point, noting that "old ties and age-long superstitions bound the villages to their old 'grannies.'" The head of the Baby Saving League in the early 1920s, the British physician Ethel Minett, condemned South Asian midwives for such "superstitions" as providing amulets and tying string around the abdomens of women during childbirth.[117] Despite her clear disdain for such practices, they may have served an important purpose. The amulets doubtless promised protection, and tying strings around the abdomen—as traditional birth attendants in nineteenth-century India did—may have been seen as familiar by the many South Asian women living in Guyana and as representing a degree of comfort in a time of anxiety.[118]

The uniforms, midwifery bags, and certificates denoted the professional status of trained midwives, distinguishing them from grannies. In the eyes of physicians, maintaining this distinction had life-and-death consequences. A decade or more after the establishment of midwife training schools, physicians described the dangers granny midwives posed to Caribbean women and their infants. Guyana's surgeon general, K. S. Wise, attributed deaths during childbirth to their ignorance.[119] A district medical officer in Jamaica longed for the day when Jamaica had more qualified midwives distributed throughout the colony, declaring that only this would save poor women and their infants from the "ill-usage of the unwashed, unkempt, unlearned old hags" who provided deadly advice about feeding and child rearing.[120] But to some physicians and matrons, they were even more dangerous than this. Ethel Minett argued that the superstitious practices of granny midwives contributed to infant deaths. The grannies bathed infants' eyes with milk or urine and rubbed a mixture of butter and "lamp-black" around the eyes of newborns. She characterized these "superstitions" as the remnants of "some old form of propitiatory and secret devil worship," an observation that resonated with long-standing negative views of popular medical practices.[121] Violet Nurse's observations, quoted at the start of this chapter, echoed Minett's conclusions.[122]

But the accoutrements of trained midwives did more than distinguish these women from the grannies. They also emphasized the difference between trained midwives and physicians who did obstetrical work. In Guyana, graduates of the midwife-training program received certificates stating that they had been "'duly trained, examined and found competent to act as a nurse midwife in the cases of simple labour.'" The words in red ink across the front of the certificate stating "'This certificate does not entitle the Holder to practice midwifery'" reminded the midwives themselves and their potential clients that they did not have licenses to practice midwifery.[123]

For physicians, this attempt to buttress their professional position had real financial consequences. Private practitioners and parochial and district medical officers earned part of their income by overseeing both simple and complicated deliveries. Private practitioners charged their patients fees for midwifery services. Parochial medical officers in Barbados, government medical officers in Guyana, and district medical officers in Jamaica received some compensation for seeing to the sick poor to whom they could charge limited fees.[124] They competed with trained midwives. The sources do not indicate the proportion of midwifery work in relation to these physicians' overall practice, but it clearly contributed to their overall income. In Barbados, for example, the medical officer in St. Peter parish relied on midwifery work to supplement his annual salary of £200.[125] Parochial physicians also offered "cheap" midwifery services at rates lower than those of private practitioners, an offer targeting the nonpauper population who were entitled to poor relief.[126] In Jamaica, district medical officers also seemed to have provided midwifery services for poor women under "certain conditions." In the mid-1920s, they were paid £1 1s for each case, an amount that seems to have been the norm for some time.[127]

They may have competed for the same business, but the relationship between physicians and midwives was to be a hierarchical one. Physicians were charged with supervising and overseeing these female birth attendants, something that the 1901 Guyanese regulations made clear. Crafted by the surgeon general at the time, David Palmer Ross, they noted that any physician was free to supervise a midwife's work. The regulations also stipulated that midwives were to call in physicians in the case of "abnormal" deliveries, such as multiple or premature births or "monstrosities," or if the patient was bleeding.[128] They were also to send cases of puerperal fever to physicians and were forbidden from attending patients with "general illnesses." Physicians were also charged with reporting any midwife who violated these rules.[129]

But the reality of the work that trained midwives were to perform undermined the hierarchical nature of their relationship with physicians. The limited number of physicians in the rural and more isolated parts of these colonies meant that the few trained midwives would have been given considerable responsibility, perhaps more than the midwifery regulations allowed. Some physicians even welcomed this. One government medical officer based in an isolated area in Guyana's interior was palpably relieved when two assistant nurses at the hospital he ran trained as midwives. The small medical facility was "far away from other trained help," and he was frequently absent.[130]

As a group, physicians were divided about the role of granny midwives. As we have seen, they hoped that the various midwife-training schemes established since the late nineteenth century would lead to the eventual replacement of the grannies by trained midwives. Guyana's Craigen spoke for many when he bluntly stated his hope "in a purely Christian spirit" that the grannies would "soon die out and give place to the better trained and more educated women."[131] By the mid-1920s, Guyana's surgeon general, P. James Kelly, believed this day would soon arrive: He was optimistic that Guyana was "within measurable distance of a happy release [from granny midwives] as a result of senile decay." However, unlike some of his counterparts, Kelly did not completely condemn all traditional midwives. He conceded that some had "no doubt done their little best."[132] Although patronizing, Kelly's comments point to a common pattern in the early years of midwife training not only in the Caribbean but elsewhere in the empire and in Britain itself. The early regulatory efforts made room for traditional midwives, albeit under restrictive conditions and under physician oversight. As was the case in Britain and colonial India, governments in Guyana and Jamaica passed legislation legalizing the work of granny midwives. In 1900, the Guyanese government passed legislation stipulating that any traditional midwife who could prove her "knowledge of simple labour" and demonstrate her "fitness to continue" in the profession by producing a certificate from a justice of the peace, "qualified medical practitioner," or poor law official could be registered and certified.[133] Some physicians were critical of this measure. Godfrey, who became surgeon general shortly after this law was passed, argued that it allowed "incompetent" and untrained midwives to be certified, the very women who should be barred from the profession.[134]

In Guyana, even unregistered granny midwives enjoyed a measure of tolerance, but its extent was determined by pragmatic considerations and individual pressure. Colonial Office officials advised the Guyanese government against prosecuting these women until the new registration system was well known.[135] Even after some time had passed, officials seemed reluctant to prosecute the uncertified grannies, especially those who practiced in more isolated areas. The magistrate in an isolated interior district of Guyana, Walter Roth, argued against prosecuting them, especially as some were skilled at their work and the "Government certified midwife" in his district could not tend to all the births.[136] A report from the early 1920s stating that officials refused to prosecute uncertified grannies practicing in areas with few trained midwives unless they actually did "harmful work" suggests that this policy continued for some time, at least in some areas.[137] However, the policy was not consistent. Police reports between 1906 and 1920 rarely singled out "uncertified midwifery" as an offense under the 1886 Medical Act, preventing an easy assessment of the extent to which this offense was prosecuted, but the 1914 establishment of the Baby Saving League seems to have been the impetus for some police activity. In its first year, four grannies were convicted, and the following year the police pursued a "few test cases" in the five districts where the league had established branches.[138] In the late 1910s, convictions rose a little, as thirteen individuals were convicted of practicing as "uncertified midwives" under the 1886 Medical Act.[139] In 1923, another effort was made, this time encouraged by Wishart. He used his new influence as the local supervising authority of midwives in Georgetown to push the police to prosecute unregistered birth attendants. They managed to round up "two or three."[140] That these examples are few in number and intermittent suggests the challenges officials faced in their efforts to craft a consistent policy, as well as the impact of local realities on this attempt.

Perhaps in reflection of local population anxieties, the colonial government in Guyana began regulating midwifery earlier than did authorities elsewhere in the region. The governments of Grenada, Antigua, and Trinidad passed legislation by the mid-1910s. Jamaican officials were familiar with these laws and considered passing something similar but delayed doing so until 1919.[141] Like the Guyanese law, it allowed experienced midwives who had been practicing for at least three years and who could produce a "certificate of fitness" from a district medical officer to register as midwives.[142] Jamaican physicians disagreed about this law. One district medical officer, J. A. L. Calder, for example, condemned "untrained midwives" and the "weak and yielding" law allowing them to practice rather than "wip[ing] [them] out." Calder argued that unlicensed and untrained midwives were "hopelessly ignorant, horribly dirty and appallingly incompetent" and their actions killed infants and left women crippled. On "behalf of the unborn children" who would certainly "be murdered" if no action was taken, he called for unlicensed midwives to take a training course, the costs of which should be paid for by the government. Calder also made an appeal in the interest of the state: "The lives of its children [were] the wealth of the state."[143] E. D. Gideon was more sanguine. He believed that some unregistered granny midwives were of "real value."[144] Despite repeated calls by John Hutson for a modified version of the British Midwives Act to be passed in Barbados, such a law was slow to appear.[145] Several unsuccessful attempts were made in the early 1920s, but no legislation regulating midwifery was passed until the approval of the Midwives and Nurses Registration Act in 1932.[146]

The decision of the colonial governments to incorporate the granny midwives into the regulated world of colonial midwifery reflected the undeniable fact that the grannies significantly outnumbered formally trained midwives. The sources do not indicate the number of uncertified traditional midwives, but in Guyana and Jamaica, a comparison of the two groups of certified midwives (those with and without formal training) indicates something of the imbalance. A Guyanese report from 1920 put the number of certified grannies at 700 as compared with the 200-odd formally trained midwives.[147] In Jamaica in 1923, of the 91 women who registered as midwives, 7 had trained at the Victoria Jubilee Lying-in Hospital, whereas the remaining 84 received certificates from district medical officers testifying to their fitness to practice their profession.[148]

Colonial and imperial officials saw the establishment of midwife training programs in the British Caribbean as offering a solution to the pressing problems of infant mortality and population decline. Although officials and physicians blamed a number of factors for this trend, they emphasized what they saw as the culpability of traditional midwives. The "filthy and ignorant" midwife was a common trope in the nineteenth century, but in the British Caribbean, as in other colonial and postslavery societies, it intersected with contemporary ideas about race as well as those of gender and class. These Caribbean grannies were seen as unskilled and ignorant, women whose birthing methods and maternal advice could be deadly and who may have used such reviled practices as obeah and bush medicine. The late nineteenth- and early twentieth-century efforts to replace the grannies with trained, certified birth attendants were undermined by the competing interests of physicians, mothers, and midwives themselves. But as the next chapter shows, trained native midwives were not limited to overseeing normal childbirths. Instead, they were increasingly incorporated into the network of infant welfare and maternal education schemes that began to emerge in the 1910s and 1920s. As the system's gatekeepers, they were responsible for shepherding poor, mostly nonwhite women into institutions administered by the respectable white and black women who dominated the world of colonial philanthropy.

CHAPTER FOUR

Infant Welfare, Maternal Education, and Uplifting the Race

CERTIFIED, TRAINED COLONIAL MIDWIVES were a crucial element in the effort to tackle the problem of infant mortality and to deal with the population anxieties of the early twentieth century. They were the birth attendants whose skill would ensure the safe delivery of newborns and whose presence would vanquish the dangerous granny midwives believed to threaten the health of infants and mothers. But their work did not end there. Officials and physicians believed that midwives should also play an educational role. Early twentieth-century worries about populations and infant health tended to focus on maternal ignorance, and poor women in particular were seen as dangerously uniformed about the best way to rear their children to productive adulthood. Trained, certified midwives, health visitors, physicians, and the volunteer members of British Caribbean baby-saving leagues labored to instruct mostly nonwhite, poor women in modern, hygienic methods of child rearing. Contemporary ideas about gender meant that paid and volunteer work in the infant and maternal welfare business was seen as best left to women, who were believed to be innately nurturing. But only the right kind of woman would do. She should be respectable, which in the British Caribbean had class and race connotations. White Britons were seen as inherently respectable and as intellectually and morally superior to black and brown West Indians, a perception that resulted in an official preference for white, "English" women as nursing administrators and educators.[1] They alone were believed capable of overseeing the work and training of native nurses and midwives. White women also played key roles in the infant and maternal welfare initiatives that emerged in this period, helping develop and run the child-saving leagues that appeared from the mid-1910s. Some were foreigners, the wives of governors and senior colonial officials; others were white creoles, but both were qualified by color and class. Ideologies of race and gender may have been seen as fitting them for this role, but in the British Caribbean, members of the nonwhite, non-British respectable classes also saw child-saving as their responsibility, part of the effort to "uplift the race."

Bad Mothers and English Nurses in the Colonies

In the British Caribbean as in other places, much of the focus on infant mortality concentrated on poor women. Regarded as ignorant and indifferent mothers, they were seen as responsible for sickly infants and high rates of infant mortality. As one speaker at the 1906 British conference on infant mortality noted, "'bad motherhood'" was at its root.[2] In the Caribbean, the early twentieth-century investigations into infant mortality and illegitimacy had argued for a link between the two, and indeed, the dangerous consequences of this purported relationship would continue to attract the attention of those worried about Caribbean populations for the next few decades and beyond. But poor women generally were represented as ignorant about hygienic motherhood and child rearing. Midwifery training and the maternal education schemes developed in the early twentieth century aimed to deal with the perceived problem of poor and ignorant mothers.

When the first midwife training programs began in the British Caribbean in the 1890s, imperial and colonial officials looked to Britain for the right kind of women to organize and administer these initiatives. Contemporary gender assumptions that women were innately maternal and nurturing made them seem the most appropriate choice. But not just any women would do. As representatives of the British empire charged with instructing native health workers and with upholding colonial hierarchies, they had to fulfill very specific requirements. They had to meet educational and professional criteria as well as those of race and class. Officials and physicians agreed that white, British nurses were needed.

The Colonial Nursing Association (CNA) was given the task of locating the right kind of woman. Renamed the Overseas Nursing Association in 1919, it was established in 1896. Over the seventy years of its existence, it provided 8,400 nurses for every part of the British empire.[3] It was not a government organization, but it worked closely with the British Colonial Office to locate nurses to work in the colonies and to assist in their placement. Through donations and subscriptions, the CNA was able to guarantee the sums needed for the salary and travel costs of the nurses and to pay outright for the costs of travel and uniforms for those destined to work in especially impoverished colonies.[4] Any nurse who broke her contract or was fired "for serious misconduct" was expected to repay her passage money.[5] Initially, the organization was to provide trained British nurses to tend Europeans in Britain's colonies in Africa, Asia, and the Caribbean, but in places like Jamaica and Guyana, CNA nurses administered the nursing staff of colonial hospitals and trained local women as nurses and midwives.[6]

CNA nurses, along with other European nurses in the colonies, were, as Sheryl Nestel has argued, "enmeshed in the nets of imperial power."[7] As trained and experienced nurses and midwives, they were to serve the interests of the empire by looking after European settlers and the troops who maintained imperial boundaries.[8] However, as Nestel has pointed out, they were also "regulators and inquisitors of native populations."[9] To carry out these duties effectively, officials required that the nurses meet class and gender expectations. Their "appearance, manner, and accent" were assessed to ensure that they were "ladies."[10] Part of being a lady also meant that they could not be openly sexual. In an effort to ensure that the nurses remained single and chaste while in the colonies, the CNA and colonial officials developed a policy that discriminated in favor of women considered unattractive in contemporary terms. They preferred hiring older, single women and those of "less attractive appearance" under the (often erroneous) assumption that such women would have limited sexual opportunities. And finally, the CNA nurses were to be nurturing and compassionate—in a word, maternal. Only such women were considered appropriate "visual representatives of the British imperial enterprise."[11] Although these women were to serve imperial interests, they had goals of their own. Some may have wanted financial independence; others, adventure. Despite the efforts to ensure that the nurses follow rigid behavioral rules, some may well have reveled in the freedom that distance from Britain provided.[12]

Some of the CNA's first appointments were made in the British Caribbean, perhaps not surprisingly, given the role that British Caribbean physicians played in the organization's genesis. Jamaica's superintending medical officer, Charles Mosse, and Guyana's head of the Public Lunatic Asylum, G. Snell, were among the group of colonial physicians who helped establish the rules guiding the appointment of CNA nurses for work in the colonies.[13] The CNA provided these colonies with British nurses to fill senior administrative and teaching positions in colonial hospitals. These appointments built on a long-standing preference for white authority figures, both male and female, in the Caribbean. In this part of the world, an ideology of white superiority ensured that senior government and institutional positions were given to whites, whether they were born in Britain or in the Caribbean itself. Contemporary gender ideologies ensured that men dominated these positions, but white Englishwomen were believed suitable for those in the nursing field, especially for infant welfare work. When the first nurse training programs developed in the 1890s, qualified English nurses were appointed to oversee the education of native women. In Trinidad, for example, an "English qualified nurse" was appointed as the superintendent of nurses in the 1890s.[14] When Jamaica's Victoria Jubilee Lying-in Hospital opened, a "highly-trained" matron was "procured from England" to oversee midwifery training.[15] And in Guyana, an Englishwoman, Mary Westwood, was appointed in 1895 to train nurses and midwives in the new training program at the Georgetown Public Hospital.[16]

After the turn of the twentieth century, the CNA provided the right kind of woman. Its representatives, along with imperial and colonial officials, determined the most suitable candidates for these positions. Once a colonial government had relayed its request to the Colonial Office, officials from the CNA pored through their files to find the right women to interview. Caribbean physicians on leave in the United Kingdom helped vet the candidates, but so did leading imperial medical figures such as Patrick Manson. When Guyana needed a matron to oversee nurse and midwife training at the Georgetown Public Hospital, the hospital's senior assistant resident surgeon, J. H. (James Hill) Conyers, participated in the interview process while on leave in England.[17] The colony's surgeon general, Joseph Godfrey, urged that Manson and Conyers be allowed to make the final choice. Godfrey wanted a "superior class of woman," one who was a competent teacher and hospital administrator, and he was confident that Conyers, a white Guyanese doctor with Edinburgh medical training, would know exactly the kind of woman he had in mind.[18]

The CNA nurses whom Conyers and others approved for service in the British Caribbean were carefully chosen to meet educational, class, and ethnic criteria. Edith Thompson, who was hired in 1912 to replace the current matron of Jamaica's Victoria Jubilee Lying-in Hospital, is one such example. Jamaica's superintending medical officer, John Errington Kerr, who participated in the interview process, proclaimed her and one other candidate to be "specially suitable."[19] Thirty-four-year-old Thompson was single and a trained and experienced nurse and midwife who had been working in this field for a number of years, mostly in London hospitals. Thompson's references praised her skills as a nurse, as a teacher, and as a manager of a female workforce. She had a "good education" and was a qualified midwife.[20] As the daughter of a naval officer, she was also from the right social class.[21]

Women with similar qualifications were hired to work in Guyana. Isabella M. Cowie was appointed in 1904 following the reorganization in nurse and midwife training at the Georgetown Public Hospital. Officials hoped that Cowie, a certified nurse who had been employed in the Western Infirmary in Glasgow, would run the program smoothly.[22] The unmarried Cowie came with glowing recommendations from members of the Royal College of Surgeons in Ireland, Sir Charles A. Cameron, and Lambert H. Ormsby. They declared her a "very suitable candidate," experienced in administering a hospital, intelligent, and an "active and zealous" worker.[23] Ormsby praised her skills as a nurse, but he also pointed out her social qualifications for the position in Guyana; she was, he noted, a "lady by birth and education" and from a family "known to [him] for years."[24]

Six years later, Cowie was replaced by Kate Drummond.[25] She also met the necessary ethnic, educational, and social criteria. A British woman, she was an experienced nurse and midwife from a family sufficiently well off to ensure that she was educated at home by a governess and later at a private school in Germany.[26] Drummond did not last long in Guyana. By December 1911, her appointment was "terminated on account of ill-health." According to Godfrey, her illness was "uterine" in nature, something that occurred in "women her age" and led to "mental instability."[27] Clearly, there were some disadvantages to hiring "older" women.

The CNA was also responsible for locating more junior nurses to work in British Caribbean hospitals. Along with the hospital matrons, they were part of a small but important network of white medical women whose presence helped maintain colonial race and class hierarchies. Three seemed the minimum number of English nurses needed to keep Guyana's Georgetown Public Hospital functioning. One acted as matron or nurse superintendent, and two more were "divisional nurses."[28] The more or less simultaneous resignations of Cowie and L. A. Gill, a divisional nurse in Georgetown's hospital, worried officials. A replacement for Gill was "urgently required," so the surgeon general did not want to waste time requiring the successful candidate to undergo training at a school of tropical medicine.[29] The first choice, Janet Wilkie, proved to be "physically unfit for nursing work in the tropics" and was quickly replaced by Ada Agnes Baird Brown.[30] But the waning months of 1911 saw a renewed staffing crisis. Drummond was sick, as was another divisional nurse, Lydia Thorpe. Brown was the only English nurse remaining, so the appointment of a new matron to replace Drummond was urgent, at least from Godfrey's perspective.[31]

For many CNA nurses, the Caribbean was just one stop on a career path that took them all over the British empire. For example, forty-year-old, Yorkshire-born Florence Parkinson had spent several years in the Hong Kong Civil Hospital before starting work as a divisional nurse in the Georgetown Public Hospital.[32] These positions offered benefits as well as risks. Lydia Beatrice Thorpe, for example, worked as a ward sister in the Singapore General Hospital for three years before taking a position in Guyana. In Singapore, she also saw private patients and seemed to have devoted much of her time to this extracurricular employment.[33] This extra work provided additional income, but it was also the source of her illness. While attending to a private patient who lived in a "very swampy" area, Thorpe contracted malaria, which forced her to return to England a few months shy of the completion of her contract.[34] Once she recovered, she took a position in the Georgetown Public Hospital. She did not last long, however, as she was soon felled by the return of her illness.[35]

With Thorpe's departure, Ada Brown was the only English nurse remaining in the Georgetown Public Hospital. But Brown was also troublesome, at least from the perspective of colonial officials. She had become engaged to a junior police officer who was not allowed to marry until he was promoted. This meant that the engagement would last for the duration of Brown's contract, something that was unacceptable to Godfrey and the hospital's resident surgeon (probably Conyers). Brown's new status as an engaged woman transformed her from a suitable nurse to one who was most unsuitable.[36] Her engagement violated the CNA's preference for single nurses. But it also threatened colonial hierarchies. Godfrey worried that "subordinate nurses" might "talk" if the English nurses received male visitors. He noted that the former tended to say "unkind things" when "disciplined by these special nurses." From the perspective of this white, male Guyanese physician and administrator, himself a representative of the colonial hierarchy, the risk was twofold. Given the financial expense of hiring these white nurses, anything that would "diminish" their "usefulness" as teachers and supervisors should be avoided.[37] Implicit in Godfrey's comments was a recognition of the tenuous nature of white women's authority. It rested on perceptions of their chastity and their ability to maintain their difference from their nonwhite female subordinates, who, in contrast, were often seen as sexually promiscuous. Maintaining their authority and their "whiteness" required that these women ruthlessly excise their sexual natures, or at least hide them. Anything else would diminish their authority. Godfrey's solution to this problem was to have all contracts with CNA nurses include a statement that women who became engaged during their appointments would have their contracts canceled and would be responsible for their travel costs back to England.[38] One Colonial Office official did not know whether such a provision "could be made or enforced," but regardless, Brown still had to resign.[39]

White female authority figures like Brown were the maternal element in benevolent colonialism. As whites who trained and supervised nonwhites, they upheld colonial racial hierarchies, and as women caring for mothers and newborns, they helped maintain gender ideologies. But in an era when ensuring infant health and survival was seen as serving a range of imperial and moral ends, including that of ensuring population growth, their work was believed to be especially crucial. As Jamaica's Michael Grabham noted, the "slightest departure from the principles of sanitation or the least inattention to any of the numerous details of treatment [could] mean not only death to mother and child but also sow the germs of puerperal disease."[40] Jessica Davis, the first matron of Jamaica's Victoria Jubilee Lying-in Hospital, was responsible for maintaining these high standards and was effusively praised for her success. Charles Mosse complimented Davis's "wise and judicious methods and counsel in the training of the pupil nurses" in the "little Colony under her immediate charge."[41]

Ideas about racial difference and white superiority underlay colonial rule in the Caribbean. However, officials on both sides of the Atlantic preferred to obfuscate this fact and deny the reality that many whites in the colonies saw the black and brown men and women with whom they came into daily contact as profoundly inferior. Whenever possible, they wanted to silence what they sometimes called the "color question." The reasons may have been strategic, especially in colonies where some nonwhite men held positions of economic and political influence, considerations that became more pronounced as the century progressed. When CNA nurse Kate Drummond was accused of being prejudiced against the nonwhite nurses and servants who worked in the Georgetown Public Hospital, Godfrey recommended that the CNA should be told to choose only "tactful" women and that the nurses themselves be informed that they would work with "black or coloured" nurses and servants who "naturally resent[ed] any slight on that account, either intentional or not."[42] Servants and nurses were not the only nonwhites with whom English-women like Drummond came into contact. Most of the patients in the colonial hospitals were of African descent, along with smaller numbers of South Asians. So were physicians, some of whom worked closely with the nurses. In Guyana, for example, Drummond was probably in regular contact with the Indo-Guyanese physician J. E. Ramdeholl, who lectured nursing students in the Georgetown Public Hospital.[43] If she had remained for another year, she would have encountered G. E. Carto and J. S. Nedd, both Afro-Guianese physicians who also gave lectures on general nursing and infant care to midwifery students.[44]

Almost fifteen years later, officials with the (renamed) Overseas Nursing Association were reminded about the color question. By the late 1920s, the growing influence of pan-Africanism and the increasingly vocal presence of creole politicians and labor leaders combined to make silencing questions about racial discrimination even more urgent, at least from an imperial perspective. In 1926 two white, English nurses, Miss F. A. Hansford and Miss E. Jackson, requested that they be released from their contracts at the colonial hospital in Trinidad. They were "surprised" and unhappy when they discovered that the hospital treated nonwhite patients. Trinidad's governor accepted their resignations, but like Godfrey some years earlier, he recommended that nurses be informed that they would work closely with "native" patients, students, and physicians.[45] The Overseas Nursing Association already did just that, but it planned to go further by having future candidates sign a document that clarified their working conditions.[46] The document itself helped disseminate racial stereotypes, pointing out several that might have been new to the nurses. They were told that they might have to do all the nursing work, as the "subordinate staff" was unreliable and possibly unacceptable to white patients, and that the "chatter" of the "native servants" meant that their accommodations would not be as quiet as they were used to. But, as compensation, they were reminded that "by [their] self-sacrifice, loyalty and cheerful devotion to duty, [they] [would] uphold the standard of what a British nurse [could] and ought to be."[47] The discomfort of Hansford and Jackson with the social reality of the British Caribbean in the 1920s had empire-wide repercussions. The secretary of state for the colonies, Leo Amery, decided that such a memorandum would also be shown to nurses hired to work in Ceylon, Mauritius, and the Seychelles, as well as those destined for the British Caribbean. Nurses headed for East and West Africa would be given pamphlets dealing with the same points.[48] Colonial Office officials believed that different parts of the empire required dissimilar approaches to the color question. One senior civil servant, George Grindle, maintained that officials could say more or less what they wanted "as regards Africa and the East." But the Caribbean and Mauritius were altogether different. In these two parts of the empire, the "colour question [was] a political issue not [to] be dealt with frankly, so far as documents that [might] leak out [were] concerned." Consequently the memorandum for the Overseas Nursing Association should be kept in-house or sent to the governors as confidential. By no means should it be sent along with other Colonial Office documents "for the clerks in the secretariat and judicial departments to see."[49]

Health Missionaries

When Ethel Minett arrived in Guyana in 1910, she was accompanying her husband, Edward Pigott (E. P.) Minett, a newly appointed government medical officer.[50] As a trained medical doctor herself, Ethel Minett was unlike most imperial spouses. With her medical training and many years of infant welfare work in Britain, she was appointed as the medical officer for the British Guiana Baby Saving League, where she supervised and trained native midwives. Her role, and that of other white women employed in senior medical positions, became more important as trained, certified midwives were increasingly employed as "health missionaries" responsible for teaching "poor, ignorant" mothers how to rear their children in a "modern," hygienic fashion.

Early in the twentieth century, physicians in the British Caribbean pondered the merits of the different approaches to maternal education in effect in Britain and elsewhere in the empire. Their education in the United Kingdom along with their reading of contemporary public health publications and attendance at conferences such as that held in London in 1913 on infant mortality familiarized them with contemporary ideas about the use of public health literature, for example. Most, such as Jamaica's James Ogilvie, believed that pamphlets could be useful.[51] Wishart, too, agreed and called for the Georgetown town council to follow Edinburgh's lead in distributing "simple [printed] directions on infant rearing."[52] Trinidad's assistant medical officer of health, J. R. Dickson, on the other hand, suspected that "educational measures of a theoretical kind" would be less effective than, for example, home visiting such as was done in Britain. He believed this approach would help reduce the "Maternal ignorance or carelessness" that caused infant mortality.[53]

Despite Dickson's opposition, educational pamphlets were distributed in Port of Spain, and by 1907 one district medical officer, J. W. Eakin, believed they had led to a fall in the "infantile diseases."[54] But most colonial physicians tended to agree with Dickson; the direct approach was most effective. They recommended trained, certified midwives be used for maternal outreach to teach poor mothers how to raise their children to healthy and productive adulthood. They established "outdoor" midwife schemes in urban areas. With their high rates of infant mortality, cities seemed especially in need of these programs, and the presence of colonial hospitals provided the necessary institutional basis. In Guyana, the combined effort of two Guyanese physicians and one Briton was responsible for the 1908 establishment of an outdoor midwife scheme based at the Georgetown Public Hospital. Two Scottish-trained resident physicians—an Englishman, Ernest Daniel (E. D.) Rowland, and a colored Guyanese man, A. J. Craigen—set up the program, but Godfrey as the surgeon general was also probably involved.[55] A few years later, in Trinidad, physicians at the colonial hospital in Port of Spain established something similar.[56] In Jamaica, two of Kingston's medical officers of health, Scotsman James Ogilvie and Jamaican L. (Louis) Oliver Crosswell, considered that this kind of measure could be useful.[57] Ogilvie believed that trained nurses could teach "poor and ignorant" new mothers how to feed and care for their infants and follow the rules of hygiene and thus help preserve "what [could], in the future, be useful and valuable citizens."[58] A local charitable organization, the Nurses Union, had provided two nurses to visit the "sick poor" of Kingston since early in the century and began seeing midwifery cases in 1918 when it began collaborating with the Child Welfare Association.[59] Despite the recommendations of Ogilvie and Crosswell, however, a more extensive system of outdoor midwives was not established in Kingston until the early 1920s, when growing internal and external pressure led to expanded public health efforts generally. The recommendations of two government inquiries early in this decade for more maternal education initiatives and an outpatient facility at the Victoria Jubilee Lying-in Hospital seemed to have helped prompt these developments.[60]

The effort to set up maternal education initiatives was an international affair, advocated by Caribbean men as well as Scotsmen and Englishmen. All agreed with John Hutson that reaching the "poorest classes" in their homes and showing them by example how to care for their infants and protect themselves against diseases was the best means to improve the health and survival of the population.[61] But the example of Barbados shows that efforts to implement accepted ideas about maternal education and infant welfare could be defeated by the combined forces of political tensions, financial concerns, and sexual anxieties. In the early 1910s, a trio of influential colonial officials in this colony—Hutson, the governor, and W. K. Chandler, the president of the poor law board—recommended that the colonial government and the parish authorities jointly fund an infant welfare and maternal education scheme. They called for the appointment of one or two nurses for each parish who were to visit new mothers with advice and assistance and to provide free milk for "deserving cases." Perhaps in an effort to facilitate efforts to launch "bastardy" proceedings and thereby save the parishes some money, the three also recommended that the nurses report to the poor law inspectors on the condition of the new mothers.[62] The representatives of the parish poor law boards rejected these suggestions and instead, echoing concerns expressed early in the century, proposed a system to register the causes of deaths, as they considered that this would help "control the death-rate of infants."[63]

The parochial medical officer for St. George parish, Norman Laurence Boxill, disapproved of this decision, declaring that "those charged with the public welfare" should "be held worthy of their responsibilities." He convinced the local authorities to implement a home visiting scheme in this parish as an "experiment" for a year.[64] The nurse who was hired, "Nurse Burrowes," like district nurses and home visitors generally, provided advice and some medical treatment and determined access to resources, including milk and doctor visits.[65] Hutson and Boxill considered the experiment a success, but it ended after a year when vestry members voted to cancel it, apparently convinced by the argument posed by one of their number that it was "a means of mothers getting support for bastard children" rather than from the children's fathers.[66] This denouement demonstrates that opposition to sexual behavior seen as immoral continued to shape infant welfare policies, but it also reflected Hutson's assessment that political divisions in Barbados could stymie such "laudable" public health initiatives, an interpretation that increasingly influenced imperial views of Barbados.[67]

In contrast, imperial officials tended to see Guyana as an infant welfare success story, a place where the theory of maternal education was put into practice. The general acceptance in this colony by government officials, physicians, and employers that population growth should be encouraged to deal with the perceived labor shortage underlay the efforts of an activist group of creole physicians to introduce infant and maternal welfare measures. This multiethnic group was part of a British-educated and influential colonial elite and included white creoles like Wishart and Godfrey as well as men of mixed African and European ancestry such as A. J. Craigen. Craigen helped implement a number of key maternal education and infant welfare initiatives in the 1910s, although his color seemed to have been held against him, at least at first. He was from a "well-known local family," had studied medicine in the United Kingdom, and practiced in British New Guinea before returning home to a position in the government medical service. He gained his position in Guyana despite a "white doctor" policy that discriminated against nonwhite physicians, especially those of African descent. The presence of nonwhite physicians in the sickroom was seen as violating colonial racial codes that represented people of African descent as intellectually inferior to white Europeans and Euro-Americans and that limited the acceptable circumstances under which black and brown hands should touch white bodies. By the 1910s, few white British physicians were willing to work in the Caribbean, a consequence of war, the employment opportunities of the British health system, and relatively low salaries for physicians in the islands. The "shortage" of white doctors was especially acute in Guyana and led to the (reluctant) employment of Afro- and Indo-creole physicians in the government medical service. When Craigen applied for employment in 1905, Colonial Office officials attempted to reconcile racial and class imperatives; they noted that he "appear[ed] to have dark blood in him" although he was not "noticeably dark." Although Governor Hodgson wanted to limit the number of African-descended men in the government medical service, imperial officials believed that Craigen's application would not present a problem, as Hodgson seemed aware of his "colour" and knew "all about his family."[68] By 1921, this earlier local knowledge seemed to have faded and class identity seemed to have trumped that of "race"; a confidential government report stated that Craigen was "British," a catchall term that referred to color and ethnic origin rather than birthplace, as the official characterization of several white Guyanese men as "British" indicates.[69]

Craigen and other colonial physicians saw maternal education as closely intertwined with that other crucial element of child-saving: trained, certified midwives. Several years after he helped establish outdoor midwife schemes in Georgetown, he and the other resident surgeons at the hospital created a drop-in infant clinic at the Georgetown Public Hospital. Their apprehensions that the city's women would not use it were unfounded, and within two years, more than 100 children were attending weekly and a second clinic had to be opened. There, babies were assessed, weighed, and measured, and mothers received advice about child rearing and "proper feeding." But access was limited to women who used the outdoor midwives or the hospital's maternity ward and to those who visited the infant clinics regularly.[70] These restrictions were educational; poor women were being systematically trained to use these services. But as the attendance numbers indicate, many women found these services useful.

As in other elements of the colonial infant welfare system, white, British women played a key, supervisory role. The outdoor midwife scheme employed two midwives initially, a number that jumped quickly to four. They tended poor women in their homes during childbirth and afterward provided advice about feeding and infant care.[71] Craigen believed that the "controlling visits" of an English nurse ensured the high quality of the midwives' work.[72] This was accomplished by "surprise visits" by the superintendent of nurses and weekly ones by the junior English nurse.[73] Indeed, the establishment of an urban outdoor midwife initiative seemed to demonstrate the need for greater training and oversight. The same year that the first two district midwives were appointed in Georgetown, the superintendent of nurses at the Georgetown Public Hospital, Isabella Cowie, instituted a new, more difficult midwifery examination, which she justified on the grounds of midwives' increased responsibilities. The new examination resulted in more failures (fifteen of the twenty-two who sat for it in 1908 failed), but Cowie was not dismayed. As she noted, education and "a certain amount of intelligence" were crucial for midwives who were to "educate the people in modern ideas of asepsis and hygiene."[74]

The British and Guyanese physicians who presided over the British Guiana Baby Saving League expressed the same certainty.[75] The league's establishment in 1914 was central to the effort to wean poor women away from the granny midwives believed to wreak such havoc. The league subsidized midwives to work wherever branches were established in the hopes that they would present competition to the grannies and gradually take over. Its establishment of antenatal clinics in 1923 had the same goal;

according to medical officer Fitzherbert Johnson, these clinics facilitated a "close association" between the expectant mothers and the league midwife in "districts which were overrun with grannies."[76] For a fee, league midwives attended to women during childbirth, but they also visited the new mothers for a week afterward, providing advice about child rearing and especially feeding.[77] They also offered free advice to pregnant women, encouraging them to use the league midwife when their time came.[78] They were health visitors and birth attendants.

Home visiting was a key element of the early twentieth-century mothercraft movement. In Britain, philanthropic groups had undertaken home visiting from the mid-nineteenth century for the purposes of public health education, including in the realm of infant welfare work. The 1907 Early Notification of Births Ordinance provided the legislative framework that facilitated the expansion of home visiting.[79] In those areas where it was implemented, the act stipulated that all births be reported to local authorities within thirty-six hours. The act was amended in 1915 as the Early Notification of Births (Extension) Act of 1915 and made birth notifications mandatory.[80] Home visitors aimed to teach poor mothers better and healthier child-rearing practices. Like others involved in the expanding mothercraft movement, their advice about sanitation and hygienic practices in the home was based on an assumption that poor mothers were ignorant and neglectful and partly responsible for their infants' deaths.[81]

Physicians in the British Caribbean saw health visiting as a useful educational tool. They were aware of British ideas about this, but Trinidad's use of health visitors to combat tuberculosis (apparently influenced by Australian approaches) seemed to have influenced Guyanese physicians.[82] In 1913, with the encouragement of Wishart, the Georgetown town council approved a health visiting scheme in the city using health visitors rather than midwives. This was the first such initiative in the region and one of the first in the empire. As in Britain, the passage of the Early Notification of Births Ordinance seemed to be a necessary first step. The Guyanese government passed the measure in 1912, described by the attorney general as based on the 1907 British law "with the necessary alterations."[83] The Georgetown town council implemented the ordinance in 1913 and promptly hired two "lady" health visitors. The following year it hired two more, the salary of one paid for by the Baby Saving League.[84] These women were to visit every newborn in Georgetown, concentrating on poor families.[85] Wishart believed that "people of the better class" generally did not want visits.[86]

Health visitors were responsible for educating poor women in mothercraft skills. They assessed the behavior of new mothers and the environment in which infants were raised in terms of contemporary medical and social ideas about the best way to ensure the survival of infants. The approach to home visiting employed in Georgetown, which was based on the British model, probably served as an example for the home visiting work rural midwives were to carry out. According to Wishart, instructions for British home visitors stated that they were to advise mothers about "the proper nurture, care, and management of young children, and the promotion of cleanliness."[87] They were to give advice about domestic hygiene and to ensure that the "environment of the infant [was] made as sanitary as possible."[88] They were also to teach mothers about "proper feeding" and encourage them to breast-feed their infants.[89] Wishart himself was certain that when this "ignorance disappear[ed], so [would] infantile mortality."[90] The visitors kept written reports for each newborn they visited, their logs constituting their assessment of the extent to which new mothers followed the medical and moral rules of child rearing. The visitors noted the substances the babies were fed (breast milk, cow's milk, tinned milk, or something else). They also identified which babies were illegitimate, the regularity with which the parents worked, and the nature of the family's accommodations.[91]

Midwives who taught mothercraft skills and the social, medical, and hygienic rules of child rearing were also seen as requiring supervision, a kind of "visiting." As with other aspects of midwife training, white, British women supervised. When the league was founded in 1914, Conyers and Godfrey chose Miss Cumming as the first "Lady Superintendent."[92] She gave talks on infant welfare in poor neighborhoods of Georgetown and visited "the homes of the people, settling difficulties and persuading wavers to employ" the midwife.[93] By 1920, the league's executive concluded that more rigorous oversight was needed over the midwives, and two new positions, medical officer and an inspector of midwives and health visitors, were created.[94] As the author of the report for 1920 noted, midwives should not be posted to areas where supervision was unavailable, as their training had not prepared them for independence. Indeed, "without help and encouragement," they faced difficulties maintaining "a high standard of cleanliness or care" when "'planted out' in country districts where no conveniences [were] to hand."[95] This use of the language of colonialism and control is telling and echoes Charles Mosse's description of the colonizing role of Miss Davis, the superintendent of Jamaica's

Victoria Jubilee Lying-in Hospital. Midwives were "planted out" like early settlers sent to civilize barbaric and newly conquered territories. But because they were themselves "natives," they needed to be trained and supervised. These sentiments must have been persuasive, as the elected and appointed members of the colonial government agreed to provide funds for this purpose.[96] Ethel Minett and an English nurse, Violet Nurse, together carried out this work.[97] Minett did not stay long; she left in 1922 to follow her husband on his professional career, this time to Hong Kong. But Violet Nurse remained in her post until the early 1930s. That Minett was not replaced by another "lady doctor," as was the practice in other British colonies, may have reflected the general difficulty Caribbean governments faced in trying to find white, British physicians, regardless of their sex, for government positions.

Drawing on her eleven years of infant welfare work in Britain, her wide knowledge of infant welfare work internationally, and her experience in Guyana as a doctor's wife, Ethel Minett threw herself into carrying out the supervisory duties for which her education and her class and ethnic identity qualified her. With her awareness of maternal and infant welfare initiatives in Europe and Australia, including milk depots and "schools for mothers" in England, she contributed to the sum of infant welfare knowledge circulating in the colony in the early 1910s. Guyana could not afford milk depots, but it had to provide education if physicians like her were "to supply the colony with healthy citizens in the next generation."[98] Minett monitored the midwives' work, visiting them in the field, checking their midwife bags, and reading their weekly reports of their cases, which she required they produce.[99] From 1920, and under Minett's direction, league policies encouraged midwives to acquire a health visitor's certificate from the English Royal Sanitary Institute. Midwifery training no longer seemed adequate to enable these women to undertake the important task of maternal education. As a bonus, they received a raise in salary, something it was hoped would attract a "better class" of midwife to country practices, as most preferred "town."[100] To further encourage excellence, Minett established the "Minett medal," to be awarded to the two midwives with the "greatest number of satisfactory cases" in a six-month period.[101]

Several years later, after she had left Guyana for Hong Kong, Ethel Minett described her belief in the necessity of oversight in a brief account she wrote for Andrew Balfour, tropical medicine expert and director of the London School of Tropical Medicine. Seeming to draw as much from the genre of early twentieth-century women's travel writing as from medical narratives, Minett adopted the persona of the courageous white woman wryly observing the environmental and cultural challenges of life in the tropics. "The supervision of midwives means anything from five to sixty miles motoring to a welfare clinic, tramping through a village in fierce sun or inches deep in mud, balancing on a coconut palm trunk bridge over ten-foot deep trenches, seeing every kind of case from a normal expecting to do her usual laundry work with a few hours old baby to an abnormal who has been hung with tied hands to a roof beam to hasten the arrival of a tardy addition to the family."[102]

Friends of the Home

Female home visitors, whether trained as midwives or not, were responsible for "improving the standard of motherhood" and bringing poor women into the world of colonial health care and child-saving. The example of Guyana shows that class and ethnic differences could present obstacles to these "friends of the home." It also reveals a gradual creolization of health visiting, as the institutionalization of health training and the establishment of a pubic health infrastructure increasingly relied on Caribbean women.

In their regular reports, Wishart and the home visitors in Georgetown constructed a narrative of improving relations and growing influence. They noted that at first, the visitors were regarded with suspicion; but relations improved quickly, and they were soon "received with greater courtesy."[103] Wishart routinely reported that the "standard of motherhood was improving": Breast-feeding was more common, homes were cleaner, and home visitors were "welcomed as friends of the home."[104] The visitors themselves observed that their poor clientele tried to carry out their advice.[105] This rendering may have reflected a gradual popular acceptance of the moral and medical rules that the health visitors were advocating or women's appreciation for the goods and services that were made available. Indeed, historians have described a similar trajectory for early twentieth-century Britain. There, the presence of middle-class women pointing out their mistakes in child rearing and domestic management initially irritated many poor women, but with time, some came to appreciate the assistance and goods to which home visitors provided access.[106] The attendance at infant clinics and the presence of poor women at public health talks by Miss Cumming show that some women were willing to use these resources and had their own ideas about what they needed. In the league's second year of operation, between thirty and forty women attended talks in the poor district of Albouystown, although the numbers were smaller for other urban districts. Accounts of these talks indicate that women were not passive recipients of advice from more privileged women. At a talk in the Salvation Army Mission Hall, some women challenged Cumming's opposition to feeding their babies "tea," arguing that this practice was crucial, as it allowed them to leave their infants with neighbors and return to work soon after giving birth. Cumming's medical objections were valid, as this practice probably did cause gastrointestinal illnesses for infants, but as these Georgetown women stated, they faced real economic pressures that limited their ability to follow Cumming's advice.[107]

In the British Caribbean, perceived class differences may well have influenced these relationships, but so did differences in ethnicity and race. Midwives charged with educating poor women in mothercraft were in regular contact with women of African as well as South Asian heritage, who comprised a significant proportion of the league's work in parts of the colony. The midwives themselves, as we have seen, were local women of African and European backgrounds, and the same was probably true for the midwives subsidized by Guyana's Baby Saving League. The handful of "lady" health visitors in Georgetown, on the other hand, were likely from a more elevated social class and probably of European birth or parentage or of mixed ancestry. They were educated, "respectable" women; they would have to be to write up their reports and act as examples for the poor women they were to tutor. In the absence of local training schemes, the first visitors had trained abroad or were certified by class and gender. One of the first women hired, Miss J. G. Lawrence, had been educated in Britain and had a home visitor's certificate from the English National Health Society.[108] Another of the first hirees, Miss E. Tennet, was described on her retirement as qualified only by her "valuable knowledge in the school of experience," although presumably her respectability was an important criterion. The city home visitors were also single, although by the early 1930s a married woman was hired.[109]

By the early 1920s, the establishment of health visitor training by the Royal Sanitary Institute in the British Caribbean enabled more local women to obtain these positions, part of the growing availability of public health training generally in this part of the world. Certification courses for health visitors and school nurses built on an earlier initiative for sanitary inspectors begun in Guyana by Edward Minett in 1913. The first examination for home visitors seemed to have been administered in Guyana by a board of examiners that was to rotate through that colony, Trinidad, and Barbados.[110] In the latter, however, examinations did not seem to have been held until 1934, when one health visitor sat for the exam.[111] The institute's home visitor training course was directed toward women who already had some medical education. By 1923, the requirements for the institute's health visitor certificate stipulated that women undergo three years of nursing education and be board-certified midwives or the equivalent and take a course with the institute.[112] Most of the nine women who applied for positions as health visitors in Guyana in 1923 met these qualifications. Four were trained nurse-midwives, and three also had health visitor's certificates. The three who were not midwives had their health visitor's certificates. The only woman without any formal accreditation was Mrs. Lillian Coates, who declared that having children of her own qualified her for the position. Even disregarding Coates's lack of formal qualifications, the official preference for unmarried women probably doomed her application. Uranie E. D. Goulding, who was eventually hired, had a health visitor's certificate and work experience as a temporary health visitor for the Tuberculosis Society and Georgetown's public health department.[113] This experience seemed to have been the deciding factor.[114] It enabled her to beat Kathleen Eloise Wilson, who had three certificates from the Royal Sanitary Institute (as a health visitor, a school nurse, and a tuberculosis visitor) and was a certified nurse-midwife.[115]

The Royal Sanitary Institute helped prepare educated, middle-class Caribbean women of African descent for these kinds of positions. Guyana's May Glasgow Hendricks and Johanna Duggin were two examples. In 1922, Glasgow Hendricks passed the examination for school nurses and home visitors.[116] Glasgow Hendricks was probably a member of the Afro-Guyanese Glasgow family that had deep roots in the Congregationalist Church in Guyana. This church advocated for poor Afro-Guyanese, but it also provided the means by which some black men could obtain clerical education and access to middle-class status, which they could then bestow upon their children.[117] Duggin, who applied for a position as a health visitor in 1923, may have been slightly more privileged as the daughter of a black Anglican minister, Rev. J. R. Moore.[118] Duggin had been educated at the Ursuline convent and taught school before her marriage. Like Glasgow Hendricks, she also had earned her health visitor's certificate, and she also had "some training at the hospital," probably in either nursing or midwifery. Two respectable professional men attested to her qualifications. A local physician, Dr. Haslem, noted her medical training, and a member of the clergy, Father Louis Quick, attested to her general respectability.[119] Unlike most health visitors, Duggin had been married, but her widowhood ensured that she was not immediately disqualified. Like the CNA, the Georgetown town council refused to hire married health visitors, perhaps preferring that women devoting their lives to the people not be distracted by male demands and appear to be chaste.[120]

Both Glasgow Hendricks and Duggin were part of a growing number of middle-class, nonwhite Caribbean women who looked to the expanding social welfare/public health sector for employment.[121] These women were part of the respectable and educated colonial middle class, but they faced challenges in finding paid employment that did not violate contemporary class or gender norms. Health visiting, nursing, and teaching were acceptable positions, along with those in various government enterprises.[122] These daughters of middle-class parents might have been rich in cultural capital, but many needed paid employment. This was especially the case for those who did not marry. Although probably not of African descent, Miss E. Tennet is an example of the economic insecurity that faced single middle-class women who had to earn their own living. Her position as a health visitor seemed to have been a crucial source of income. Still making her rounds by bicycle some fifteen years after she was hired, she appealed for an increase in her traveling allowance in 1928, citing her age and a bicycle accident as justifications. She skidded and fell and was injured when riding her bicycle one day. The town council agreed to give her a "nonpensionable personal allowance" of $5 a month for twelve months.[123]

Maternal Philanthropy

As the example of the British Guiana Baby Saving League shows, the state-supported infant and maternal welfare initiatives that emerged in the first two decades of the twentieth century were closely allied with philanthropic organizations, notably the baby-saving leagues that developed after the mid-1910s. Privileged white and colored women played key volunteer roles in these organizations; their involvement reflected contemporary views about the obligations of such women to help their less fortunate sisters and their purportedly innate nurturing abilities. But the involvement of physicians and trained midwives and home visitors in the baby-saving leagues indicates the extent to which these twentieth-century social welfare undertakings intersected with imperial and colonial official interest in population growth.

Governments, church groups, and philanthropically minded members of the colonial political and social elites provided some support for their impoverished countrymen and -women. Verifiable poverty qualified one for aid distributed from parish or municipal governments through the poor law system, but religious affiliation seemed to have been the requirement to receive assistance from various religious groups.[124] White women from the more privileged classes were involved in some of these early initiatives, which targeted respectable women who themselves were often white. One of the oldest such organizations was established in Barbados in the 1820s, the Ladies Association for the Relief of the Indigent, Sick and Infirm. During the period of slavery, it focused on poor whites, but by the 1830s its mandate expanded to include poor Afro-Barbadians.[125] It was still in existence in the early twentieth century, but if the size of its board is any indication, it did not seem to enjoy much "elite" support. Three women sat on the board, one of whom was John Hutson's wife.[126] Other organizations that focused on respectable women fallen on hard times included Jamaica's Women's Self-Help Society, Trinidad's Home Industries and Self-Help Society, Barbados's Women's Self-Help Society, and the British Guiana United Home Industries and Self-Help Association, founded in 1914. Socially and economically privileged men and women also saw children and young people as worthy targets of their concern. In Guyana, they established the Society for the Protection of Children in 1889, and in Jamaica, the Upward and Onward Society in 1902 helped young girls at risk of being led astray find more respectable ways of earning a living.[127]

The population anxieties of the late nineteenth and early twentieth centuries, the growing attention of governments to the health of the young, and contemporary gender norms that represented women as innately nurturing and maternal came together in the establishment of baby and child welfare organizations in the 1910s and 1920s. They aimed to educate poor mothers and save young lives. As Judith DeCordova, chairwoman of Jamaica's Child Welfare Association, noted, this organization was founded to help reduce the rate of infant mortality and to "create for the state a more useful population."[128]

An international conference held in London in 1913 on infant mortality was part of the impetus behind the establishment of the Baby Saving League in Guyana the following year. It attracted physicians from Europe, North America, and much of the British empire, including the chief medical officers from Guyana, Jamaica, Trinidad, Belize, and St. Vincent.[129]

Joseph Godfrey was the Guyanese representative, and he returned home filled with "enthusiasm and inspiration" and determined to inform the government and the public about the subject. With the support of the governor's wife, Louisa Egerton, a meeting in the Georgetown town hall barely six months after the London conference brought together physicians, clergymen, and politicians long interested in infant health and population growth. The group resolved to disband the older Children's Protection Society and create a baby-saving league instead.[130] Two years later, at a similar meeting in Kingston called to address the problem of infant mortality, Oliver Crosswell suggested that a baby-saving league be formed in Jamaica along the lines of that in Guyana.[131] Trinidad followed in 1918, St. Kitts and Belize in 1920, Barbados in 1921, and St. Lucia in 1929.[132]

A combination of imperial, regional, and local factors shaped these organizations. Colonial Office officials facilitated the spread of information about the Guyanese initiative, which they described as "pioneer[ing]." They sent copies of its reports to officials in other British Caribbean colonies as well as to Ceylon, Hong Kong, Mauritius, and the Seychelles, and the secretary of state for the colonies urged other tropical colonies to attempt something similar if possible.[133] Officials also distributed the views of K. S. Wise, Guyana's surgeon general, as to the key elements required for baby-saving league success. Wise emphasized local factors, namely the "co-operation and active participation" of influential inhabitants, a population educated about the merits of such initiatives, and trained midwives. He also noted that Englishwomen were crucial, recommending the appointment of a "well qualified [English] Lady Superintendent" with "English" certification and training in midwifery, health visiting, and nursing.[134]

The official support that these organizations attracted indicates the extent to which they were believed to be doing work that served the interest of the colonies. The leagues obtained financial and other support from the colonial governments and local authorities. In Jamaica, for example, the Kingston town council provided £50 a year, and by 1917, the colonial government had started to pay for the costs of two nurses and the premises for a crèche.[135] In Barbados, the parish authorities in St. Michael gave £50, and in its second year (and in response to imperial pressure), the colonial legislature provided a grant of £150.[136] As in Guyana, the support by parish and municipal authorities reflected concerns about the unsanitary state of urban areas, their various public health problems, and their high rates of infant mortality. But cities were also home to a number of influential members of colonial society who increasingly saw infant welfare and the related problem of population growth as strategically important and as a matter of civilization.

For the first decade or so of their existence, the child welfare organizations in Jamaica and Barbados remained mostly urban undertakings and limited their activities to the main cities. In Barbados, that meant Bridgetown and St. Michael parish; in Jamaica, the larger Kingston area. In Barbados, an attempt was made in 1923 to establish an infant welfare clinic in St. Peter parish, but the "'lack of financial support from estate owners'" seemed to end this effort.[137] The following year, Hutson called for at least two additional "baby welfare centres" for Bridgetown and St. Michael and a minimum of one for the other parishes, declaring that the "time ha[d] come when the local health authorities in each parish should wake up to the fact that throughout the civilised word baby welfare work [was] regarded as one of the functions of health authorities."[138] By the late 1920s, Jamaica's Child Welfare Association (called the Child Saving Association until 1927) was active in ten districts in the Kingston area, although in 1925 an attempt was made to start one in Montego Bay.[139]

In Guyana, the early involvement of different levels of government in infant welfare philanthropy resulted in a different pattern. The league emerged around the same time as a parallel, municipal infant welfare network in Georgetown. While it was active in the city, the league paid the salary of one of the Georgetown health visitors, who in turn encouraged women to visit the league midwives and its two clinics.[140] But concerns about what was seen as an overlap between the two saw the town council take over the league's work in Georgetown in 1924. (By this time, the league had been renamed the Infant Welfare and Maternity League of British Guiana, in "conformity with the custom prevailing in other parts of the Empire.")[141] Unlike in Barbados and Jamaica, the Guyanese child-saving organization expanded quickly outside the main urban areas. In its first year, branches and clinics were founded in New Amsterdam and four other districts; by 1919, there were 12 branches, a number that had grown to 23 by 1923 and to 45 branches in the villages and on some plantations by the late 1920s.[142] By that point, league midwives attended a little over 21 percent of all registered births in the colony.[143] The colonial government supported this expansion. It placed its own subsidized midwives under the league and included league work as part of the duties of the government medical officers.[144] Its 1921 appeal to government medical officers that they treat "League babies" for a reduced amount was successful: All but one agreed.[145]

Early twentieth-century accounts of the Caribbean baby-saving leagues tended to emphasize the foundational role of governors' wives and ongoing support of these elite women.[146] The symbolic value of this official support was important, indicating the approval that this work enjoyed. In 1930, for example, the queen agreed to be a patron of Jamaica's Child Welfare Association.[147] This was approval at the highest levels. These organizations also enjoyed the support of the local and foreign-born elites who were involved with other kinds of philanthropic enterprises. Representatives of the Anglican Church and colonial officials and their wives sat on the committees or held executive positions. In a reflection of the public health goals of these organizations, physicians (and their wives) also played important roles, notably the chief medical officers and those holding senior positions in the colonial medical administration. They also publicly supported these organizations, turning out for lectures given in their support or to the annual baby shows that highlighted their accomplishments.[148]

Urban-based members of the professional (especially medical) and commercial classes played key roles in these organizations. In Jamaica, for example, a number of the women who sat on the executive board of the Child Welfare Association had married into or were born into these families, some of which were from the increasingly intertwined world of commerce and plantations. Women from the prominent DaCosta, Ashenheim, and DeCordova families sat on the association's executive board. These were Jewish families, members of the Jewish Jamaican population of Portuguese ancestry who had lived on the island since the sixteenth century.[149] By the turn of the century, many lived in the Kingston area, and some of the wealthier merchant families had joined "high society" and enjoyed some political influence.[150] Judith DeCordova played a particularly important role in the emergence of infant welfare work in Jamaica. She helped establish the Women's Social Service Club in 1918 and held a leadership role in the Child Welfare Association for many years. She and Nellie Latrielle, a white Jamaican woman who supported the anti–venereal disease campaign of the 1910s and woman's suffrage, were long-serving members of the association, active in many of its activities throughout the 1920s.[151]

Some of the Caribbean women active in infant welfare work seemed to have become involved through the professional and familial worlds of medicine. In Jamaica, for example, some members of the Child Welfare Association were married to physicians and were thus part of medical families, but one woman was a physician herself, Dr. Marie Cassidy. Cassidy was the treasurer of the Child Welfare Association.[152] In Barbados, the "guiding spirit" of the infant welfare association, Florence Sinclair Browne, may have come to this work in a similar manner. She headed the organization and allowed her home to be used as its clinic until the early 1930s.[153] Like many of those involved in social welfare work targeting children, Browne was married to a physician. She also worked in the medical field; for a while, she was a druggist, one of only two female druggists listed in the 1914 colonial directory.[154]

Interest in medical care and philanthropy brought many women to these organizations, but the example of Jamaica shows that money and racialized social networks could limit access to this philanthropic work. Members of the Child Welfare Association were charged a guinea, and prospective members required the recommendation of a current one. Respectable, educated Afro-Jamaican women resented what they saw as their exclusion from this organization. According to Mary Morris-Knibb, a black Jamaican teacher involved in social welfare activities, nonwhite women like her were not permitted to join the Child Welfare Association. When Morris-Knibb and other Afro-Jamaicans asked to join, they were told to form an "auxiliary," something that Morris-Knibb argued was impossible on financial grounds and forced them to "remain out."[155] Some of the "Coloured people," as she noted, formed an affiliated group and eventually created a separate organization. This was probably the Save the Children Fund, which Morris-Knibb and other nonwhite ("shady," to use her word) women created in 1938.[156] Its members visited the homes of the poor and helped "[look] after the children," activities that reflected the desire of Morris-Knibb and other Afro-Jamaican women ("ladies of my type," as she noted) who wanted to "help rectify things" by going into the homes of "our people."[157] To Morris-Knibb, reflecting on these developments from the very different political and social context of the 1930s, this exclusion was the result of prejudice on the grounds of biological race. In written testimony submitted to the West Indian Commission investigating the protests of the 1930s, Morris-Knibb and the other members of the Jamaica Progressive League declared that a "certain select element of [the] community" saw "welfare" as its "prerogative" and that "the services of capable women" seemed to have been rejected "on the grounds of colour."[158] She noted that only one black woman sat on the committee,

Mrs. Walter Brown, the "wife of the Rector of a church situated in a poor area."[159] DeCordova used the pages of the *Gleaner* (a newspaper her husband's family had founded) to defend herself and the Child Welfare Association. She declared that the association was always open to "black" members and had "black ladies working on its committees." She attributed the small numbers to the "apathy and indifference" of well-off Afro-Jamaicans.[160] As Morris-Knibb suggested, DeCordova's interpretation underestimated the financial obstacles that prevented black Jamaican women from becoming involved. It also ignored a more general indifference to this cause. The association's 1926–27 report noted that although a plea for help that year encouraged many women to join the visiting committee, many did not last long; most soon resigned, defeated by the "sun and the cobbles."[161]

Respectability and class also determined membership in the British Guiana Baby Saving League, but its rapid expansion to the villages and plantation zones and the involvement of government medical officers made it more ethnically diverse. By the 1920s, the government medical service included men from most of the colony's ethnic groups (British, Dutch, Portuguese, Chinese, South Asian, and African). The league attracted some of these men as well as other members of the multiethnic respectable classes, including politicians, town council members, and male and female adherents of the Congregational Church. Indeed, the Baby Saving League relied on "respectable families." Sometimes members of the same families held complementary executive positions. For example, Rev. T. B. Glasgow, the Afro-Guyanese Congregationalist minister, and his wife, Mrs. T. B. Glasgow, sat on the committee of the Den Amstel; the minister served as vice president in its first year and then as president between 1919 and 1924. Mrs. T. B. Glasgow was the honorary secretary in the years he was president.[162] Female members of these medical and religious families undertook much of the work in the league, both in Georgetown and outside the city. In 1926, for example, Miss T. B. Glasgow, a younger member of the Glasgow family, was the secretary of a league branch and helped organize one of that year's baby shows. She used the opportunity to describe the "benefits" of joining the league.[163]

As Miss Glasgow noted, child welfare associations could provide a number of benefits for poor women and their children. The volunteers and (few) paid staff members operated clinics where poor women could bring their children to be assessed or receive medical care if they were ill. They could also obtain advice about child care and feeding and sometimes food and milk. Indeed, clinics were sites of maternal education, health care, and social welfare assistance. In Barbados, for example, the clinic in St. Michael parish provided food for women and their children as well as medical care.[164] Clinic visits could cost, but in Jamaica many women (almost 1,400 in 1927) were given tickets that entitled them to free visits.[165] The fee for league membership that provided free access to the clinics with medical care and free medicine cost a shilling in Guyana.[166]

Female volunteers also undertook home visiting. In Guyana, volunteer home visiting under the auspices of the league began in conjunction with its establishment, and in Barbados, a small network of volunteer "enquiry officers" seemed to have been established in 1924, the same years the visiting committee was formed in Jamaica.[167] These women facilitated access to a number of benefits offered by these associations. In Jamaica, for example, members of the volunteer committee distributed admission tickets for the baby clinics as well as food tickets.[168] Volunteers also provided access to the poor law system, specifically through the bastardy laws. In Jamaica and Guyana, volunteer visitors reported "bastardy cases," and those in Barbados probably did the same.[169] Doing so was part of the ongoing attempt to compel men to support their children and save them from the early death that physicians, officials, and philanthropists were certain would result from maternal poverty. Perhaps this mission also reflected a desire by those involved with the child welfare associations to counter accusations that they encouraged "immorality" and "illegitimacy."[170]

The volunteer members of Caribbean child welfare associations endeavored to bring poor women into the world of colonial medicine through access to midwives, nurses, and physicians and to teach them modern mothering skills. The crèches that were established shortly after the founding of the associations played an important role in this respect. Access was limited by the small size of the premises; the crèche operated by Jamaica's Child Welfare Association had space for only twelve children when it opened.[171] Fees also limited access, although in Jamaica the philanthropically minded were encouraged to buy tickets for needy children.[172] But their reach and their ambitions were larger than this. Crèches trained women in mothercraft. In Guyana, for example, by the early 1920s, the Georgetown crèche taught young girls how to care for the infants it looked after in the hope of influencing the "standard of town infant life."[173] By 1927, the crèche in Jamaica began offering training courses for "children's nurses."[174]

The annual baby shows had a similar function. They served an important propaganda purpose, showing officials in London and the colonies and members of the colonial middle classes that their support was effective. They were also an opportunity for the latter to demonstrate their own commitment to this project. In Guyana, members of the colonial hierarchy showed up, as did the governor's wife on occasion. And physician supporters were also present. For example, the Afro-Guyanese physician Frederick Gardner Rose was the judge at one baby show.[175] Baby shows were also directed to nonelite Caribbean women, demonstrating the results of infant welfare initiatives and, indeed, colonial medicine as a whole. At the Berbice Baby Show, for example, one physician noted that the event showed the "value of regular attendance at the Clinics" and expressed the wish that the new generation "would seek medical aid as readily as their parents sought it on their behalf."[176] In Guyana, mothers were encouraged to attend the shows by the prizes given to the winners and the gifts of clothing to all who attended. The prizes recognized infant health and maternal competence and domestic skills, everything that health visitors, local philanthropists, and midwives had been teaching. Thus, awards were given for the "best conditioned baby," the "best breast-fed baby," and the "most sensibly-dressed baby," as well as for infants who had attended the clinic with the greatest regularity and for mothers who had the "cleanest kept home." In a recognition that in Guyana at least, child-saving was a multiethnic enterprise, a prize was also given for the "best East Indian baby."[177] Guyana's surgeon general, who presided over the 1927 baby show at the Nabaclis-Bachelors' Adventure branch of the league, was pleased to see that "all the races had been represented." It had attracted 65 babies, including 8 of "East Indian parentage."[178] Indeed, the prizes and refreshments offered could attract sizeable crowds. A baby show in New Amsterdam, for example, pulled in 110 babies from the town itself and the surrounding villages.[179]

Uplifting the Race?

Nonwhite women who were active as volunteers in these infant welfare organizations or who were paid employees had to negotiate perilous social terrain. These middle-class women were charged with advising poor women in domestic management, many of whom may have resented advice offered by socially more advantaged women despite their shared sex and similar ethnic backgrounds. Race, gender, and class identities came into conflict. In colonial and postslavery territories, the representation of the domestic practices of non-Europeans as uncivilized and unrespectable and as posing a threat to infant health presented particular challenges to nonwhite, non-British women from the middle classes.

In the British Caribbean, the growth of a non-British middle class was the result of education, government expansion, and economic diversification. During the period of slavery, a tiny and relatively privileged group of West Indians of mixed African and European descent had some wealth and access to higher education. During the postemancipation period, this nonwhite middle sector grew as some former slaves and descendants of slaves acquired the wealth and education required for membership. Education in the Caribbean could lead to respectable, nonmanual work, such as teaching or employment as a clerk or civil servant, and studies in the United Kingdom and North America prepared Caribbean men for professional careers as lawyers and doctors. The cost of advanced, foreign education was prohibitive for most, but a fortunate few had access to family money or won one of the handful of educational scholarships available and were able to train for the professions. Economic diversification and an expanding commercial sector also provided a means of social mobility. Although by the late nineteenth century, Jamaica's banana industry was dominated by the United Fruit Company, a U.S. company, some African-descended Jamaicans owned banana estates. In Guyana, men of Portuguese and Chinese descent made money from industries such as timber and balata. And everywhere, the region's towns and cities saw the emergence of a merchant class, whose members hailed from the many non-British groups represented in these colonies.

Many used their positions, education, and social connections to become involved in philanthropic initiatives, such as those addressing infant and maternal welfare. To many members of this class, involvement in philanthropic activities reflected their sense of responsibility to their less fortunate countrymen and -women. Philanthropic activities gave middle-class, nonwhite Caribbeans opportunities to exert cultural and social influence in the face of the widespread racial discrimination that served to limit their employment opportunities and their ability to exercise the political influence for which they believed their educational and cultural achievements qualified them.[180] Involvement in charitable work that was infused with the moral and scientific certainties of public health only added to the stature and influence of the nonwhite colonial middle class. It also provided a measure of protection against contemporary representations of nonwhites as uncivilized.

The emergence of Afro-creole oppositional organizations in the early 1920s provided opportunities for middle-class African-descended women to address the importance of infant and maternal welfare work, but they also indicate some of the tensions involved in these maternalist initiatives.[181] The Black Cross Nurses, a Garveyite social welfare initiative, and the Guyanese Negro Progress Convention are two such examples. Women involved in these organizations expressed a "maternalist" perspective and represented themselves as peculiarly responsible for teaching domestic and mothercraft skills to their poorer countrywomen. They made their case on the grounds of biological race, gender, and class. But they were also motivated by self-interest. Scholars of African American philanthropy in the postslavery United States have argued that black middle-class activists worried about the extent to which negative views about African Americans generally informed how they themselves were seen. Despite their undoubted sincerity in wanting to improve the lives of poor men and women and help more children survive to adulthood, they were impelled by the assumption that "uplifting the race" would benefit all African-descended peoples.[182]

In the 1910s and early 1920s, branches of the Universal Negro Improvement Association (UNIA) were established throughout the British Caribbean. Marcus Garvey established the first one in Jamaica in 1914, and by 1919 branches had appeared in Guyana and Barbados and, soon afterward, in Trinidad.[183] The strikes and popular protests that occurred in several British Caribbean colonies in the late 1910s and early 1920s provide some of the context for the establishment of UNIA branches, as did unhappiness with the economic and race-based inequalities experienced by members of the working and lower middle classes and significantly by demobilized soldiers in the aftermath of World War I.[184] The UNIA branches included similar components, including regular meetings at a Liberty Hall and the establishment of auxiliary organizations such as the Black Cross Nurses. This organization was created in 1920 to "provide an arena for respectable female community service."[185] The nurses provided some medical instruction and, in Belize, undertook maternal education and social welfare work.[186] In this British colony, although they supported women's suffrage and other similar causes, the Black Cross Nurses were essentially "middle-class reformers" who espoused a class-based "maternalist" obligation to poor black women. As Anne Macpherson has argued, for the most part they did not "threaten colonial, middle-class, or Garveyite masculine authority."[187]

Although Guyana's Negro Progress Convention did not provide infant and maternal welfare initiatives similar to those of Belize's Black Cross Nurses, it created a discursive space for at least one of its female members to consider the same kind of issues. Established in 1922, the Negro Progress Convention, like the Garveyite movement, reflected some of the economic and social concerns of black middle-class men and women, including the importance of black economic development. It aimed to help its members develop the "virtue of self-help and thrift" and encouraged them in the "fields of economic and industrial development."[188] It was founded by members of the Afro-Guyanese professional class, M. E. F. Fredericks, a barrister, and Theodore Theophilus (T. T.) Nichols, a physician. Hubert Critchlow, who founded and headed the British Guiana Labour Union, was also involved.[189] Its organizers were, in the words of one British governor of the colony, "a small group of educated negroes, lawyers, doctors and ministers of religion."[190] Although it was not a pan-Africanist organization in the mold of the UNIA, it did look to African Americans for support and a kind of inspiration, as a speech by Princess Maud Kendall demonstrates. An editorial in the *Argosy* newspaper written in the aftermath of violent labor protests in Georgetown saw the Negro Progress Convention in a much more negative light. Its author blamed "negro firebrands" and "apostles of racism" for encouraging the "unrest" in the colony and noted that when "feather-brained" Afro-Guyanese returned home from their travels, they were filled with "race hatred because of fancied slights and indignities" they had experienced while abroad. To the editor, Fredericks seemed one example, an "Americanized self-appointed Negro champion."[191]

In a speech at a 1926 meeting, a female member, Princess Maud Kendall, expressed the same gender- and class-based argument for black middle-class female involvement in social welfare work as that articulated by some Garveyite women. She saw the African American example as a positive one. Kendall noted that women could exercise great influence, both as mothers and more generally as "earnest women engaged in creating for themselves a higher sphere of usefulness to the world." She called for the establishment of "Women's Societies" that would encourage women to become involved in these laudable endeavors and to address such subjects as "Infant Welfare, Child Training, Management of the Home, [and the] Peculiarities of Husbands." She noted that all women should be aware of their "dut[ies] in the woman's field of work" regardless of "race," but her main concern was for privileged Afro-creole women. They had an obligation to "teach race pride and race independence." These Caribbean women's societies should follow the lead of the U.S. National Association of Colored Women and use its motto, "Lifting as we climb." Kendall believed that Afro-Guyanese women would do well to model themselves in their mission of uplift on African American women such as Phillis Wheatley, Ida Wells Barnett, and Mrs. Booker T. Washington, all of whom were worthy of emulation. Kendall argued that "women of culture and education of the Negro race" should help "uplift" their "less fortunate sisters." "Duty" and "humanity" demanded that they "go down among the lowly, the illiterate, and even the vicious to whom they [were] bound by ties of race and sex," but so did "self-preservation." Women such as her listeners knew that they could not "escape altogether the consequences of the acts of their most depraved sisters." The women's societies for which Kendall was calling would help "[reach] the masses" and "inaugurate the reforms" that were needed for the "race" to thrive.[192]

In pointing to these figures from the United States, Princess Maud Kendall emphasized the different influences at work in the British Caribbean in the early twentieth century. Men and women in these Caribbean colonies imported British models of infant welfare work and maternal education to help defeat infant mortality and help the populations grow. This was to be a task for educated, respectable women. For some women, infant welfare work and maternal education was paid employment. Positions in the expanding social welfare sector provided work in a world of limited employment opportunities for middle-class women. But for some women it was a duty to country and to the "race." As the next chapter shows, economic and political imperatives underlay this duty. Worries about shrinking populations and the impact of tropical diseases supported efforts to encourage population growth and the survival of the race.

CHAPTER FIVE

International Public Health and Caribbean Child-Saving

It has been said that a nation's health is a nation's wealth. Nowhere is this more true than in the West Indies, where prosperity is as largely dependent on the health and efficiency of the field labours as it is on the introduction of capital. . . . The death of a child before the completion of its first year, in Great Britain, is estimated to be an economic loss to the State of two hundred pounds. . . . If this value is put at one hundred pounds in the West Indies, the loss of economic wealth is obviously considerable.

—G. B. Mason, "British West Indies Health Services," 1922

IN 1922, A WHITE BARBADIAN PHYSICIAN, G. B. Mason, published an article in which he argued that a large and healthy workforce was necessary for the economic survival of the British Caribbean. In particular, he emphasized the impact of infant mortality on the region's economic health. To a significant extent, these sentiments underlay the early twentieth-century child welfare initiatives discussed in the previous two chapters. They were especially pronounced in a period when migration and tropical diseases were seen as obstacles to population growth. To imperial and colonial officials and members of the multiethnic West Indian middle and professional classes, attracting immigrants and eradicating diseases that led to shrinking and weakened populations were the main solutions. These discussions were imperial in scope, involving British officials and tropical medicine researchers and disseminated in empire-wide publications such as the journal of the Royal Colonial Institute, United Empire, the vehicle for Mason's 1922 article. By the 1910s, however, the Americans were also involved, newly arrived in this part of the world as public health saviors. Their presence indicates the extent to which questions about the size and health of British Caribbean populations had become part of U.S. strategic interests. To these British and American researchers, and to some white West Indians, infant mortality and the diseases that caused it were the product of "racial habits" and raised questions about the "value" of the "degenerate" offspring of sickly parents. To many Caribbean men and women, however, child-saving was an economic and a moral imperative and one upon which their reputation as civilized people rested.

Shrinking Populations and Colonial Economies

In 1957, a member of the first generation of Caribbean-born social scientists, George Roberts, observed that the 1920s represented the beginning of a new demographic era in the British Caribbean. Mortality levels were starting to fall and a "demographic phase much less wasteful of human life than that prevailing in the past was emerging."[1] That there would be cause for such optimism was not apparent from the vantage point of the late 1910s and early 1920s. Imperial officials, tropical medicine researchers, and members of the Caribbean middle and professional classes worried about the combined effects of migration and disease on their colonies.

To officials in the Caribbean and in London in the 1910s and 1920s, maintaining the size and health of the colonial population was an economic imperative, just as it was in the nineteenth century. Key areas of the colonial economy relied on healthy workers. From an imperial perspective, the sugar industry and other agricultural enterprises were valuable. Despite the fall in sugar prices in the 1920s resulting from excess supplies and renewed competition by revitalized European beet sugar producers after World War I, cane sugar remained the most significant export for most British Caribbean territories in this period. The British companies and West Indian merchants and others who owned sugar production facilities in the Caribbean all had an interest in seeing the industry thrive, as did the British banks who lent to them.[2] During his visit to the region in the early 1920s, the British undersecretary of state for the colonies, E. F. L. Wood, made these very points. Wood had been dispatched to this part of the world as part of the effort of the British government to assess the colonies' readiness for more self-governance than that permitted under the existing crown colony system. In almost every British Caribbean colony he visited, Wood was told about the crisis in the sugar industry, and he was convinced that this was the most serious problem facing the region. Wood recommended that the British government "favourably consider" calls from Caribbean governments and planters for preferential treatment for West Indian sugar. The capital investment of many Britons in the Caribbean and the taxes they paid were at risk, as were the profits of the British factories that produced the equipment planters relied upon but were unwilling to purchase in the current economic climate. Indeed, the very future of "Empire-grown sugar" seemed to be uncertain without such policies.[3]

But more than profits were involved. Echoing views expressed by imperial officials in the immediate aftermath of emancipation, Wood argued that a collapse of the sugar industry could threaten the colonies' "stability and progress." To survive and flourish, the British Caribbean needed a "European element," but that was only possible if the sugar industry continued to exist. It was, Wood argued, the "chief means of attracting and maintaining the European population." Europeans were needed to ensure that the sugar industry functioned smoothly and to oversee and administer "local" workers. For economic and political reasons, he declared, the British government must help the Caribbean sugar industry survive.[4]

To survive, however, the industry required workers, the "local labourer," as Wood noted. At the time Wood penned these words, the number of laborers was threatened by the combined effects of high death rates and migration. Mortality rates in the British Caribbean were considered to be dangerously high largely due to significant numbers of infant deaths. (See Table 2.) These concerns were expressed even in populous colonies such as Jamaica and Barbados. Jamaica's population was growing steadily despite high levels of emigration, but its officials worried about the impact of high death rates. In 1918, Jamaica's registrar general for the first two decades of the twentieth century, David Balfour, noted that almost a fifth of all deaths occurred among infants under a year. He lamented that Jamaica's infant mortality rate was nearly twice as high as that in England and Wales and worse than in some places in the British Caribbean. He did find a measure of "poor consolation" in the fact that the situation was worse in Guyana. The influenza epidemic of the late 1910s also contributed to higher than usual mortality rates that, in combination with emigration, resulted in a fall in the colony's population.[5] To Balfour's Barbadian counterpart, Henry Lofty, the colored merchant and political representative for the urban parish of St. Michael and Bridgetown in the early twentieth century, the situation in his small island was even worse.[6] He noted that the island's population in 1921 was scarcely higher than it

Table 2. Infant Mortality Rates in the British Caribbean (per 1,000 live births)

COLONY	1900–1904	1903–4	1912–16	1920–21
Barbados	282	—	293	270
Belize	139	—	—	123
Grenada and Carriacou	—	169.68 (Grenada, 1900–1904)	—	115
St. Vincent and Grenadines	—	—	—	105
Nevis	197	—	—	173
Antigua	—	350.89 (1903)	—	233.34
St. Lucia	—	—	—	143
St. Kitts	247	—	—	322
Trinidad	162	173.04	164	174.93
Jamaica	171	187.02	248	172.51
Guyana	185	200.63 (1904)	183	148

Source: This table includes infant mortality statistics from a number of key colonial reports chosen due to their influence on colonial and imperial thinking about this subject. For 1900–1904, see Minutes of the British Guiana Combined Court, *Report of the Commission Appointed to Enquire into and Report upon the General and Infantile Mortality*, 1906, 11, ICS; for 1903–4, see Knaggs, "Minute by the Colonial Secretary," December 2, 1905, in Barbados Infant Mortality Report, 1905, LSTM; for 1912–16, see, *Report of the Proceedings of the West Indian Medical Conference*, 1921, 62, ICS; for 1920–21, see Mason, "British West Indies Medical Services," 694. Barbados's John Hutson noted that his wife helped him draw up a series of "diagrams" from these numbers. See *Report of the Proceedings of the West Indian Medical Conference*, 62, ICS.

had been in 1861 and had increased by slightly more than 4,000 souls over sixty years; he blamed infant mortality and emigration.[7] But emigration weakened the colony in another way, at least in Lofty's eyes. As had his predecessors in the late nineteenth century, he believed that Barbados was losing "the better class of industrial labourer and industrial worker."[8] Guyana's population was also falling, something that Wood, along with colonial and imperial officials and many members of the colonial elites and the middle and professional classes, noted with considerable alarm. It had declined by several thousand since the early twentieth century, and high mortality rates due to tropical diseases as well as the recent influenza epidemic were the cause.[9]

In the immediate aftermath of emancipation, officials and planters had turned to immigration as one of the solutions to perceived inadequate labor supplies. By the late nineteenth century, South Asia was the source of immigrants destined for the plantations. By the mid-1910s, growing opposition in India to the indentureship system threatened this remedy.

Its end in 1917 prompted the British government as well as planters and government officials in Guyana, Trinidad, Jamaica, and Fiji (which had also imported South Asian workers) to find a means to resuscitate some version of it.[10] Their effort to convince the Indian government to cooperate on a migration scheme was not successful, due to continuing opposition in India.[11]

In Guyana at least, immigration advocates did not give up. They continued to press for immigration, but in a reflection of local political realities, officials were forced to look to Africa and the diaspora as well as India for workers. Guyanese from a number of backgrounds as well as British officials supported what was dubbed the colonization scheme, indicating the widespread nature of the "population anxieties" in this period. It included representatives of the large companies that operated the colony's plantations and men from the expanding merchant and professional classes who were starting to exercise more political influence. Some examples include P. N. Browne, an Afro-creole lawyer and politician, and J. V. Evan Wong, a Chinese-Guyanese man whose family was involved in the new gold and bauxite industries of the colony's interior. They were joined by E. A. Luckhoo, the Indo-Guyanese mayor of Guyana's second largest city (New Amsterdam), and Francis Dias, the (Portuguese-Guyanese) former mayor of Georgetown. Some of these individuals were also involved in the Baby Saving League, notably Browne, Dias, and Luckhoo, suggesting the extent to which these men saw both initiatives as necessary for the colony's health. Organized labor was also represented in the person of Hubert Critchlow, the Afro-Guyanese head of the British Guiana Labour Union. At a 1919 meeting in the Georgetown town hall to address the need for more immigration, those present agreed that the end of indentureship had led to a labor shortage that "threaten[ed]" the sugar industry and that the situation would worsen if large numbers of Indians returned to India.[12] Governor Wilfred Collet seemed to speak for many with his declaration that "what we want is a colonization scheme."[13] The governments of India, Guyana, and Britain continued to address this matter over the next eight years, but they were ultimately unsuccessful. By 1926, when the Indian government agreed to permit immigration, the financial cost seemed to have dissuaded the Guyanese government from proceeding.[14] Perhaps perceptions of population growth in Guyana were also a factor. By the late 1920s, it was increasing, albeit slowly, and births were outnumbering deaths.[15]

Some Afro-Guyanese wanted to make sure that immigration was "balanced." Years of South Asian migration had left people of African descent in a slight minority in the colony, a development that worried Afro-Guyanese members of the UNIA and the Negro Progress Convention. They pushed for the colonial government to recruit laborers from Africa and other British Caribbean territories as well as from India.[16] In 1924, with a new push for immigration, they repeated their demand for involvement in the process and for numerical parity, arguing that it was a matter of justice; anything else, they declared, would undermine the British goals of emancipation. They also made a claim on behalf of their role in Guyana's history and their "civilization," noting that Afro-Guyanese, as longtime "settlers" in the colony, had developed the sugar industry and the new industries of the interior and had acclimatized to "Western civilisation."[17]

This representation of themselves as settlers, not former slaves, but as also entitled to consideration on the basis of emancipation, probably did less to convince the new governor, Graeme Thompson—who had replaced the disliked Collet—than a recognition of their political and economic clout and perhaps their general respectability. The attorney general, Joseph Nunan, described the members of the convention as "courteous and considerate" and able to make "business-like and prompt decisions at a time when important decisions had to be hurriedly made." He also characterized them as "authoritative representatives of educated African creole opinion in this Colony," a point that Thompson echoed in his exchanges with the secretary of state for the colonies, noting that they enjoyed considerable support by some elected members of the government.[18] Thompson's queries to the governors of Sierra Leone, Gold Coast, and Nigeria about their supplies of "surplus labour" and willingness to allow family groups to emigrate to Guyana (paid for by the Guyanese government) were disappointed. Workers in these colonies were apparently needed for "local production." Thompson did not give up. If a "a surplus supply of negro labour" could be found "in any dependency within the Empire," he was willing to facilitate their importation. At the same time, the Guyanese government improved the terms for immigrants from Barbados, the only place in the British Caribbean with an "available supply of negro labour," according to Thompson.[19]

These plans, though, were threatened by Guyana's poor reputation, which was believed to discourage the very migrants whose presence was needed to compensate for the high number of deaths. Those at the 1919 colonization meeting were told that convincing Barbadians and Jamaicans to emigrate to Guyana depended upon whether "they could overcome the terror that appeared to obtain in respect of local health conditions."[20] The authors of the report on the colonization scheme observed that Guyana was healthy, much more so than "most tropical countries," including India, and that the "erroneous impression" of this colony as "unhealthy" was a relic of the past when epidemics of cholera and yellow fever were common. Nowadays, both had "vanished," and Guyana only suffered from "ordinary tropical diseases" like malaria and hookworm and was tackling these energetically and systematically. Indeed, supporting sanitary improvements was a "vital part" of the "colonisation movement."[21]

Jamaicans also worried about the impact of disease and migration on labor supplies. To Oliver Crosswell, Jamaica's position and future prosperity were threatened by its failure to address health problems and the "labor problem." In a talk before the colony's medical association and published in the Gleaner, Crosswell argued that the end of immigration in combination with migration to Panama presented an obstacle to the island's "future improvement." Jamaica's "principal position among the islands of the Western hemisphere and as a useful link in the chain of the overseas Empire" meant that this problem had to be addressed. But the "backward" and "uncivilized" state of the island's health also presented a problem. Sanitary arrangements were "backward"; hookworm, malaria, and venereal diseases were too common; and infant mortality rates were too high. This last in particular was a matter that was "receiving attention in all parts of the civilized world." This situation had "serious consequences" for the island's "industrial interests," including its "production of valuable products," by which Crosswell probably meant bananas and sugar but also tourism. He declared that its beauty and "equable" climate were "valuable assets" that should help Jamaica get "a share of the prosperity" that Bermuda and Nassau received as tourist destinations.[22] In the late nineteenth and early twentieth centuries, efforts to sell Jamaica as a tourist destination had not been very successful, but Crosswell clearly believed that this could be revitalized.[23]

That Crosswell's speech was published in the Gleaner is not surprising. The Gleaner played a key role in disseminating current ideas about public health problems and their avoidance.[24] The involvement of the DeCordova family also suggests the wide-ranging influence of respectable colonial families in spreading public health information. This newspaper regularly covered public health and medical stories in Jamaica and internationally, reprinting health stories from British and British Caribbean newspapers. It also published the proceedings of medical conferences in the Caribbean and the wider region and in Britain that dealt with hemispheric or imperial health matters. From 1904 to the 1940s, Herbert George de Lisser, a white Jamaican of Jewish-Portuguese ancestry, edited the newspaper, the same period when it was under the directorship of Judith DeCordova's husband, Michael DeCordova, whose family had founded it in 1834.[25] During this period, the paper published many editorials about health matters, at times calling for the colonial government to play a stronger, more interventionist role in improving health and sanitation in the colony. In an editorial in 1909, the *Gleaner* praised the public health and sanitation work undertaken by the Americans in Cuba and Panama as an example of the need for governments and the population in a "tropical country" to work together to "keep it sweet and clean," an effort that the government and population of Jamaica should recognize. It declared that in a "tropical, mosquito-plagued, fly-haunted country, the motto should be sanitation and yet more sanitation."[26]

Colonial Diseases

As Crosswell noted in his speech, a trio of colonial diseases—malaria, hookworm, and venereal diseases—were seen as constituting a serious threat to the health of Caribbean populations and their economies. Imperial officials agreed. The undersecretary of state for the colonies, Wood, made this point following his visit to the region. He identified malaria, hookworm, and venereal diseases (which he argued were "rife") as largely responsible for high death rates.[27] Tropical medicine researchers Andrew Balfour and Henry Scott said much the same, arguing that they weakened colonial populations and contributed to the production of sickly offspring and high rates of infant mortality.[28] To officials and physicians in the Caribbean, as well as to concerned members of the middle classes, these diseases needed to be eradicated. In an era when adherence to sanitary precepts and good health was seen as synonymous with civilization as well as necessary for population growth and economic development, a poor reputation in this respect could rankle as well as having real economic consequences.

Malaria was seen as especially dangerous in this regard. Spread by mosquitoes carrying parasites, especially *Plasmodium vivax* and *Plasmodium faliparum*, that flourish in warm weather, malaria is today considered one of the most deadly diseases known to humanity and particularly lethal for children.[29] Early twentieth-century physicians in the British Caribbean were aware of malaria's impact on population growth. Medical schools and especially the schools of tropical medicine in Liverpool and London established at the end of the nineteenth century disseminated this information, as did medical journals and international and regional medical gatherings. Meetings of the local branches of the British Medical Association allowed colonial physicians and tropical medicine itinerants to discuss recent findings. In Jamaica, the Society of Medical Officers of Health (established in 1914) also facilitated such exchanges.[30] Physicians based in Guyana paid particular attention to this scourge, which they argued led not only to high death rates but also to low birthrates. In 1916, Wise argued that the fall in birthrates (which were the lowest since 1896) was largely due to malaria.[31] Edward Minett based his appeal for antimosquito and antimalarial measures on its threat to children. Dealing with the "mosquito problem," he argued, was the means by which the death rate, especially among infants, could be reduced.[32]

Malaria was the source of economic and eugenic anxieties. K. S. Wise argued that it was the "most incapacitating disease to which man [was] liable." It weakened those it did not kill outright until they could "no longer support even the facile, sheltered life of the tropics." Intellectual and physical capacities were diminished; "mental activity" became "dull and slow" and "muscular action inert and effortless."[33] As well as weakening laborers, it also attacked Europeans, whose presence was still seen as necessary for these colonies to flourish. Minett described them as "the pioneers of civilisation, the trader, the planter, the missionary, and the soldier." Malaria, he concluded, was the "greatest ally of ignorance, prejudice, and misery."[34] Minett and Wise were probably influenced by Ronald Ross's conclusions about the impact of this disease; he too saw it as "the great sapper of civilisations [and] the destroyer of imperial races."[35] To Wise, malaria was a "racial poison," the effects of which were dramatic and ubiquitous, at least in tropical territories such as Guyana. In this unfortunate land, malaria was as "omnipresent as the light and wind," its people "bathed" in the disease, "saturated with its poison." The consequences were clear and devastating. It led to an "enormous loss of individual efficiency, [a] steadily recurring loss of prosperity . . . , [and a] subnormal character of physical, educational, and moral life."[36]

Worries about the impact of diseases such as malaria that were spread by mosquitoes animated British imperial officials familiar with the findings by men such as Ross. British tropical medicine researchers journeyed to the Caribbean in the early twentieth century to study these diseases and to spread the word about their seriousness.[37] In 1901–2, the London School of Tropical Medicine's George Carmichael Low gave a series of lectures on malaria and mosquitoes to physicians in Barbados and Guyana while he was in the Caribbean investigating mosquito-borne diseases.[38] The Colonial Office under Joseph Chamberlain helped disseminate researchers' findings and encouraged colonial governments to implement public health measures.[39] Chamberlain also called on colonial governments to investigate tropical diseases and to contribute to educational initiatives to train physicians in tropical medicine. Guyana's Governor Walter Sendall responded enthusiastically, declaring that "every possible means" should be taken to publicize Patrick Manson's findings about the relationship between malaria and mosquitoes and that medical officers should monitor civil servants for compliance in antimosquito measures. The Guyanese government also agreed to contribute to the tropical medicine educational fund.[40] Within the next few years, the government expanded its antimosquito measures following the advice of tropical medicine experts. It provided free quinine for select groups (policemen and their families, individuals in colonial medical and judicial establishments, and residents on sugar estates) and subsidized its sale to others. Guyanese officials also attempted to eradicate mosquito breeding areas. Following the 1909 visit by the tropical disease researcher Rupert Boyce to the Caribbean, municipal and colonial governments in Guyana passed laws and regulations stipulating that houses and yards be inspected, trenches and drains filled in, and water receptacles removed or covered up.[41]

Barbadian officials were happy to note that their island suffered much less severely from mosquito-borne diseases such as malaria and yellow fever than did other places, a (generally accurate) perception that helped shape their responses to imperial officials in this period. Colonial legislators refused Colonial Office pleas to contribute to the tropical medicine education fund on the grounds that the island did not suffer from "dangerous malarial fevers." Governor Hodgson, perhaps familiar with the impact of malaria from his time as governor in the Gold Coast, promised to try to convince the executive to change its collective mind. He planned to publish Chamberlain's circular about mosquitoes and disease in the *Official Gazette* and to send copies to every doctor in the colony. And he asked for pamphlets and anything else he could use to demonstrate to "the people the advantages to be obtained by common activism and disadvantages of isolation."[42] The yellow fever epidemic that appeared in Barbados five years later seemed to convince Patrick Manson at least that the colony's government was not entirely rational about health matters, a criticism that would be repeated over the next few decades. The Colonial Office responded by dispatching Boyce to the region to investigate mosquito control measures generally, but Manson hoped that he could convince the Barbadian government in particular to act. As Manson noted, this was a "good opportunity" to "bull[y] the high-handed" Barbadian legislature into adopting "sensible measures" following its dismissal of Low's earlier advice. He saw this as an opportunity to "initiate valuable measures," but as one Colonial Office official told Ronald Ross, criticisms could backfire.[43] Writing for the secretary of state for the colonies and relaying a message from the Advisory Committee for the Tropical Diseases Research Fund, Francis J. H. Hopwood reminded Ross of the limits of metropolitan power. The secretary of state could not "dictate to the local [Barbadian] Legislature" about the initiatives that should be undertaken. "Hearty co-operation" was needed to implement desired "sanitary measures."[44] Boyce agreed with colonial officials that endemic malaria was not present in the island, but he encouraged them to prevent further yellow fever outbreaks by removing receptacles where the mosquitoes could breed, thereby making the colony "mosquito-free and the envy and admiration of the rest of the tropical world."[45] After Boyce's visit, Hutson submitted a report on malarial and other fevers to imperial officials. He echoed Boyce's conclusion that malaria was not endemic to Barbados and speculated that cases in the colony probably came from Guyana or nearby Caribbean islands, or perhaps even farther afield from Panama or Brazil.[46] Governor Leslie Probyn observed that as Barbados did not have a medical department, sending a similar report each year would be "difficult," and he quoted Hutson's conclusion that any such report would be "meager," given the "absence of malaria" and the rarity with which yellow fever occurred.[47]

Malaria was believed to pose a threat to Jamaica and for many of the same reasons as in Guyana and other colonies. According to tropical medicine researcher W. T. (William) Prout, it affected the "general health and death-rate" of the population and "the agricultural development of the colony." Formerly a medical officer in Sierra Leone, Prout had addressed the impact of malaria on white Europeans and recommended "'[European] segregation from the native'" as a solution. In Jamaica, as part of a team from the Liverpool School of Tropical Medicine in the colony in 1908, he was more concerned about the protection of nonwhite agricultural workers.[48] He observed that "malaria-carrying mosquitos [bred] in great abundance" in banana- and sugar-growing zones, where they attacked indentured South Asian workers.[49] Prout estimated that malaria was responsible for almost one-fifth of the colony's deaths and about a third of admissions to its hospitals and was costly in terms of treatment and lost work time. Following Prout's visit and a local outbreak of the disease, the colonial government established its own malaria commission in 1910 and followed up with a number of antimalaria initiatives. These included the beginnings of an education campaign, the passage of a new public health law, training for sanitary inspectors, the sale of cheap quinine in the post office, and government recommendations that district medical officers take on the work of medical officers of health.[50] These developments convinced Prout that the "anti-malarial campaign in Jamaica [had] been fully started."[51] This may have been so, but it was short lived. Within a few years, many of these measures had been abandoned, probably for financial reasons.[52]

A Nation's Wealth

Deaths from tropical diseases and other ailments, especially among the very young, were personal, family tragedies. To colonial and imperial officials and to physicians and other members of the colonial educated middle and professional classes, high rates of infant and child mortality were a threat to economic survival as well as to reputations. The author of the 1915 report for Guyana's Baby Saving League quoted a "well-known [English] authority" who declared that "'carelessness in connection with Infant life [was] a sure sign of degeneracy in any country.'"[53] Despite these imperatives, not everyone agreed on the actions to be taken. Many members of the educated colonial classes wanted to ensure that all children survived to healthy adulthood, but some echoed more disturbing contemporary views that worried about the economic and eugenic cost of survival.

Anticipating the comments by Barbadian G. B. Mason, a Jamaican district medical officer argued that economic considerations meant that the colonial government should help preserve young lives. Henry Tillman made his comments in the aftermath of the Jamaican Malaria Commission, but his comments applied more broadly to public health measures directed at children. He argued that the colonial government should devote financial resources to combating malaria. He noted the cost of health education and free medicine for children, but he argued that these would address the "gross ignorance" and poverty that condemned so many to premature death and poor health. Indeed, these factors were responsible for the deaths of "young children," rather than illegitimacy "as many claim[ed]." Tillman maintained that malaria's devastating impact on the young demanded no less and that the effects of a public health campaign would be long lasting. Tackling malaria would "work wonders for the physique of [the] future generation of labourers" and keep alive children so they could become "assets to the State." In Tillman's eyes, children were potential "consuming unit[s]" as well as future "pro-creating unit[s]."[54]

The philanthropic and state child welfare initiatives discussed in the previous chapter were part of this effort. The first few reports of Guyana's Baby Saving League justified its work on these grounds, noting that the "State march[ed] forward on the pattering feet of its little children."[55] Echoing Tillman, the author of the league's second report (probably Wise) declared that premature death of the young was "a deplorable waste of life." But he also expressed some ambivalence, worrying that those children who were ill but survived could end up living weakened lives of "impaired vitality" and that the potential economic and eugenic consequences were worrisome. He argued that "damaged and weakly infants" would become physically and mentally weak adults, destined for "the hospitals, alms house, and prisons" and potentially contributing to the "physical deformity of the race."[56]

Wishart, writing at the beginning of the 1920s, did not seem as worried by such predictions, suggesting that infant welfare measures could help prevent their realization. Indeed, he argued that infant welfare measures helped create a healthier, stronger race of West Indian men and women, fitted for survival in this part of the world. Wishart believed that efforts should be made to save all children, including those whom an earlier generation had condemned as future members of an impoverished, debilitated residuum. He saw "legitimate" and "illegitimate" children as "potential assets to the State and from the broad point of view of equal value."[57]

The perspectives expressed in the Baby Saving League report from 1915 may have owed something to Wise's more or less contemporaneous writings about the impact of malaria; both emphasized the consequences of illness on the health of the race and the burden that sickly survivors were believed to pose to families and state-supported welfare institutions, such as the poor law system.[58] But they also echo views expressing some unease about the potential consequences of infant welfare initiatives. Andrew Balfour and Henry Scott summed up some of these in their wide-ranging survey of health problems and medical services in the British empire.[59] Under the heading "Some Imperial Burdens," they discussed some of the efforts to deal with infant mortality, arguing, for example, that early notification of births legislation and the presence of trained midwives and health visitors, along with enhanced training schemes, could help solve this problem in Britain's "tropical possessions."[60] Balfour and Scott praised the infant welfare initiatives undertaken by physicians and "laywomen" in parts of the British Caribbean, including Jamaica, Guyana, and Trinidad.[61] But the two men wondered whether child-saving measures could be excessive. To what extent should the "State" care for children as they grew? They saw the question of "fostering and tending to the weakly and the unfit and allowing them to propagate their kind" as a "difficult one." If they were not to be euthanized, they needed to be cared for, both for their "own sake and for that of the race."[62] Balfour and Scott noted that "some" identified the harmful effects of excessive cosseting of children in the form of clinics and "free meals" and the provision of "cheap or free" medical care for adults. They themselves were concerned about potential political consequences. Labor strife might result once children grew to become adult workers who made unreasonable demands and ended up as pawns of "irresponsible agitator[s]."[63] The survival of the nation and, indeed, the empire was also at risk. Balfour and Scott maintained that the endurance of hardships and the consequent survival of the fittest, not the "*undue* fostering of the weak, [had] made Britain a glorious nation, and enabled her to maintain her supremacy against countless difficulties." The "weak and sickly" should be helped but "in a reasonable and sensible way."[64]

Sex, Venereal Disease, and Caribbean Populations

Concerns about helping the "sick and weakly" were expressed in British Caribbean discussions about venereal diseases, especially syphilis, in the late 1910s and early 1920s. An editorial in the *Gleaner* declared in 1916 that venereal diseases had a "deteriorative effect not only on those who contract[ed] them but on yet unborn offspring" and that their "sterilising influence" prevented population growth.[65] Representations of venereal diseases in the British Caribbean echoed those associated with other maladies, especially malaria. Both were seen as a kind of "racial poison" that threatened reproduction. Venereal diseases were also associated with contemporary representations of the purportedly immoral and uncivilized sexual practices of colonial peoples. These, it was argued, made them especially susceptible to such dangerous diseases.

In Britain and its empire, perceptions about venereal diseases in the early twentieth century were linked to worries about the declining "fitness" of the population and the deficit of healthy men to defend the empire.[66] As Philippa Levine has argued, venereal diseases were believed to "weaken racial strength, sap civilization, and potentially threaten the [British] empire."[67] In the second half of the nineteenth century, prostitutes were the main targets of attempts to halt their spread. In Britain and parts of its empire, concerns about the health of sailors led to the passage of Contagious Diseases Acts, which tried to compel prostitutes to undergo testing and treatment for these illnesses. By 1870 the Contagious Diseases Acts had been implemented in more than twelve British colonies, including the Caribbean colonies of Barbados, Jamaica, and Trinidad. Following a campaign by female activists, they were repealed in Britain in 1886 and later in the colonies.[68]

Venereal diseases continued to be the subject of considerable anxiety after the abolition of the acts. Britain's Interdepartmental Committee on Physical Deterioration pointed to the hereditary nature of syphilis, observing that parents could pass this debilitating illness to their children.[69] Indeed, Balfour and Scott listed it as one of the causes of infant mortality.[70] In the early twentieth century, researchers identified the cause of syphilis in a microorganism, *Treponema pallidum*, and devised more accurate diagnostic tests and more effective treatments.[71] These years also saw advances in the treatment of venereal diseases, including a diagnostic test for syphilis, the Wassermann test, developed by August Wassermann in 1906. In 1909, the German physician and medical researcher Paul Ehrlich discovered Salvarsan as a treatment for syphilis, the so-called magic bullet. Despite these developments, diagnosis and treatment were far from perfect. The Wassermann test was costly, "complicated," and not entirely accurate, and once syphilis was diagnosed, treatment could last for some time and lead to side effects.[72] Concern about the impact of venereal diseases led the British government to establish a commission to investigate their treatment and prevention. The commission issued its report in 1916 and recommended free clinics be founded for diagnosis and treatment as well as a "public education campaign" to spell out the consequences of contracting venereal diseases and detail how they could be prevented.[73]

The committee's recommendations provided the basis for public health policy decisions in some British Caribbean colonies where concerns about the impact of venereal diseases were frequently expressed. In 1916, Wise noted that "in conformity with the recommendations of the Royal Commission on Venereal Diseases," Guyanese physicians began treating patients with Salvarsan, and the colonial bacteriology department started to use the Wasserman test.[74] Jamaican physicians undertook similar measures.[75] In this colony, the Royal Commission also prompted colonial officials and physicians to participate in the anti–venereal disease campaign. Crosswell, for example, developed educational lectures along the lines suggested by the commission, and the Central Board of Health distributed information pamphlets. The colonial government also made a significant financial commitment to the battle, promising £2,500 to establish a venereal diseases clinic in Kingston, a large amount of money for the period.[76] The Kingston Public Hospital began offering free treatment and in 1917 instituted evening clinics for sufferers.[77] The response of the government in Grenada was the most dramatic and apparently unique in the British Caribbean in this period. In 1917, it passed legislation compelling sufferers (both adults and children) to undergo medical treatment. Physicians were to report delinquent patients to the police, and fines could be imposed on anyone convicted of knowingly spreading venereal disease or "permitting any acts" that might lead to its spread.[78] The governor believed the legislation was "useful," but the surgeon general, P. W. Paterson, was a little less enthusiastic. He noted unhappily that patients refused to show up for their treatment and vanished.[79] It was also not implemented as fully as possible. In 1921, Paterson noted that existence of the legislation was useful but that considerable "leniency" was exercised.[80]

The response of the Barbadian government to the crisis posed by venereal diseases reflected the same kind of tension between medical paternalism and local sentiments as seen in other public health discussions in this colony. The colony's governor, Leslie Probyn, suggested that the apparently high rates of venereal disease among the Afro-Barbadian recruits to the British West Indies Regiment warranted a consideration of the Grenadian law. Like other members of the colonial governments and many physicians, he believed this problem was widespread.[81] Some of the colonial physicians whose opinion Probyn solicited on this matter believed that legislation was necessary to combat the destructiveness of the disease. To the coroner, Eustace Greaves, legislation was needed in Barbados because syphilis ("both in its acquired and congenital form") was "striking at the very root of the prosperity of the island, namely the virility of the agricultural class."[82] A number of physicians approved of the legislation in theory but suspected that it could not be enforced or implemented for various reasons. John Hutson, for example, thought that fines might be impractical.[83] E. H. (Edward Howard) Bannister, a parochial medical officer for St. Michael parish, thought that the law was "well nigh perfect" and that perfection itself could be achieved with the establishment of a clinic at the general hospital, which currently had no facilities for treating venereal diseases, and the free provision of Salvarsan and other medication for paupers. He also recommended that poor "private patients" be sold the medication at cost.[84] Norman Boxill saw cost as the main impediment and as a moral problem; the legislation might be effective, but its prohibitive cost would mean "endless heartburn both to the patients" and their physicians.[85] The government did not adopt the law, concluding that it was, as Hutson noted later, "too drastic" for Barbadians. Hutson's comments several years later indicate some uncertainty, however. He had heard the law described as "very nearly approaching Prussian," a harsh criticism in the aftermath of the war, but he also admired the Grenadian government for its paternalism and "courage" in passing the law and the "docility" of Grenadians in obeying it.[86]

Concerns about the health of fighting men and the outbreak of World War I prompted these discussions and policy decisions, both in Britain and in the empire. In Britain, the presence of young soldiers and a more independent and public role for many young women during the war years contributed to the view that sexually immoral behavior was more common and that rates of venereal disease were rising. The health of the population and especially of the troops was believed to be at risk.[87] Racial fears aggravated these anxieties. The war brought nonwhite colonial troops, many of whom were from the Caribbean, into Europe and other theaters of the war.[88] Following an initial ban on nonwhite Caribbean men as military combatants on the grounds that their purported lack of civilization made them unreliable and inadequate soldiers, some 15,000 men from the British Caribbean ended up participating in the war.[89] But these nonwhite colonial men were seen as dangerous; their assumed excessive sexual desires and bodies contaminated with venereal diseases were believed to place white women at risk.[90] E. F. L. Wood spoke for many when he declared that the purported pervasiveness of venereal diseases in this part of the world reflected the "low" "standard of sexual morality" in the region.[91]

After the war, concerns about the impact of venereal diseases on the size and health of colonial populations prompted the British government and the National Council for Combating Venereal Diseases to dispatch commissions of inquiry to Gibraltar and Malta, the "Far East," and the

British Caribbean. The two physicians given the task of visiting the British Caribbean, Letitia Fairfield and Archibald Francis (A. F.) Wright, were to discuss with colonial governments the "preventative and curative" measures that could be taken.[92] Fairfield and Wright concluded that apart from Trinidad and St. Kitts—where the government was making a "very plucky effort"—anti–venereal disease measures were generally inadequate.[93] This was a problem, given the high rate of infection, something that medical inspections of the troops during the war had revealed and which Fairfield emphasized.[94] For these researchers, the impact on Caribbean health and society was clear. Like malaria and hookworm, these diseases caused sickness and death and weakened the population's "wage-earning capacity."[95] As they noted in their public talks in Jamaica, treatment, prevention, and improved living conditions made financial sense in the long run, as did more clinics and the provision of free treatment.[96]

In Jamaica, the presence of Fairfield and Wright provided members of that colony's educated, professional, and middle classes with an opportunity to call on the colonial government to address these public health problems. In a talk republished in the *Gleaner*, Fairfield advised Jamaicans to support organizations addressing infant mortality (which was one of the consequences of venereal diseases) and appealed to her listeners to "carry on the work" begun with the commission's visit. Venereal disease, she told them, was an imperial "problem," and she and Wright wanted the elite and middle-class Jamaicans in the audience "in the name of the Empire" to "make a little sacrifice in this cause."[97] Wright's talk a few days earlier, with its blunt description of poor sanitation and health in Jamaica, prompted the Women's Social Service Club to call on the colonial government and the U.S. firm United Fruit Company to act. Its members expressed shock and some embarrassment at the "serious condemnation" by Wright (whom they described as "a doctor holding a very responsible position") that venereal disease was "spread all over the island" and that Jamaica was—as the *Gleaner* quoted Wright in large, bold type— "Competing with Port Said for World's Cesspit."[98] The colonial government should take immediate steps to "remove the reproach of being a 'Cesspit of the world' from our lovely island" and to "prevent our island being so over-run by disease germs that no one could live in it and still keep healthy and uncontaminated." As Judith DeCordova noted in her letter to the governor on behalf of the Women's Social Service Club and printed in the *Gleaner*, these conditions must appall the governor as they would "all thoughtful and intelligent people."[99]

In the early twentieth century, the impact of venereal diseases led some Caribbean and British physicians in the Caribbean to speculate about the "value" of the victims' "tainted" offspring. Some of the participants of the early twentieth-century investigations into infant health had identified congenital syphilis as a contributing factor to high rates of infant mortality.[100] But to Barbados's Edward Deane, their survival also posed a problem. The parochial medical officer for St. Michael's parish in Barbados observed that the incidence of syphilis had increased "among the lower classes" following the closure of the Lock Hospital some twenty years earlier. Deane was of two minds about this development. He felt "pity" for those infants who died young. But he also saw their deaths as the "merciful" action of "Providence" that "rid society of these unfortunate and tainted beings." If they survived, they would only "beget offspring who would add greatly to the sum of human suffering and misery."[101] The eugenicist impulse behind these words was expressed more explicitly by Conrad Arthur, a medical officer of health in St. Vincent in the early 1910s. Like other physicians, he worried that the "unhealthy" and "degenerate" adults populating the Caribbean contributed to the "propagation of inferior stocks." He noted that the more extreme solutions to this problem included sterilizing "unfit adults" or "destroy[ing] their progeny" but concluded that both were "impossible" and "impractical."[102]

Although some contemporaries still regarded these children as "tainted" a few years later, the availability of new treatment methods may have made them seem "salvageable." To J. A. L. Calder, a district medical officer in Jamaica, addressing the problem of venereal disease (he favored the compulsory approach) was part of the larger project of ensuring the health and survival of children.[103] New treatment methods and the acceptance that child-saving was needed for healthy colonies seemed to have shaped the thinking of some. Ethel Minett, for example, observed that venereal disease should be treated to ensure that children did not become infected and grow to become "diseased and crippled" adults who produced unhealthy "future generations." Otherwise, she observed, they might not have been "worth the saving."[104]

Public Health and Infant Welfare in an "Ever-British Colony"

These discussions about venereal diseases, infant mortality, and the moral calculations about the value of children's lives were part of the demographic anxieties of the late 1910s and early 1920s. They prompted governments and philanthropists to combine venereal disease treatment and prevention with infant welfare work, an expenditure deemed worthwhile, given the disease's physical, social, and economic costs. In Barbados, as in Jamaica, the visit by Fairfield and Wright helped prompt some members of the white elite to undertake these initiatives. Their actions were more than the reflexive responses by colonial elites reacting to imperial critics, however; they also emerged out of long-standing discussions in Barbados itself about population health. But for some imperial officials, health problems in Barbados and its excessive levels of infant mortality challenged the accepted intersection of race and civilization.

The visit by Fairfield and Wright led to a "great awakening of interest" in Barbados, according to John Hutson. During their visit, the two Britons met with politicians and officials from the colonial and local governments, physicians, and members of the "general public."[105] They recommended the establishment of an anti–venereal disease clinic in Bridgetown, advice that found a receptive audience among Barbadian physicians who had already called for similar measures.[106] The previous year, the colonial government had created its own venereal disease committee, which recommended a network of clinics throughout the island, based in the general hospital and the almshouses, offering "free and strictly confidential" treatment. It was thought best to wait for the British commission to arrive, however, before implementing these measures.[107] By the time Fairfield and Wright delivered their suggestions, the colonial government's enthusiasm had waned, the result of a postwar fall in sugar prices that left "general revenues" unable to fund such initiatives. Female philanthropists stepped in, with the newly formed Women's Social Welfare League under the presidency of Mrs. E. H. Bannister quickly establishing a venereal disease clinic at the general hospital. In the absence of government financial support, the league turned to Barbadian and British philanthropists (including Mrs. A. R. Fellowes, a planter's wife, and "her friends in England") for the equipment and funds necessary to operate the clinic. As part of a medical family, Bannister was doubtless aware of the suggestion for just such an initiative offered by her husband, E. H. Bannister, several years earlier.[108] The Women's Social Welfare League also founded a baby-saving league, and by the late 1920s, the two were working closely together. Medical staff at the infant clinic channeled infected mothers to the venereal disease clinic for treatment.[109]

These policies were implemented in a colony that increasingly found itself condemned by imperial officials as a public health laggard. The refusal of colonial politicians to support the kinds of public health measures that other colonial governments in the region were undertaking played a role in this. For example, when Hector Howard, the U.S. director of the International Health Board's anti-hookworm campaign, visited Barbados in 1919, he found evidence of the disease in a number of parishes and proposed an extensive and expensive campaign to combat it. Most of the parish-based commissioners of health either refused the request that they contribute to the cost or did not reply, leading the governor to reject Howard's offer of Rockefeller Foundation assistance.[110] In the aftermath of their visit to Barbados, Fairfield and Wright used this episode as an example of purported Barbadian indifference to implementing public health measures, noting caustically that nothing further was done and that "the hookworm remain[ed] the master of the situation."[111]

Wright and Fairfield contributed to Barbadians' poor reputation. Once back in England after their Caribbean tour, they wrote a confidential report for the Colonial Office and its medical and sanitary advisors in which they harshly criticized what they saw as Barbados's general neglect of public health. They also condemned as ineffective its decentralized medical system that gave individual parishes considerable leeway in making their own sanitary and public health decisions. They especially emphasized its impact on infant health. With considerable impatience, the two medics noted that the "question of Infantile Mortality ha[d] been under discussion for 15 years" in Barbados. They cited the failed attempt in 1912 to create a network of district nurses to visit newborns as one example. Instead, they noted, the "unfortunate babies continue[d] to die and attempts to stimulate the Parishes to save them [were] met by ill-spelt, childish and pitifully conceited letters of refusal."[112] Fairfield and Wright saw this as part of a larger political and social problem in Barbados. They condemned the assembly as "probably the most conservative and reactionary body in the world," motivated almost entirely by "fear of an income tax" and an effort to ensure that money for public expenses was limited to what could be raised by "taxing the necessities of life." They would have been more sympathetic during the current financial crisis if government members had instituted an income tax or used some of that money to support charitable initiatives during the prosperous war years.[113]

The Australian-born Fairfield's Fabianism may well have influenced her views, but she and Wright were probably also influenced by John Hutson, who was one of their sources.[114] Many of the criticisms offered by Fairfield and Wright echoed points that this Barbadian physician had been making to colonial and imperial officials and politicians for almost twenty years. To a significant extent, Hutson helped shape imperial views about health policies in Barbados. On reading the report by Fairfield and Wright, imperial officials asked Hutson for information on any "sanitary and medical" matters on which the Colonial Office could "usefully intervene with a view to improvement."[115] In his written and oral response to the Colonial Advisory Medical and Sanitary Committee, Hutson repeated his long-standing arguments about the deleterious effects of Barbados's decentralized medical and health system on the colony's ability to craft a coherent and unified approach to public health problems and his view that the government's response to high rates of infant mortality was inadequate.[116]

Hutson was not the only white creole who criticized Barbados's policies. He was joined by G. B. Mason, a former district medical officer for the Leeward Islands and St. Vincent and whose words opened this chapter. Like Hutson, he was an influential figure, at least in imperial eyes. He belonged to the Royal Colonial Society and was the founder of the West Indian Club, where he would have socialized with past and present governors, planters, and white West Indians based in London.[117] He occasionally testified to the Colonial Office imperial medical advisory committee about Caribbean health matters and relayed his views in specialist and more popular publications.[118] Mason had some harsh words about his home colony. In an article in the *Gleaner*, he observed that Barbados had the highest rate of infant deaths in the region. He expressed astonishment that a colony "so advanced in many ways"—with its "pipe-borne portable water" and a "stringent anti-Mosquito Act"—could be "so indifferent to this terrible waste of human life." Despite its "representative institutions" and elected assembly, Barbados was behind all the other colonies in "the struggle for infant welfare, being badly beaten by the Crown Colonies around them." He noted caustically that "rear[ing] labourers for emigration [did] not appear to appeal to the Barbadians" whose infants, he declared, did not "get a fair chance."[119]

As Mason suggested, representations of Barbados as a special kind of British colony, a "little England," as some contemporaries called it, were intimately entangled with discussions about health and social welfare initiatives. Barbados was one of Britain's oldest colonies, dating back to the early seventeenth century. Unlike the "crown colonies" dismissingly referred to by Mason, it had an elected government, albeit with a tiny electorate, and "English" political and administrative structures, such as vestries, parishes, and the like. It also had white people. In the early 1920s, "whites" (people of European ancestry) comprised just under 7 percent of Barbados's total population, a higher percentage than in other British Caribbean colonies.[120] As we have seen, it was also believed to be healthy, much more so than places like Guyana. A certain degree of civilized behavior was expected of this "little England," and by the early twentieth century, civilization was increasingly indicated by an adherence to modern sanitary and public health policies. This was the standard by which nonwhite colonized peoples were regularly assessed in this period. The widely perceived failure of these groups in India, Africa, and the Caribbean to follow metropolitan-approved rules of sanitary behavior saw them condemned as "uncivilized."

Imperial officials seemed to be of two minds about white Barbadians. Fairfield and Wright were contemptuous of them. "Their pride," they argued, "pass[ed] all belief and [was] impervious to reason or ridicule."[121] But the secretary of state for the colonies and the members of the Colonial Advisory Medical and Sanitary Committee were more disappointed than anything else. They seemed to have expected more of this "little England." After having read the reports by Hutson and Fairfield and Wright and having talked to Hutson himself, they described themselves as "surprised" at the uncivilized sanitary behavior by Barbadian officials. They had expected that this colony, with its "ancient history of British influence and settlement," would demonstrate more "appreciation of the vital importance of good sanitation to the health and welfare of the community." They, like many Barbadians themselves, saw the colony as "naturally healthy," or at least one that should have been healthy due to its "natural advantages." Instead, it was among the least healthy places, and its rate of infant mortality was the highest the committee members had seen in any part of the empire.[122] They acknowledged the impact of poor economic conditions, but they also pointed their collective fingers at government neglect. Rather than taking on the task of infant welfare work itself, the colonial government left this to charity.[123]

Hutson and Mason did not speak for all white Barbadians. In an inquiry into public health subsequently called by the acting governor of Barbados, committee members A. J. Hanschell and James Walker Hawkins (a planter and physician) heatedly disagreed with the majority, who repeated Hutson's calls for change. This group included two Barbadians who had long agitated for infant welfare measures, Norman Boxill and John Hutson.[124] Among their wide-ranging public health recommendations, they called for the establishment of clinics that offered maternal education and medical assistance by physicians and midwives.[125] Hawkins and Hanschell defended the current system of health and sanitary administration. Its decentralized nature, rather than the blight seen by Hutson, reflected Barbados's "English" heritage. This vestry-based system was based on the "English method"; the vestries and their boards of poor law guardians were analogous to the "English Parish and County Councils," and the general board of health (which supervised and coordinated health matters) was similar to the "English Ministry of Health." They argued that this approach should be "continued and improved in an ever British colony like Barbados."[126]

In defending Barbados's "Britishness," Hawkins and Hanschell attacked Hutson and others for their scurrilous and unfair characterizations of the colony as "unhealthy," something that their own "experience" disproved. They condemned Hutson's views as mere "opinion" that rested on "insufficient data and knowledge of conditions." They appealed to social Darwinism and contemporary ideas about race to buttress their argument that rather than being unhealthy, Barbados was in fact a public health success story. They pointed out that in terms of population density, Barbados was able to keep alive "twice as many people" as England and more than double that again than did Trinidad. They suggested that the death rate did not point to poor sanitation, something they associated with population density, race, and class. Barbados, they argued, was much more "densely populated" than was England, and its population was "poorer and black." In an island as "saturated" with people as was Barbados, the death rate had to be "high" to ensure that the "present saturated point" was maintained. The "universal law of nature, 'The survival of the fittest,'" dictated that a proportionate number of the "weakest" must die ("be sent to the wall") to approximately offset births. They noted that the "weakest" were babies, especially those of illegitimate birth. To Hanschell and Hawkins, the high birthrate "could not be prevented in a tropical island like Barbados, except by moral education, and prevention of the most unfit from having children, if that [was] practicable."[127]

Between Two Empires

In his 1919 talk before Jamaica's medical association, Oliver Crosswell noted the public health efforts of the Americans and the British in Jamaica in targeting diseases such as hookworm and venereal disease.[128] By the 1910s, the Americans had joined Britain in its public health mission in the

British Caribbean. From the late nineteenth century, U.S. public health initiatives had been carried out in this part of the world under the auspices of the army and in the context of military occupation. The eradication of yellow fever in Cuba and Panama stands out as an example of U.S. military accomplishment.[129] It also led U.S. officials to express some interest in health matters in the British Caribbean. In 1912, for example, U.S. officials asked the British secretary of state how the various governments in the British Caribbean were dealing with "yellow fever" mosquitoes, prompting the British official to poll the region's governments on this matter.[130]

Although the United Fruit Company had a medical presence in Jamaica in the early twentieth century, the Rockefeller Foundation was the most prominent U.S. public health presence in the British Caribbean in the 1910s and early 1920s. As Steven Palmer has suggested, the "glow of the [American] imperial public health array forged" between 1898 and 1903 provided part of the background to the Rockefeller Foundation's international activities in the British Caribbean.[131] The international arm of the Rockefeller Foundation, the International Health Board, set up a series of relatively short-term cooperative anti-hookworm projects in parts of the Caribbean and Central America. The first was in Guyana in 1914, followed quickly by ventures in Trinidad, Grenada, St. Vincent, St. Lucia, Jamaica, and Antigua. Guyana's ran from 1914 to 1919 and Jamaica's from 1919 to 1926.[132] The Americans worked closely with British officials to negotiate their role in these colonies.[133]

The effects of hookworm disease (ankylostomiasis) on labor productivity convinced medical researchers and those who funded their work that it needed to be eradicated. Caused by parasites that left victims anemic and weak, it was spread among workers in areas of intensive economic development, such as plantations, where sanitary facilities were inadequate and workers were often barefoot and underfed. Hookworm disease was recognized as a major public health problem in places such as India, Egypt, and parts of the British Caribbean by the nineteenth century. Physicians in Guyana, Trinidad, and Jamaica discovered its presence in the 1880s, and by the late 1890s, some district medical officers in Trinidad and Guyana were treating it on the plantations.[134] In 1908, a British government committee studied hookworm and relayed its findings to various colonial governments, including those in the British Caribbean.[135] The following year, as part of his public health fact-finding tour of the region, Rubert Boyce assessed anti-hookworm measures in place on estates where indentured workers were employed. He noted with approval that "health authorities" in Guyana, Trinidad, St. Lucia, and Grenada were "giving their attention to the eradication of this disease."[136] When officials with the Rockefeller Foundation arrived in these colonies several years later, they had to work closely with the colonial physicians and health initiatives already in place.[137]

Like malaria and venereal diseases, hookworm was a locus of population anxieties. It was seen as weakening workers and making them lazy. Rubert Boyce characterized hookworm as a "labour-paralysing disease."[138] It also threatened population growth; anemic women often miscarried their infants, as the author of the 1915 report of the British Guiana Baby Saving League noted.[139] In the British Caribbean, as in other tropical areas, hookworm disease was entangled with ideas about race, civilization, and sanitation; as Anderson has noted for the Philippines, the anti-hookworm campaign constituted a "colonial civilizing project."[140] In the Caribbean, the presence of this illness among South Asian plantation workers and its transmission among those who walked barefoot on (feces-)infected soil gave it particular symbolic weight in an age when hygienic, sanitary practices were so closely associated with civilization. Its eradication served economic ends as well as helping burnish a colony's reputation. In 1919, the Guyanese involved in the colonization scheme called on the colonial government to invite the International Health Board to remain in the colony and expand its activities. Apparently, the presence of hookworm disease in the colony discouraged potential immigrants.[141]

In Jamaica, individuals reflecting a similar constellation of overlapping business, philanthropic, and medical interests called on their government to invite the Rockefeller Foundation into their colony. In 1917, the members of the Agricultural Society appealed to the colonial government to accept the help of the International Health Board to eradicate "hookworm, malaria, and other diseases which [were] widespread and preventable," as a matter of "vital importance to the welfare of the colony."[142] Two years later, the Jamaican Imperial Association echoed this plea. Its own investigation had revealed that hookworm, venereal diseases, and malaria were a particular menace.[143] This pressure seemed to have helped convince an initially reluctant Jamaican government to agree to the International Health Board's proposed hookworm campaign, despite worries about the cost.[144]

Working with the colonial government and physicians in Jamaica, the International Health Board tackled hookworm. The public health education campaign its officials initiated in 1926 in alliance with the Jamaican government reflected the perception of Benjamin Washburn, the board's representative in Jamaica, that attacking hookworm could transform the way Jamaicans saw health. Indeed, Washburn wanted a "public health consciousness" to emerge in Jamaicans.[145] But he also wanted to see a more vital, healthy population and argued that the "main causes of lowered vitality among Jamaicans" were hookworm disease, malaria, and venereal diseases.[146] As part of this effort, Washburn collaborated with the Jamaican government to create a Bureau of Health Education. Established in 1926, it aimed to "change the habits and customs which interfere[d] with the highest mental and physical development of the people" by devising a public health propaganda campaign that included films, slide shows, and public lectures. It also published *Jamaica Public Health* monthly. At first, 5,000 copies were printed, given for free to "any citizen of the colony who asked for it." By 1927, its circulation had risen to 10,000, and copies were sent to other parts of the world, including Europe, Asia, Latin America, and the Caribbean. Issues addressed a range of health problems including "malaria, smallpox and vaccination, typhoid fever, tuberculosis, house fly, bad cold, family health, vital statistics, and infant mortality." They also included stories or plays "designed to interest children in sanitation and personal hygiene."[147]

An emphasis on child-saving lay at the core of the bureau's work, a key element in creating a "successful nation," as Washburn noted. He saw the two as intimately intertwined, arguing that the "causes of infant mortality" were "interwoven with the life and habits of the people" and that "the health of the children, the future citizens," must be preserved. Washburn and other bureau officials worked closely with the Jamaican Child Welfare Association and praised their work.[148] Washburn used their meetings to talk about the importance of sanitation and public health education for good health, especially in the schools.[149]

The language and institutions of Britain and the empire shaped and supported the work of the Rockefeller Foundation in Jamaica. Officials such as Washburn quoted British political luminaries to buttress their arguments. In arguing for infant welfare work, for example, Washburn quoted Lloyd George as declaring the impossibility of "'maintain[ing] an A1 nation with a 3C population'" and that caring for the "'health of the people is the secret to national efficiency.'"[150] One of the bureau's officials, Mrs. Passingham, used Arthur Newsholme's words to make the case for infant welfare work, stating that "'infant mortality [was] the most sensitive index . . . of social welfare.'"[151] Washburn also associated himself and, by extension, the American Rockefeller Foundation with Britain, characterizing public health initiatives as part of "our English civilization."[152] Citing British political and medical authorities and associating themselves with the British empire may have given these Americans a degree of legitimacy in their work in these British colonies. As Palmer has noted for the anti-hookworm campaign, U.S. Rockefeller officials were confronted with the challenges of dealing with (British) colonial health policies and political and medical officials. They also faced the anti-Americanism of imperial officials and colonial physicians and the reality of "turf politics."[153] Associating themselves with Britain may also have been linguistically convenient for Americans such as Washburn, providing ready-made imperial language for an incipient empire.[154] After all, both nations now carried the "white man's burden," a joint responsibility only made more apparent by an appeal to a shared "Englishness."[155]

The enthusiasm with which Washburn and other Rockefeller officials in Jamaica threw themselves into the ritual of Empire Health Week is a striking example of this imperial indebtedness. Starting in 1912, Empire Health Week was held throughout the British empire to spread information about sanitation, public health, and infant welfare. Guyana seems to have been the site of the first Empire Health Week in the British Caribbean, holding its first one in 1919, followed by Jamaica in 1923.[156] Barbados's first health week was held in 1929, organized by health commissioners in the parish of St. Michael but implemented throughout much of the island. In the words of Governor William Robertson, they wanted to undertake a "general clean-up" of this parish, and the initiative spread from there.[157] "Cleaning-up" was the goal of health week in many places, but it also served an important educative function. As an editorial in the *Gleaner* noted, "setting aside one special week" helped "focus public attention upon the importance of health and to arouse in everybody a sense of personal responsibility for health."[158] Colonial political and social elites spearheaded these Caribbean health weeks, and they enjoyed the support of secular and religious institutions. Using government buildings, schools, and churches, politicians and clergymen gave talks extolling the importance of following the rules of hygiene and health. Ministers in Jamaica and Guyana used their pulpits to address these matters; ministers were encouraged to use health week to show their followers the importance of public health, and organizational meetings were held in churches.[159] Schools also played an important role. Children were encouraged to perform "health plays" addressing particular health problems, and essay competitions were held.[160] In Jamaica, the International Health Board was an enthusiastic supporter. Washburn gave public lectures that were attended by members of the religious and secular hierarchy and covered in the *Gleaner*.[161] In 1927, *Jamaica Public Health* began publishing a special Empire Health Week issue. Ten thousand copies were published, and Washburn saw this as responsible for the success of health week that year.[162] Readers were reminded that "cleanliness of person, home, shop, yard, or premises help[ed]" ensure overall health. But they were told that the consequences were larger than this. Cleanliness was described as a duty to the British empire, and they were enjoined to "remember [their] duty to empire."[163]

Imperial Circuits and the Politics of Reproduction

In 1921, colonial physicians from around the Caribbean and tropical medicine researchers from Britain gathered in Georgetown, Guyana, to discuss the health problems afflicting these territories and the best way to eradicate them. Ensuring that colonial populations continued to grow was an imperial duty, as the American Washburn had reminded Jamaicans. Perceptions of race and class were entangled in these discussions, much as they had been in exchanges earlier in the century. But these Caribbean physicians had their own ideas about race and fit populations, ones that were indebted to current medical and social thinking but that also intersected with Caribbean concerns.

The meeting in 1921 was the third medical conference held in the Caribbean since the turn of the century, following earlier ones in 1903 (on quarantine laws) and in 1913 (on tuberculosis). Imperial officials helped establish the parameters of this meeting. At the request of the secretary of state for the colonies, Alfred Milner, Patrick Manson and G. C. Low drafted questions for the participants to consider. Much to Manson's irritation, imperial officials did not use them. One Colonial Office official criticized his questions as more appropriate for a meeting of "scientific experts" than for colonial medical officers, who were to be the main participants.[164] Their number included the "principal medical officers" for the colonies and researchers from the School of Tropical Medicine in London.[165] Physicians based in Guyana, Barbados, St. Lucia, Jamaica, Grenada, and Trinidad attended, as did the government bacteriologist from Suriname, J. Wolff. Belize did not send a representative, nor did the Leeward Islands, much to the regret of Mason. He believed that representation from the Leewards would have "strengthened" the conference, which would have "benefited by their experiences in tackling the many serious problems under discussion."[166] Milner's questions focused on health, "racial habits," and the size and "vitality" of populations. He instructed the delegates to consider the factors that determined population size and health, especially emigration and what he called "local and racial habits." He wanted to know whether the "best stocks" were leaving the region and whether the "loss of the more vigorous elements in the population" contributed to "certain diseases." He also asked them to consider the necessity for a "medical survey" to see if "local and racial factors," including "racial habits," led to disease, "poor physique and industrial inefficiency."[167]

These questions reflected contemporary ideas about the health and "vitality" of populations. They may have been provided by imperial officials, but they also reflected colonial concerns. Milner's question as to whether the "West Indies [was] being denuded of their best stocks by emigration" had been addressed by Barbadian officials, such as Lofty, worried about the economic and eugenic consequences of emigration. Hutson's comments at the conference echoed some of Lofty's earlier points. He maintained that the "best stock" was leaving the colony, the most "active" and "ambitious" Barbadians or, to use Leiper's phrase, "'stocky families.'"[168] Jamaica's delegate, E. D. Gideon, also believed that emigration weakened populations, but he argued that this was the result of its (indirect) impact on infant mortality. Gideon maintained that men who did not emigrate were of "inferior physical and moral character" and that they inevitably produced illegitimate children who were vulnerable to early death, declaring that "illegitimacy . . . contribute[d] to infant mortality."[169] These comments indicate that for at least some colonial physicians, an acceptance of the purported relationship between illegitimacy and infant mortality continued to shape their interpretations of colonial health, much as it had decades earlier.

As well as pressing the delegates about the impact of emigration on population health, imperial officials also wanted to uncover the impact of "race and racial habits" on disease.[170] For many contemporaries, "race" was at once a "physical entity" and a "cultural artifact," and the "habits" or "customs" of particular population groups were seen as contributing to the presence and spread of disease.[171] Tropical medicine researcher John Anderson, in Guyana as part of a team from the London School of Tropical Medicine studying filariasis, seemed to accept "racial habits" as a concept but considered that Caribbean history rendered it irrelevant as the basis for medical research in this part of the world. He maintained that the Caribbean social environment weakened "racial habits." In these British colonies, he argued, sanitary regulations and public health campaigns prevented people of African and South Asian descent from practicing their "natural racial habits." Anderson saw this process as positive; suggesting that nonwhites could be taught modern European and Euro-American sanitary practices indicated the possibility of sanitary (and cultural) progress and civilization.[172]

Caribbean physicians were more cautious about incorporating a consideration of race into their analysis of disease. Hutson and Paterson, for example, maintained that their colonies were not suitable places to investigate this issue. Hutson based his conclusion on what he saw as Barbados's relative homogeneity; the colony had "few races" and did not experience high rates of tuberculosis, one of the diseases under discussion.[173] For Paterson, in Grenada, social conditions, not race, were to blame for diseases such as tuberculosis.[174] Gideon, on the other hand, accepted the existence of "racial habits" but, like Paterson, interpreted them as at least partially socially determined. He argued that working conditions and social practices were more relevant. He maintained that South Asians' scanty clothing made them susceptible to tuberculosis and that the "habit of overcrowding" among Afro-Jamaicans had similar results. These, he concluded, were really "sanitary matters" and could be uncovered in "ordinary investigations" rather than those focusing on race.[175] Despite these views, the delegates passed a resolution calling for more research on this matter, a decision that may have reflected their belief that particular ethnic groups were inclined to behave in unsanitary ways.[176] But their discussion also suggested a willingness to reject the permanence and inevitability implied by the concept of race itself, something that may have been unacceptable to this multiethnic gathering that included creole physicians of African, European, Chinese, and African origin. The "sanitary habits" to which Gideon pointed could be rectified. The delegates' passage of resolutions emphasizing the need for sanitary and public health measures to address venereal diseases and malaria and the importance of infant and material welfare suggests an acceptance of amelioration.[177]

The results of the conference influenced approaches to these health problems. Imperial officials used the resolutions to monitor colonial progress and pushed individual governors to put them into effect. For example, imperial pressure seems to have convinced the governments of Guyana and Barbados to provide more money for the volunteer-run child-saving organizations.[178] Some of the participants used the discussions in Guyana as the basis for considering changes to the health policies in their own colonies, such as H. E. Sutherland Richards, St. Lucia's chief medical officer. He had attended the meeting with the goal of discovering whether Guyana's approach to infant welfare work could be useful for his colony.[179] Although he was not a delegate, G. B. Mason wondered whether the kind of government subsidies used in Guyana to support district midwives could help in the fight against untrained midwives in Antigua and St. Vincent and whether maternity facilities should be established.[180] Caribbean physicians continued to address these issues at other, subsequent meetings and to call for more improvements to sanitary infrastructure and public health education. In 1926, at a West Indian health conference held in London, Andrew Balfour was pleased to note the considerable progress in the British Caribbean and pointed to the baby-saving leagues that helped reduce infant mortality, the "wasteful" and "wicked" deaths of infants, or "potential labour" as he called them.[181] But he argued that these measures were only useful if they were part of a wider, more comprehensive project of health reform.[182] Three years later, the Caribbean delegates to the 1929 medical conference held in Barbados asked the imperial government to send experts to show their governments the best way to solve the pressing sanitary problems.[183] But Dr. Thomas Stanton, the medical advisor to the Colonial Office, noted with some impatience that experts were not needed. Stanton believed that these problems required, above all, a political solution, as those who knew about these problems did not have the power or the money to fix things.[184]

These exchanges were conducted among colonial and imperial officials, but they were also spread outside these official circles in the pages of local newspapers. Under its editor A. R. F. Webber, the Guyanese *Daily Chronicle* covered the conference, as did the colony's other major newspaper, the *Daily Argosy*.[185] The *Gleaner* published several accounts of the 1921 conference and reprinted a story from the *Chronicle*.[186] Mason played an important role in disseminating the conference proceedings in Caribbean and imperial newspapers. He published an article in the British-based *West Indian Circular* (which was eventually reprinted in the *Gleaner*) and the journal of the Royal Colonial Institute, *United Empire*, and some of his work made its way into Balfour and Scott's book.[187]

The details about death and disease in the British Caribbean as described in the conference proceedings and imperial publications such as that by Balfour and Scott may have surprised many readers who did not live in this part of the world. But for the Caribbean men and women who read local newspapers and who were in attendance, it was not news. They already knew that most of their countrymen and -women lived and worked in poor conditions and that many died young. The men and women who sat in the audience in 1921 included physicians, politicians, merchants, journalists, and philanthropically minded West Indians active in infant welfare work. Often these categories overlapped. Some were British, whereas others were white West Indians, such as Wishart, or members of the colored population, such as the physicians Rose and Craigen. But the audience also included a member of the Glasgow family and supporter of the Baby Saving League, Mrs. T. B. Glasgow, and Afro-Guyanese men from the middle and professional classes, including T. T. Nichols.[188] Their presence indicates the keen interest that members of this class took in this issue and their involvement in its amelioration. Nichols's attendance also suggests the extent to which organizations such as the Negro Progress Convention saw the problem of population and health as aligning with their interests. The conference's location in Guyana meant that most of the audience was Guyanese. If it had been held in Jamaica, it could well have attracted Oswald Anderson, an Afro-Jamaican physician who devoted much of his professional career to critiquing inadequate medical facilities in Jamaica.[189] A similar conference held a few years later probably would have involved the Afro-Barbadian physician Charles Duncan O'Neale, recently returned from Britain to Barbados, where he helped found the colony's first political party, the Democratic League; it expressed some of the social and political concerns of the black Barbadian middle and working classes, including infant and child welfare.[190] As the Conclusion shows, the political and ideological turmoil of the 1930s provided the context for these developments.

Social Welfare Policies and
Population Questions in the 1930s

Someone referred to the [Moyne] Commission as a "Confessional,"
and that it really proved to be. Not only were these evils known to exist
brought to its attention but topics that were considered taboo and non-existent
were not only dragged out into the open (some were thrown straight
in one's face) but were given foundation in facts.

—Eulalie Domingo, "Middle Class Inertia," 1938

IN AN ARTICLE THAT APPEARED in the Jamaican publication *Public
Opinion*, Eulalie Domingo reflected on the ways in which Caribbean men
and women used the Moyne Commission, the eponymous British government inquiry held to investigate the causes of the violent protests
that roiled much of the British Caribbean between 1934 and 1938. As this
Afro-Jamaican woman noted, men and women from throughout the region took advantage of the hearings to describe the many political, economic, and social problems afflicting the colonies in the 1930s and to
recommend solutions. The events of the 1930s are rightly seen as part
of the lead-up to important developments in the post–World War II era,
including the legalization of trade unions, the establishment of more
representative political structures, the emergence of political parties,
and ultimately, independence for most colonies. As well as addressing
labor and political concerns, those who participated in the hearings of the
West India Royal Commission (the Moyne Commission) also discussed
long-standing social issues, many of which, as Domingo noted, had been
considered taboo. As this Conclusion shows, men and women from the
Caribbean and Britain used the West India Royal Commission to express

their views about sex, reproduction, and morality. They repeated points that they and their predecessors had made in earlier decades and which have been addressed throughout this book. These exchanges were conducted in the context of growing imperial and colonial concerns about population surplus rather than the population deficit that underlay the introduction of infant welfare institutions in the early twentieth century. Worries about excessive population growth were not entirely new in this part of the world, as earlier discussions in this book about "overpopulated" Barbados have shown. But what had changed by the 1930s was the scope of these anxieties; by this point, the problem seen as afflicting Barbados appeared to have become a regional malady. The above quotation by Domingo points to another element of continuity, the involvement of men and women from the Caribbean in advancing social welfare issues. They continued to shape imperial views and colonial social policies.

In the 1930s, men and women throughout the Caribbean protested low wages, poor working and living conditions, and social and political inequalities in often violent strikes and protests, some of which threatened the political status quo. Places as disparate as Cuba, Belize, Puerto Rico, Jamaica, and Guadeloupe experienced some degree of unrest in this period, although the intensity varied significantly from place to place. In Cuba, this took the form of a political revolution that overthrew the government.[1] In the disturbances in the British Caribbean between 1934 and 1938, governments did not fall, but the violence was real and protests were extensive. Sugar estates in St. Kitts, Barbados, St. Vincent, Jamaica, and Guyana were the scenes of protests and strikes, as were the oil fields of Trinidad and the wharfs of Kingston, Basseterre, and Bridgetown. Workers protested and struck work, joined by many of their rural and urban countrymen and -women. Repressive action by colonial authorities in many cases contributed to the ensuing violence. In the region as a whole, around 50 people were killed and more than 100 were injured, mostly in Barbados, Jamaica, and Trinidad. More than 1,000 were arrested.[2]

Historians of the English-speaking Caribbean have identified numerous and interrelated economic, political, and social factors as contributing to these protests. The worldwide economic depression of the early 1930s was an important catalyst. The fall in prices for staple agricultural products and the return of many migrants expelled by neighboring governments themselves grappling with the crisis increased already high rates of unemployment.[3] The introduction of political and labor reforms in the late 1920s and early 1930s was also important. As Nigel Bolland has suggested, they just made West Indians hungry for more. The slow expansion of the franchise led them to press for more improvements, as did the growth of a trade union movement that had a regional and imperial reach. Labor leaders in individual British Caribbean colonies and in Britain came into contact through a series of labor conferences held in the late 1920s and early 1930s, and these exchanges energized the movement in the Caribbean.[4] This period was also marked by considerable intellectual and ideological ferment. Marxism, pan-Africanism, and anticolonialism were influential and motivated Afro–West Indians and other members of the African diaspora to organize politically and to search for opportunities to express their ideas about race, history, and modern-day inequalities. For many, Italy's invasion of Ethiopia (Abyssinia) and the perceived reluctance of other European powers to come to the rescue of the African country was especially significant.[5] Biblical references to Ethiopia and its military defeat of European troops during the "scramble for Africa" gave it considerable symbolic weight in the eyes of blacks and led to the emergence of a number of pan-African protest organizations based in Europe.[6] This political, intellectual, and cultural activity occurred in the Caribbean and in North America and Europe, especially London in the case of British West Indians. Something of this energy can be seen in organizations such as the League of Coloured Peoples, founded by the Afro-Jamaican physician Harold Moody, and the International Service Bureau, established by Trinidadians George Padmore and C. L. R. James and the West African Jomo Kenyatta in response to the invasion of Ethiopia.[7] As Thomas Holt has noted, the "synergy" created by the presence of "increasing numbers of West Indian and African political activists, students, and other intellectuals" in North American and European cities "created a new international black literature and sharpened political consciousness and commitment throughout the black world."[8]

Black Caribbean women such as Eulalie Domingo were part of this development. Their political and social views were influenced by the same intellectual and ideological currents that were buffeting Caribbean men. Like Caribbean men, they advanced their concerns in the pages of local publications, such as Jamaica's *Daily Gleaner* and the short-lived *Public Opinion*.[9] Domingo was a musician and a teacher and, as was the case with many Caribbean people in this period, spent time abroad in New York, where she was part of UNIA circles.[10] Along with Amy Bailey, also a teacher (and whom Joan French has described as an "early black Jamaican feminist"), and Mary Morris-Knibb, Domingo founded the Jamaican Women's Liberal Club in 1936.[11] Bailey herself, along with the Afro-Jamaican writer Una Marson, also inaugurated the Jamaican Save the Children's Fund.[12] Like the generation of educated women who founded social welfare organizations in the 1910s and 1920s, they articulated a maternalist perspective that represented women of their class as particularly responsible for improving the lot of poor children and their mothers and, more generally, for improving civic life. Women like Bailey, Morris-Knibb, Marson, and Domingo were educated women from the middle class, teachers for the most part and, in the case of Bailey, the daughter of a teacher.[13] Veronica Gregg has argued that Bailey "encapsulate[d] the paradoxes and inhabit[ed] the contradictions of her historical moment," citing as evidence her comment that the colony's population should be "'forced to be decent even against their will.'"[14] But the aims and actions of the Women's Liberal Club also had a radical element. The organization encouraged women to become politically and socially active, to be informed about local and international events, and to study "Negro History, native and foreign."[15] As Patrick Bryan has argued, it showed the influence of a "black political consciousness."[16] As was the case for middle-class Afro-Caribbean men, the popular disturbances of the 1930s seemed to convince women from this class that the time required political and social action. Many years later, Bailey described herself as "inspired" by the protests to become active.[17]

The extent and scale of the Caribbean disturbances in the 1930s and the fact that strikes and protests also occurred in some of Britain's African colonies during the same period convinced British officials and politicians that a comprehensive official response was needed.[18] Following what Thomas Holt has described as a "century-old tradition" and a favored means of inaugurating new policies, they called for a commission of inquiry.[19] Imperial officials hoped this latest iteration would "restore calm" and show West Indians and Britons that the British government cared about its Caribbean colonies and was a "'benevolent' colonial power."[20] The commission's mandate was broad, encompassing "all aspects of life in the West Indies," including economic conditions, social structure, agriculture, administration, public finances and taxation, housing, labor and trade unions, and "social services," such as education and health.[21] Headed by Walter Guinness (Lord Moyne), a former member of Parliament, government minister, and chair of previous imperial commissions, the commission included British men and women, many of whom had imperial experiences, such as Mary Blacklock, a British physician who had practiced in Sierra Leone and, as a current member of the Colonial Advisory Committee, regularly weighed in on imperial discussions about Caribbean health matters. The inclusion of Rachel Crowdy, who led the League of Nations' Social Questions sections in the 1920s, indicates the growing role of this international body in addressing issues about the health and welfare of children and populations as a whole.[22] Significantly, it did not include a Caribbean representative, something that the secretary of state for the colonies, Malcolm MacDonald, did not seem to have considered.[23]

The commission and its recommendations can be seen as reflecting the views of British officials that the country needed to "reinvigorate" "its mission civilisatrice" and as an effort to postpone the "inevitable, irresistible demands for decolonization" and ensure continued British sway once that day arrived.[24] Between September 1938 and June 1939, these British men and women heard from hundreds of West Indians as well as fellow Britons in written and oral testimonies gathered in London and throughout the Caribbean. They called for expanded political rights and the legalization of trade unions as well as for improvements in the realm of social welfare and health. These included increased facilities for medical training, unification of the region's medical services, and institution of preventative measures, especially those focusing on infants and children.[25] Significantly, they recommended that the British government pay for many of the suggested social reforms. The result was the Colonial Development Welfare Act of 1940.[26] Earlier suggestions that the British government fund health, social welfare, and economic development measures had led to the establishment of the Colonial Development Fund in 1929, but the economic crisis of the 1930s seemed to have limited its effectiveness.[27] The commissioners observed that the fund was inadequate for the purposes they had in mind and that the region's governments did not have the resources.[28] They believed that Britons themselves were increasingly convinced of their government's obligation to colonial populations, but they also argued that the Caribbean deserved special attention when a new colonial development fund was created. Its populations had been removed from their original homelands, scattered over numerous little islands, and stripped of "their original native cultures." Proximity to "white folk" and Americans meant they were well aware of the poor conditions under which they suffered, something which the current economic problems made difficult to solve. In the eyes of the commissioners, the British government had to help.[29]

To imperial officials in the first half of the twentieth century, few subjects so represented the "civilising mission" as health and social welfare. The West India Royal Commission was just the latest official effort to collect information about the size and health of Caribbean populations with an eye to suggesting reforms. The annual reports submitted by the chief medical officers and studied by the members of the Colonial Advisory Medical Committee were the main official source of information, but the committee also sent its own members to the Caribbean. Arthur John Rushton (A. J. R.) O'Brien visited the region in 1930, perhaps in response to the pleas of the delegates at a 1929 health conference in Barbados for an expert to advise their governments.[30] Colonial and imperial officials monitored the incidence of the diseases that had concerned them since early in the century, such as malaria, venereal diseases, and hookworm, and tracked changes in mortality and birth rates. By the early 1930s, vital statistics had improved markedly for a number of colonies, including Guyana, Jamaica, Grenada, Antigua, and Belize.[31] But epidemic diseases like malaria still had effects. A serious outbreak occurred in Guyana and Barbados in the late 1920s, for example; in Guyana's case, this continued to be felt into the next decade.[32] Official reports also pointed to the impact of the economic crisis of the 1930s on the ability of colonial governments throughout the region to pay for health care.[33]

The Britons who sat on the commission drew conclusions that reflected their own views as much as those of the witnesses. Notably, Mary Blacklock's long-standing professional interest in infant and maternal welfare was apparent in her questioning of the medical informants, one of whom was O'Brien, by this point the chief medical advisor for the Colonial Office.[34] O'Brien was an important source for the commissioners; he had been a medical officer with the West African Medical Service before joining the Colonial Office in the late 1920s and had visited the British Caribbean in 1930 to investigate public health conditions and medical administration.[35] O'Brien was just one of many British physicians who testified before the commission. Some were based in Britain and had traveled in the region on fact-finding tours, and others were colonial doctors, often the heads of the colonial medical services or representatives of the local branches of the British Medical Association.[36] The commissioners and the British government welcomed the views of some Caribbean physicians, notably John Hutson, although he was long-retired by this point.[37] Hutson used his memorandum to the commission to repeat some of his long-standing recommendations for public health improvements in Barbados.[38]

The broad subject of infant welfare received considerable attention from other medical witnesses and in the final report issued by the members of the Moyne Commission. They concluded that the residents of the British Caribbean were healthy compared with those in other parts of the tropical empire, but that they were afflicted with "chronic" diseases such as hookworm, venereal disease, and malaria. Rates of infant mortality remained high. In the region as a whole, it was 100 per 1,000, and in some places as high as 200 per 1,000. (By comparison, it was 60 per 1,000 in England.) The commissioners echoed the views of J. L. Gilks and D. G. Anderson, two representatives of the British Medical Association, in their conclusions about infant health; in their testimony, the two men blamed infant mortality on "poor social conditions" and "ignorance of personal hygiene and cleanliness."[39] Inadequate medical services and poor living conditions were seen as contributing to some of these problems, but so was "ignorance," especially among the poor; their "lack of knowledge of the elements of nutrition and hygiene" led them to make bad choices.[40] The commissioners called for the expansion of existing health and medical institutions and greater emphasis on prevention, including more infant and maternal services.[41] O'Brien's emphasis on the positive effects of infant welfare work probably influenced the commissioners' conclusions about the need for more prevention. Like many imperial observers before him, he concluded that although infant mortality rates in the region were falling, they were still generally high, especially in Barbados, Jamaica, Belize, and St. Kitts. He believed that in these cases, more child welfare work would make a difference. O'Brien compared these colonies with Trinidad and Grenada, where infant mortality rates were lower, and "Infant Welfare work [was] well established and . . . run on proper lines."[42] "Proper lines" meant government support for training and deploying midwives and facilities that could oversee new mothers. By the late 1930s, most British Caribbean governments had some of these elements. Governments provided some support for midwifery training, except in Barbados, where it continued to be funded at the parish level, and volunteers operated the baby-saving leagues located in most of the main cities and the estate zones in Guyana and Trinidad.[43]

The commissioners relied on traditional sources of medical information to draw conclusions about infant welfare and other British Caribbean social issues. But they also heard from Afro–West Indians such as Harold Moody.[44] He and others lobbied imperial officials and the British public through their publications, speeches, and letters to the editors of English newspapers. This pressure seemed to have helped convince Lord Moyne to hear his testimony as well as that of George Padmore and Peter Blackman (the three had jointly written a submission for the commission) despite Colonial Office views of Moody as a "busy body."[45] Crowdy's observation that denying them an interview might indicate that the commissioners did not want to "hear the evidence of negroes but only that given by the white" seemed to have had an impact.[46]

The perspectives of these men as representatives of three distinct organizations colored their submission. Moody was the founder and head of the League of Coloured Peoples, a group that lobbied for the rights of black residents of the British empire and addressed the discrimination they suffered in Britain. Padmore was a former member of the Communist Party and was active in the International African Friends of Abyssinia, an organization founded by fellow Trinidadian C. L. R. James, and its successor organization, the International African Service Bureau.[47] The Barbados-born Peter Blackman, whom David Killingray has described as a "pan-Africanist Marxist," was involved with similar causes.[48] Like Padmore, he belonged to the Communist Party for a while and to Moody's League of Coloured Peoples.[49] With some justice, Harold Moody is often represented as less of a radical than men like Padmore and Blackman, but the events of the 1930s brought the three together and saw them articulate a criticism of the region's social, political, and economic ills. They condemned low wages, poor conditions among agricultural workers, substandard housing, and inadequate support of education. They called for the British government to address these problems by improving the education system, legalizing trade unions, improving the provision of health care, and reforming agriculture and land tenure.[50] The trio associated these reforms with economic matters, arguing that improvements to social welfare would lead to economic development.[51]

Moody, Padmore, and Blackman also reminded the commissioners about a recent controversy over race, population, and birth control in the Bahamas. This issue had attracted attention on both sides of the Atlantic and showed the extent to which representations of colonial populations as growing uncontrollably were coming to dominate discussions over the debates about population size by the 1930s. In the mid-1930s, a government committee in Bermuda had recommended that a series of measures be undertaken to deal with the "pressure of population," the result of a lack of jobs at home and restricted opportunities to migrate abroad for work. It recommended the establishment of birth control clinics and compulsory sterilization legislation for sections of the population: "mental defectives," those convicted of rape or other "unnatural offences," women who had given birth to two "illegitimate" children, and men who had fathered one. In their explanatory comments, the committee members cited recent measures allowing for the sterilization of "mental defectives and habitual criminals" in Germany and the United States.[52] The colonial secretary at the time, E. J. Waddington, doubted these provisions would be implemented as legislation, describing them as "startling" but noting that the committee members had no intention of seeing them become law. Instead, they wanted to emphasize the "seriousness of the over population menace."[53] The secretary of state for the colonies, Malcolm MacDonald, was appalled at the suggestion that the parents of illegitimate children be sterilized, calling it a "disgrace to the whole British Empire" if carried out.[54] But in his letter to Nancy Astor, the British member of Parliament who had brought this matter to his attention, he suggested that racial considerations were at the root of the problem. He noted that health officials in Bermuda were worried about "over-population, due to the rapid increase in the coloured population" that could not emigrate.[55] The comments by the new governor shortly afterward about the need for birth control clinics suggested much the same. Reginald Hildyard noted the "necessity of checking the growth of the coloured population of the island."[56] The prospect of questions in the British House of Commons as to whether the government in Bermuda was putting into effect the sterilization proposals from 1935 led to an exchange of telegrams across the ocean and the assurances of the island government that it intended no such thing.[57]

The rapidity with which this matter became a public political issue reflected the lobbying efforts of pan-Africanist organizations on both sides of the Atlantic. The Communist Party publication the *Negro Worker* played an important role. Its mandate to publish articles dealing with working-class issues throughout the African diaspora and its editorial board that included members from the United States, Britain, South Africa, and the Caribbean (including Guyana's Hubert Critchlow) facilitated this dissemination. It published a highly critical article about the matter and highlighted what it saw as the racist nature of the governor's comments. To Charles Alexander, the article's African American author, the governor's justification of the measure on economic grounds, namely that a growing black population was leading to widespread poverty, represented a return to "discredited" Malthusian views of population growth. Rather than calling for higher wages or assistance for the unemployed, Alexander maintained that the governor instead had proposed sterilizing the island's population, essentially to "make barren Negro men and women in order to prevent them from having children."[58] The connections that Padmore and Blackman had with leftist groups in London doubtless helped bring this matter to their attention. In their written submission to the West India Commission, they strongly "condemn[ed]" those who suggested sterilization as a "cure for the illegitimacy problem."[59]

This debate occurred in the context of increasing concerns about excessive population growth, a change from earlier worries about population shortages and race suicide. The problem of overpopulation was on its way to becoming one of the defining problems of the "third world."[60] Colonial officials in Asia and Africa increasingly fretted about the economic consequences of growing populations; overpopulation was seen as an economic burden for countries. Something of the same can be seen in imperial views of the British Caribbean in the 1930s. The members of the Moyne Commission argued that population growth in the early twentieth century, especially since the 1920s, had occurred within the context of expanding colonial economies and high rates of emigration. After the 1930s, restrictions on immigration by many of the traditional receiving countries, such as Cuba, meant that emigration could no longer "relieve the growth of population," a problem that was worsened by the forcible repatriation of many emigrants themselves. At the same time, declining death rates and high birthrates in much of the British Caribbean meant that populations were growing steadily, something the commissioners did not think would end soon. They noted with some concern that at the present rate of population growth, which was between 1 and 2 percent a year, the overall population could well double in a few decades.[61] In fact, some colonies, such as Barbados, seemed to have already reached a danger point. They suffered from "absolute over-population."[62] Even those colonies where the ratio of population to area was less worrying were at risk, as much of their land mass was mountainous and thus not easily cultivable. At the same time, the market for their main agricultural goods was more limited than in the past.[63]

The commissioners reached these conclusions about relentless population growth despite the serious concerns of at least one demographer.

Colonial Office officials asked P. Granville Edge, a demographer based at the London School of Hygiene and Tropical Medicine, to predict population growth for these colonies over the next decade. Edge concluded that populations in the British Caribbean were increasing, but he reminded officials that the unreliable nature of the population data posed serious problems. He had long critiqued the ways in which population statistics were gathered in this part of the world, concerns that he expressed in his submission to the commissioners.[64] He noted that twelve of fifteen colonies had not held censuses since 1921 and that although the methods by which vital statistics were gathered had improved, they were still "defective" in a number of the colonies. As a result, he doubted that he could provide accurate estimates of the colonies' populations a decade or more into the future, stating that "estimates based on such unreliable data, . . . [were] likely to prove grossly misleading."[65] He was adamant that "population figures" would be "largely conjectural" until "regular decennial censuses [became] a recognized unit in the administrative machinery of these territories."[66] O'Brien was more sanguine and observed that the numbers of births and deaths were accurate, a view that probably helped convince the commissioners that the population numbers in their report, although "subject to a large margin of error," could be "accepted as at least broadly true."[67]

As this book has shown, for most of the late nineteenth and early twentieth centuries, official concerns about population in the British Caribbean focused on population shortages. Barbados, though, was always seen as something of an exception. Officials in the colony itself and in London had regularly described it as overcrowded and had worried about some of the social and economic consequences of its population density. During the Moyne Commission hearings in the 1930s, members of the commission repeated some of these views, as did officials based in Barbados itself. But by this point, Barbados did not seem as much of an anomaly as a harbinger of the Malthusian future.

Two Barbadian officials contributed to these views. N. V. Wase-Bailey, the current chief medical officer for Barbados and the former surgeon general for Guyana, carefully detailed the many interrelated consequences of overpopulation as he saw them. These included malnutrition, congestion in schools and homes, and unemployment, each of which led to other serious social and health problems, such as reduced intellectual ability, increased rates of infant mortality, disease (including venereal diseases), promiscuity, and a worsened standard of living. This population surfeit also led to lower "social and moral status" and "lack of parental responsibility."[68] Barbados's governor, John Waddington, formerly the colonial secretary of Bermuda, was also concerned about the population problem in Barbados. And like Wase-Bailey, he too saw it as entangled with a variety of social problems, notably sexual practices. He described what he saw as the propensity of the "lower classes [to] drift naturally into irregular alliances" and quoted poor law officials who noted that poor women gave birth to large numbers of "unwanted," "illegitimate" children for whom they were unable to care.[69] Barbados's "principal problem" of population growth was so pressing that it even made him question the advisability of dealing with syphilis, which he saw as "contaminating" much of the population and as contributing to the high rates of infant mortality.[70] Waddington wondered whether the laws governing reproduction and population growth operated differently for whites and blacks. He argued that "modern statisticians" had only been able to "[disprove] the Malthusian theory of saturation" for "European countries" but not for "coloured races." In a place like Barbados, Waddington saw Malthusian principles as operating.[71] He believed that a solution could be found in combining "contraceptive instruction," venereal disease examination and treatment, and "relief work." He believed that unmarried women with many children would "welcome" some kind of birth control method that "would prevent them from burdening their lives with the responsibility of numerous children."[72] His role in overseeing the establishment of birth control clinics in Bermuda a few years earlier likely influenced his ideas about limiting population growth in Barbados.[73] But he may well have been echoing views expressed in Barbados. As Barbados's chief medical officer, John Haslam, noted in his report a few years before the commission, there were "private" discussions "even among responsible medical men" in Barbados about the advisability of establishing the kind of "maternal and child organisation" that was in place "practically everywhere else." They wondered whether "efforts at saving child life [were] undesirable" because Barbados was overcrowded. For his part, Haslam believed "mortality" was not a "sufficient remedy" for overcrowding.[74]

These interpretations about overpopulation and its relationship to Caribbean family forms seemed to have found a place in the final report by the West India Royal Commission. The commissioners argued that the "prevalence of temporary and often casual unions between the sexes [and] the absence too often of any settled family life" contributed to rising birthrates and to population growth.[75] Echoing views expressed by physicians and officials for well over a hundred years, they argued that these unions, which they described as promiscuous, also contributed to infant mortality. Citing prison and reformatory officials, they argued that children produced by "promiscuous unions" died young or led debilitated and weakened lives.[76] "High rate[s] of illegitimacy combined with large families and the lack of parental responsibility" contributed to "ill-health and death, . . . especially among young children."[77] The commissioners associated the high rate of illegitimacy with the absence of family life in the Caribbean, something that affected "every aspect of social conditions," especially health. They argued that this was probably one of the main causes of infant mortality, a problem that could not be remedied until the "family [was] recognized as the normal unit of human existence and the responsibilities of parentage [were] accepted in the West Indies."[78] The problem was especially serious due to the numbers of illegitimate children involved, more than 60 or 70 percent of all births.[79]

Despite the certainty with which the commissioners and some of their witnesses associated illegitimacy with various social ills, they also acknowledged that the sexual practices that produced illegitimate children had diverse social implications. Not all were socially dangerous. One person who submitted written testimony to the commission was a white Jamaican woman, Edith Clarke, whose ideas about Caribbean family forms seemed to have influenced the commissioners' conclusions in this respect. In her testimony, she observed that "as long as a couple [was] living together, there [was] no essential difference as far as the children [were] concerned." The real problem, according to Clarke, was "temporary concubinage." Under this arrangement, paternal support was less assured and children did not receive the same "assistance or discipline" that they would have experienced if they lived in a family.[80] In her 1957 book *My Mother Who Fathered Me*, part of which was based on her contribution to the Moyne Commission, Clarke defined "promiscuity" as "indiscriminate casual mating" without the intention to establish a permanent relationship and "concubinage" as "the conjugal union in cohabitation of a man and woman without legal and religious sanction."[81] The commissioners likewise distinguished "promiscuity" from "permanent unmarried cohabitation" or "faithful concubinage." Echoing Clarke, they argued that the former was similar to marriage and allowed for stable domestic and family life, whereas the latter constituted a "grave danger to the social stability of the West Indies."[82] In her own discussion of the "illegitimacy problem," Amy Bailey, like Clarke, distinguished promiscuous relationships from more permanent ones. Bailey argued that men and women could live together with "constancy and devotion" without being married.[83] To this Jamaican woman, parental (especially paternal) neglect by parents in temporary relationships put their children at risk. She argued that men were more likely to support their children if they were the product of permanent cohabitation rather than transitory encounters. Children from the latter were the "most dangerous."[84] But Bailey, unlike the commissioners, noted the difficulty of identifying the extent of this problem with any statistical certainty. The censuses did not distinguish the number of illegitimate children born to parents who cohabited from those involved in more temporary relationships.[85] All were deemed illegitimate.

In their attempt to identify the causes of illegitimacy, the commissioners emphasized social factors ranging from poor housing to insufficient recreational facilities and inadequate education in "civil responsibility and sex hygiene."[86] But they also suggested that ideas about race and culture continued to be significant. The commissioners argued that one of the main causes of "this grave social evil" was the lack of a "strong opposing public opinion among a people whose immature minds too often [were] ruled by their adult bodies."[87] This representation resonated with views expressed by nineteenth-century imperial officials and other well-meaning Britons. In the 1930s, the purportedly innate flaws of Caribbean people were still seen as responsible for serious social problems.

Sex posed another kind of problem. It was seen as leading to over-population and its various social and economic ills. The members of the West India Royal Commission noted that the high birthrates that were contributing to overpopulation were "deeply rooted in social customs" and could not be "quickly [or] easily corrected."[88] As had some of their predecessors in the nineteenth century, many of the Barbadian witnesses recommended a scheme be set up to facilitate emigration to St. Lucia or Guyana, but the commissioners did not think that these solutions were likely to be successful.[89] The commissioners saw limiting reproduction as a better idea. Indeed, doing so was "in one sense, the most pressing need of the West Indian Colonies."[90] Without it, the "standard of life" would stagnate or even fall.[91] They called for a propaganda campaign to awaken the region's population to the necessity that the birthrate be limited, but they did so cautiously, observing that birth control clinics could be useful in colonies where public opinion was already receptive to the important issue of limiting births.[92] This caution may have reflected disagreements in the Colonial Office about family planning. Some officials, such as O'Brien, supported it, whereas others were opposed. By the late 1930s, Colonial Office officials were taking a more or less neutral view of birth control initiatives in the colonies, allowing them to function providing that laws were not broken and that private organizations did not receive state support.[93]

Controlling the size of populations and limiting births was a subject of interest to Caribbean men and women as well to these officials. In 1927, attendants at a Women Workers' Conference in Guyana passed a resolution calling for the government medical service to establish birth control clinics in the colony "for the sole purpose of instructing the women of the working classes on the subject of birth control." Among those present were Hubert Critchlow and the male and female representatives of the colony's friendly societies.[94] The subject was debated several years later by members of the British Guiana Branch of the British Medical Association.[95] In Jamaica, support for birth control was expressed by black and white male and female members of the middle and professional classes.[96] In the late 1930s, for example, the *Daily Gleaner* became a major forum for discussions about this subject.[97] Bailey also called for the dissemination of information about birth control, but in a fashion that expressed contemporary class biases as well as a kind of incipient feminism that emphasized the importance of empowering women. Many years after the events of the 1930s, Bailey recounted the story of a woman, a local fish seller, who had given birth to many children. When she asked the woman why, the woman asked what could she do, a response that convinced Bailey that the woman did not "know how to stop them from coming."[98] Bailey concluded that the "State" should give the "poorer classes" access to information about birth control as well as facilities to undertake it. But in a reflection of the influence of current ideas about class and morality on her thinking, Bailey declared that women needed to be shown that they were "committing a social and economic offence against the State when [they] persist[ed] in having children, who, lacking parental control and care, grow up to be a menace."[99] Bailey took advantage of the international birth control work of British women to advance this issue. She encouraged Edith How-Martyn, the British birth control advocate, to visit Jamaica in the late 1930s. Along with Margaret Sanger, the U.S. supporter of birth control, How-Martyn played a leading role in developing the Birth Control International Information Centre and the National Birth Control Association (itself funded by the Eugenics Society through its Birth Control Investigation Committee). The two women were part of an effort to spread information about birth control throughout the empire, not only to Jamaica. As Bailey noted many years later, "We launched a birth control society right there at the Ward Theatre with Mr. [Norman] Manley."[100]

———————————

Amy Bailey's comments remind us that the questions about social welfare policies, population health, and reproduction that this book has explored would continue to be addressed as the colonies of the British Caribbean moved toward independence in the second half of the twentieth century. A new generation of Caribbean political and labor leaders would be involved, as would other educated members of the middle and professional classes such as Bailey. But the discussions and recommendations that emerged from the Moyne Commission hearings in the late 1930s and that West Indians conducted in the pages of local publications and in public meetings also looked to the past. Perceptions of the economic importance of populations and interpretations of the social, cultural, and biological factors responsible for their size and health held echoes of exchanges reaching back to the late nineteenth and early twentieth centuries. Then as in the 1930s, poor health and mortality, especially among the very young, were attributed to unsanitary living and working conditions and to tropical diseases such as malaria and hookworm and to venereal diseases. Despite the emergence of new medical ideas about disease causation, much of the blame was placed on social factors, including the nature of Caribbean family forms and sexual practices.

The infant and maternal welfare initiatives addressed in this book were an attempt to solve contemporary population problems. This book has emphasized the role played by a multiethnic group of Caribbean men and women from the middle and professional classes in developing and implementing public health and social welfare policies in the first few decades of the twentieth century. It also has pointed to the role of Britons and Americans, indicating the extent to which these initiatives were regional as well as imperial and hemispheric in their scope. Influenced by contemporary notions of gender, class, and race and by their perceptions of their home islands, Caribbean men and women constructed laws, policies, and institutions to ensure population growth and protect young lives, drawing on approaches originating in Britain and its empire, in the United States, and in the Caribbean itself. By the 1930s, a discourse of overpopulation had started to replace the worries about falling populations that were expressed in the late nineteenth and early twentieth centuries

Crowd assembled in the grounds of Queen's Park, Bridgetown, Barbados, to listen to
the proceedings of the West India Royal Commission relayed by loudspeaker (BPP,
"WIRC Report," after p. xviii, plate 1, CO 950/907, NA)

and that initially underlay these initiatives. Views about declining populations were commonplace in this period, but in the British Caribbean they
were tied to assessments of emancipation itself. The shape of the health
and social welfare undertakings addressed in this book may have varied
from colony to colony, but a shared history imposed a degree of similarity.
Equally important were the lively exchanges of ideas about policies and
plans that occurred in this period, sometimes circulating through Britain
but often bypassing the imperial center and traveling directly from one
colony to another.

   During the hearings of the West India Royal Commission in early 1939,
loudspeakers and microphones were set up in public spaces in Barbados
and Guyana. The final report of the commission included an image of a
large crowd gathered in Queen's Park, in Bridgetown, Barbados. The photograph conveys an impression of quiet and order, a striking counterpoint

to earlier pictures of the rioting mobs that led to the commission. But it also depicts black, brown, and white men and women listening and talking about what they saw as the problems in their societies and how they could solve them. This was not the first time they had done so, of course, but with the promise of more political rights and independence in the future, their voices would be amplified even more.

Notes

Abbreviations

BGBBMA	British Guiana Branch of the British Medical Association
BPP, "WIRC Report"	United Kingdom, House of Commons, "West India Royal Commission Report, 1944–45," *British Parliamentary Papers* [Cmd. 6607], House of Commons Parliamentary Papers Online, 2006
BSLBG	Baby Saving League of British Guiana
CNA	Colonial Nursing Association
CO	Colonial Office
Correspondence Relating to Cholera	"Copies or Extracts of Despatches and other Documents relating to the Outbreak of the Cholera in the island of Jamaica, and respecting any Applications made to Her Majesty's Government for the adoption of Measures to meet the Difficulties thus brought upon the Colony, 1851," in Milroy, *Report on the Cholera*, New York Academy of Medicine
CPP	College of Physicians of Philadelphia, Historical Library and Wood Institute, Philadelphia, Pa.
DABB	Department of Archives, Bridgetown, Barbados
DG	*Daily Gleaner*
ICS	Institute of Commonwealth Studies, London
IWMLBG	Infant Welfare and Maternity League of British Guiana
JPL	Jamaica Progressive League
LSTM	London School of Hygiene and Tropical Medicine
Milroy, "Report on Cholera"	Gavin Milroy, "Report of Dr. Milroy," encl. 1 in no. 1, in "A Copy of the Report made by Dr. Milroy to the Colonial Office, on the Cholera Epidemic in Jamaica, 1850–51; and Copies of Extracts of Despatches addressed to and received from the Governor of Jamaica in relation to the said Report," in Milroy, *Report on the Cholera*, New York Academy of Medicine
MTC	*Minutes of Georgetown Town Council*, National Archives of Guyana, Georgetown
NA	National Archives, London, United Kingdom
NATT	National Archives of Trinidad and Tobago, Port of Spain
NCCVD	National Council for Combating Venereal Diseases
NDC	*New Daily Chronicle*

RAC Rockefeller Foundation Archives, Tarrytown, N.Y.

Report of the British Minutes of the British Guiana Combined Court, No. 344, *Report of*
Guiana Mortality *the Commission Appointed to Enquire into and Report upon the General and*
Commission *Infantile Mortality* (1906), ICS

VJLH Victoria Jubilee Lying-in Hospital

WIRC West India Royal Commission (CO 950 series of correspondence)

Introduction

1. Details about Catherine Barrow's case can be found in *Twenty-Sixth Half-Yearly Report of the Poor Law Inspector* [1893], 58, DABB. I discuss this case in more detail in Chapter 3. "The discovery of the child" is Manderson's phrase. See Manderson, "Shaping Reproduction," 28.

2. Terms denoting ethnicity and nationality are inevitably reductionist and imprecise and reflected imperial and colonial categories of difference. Despite these caveats, ethnic and national affiliations, whether self-imposed or attributed by others, were significant conceptual categories in the British Caribbean in this period. They provided the basis for political and social organizations and exclusion. Following convention and a desire to avoid using unwieldy hyphenated words, I have opted to use the following terms: "colored" for those of mixed African and European ancestry; "white" to refer to those accepted as phenotypically "white" and of European birth or origin; "black" for those of mostly or entirely unmixed African ancestry. I generally use "Indo-" and "Chinese-" as prefixes to refer to individuals born in the Caribbean, but otherwise I use "South Asian," "East Indian," or "Chinese." I have tried to limit my use of "Portuguese" and "British" to refer to men and women born in Portugal and Great Britain. Where necessary, I use various class and national qualifiers along with these terms.

3. United Kingdom, House of Commons, "Report by the Honourable E. F. L. Wood," 11; Brereton, *History of Modern Trinidad*, 166.

4. Lewis, *Growth of the Modern West Indies*, 99.

5. Bryan, *Jamaican People*, 14, 15; Moore and Johnson, *Neither Led nor Driven*, 4.

6. BPP, "WIRC Report," 378, 379.

7. This discussion focuses on the British Caribbean; for some of the patterns in political arrangements and protest in the wider region, see Knight, "Caribbean in the 1930s." For some of the recent scholarship, see Brereton and Martinez-Vergne, *General History of the Caribbean*, vol. 5, for the nineteenth century, and Laurence, *General History of the Caribbean*, vol. 4, for the twentieth.

8. Craigen, untitled talk, 131, 132.

9. Belize, or British Honduras as it was known during the colonial period, is the other mainland territory of the British Caribbean. Guyana, or British Guiana as it was known before independence in 1966, was three colonies, Demerara, Berbice, and Essequibo, before being united in 1831. I will refer to these places as Belize and Guyana in this book.

10. De Barros, *Order and Place*, 32.

11. Balfour, *Census of Jamaica and Its Dependencies*, 1911, 7.

12. Roberts, *Population of Jamaica*, 330, 331; Leeward Islands, *Census 1891*, table A; Clark, *Census of the Colony of Trinidad*, 1.

13. I use the term "Great Britain" to refer to the geographic/political territory that comprises England, Scotland, and Wales, and "British" to refer to its inhabitants. The only exceptions are for those instances when individuals described themselves in ethnic terms as "English."

14. Lawance, *Census of Barbados*, 28.

15. Balfour, *Census of Jamaica and Its Dependencies, 1911*, 7; De Barros, *Order and Place*, 32. In Guyana, the census reports used "European" rather than "white." See Lawance, *Census of Barbados*, 14.

16. Cassedy, "Hygeia," 221.

17. J. B. Alberdi, *Bases y puntos de partidos para la organización política de la República Argentina* (Buenos Aires: Librería de la Facultad de Juan Roldán, 1915), qtd. in Stepan, "Hour of Eugenics," 43; Meik, "Disease and Hygiene in the Construction of a Nation," 76.

18. Dwork, "Childhood," 1075, 1076; Klaus, "Depopulation and Race Suicide," 200, 201; Davin, "Imperialism and Motherhood"; Mead, "Beneficient Maternalism," 124–26.

19. Francis Galton, *Inquiries into Human Faculty and Its Development* (London: Macmillan, 1883), qtd. in Paul and Moore, "Darwinian Context," 36.

20. Bashford and Levine, "Introduction," 3, 4. Despite the variations in eugenicist thought in different countries, there was some similarity especially in terms of thinking about the significance of environment. On these points, see Stepan, "Hour of Eugenics," 87, 88; Klaus, "Depopulation and Race Suicide," 202, 203; Davin, "Imperialism and Motherhood," 19; and Stern, "Responsible Mothers and Normal Children," 389 n. 18.

21. Roberts, *Infectious Fear*, 50, 51.

22. Marks, "What Is Colonial about Colonial Medicine?," 210. And see Ernst, "Introduction," 4.

23. Hall, *Civilising Subjects*, 338.

24. Holt, *Problem of Freedom*, 309.

25. See Drescher, *Mighty Experiment*, esp. chap. 3, on this point.

26. Arnold's use of this term to characterize the outbreak of cholera in India is useful for the Caribbean context; see *Colonizing the Body*, 159. Arnold and other historians have demonstrated the extent to which the response to epidemic diseases reflected political and social concerns. See Peckman, "Infective Economies," on plague in Hong Kong in this respect. I also found Charles Rosenberg's elegant definition of disease as both a "biological event" and a "generation-specific repertoire of verbal constructs" very helpful in shaping my own thinking about these issues. See Rosenberg, "Introduction," xiii.

27. These concepts are useful for thinking about representations of disease and populations in various contexts. Briggs's work focuses on a late twentieth-century cholera epidemic in Venezuela, but these ideas can be usefully employed in the context of the postemancipation British Caribbean. See Briggs with Mantini-Briggs, *Stories in the Time of Cholera*, 10.

28. Stern, *Eugenic Nation*, 29, 30.

29. Worboys, "Colonial World as Mission and Mandate," 208, but see also 212. And see Farley, *Bilharzia*, 4. Early work by Curtin, Headrick, and Arnold helped establish many of the questions and themes about the intersection of tropical medicine and the goals of empire-building and their impact on the colonized and colonizer. See Arnold, *Warm Climates and Western Medicine* and *Imperial Medicine and Indigenous Societies*; Headrick, *Tools of Empire*; Curtin, *Death by Migration*; and MacLeod and Lewis, *Disease, Medicine, and Empire*. The field has expanded significantly over the past decade or so as historians have explored imperial medical networks and the roles of individual researchers, compared approaches taken by different governments, and identified the intersection between tropical medicine and other imperial methods of surveying, classifying, and monitoring colonial populations. For example, see Johnson, "West African Medical Staff"; Crozier, *Practising Colonial Medicine*; Manderson, *Sickness and the State*; and Anderson, *Colonial Pathologies*.

30. Arnold, "'Ancient Race Outworn,'" 125.

31. See Marks, "What Is Colonial about Colonial Medicine?," 211, on "racial anxieties" and colonial medicine.

32. Anderson, *Colonial Pathologies*, 3, and see Arnold, *Colonizing the Body*, chap. 6. On the "civilizing mission" in the French imperial context, see Conklin, *Mission to Civilize*, esp. 51–54, 56, 59–65.

33. The name was later changed to the International Health Board. On U.S. public health and tropical medicine in areas of U.S. influence and the intersection between, see Anderson, *Colonial Pathologies*, and Stern, *Eugenic Nation*.

34. For a recent summary of some of the literature on the history of medicine in the Caribbean, see De Barros, Palmer, and Wright, introduction to *Health and Medicine in the Circum-Caribbean*, 1–18. Since then, Margaret Jones's book on public health in Jamaica has been published; see Jones, *Public Health in Jamaica*.

35. Palmer, *Launching Global Health*, 58. See Wilkinson, "Burgeoning Visions of Global Public Health," on the relationship between the Rockefeller Foundation and British tropical medicine institutions. Several other works have helped advance our understanding of the impact of the Rockefeller Foundation on Caribbean public health, including Pemberton, "Different Intervention"; Riley, *Poverty and Life Expectancy*; Hoefte, *In Place of Slavery*, esp. chap. 8; and Jacklin, "British Colonial Healthcare."

36. On this point, see Power, "Calcutta School of Tropical Medicine," 197; Arnold, *Colonizing the Body*, 294; and Arnold, "'Ancient Race Outworn,'" 139, 140. Scholarship on black physicians in the United States and creole researchers and physicians in Latin America demonstrates similar patterns and the emergence of creole interpretations of disease and health. See Roberts, *Infectious Fear*, and Peard, *Race, Place, and Medicine*.

37. Birn, "Child Health in Latin America," 682, 683; Birn, "Historiography of Child and Infant Health." See esp. Mead's comparative article "Beneficient Maternalism."

38. Rooke and Schnell, "'Uncramping Child Life,'" 189, 190, 195; Birn, "Child Health in Latin America," 691, 692; Sanders, "Protecting Mothers," 150. On Ceylon, see Jones, "Infant and Maternal Health Services," 267–69. For a useful summary of some of these developments in Europe and North and South America, see esp. Birn, "'No More Surprising Than a Broken Pitcher?,'" 20–24.

39. Pedersen's quotation provides a useful way for thinking about "maternalism"; see "Maternalist Moment," 165. Historians of the United States and Latin America have explored the extent to which these activities can be considered feminist. See Birn, "'No More Surprising Than a Broken Pitcher?,'" 24; Guy, *Women Build the Welfare State*; and Ladd-Taylor, "Toward Defining Maternalism." See van der Klein, Plant, Sanders, and Weintrob, *Maternalism Reconsidered*, esp. Plant and van der Klein's "Introduction," for some of the recent trends in this scholarship. Also see Michel, "Maternalism and Beyond." In the U.S., historians have noted the role that black and white women played in the emergence of the welfare state. See Koven and Michel, "Introduction," 2, 3, 11, and Dayton and Levenstein, "Big Tent of U.S. Women's and Gender History," 811. Thanks to Karen Balcom for telling me about this article.

40. Koven and Michel, "Introduction," 2, 3, 11.

41. On this point for some Latin American countries, see Sanders, "Protecting Mothers," 149, 150, 163.

42. Gilmore, *Gender and Jim Crow*; but see also Gordon, "Black and White Visions of Welfare," and Boris, "Power of Motherhood." Anne Macpherson has demonstrated a similar pattern in Belize; see Macpherson, "Colonial Matriarchs" and *Women Activists*.

43. Manderson, "Shaping Reproduction," 38; Allman, "Making Mothers," 25.

44. Ramusack, "Cultural Missionaries," 319; Allman, "Making Mothers," 25.

45. Rafferty and Solano, "Rise and Demise of the Colonial Nursing Service"; Birkett, "'White Woman's Burden'"; Nestel, "(Ad)ministering Angels"; Jones, "Heroines of Lonely Outposts."

46. The term is from Plant and van der Klein, "Introduction," 8.

47. Levine, "Sexuality, Gender, and Empire," 136. Stoler has made an important contribution to this scholarship, demonstrating the extent to which "matters of the intimate [were] critical sites for the consolidation of colonial power" ("Intimidations of Empire," 3, 4). And see Stoler and Cooper, "Between Metropole and Colony," 11, 26, 27.

48. Scully, "Rape, Race, and Colonial Culture," 338; Scully "Narratives of Infanticide," 89.

49. Briggs, *Reproducing Empire*, 35. Like many scholars, my thinking about empire and venereal diseases has been influenced by Levine's work. See Levine, *Prostitution, Race, and Politics*. See also the following: for the British Caribbean, Challenger, "Benign Place of Healing?," and Green, "'Abandoned Lower Class of Females,'" 173, 174; for Puerto Rico, Findlay's *Imposing Decency*, esp. chap. 4, and Briggs's *Reproducing Empire*, esp. chap. 2; for the Dominican Republic, Lord, "Quarantine in the Fort Ozama Dungeon."

50. Moore and Johnson, *Neither Led nor Driven*, 96–98. See also Jones, "Contesting the Boundaries of Gender," and Altink, "'I Did Not Want to Face the Shame of Exposure.'"

51. Stoler and Cooper, "Between Metropole and Colony," 11.

52. Levine, *Prostitution, Race, and Politics*, 199, 200.

53. Anderson, *Imagined Communities*, 163.

54. For thoughtful discussions about the discourse of colonial overpopulation, see van Beusekom, "From Underpopulation to Overpopulation"; Bashford, "Nation, Empire,

Globe"; Cordell, Ittmann, and Maddox, "Counting Subjects"; Ittmann, "'Where Nature Dominates Man'"; and Ittmann, "Colonial Office and the Population Question." For the Caribbean, see Bourbonnais, "'Dangerously Large,'" and Briggs, *Reproducing Empire*.

Chapter One

1. Buxton, *Slavery and Freedom*, 18.

2. Ibid., 19, 20.

3. On the U.S. views of emancipation in the Caribbean, see Clayton, "Managing the Transition to a Free Labor Society," 90, 91, 95.

4. On the expectations of former slaves after the end of slavery, see Marshall, "'We Be Wise to Many More Tings.'"

5. The demographic performance of slave populations varied across the Americas. Despite a number of important exceptions, overall, British North American slave populations saw the greatest rate of natural increase as opposed to those in most of the Caribbean and Latin America, where deaths outnumbered births. Historians have pointed to a range of factors, including labor regimes, disease, planter policies, and the actions of slaves themselves. See Tadman, "Demographic Cost of Sugar," 1534, 1539, 1540; Kiple, *Caribbean Slave*; Higman, *Slave Populations*, chap. 9; and Bush, "Hard Labor."

6. Drescher, *Mighty Experiment*, chap. 2, 34, 35. Some of the other works that address the factors leading to the end of slavery include Williams, *Capitalism and Slavery*; Drescher, *Econocide* and *Capitalism and Antislavery*; and Davis, *Problem of Slavery*. Ryden's *West Indian Slavery*, esp. chap. 1, has a good, recent summary.

7. See Drescher, *Mighty Experiment*, chap. 3.

8. United Kingdom, *Hansard Parliamentary Debates*, "Slave Trade Abolition Bill," February 5, 1807, 657–60.

9. United Kingdom, *Hansard Parliamentary Debates*, "Slave Trade Abolition Bill," February 23, 1807, 950, 951; Drescher, *Mighty Experiment*, 45.

10. Higman, *Slave Populations*, 6, 7; Titus, *Amelioration and Abolition of Slavery in Trinidad*, 18–21.

11. Higman, *Slave Populations*, 7, 8.

12. Ibid., chap. 2, 321, 322.

13. On the growth of Barbados's population during the period of slavery, see Tadman, "Demographic Cost of Sugar," 1565; Inniss, "From Slavery to Freedom"; and Higman, *Slave Populations*, 72, 75, 77, 307–11. On demographic patterns after the end of the transatlantic slave trade, see Higman, *Slave Populations*, 72–77, 307–14, and Higman, "Slavery and the Development of Demographic Theory," 167, 168.

14. Higman, *Slave Populations*, 304; Drescher, *Mighty Experiment*, 47, 48.

15. Higman, *Slave Populations*, 305.

16. Stephen, *Slavery of the British West Indian Colonies Delineated*, 2:79, qtd. in Higman, *Slave Populations*, 306.

17. For a discussion about the goals of amelioration legislation, see Holt, *Problem of Freedom*, 18, and Ward, *British West Indian Slavery*.

18. Turner, *Slaves and Missionaries*, 104. On the use of the whip as a symbol of planter control, see Higman, *Slave Populations*, 200; Paton, "Decency,

Dependence and the Lash"; Brown, "Spiritual Terror"; and Ryden, *West Indian Slavery*, 135, 136.

19. Ryden, *West Indian Slavery*, 175, 176, 197. On Edward Long, see Lewis, *Main Currents in Caribbean Thought*, 109–13. On the health of slaves and reproduction, see Kiple, *Caribbean Slave*, chap. 8.

20. Higman, *Slave Populations*, 350–52; Bush, "Hard Labor," 87.

21. Holt, *Problem of Freedom*, 43, 45, 53.

22. Ibid., 48, 49; Green, *British Slave Emancipation*, 80, 81, 119–24.

23. United Kingdom, House of Commons, "Report from the Select Committee on Negro Apprenticeship," i, vi, 14, 26, 49, 58, 96; Sturge and Harvey, *West Indies*, 132, 133, 362, 363.

24. Thome and Kimball, *Emancipation in the West Indies*, iii, iv, 438, 439.

25. Inniss, "From Slavery to Freedom," 256–58; Boa, "Experiences of Women Estate Workers"; United Kingdom, House of Commons, "Report from the Select Committee on Negro Apprenticeship," viii.

26. United Kingdom, House of Commons, "Report from the Select Committee on West India Colonies," iii, iv, 115, 116.

27. Sturge and Harvey, *West Indies*, appendix, sec. 4.

28. Ibid., xlviii, 132, 133, 362, 363. Catherine Hall has described the visit of Sturge and Harvey to evaluate the apprenticeship system and the significance of the book in their anti-apprenticeship campaign. See Hall, *Civilising Subjects*, 316–18.

29. Hall, *Civilising Subjects*, 318.

30. Paton has argued that apprentice resistance in Jamaica to the treadmill as a method of punishment played a role. See Paton, *No Bond but the Law*, 83.

31. Marshall, "Termination of the Apprenticeship"; Green, *British Slave Emancipation*, 157–59.

32. On emancipation as a "mighty experiment," see Drescher, *Mighty Experiment*, esp. chaps. 8 and 9, and Holt, *Problem of Freedom*, chap. 1.

33. No. 56, John Russell, February 15, 1840, in United Kingdom, House of Commons, "Papers Relative to the West Indies," 71.

34. Holt, *Problem of Freedom*, 43, 45, 53.

35. Eltis, "Abolitionist Perceptions," 199; Trotman, *Crime in Trinidad*, 41; Adamson, *Sugar without Slaves*, 41.

36. For a summary of the debates addressing the "flight from the estates" and the "land-labor ratio," see Marshall, "Post-Slavery Labour Problem," 118–20; Eltis, "Abolitionist Perceptions," 199; Bolland, "Systems of Domination"; Green, "Perils of Comparative History"; and Bolland, "Reply," 120–25.

37. Marshall, "'We Be Wise to Many More Tings.'"

38. Drescher, *Mighty Experiment*, 56–58; Green, *British Slave Emancipation*, 117, 404.

39. Marshall, "Post-Slavery Labour Problem," 117.

40. Ibid., 117, 118; Holt, *Problem of Freedom*, 199; Green, *British Slave Emancipation*, 266.

41. Froude, *English in the West Indies*, 36.

42. Eltis, "Abolitionist Perceptions," 205.

43. On the "proto-peasantry" during slavery, see Mintz, *Caribbean Transformations*, 151, 152, and Mintz and Hall, "Origins of the Jamaican Internal Marketing System."

44. Holt, *Problem of Freedom*, 144–46; Rodney, *History of the Guyanese Working People*, 60, 61; Brereton, *Race Relations in Colonial Trinidad*, 9. On the emergence of sharecropping, see Marshall, "Metayage in the Sugar Industry"; Marshall, "Emergence and Survival of the Peasantry"; and Bulmer-Thomas, *Economic History of the Caribbean*, 60.

45. Holt, *Problem of Freedom*, 284 and n. 9. Hall's work has provided an important basis for Holt and others on this subject. See Hall, *Free Jamaica*, esp. chaps. 5 and 6, and Bolland, "Systems of Domination," 599.

46. These figures are from Rodney, *History of the Guyanese Working People*, 61. Adamson notes the same number of estate residents in 1850 and somewhat fewer nonresidents, 42,755; see Adamson, *Sugar without Slaves*, 38, 39. And see J. Hadfield, "Population of British Guiana," December 20, 1842, 29, in United Kingdom, House of Commons, "Copies of the Last Census," 331. For a summary of these developments in the wider region, see Marshall, "Emergence and Survival of the Peasantry," 174–78. For many, wage labor complemented small-scale agriculture. On the emergence of a South Asian smallholding group, see Rodney, *History of the Guyanese Working People*, 61–62, 70, and Will, *Constitutional Change*, 97.

47. Bulmer-Thomas, *Economic History of the Caribbean*, 60; Adamson, *Sugar without Slaves*, 57–60; Rodney, *History of the Guyanese Working People*, chap. 3; Marshall, "Emergence and Survival of the Peasantry," 179.

48. Gibbs, "Establishment of the Tenantry System."

49. United Kingdom, House of Commons, "Report from the Select Committee on West India Colonies," 762, iii.

50. Ibid., iv.

51. Holt, *Problem of Freedom*, 50.

52. Ibid., 297, 424.

53. No. 16 (no. 50), Metcalfe to Russell, March 30, 1840, 91, and no. 17 (no. 82), Russell to Metcalfe, April 5, 1840, 93, both in United Kingdom, House of Commons, "Papers Relative to the West Indies."

54. Phillippo, *Jamaica*, 218, 231, 232; see also Sturge and Harvey, *West Indies*, vi, 76, 77. And see Hall, *Civilising Subjects*, 178, 179.

55. No. 16 (no. 50), Metcalfe to Russell, March 30, 1840, in United Kingdom, House of Commons, "Papers Relative to the West Indies," 88.

56. United Kingdom, House of Commons, "Report from the Select Committee on West India Colonies," iii, v.

57. See Drescher, *Mighty Experiment*, 129–34.

58. No. 16 (no. 50), Metcalfe to Russell, March 30, 1840, in United Kingdom, House of Commons, "Papers Relative to the West Indies," 88.

59. United Kingdom, House of Commons, "Report from the Select Committee on West India Colonies," 272, 281, 351, 381, 406.

60. Sturge and Harvey, *West Indies*, appendix A, "Antigua."

61. United Kingdom, House of Commons, "Report from the Select Committee on West India Colonies," 756, 758, 759. The decision of planters to emphasize sugar cultivation at the expense of food production aggravated the effects of the drought that had begun in 1838. See Brown and Inniss, "Family Strategies," 178, 179.

62. United Kingdom, House of Commons, "Report from the Select Committee on West India Colonies," 675, 676.

63. Ibid., 426.

64. Ibid., iii–v.

65. Ibid., 348, 350, 351.

66. Ibid., 391, 406, 409.

67. Christopher, "Quest for a Census," 273.

68. Elgin to Stanley, November 7, 1844, in United Kingdom, House of Commons, "Copies of the Last Census," 331.

69. Chace, "Protest in Post-Emancipation Dominica," 129, 130; Roberts, *Population of Jamaica*, 6.

70. Grey to Stanley, October 4, 1844, in United Kingdom, House of Commons, "Copies of the Last Census," 335. In 1885, Barbados received its own governor; see Richardson, *Economy and Environment in the Caribbean*, 30.

71. FitzRoy to Stanley, June 7, 1844, in ibid., 345.

72. Baynes, "Report of the Census of the Population of Montserrat," September 3, 1844, in ibid., 348, 349.

73. Light to Stanley, February 28, 1843, in ibid., 355.

74. Light to Stanley, November 30, 1844, in ibid., 396.

75. Grey to Stanley, October 4, 1844, in ibid.

76. Light to Stanley, November 30, 1844, in ibid., 395.

77. No. 18, Light to Grey, May 3, 1848, in United Kingdom, House of Commons, "Sugar Growing Colonies," 131; Rodney, *History of the Guyanese Working People*, 33.

78. No. 18, Light to Grey, May 3, 1848, in United Kingdom, House of Common, "Sugar Growing Colonies," 132, 133.

79. Cateau, "Crisis of the Plantation," 89.

80. This conclusion is based on numbers in Green, *British Slave Emancipation*, 246. See also Cateau, "Crisis of the Plantation," 90 nn. 53–55.

81. Drescher, *Mighty Experiment*, 175–77, 179, 180; Holt, *Problem of Freedom*, 119; Marshall, "Metayage in the Sugar Industry," 64.

82. Drescher, *Mighty Experiment*, 181–82.

83. Ibid., 180, 182. Samuel Wilberforce, *Cheap Sugar Means Cheap Slaves: Speech of the Right Reverend the Lord Bishop of Oxford in the House of Lords, February 7th, 1848* (London: James Ridgeway, 1848), 4–10, qtd. in Drescher, *Mighty Experiment*, 180.

84. Hall, *Civilising Subjects*, 176.

85. Holt, *Problem of Freedom*, 307, 308; Drescher, *Mighty Experiment*, 218.

86. Hall, *Civilising Subjects*, 338. Carlyle published this work anonymously in 1848 and reissued it in 1853 under his name and with a new and more aggressive title. See Holt, *Problem of Freedom*, 455 n. 37, and Hall, *Civilising Subjects*, 349.

87. Holt, *Problem of Freedom*, 280–83.

88. Ibid., 284; Hall, *Civilising Subjects*, 350, 351.

89. Holt, *Problem of Freedom*, 284, 285; Henry Taylor, Colonial Office, "State of the West Indies in 1862," July 1862, CO 884/1/1, no. XII, 8, 10, 12, NA; H. T., "State of the West Indies in 1855," March 24, 1856, CO 884/1, no. XI, NA.

90. Carlyle, "Occasional Discourses," 671, 672.

91. Holt, *Problem of Freedom*, 302, 303, chap. 8; Hall, *Civilising Subjects*, chap. 4; Heuman, "Killing Time"; Bolt, *Victorian Attitudes towards Race*, chap. 3.

92. Holt, *Problem of Freedom*, 307, 308.

93. Porter, *Health, Civilization, and the State*, 91. Cholera is still quickly fatal for most of those afflicted if treatment is not administered quickly. See Briggs with Mantini-Briggs, *Stories in the Time of Cholera*, 1, 2, and Kiple, "Cholera and Race," 161.

94. Kiple, "Cholera and Race," 175.

95. Porter, *Health, Civilization, and the State*, 91, 94; Rosenberg, *Cholera Years*; Kiple, "Cholera and Race," 174–75. And see Christina Fryer's recent and interesting article "The Moral Politics of Cholera in Postemancipation Jamaica."

96. The outbreaks lived on in people's memories and were used as lessons in the need for sanitation. As an 1892 editorial in the *Daily Gleaner* noted, many were still alive who had experienced the epidemic but that "personal cleanliness and moral health" would prevent a return. They were also the best ways of "creating and maintaining a vigorous and virile national existence" ("The Black Cloud," DG, August 1, 1892, 4). Jean Besson has noted that memories of the epidemic also lived on in the tales of late twentieth-century Jamaicans who identified plots of land as "cholera-ground" where "slaves" were buried, but that they were probably referring to the epidemic of the 1850s. See Besson, *Martha Brae's Two Histories*, 114, 115, 331 n. 41.

97. Kiple, "Cholera and Race," 157, 162–63, 165, 167.

98. Gavin Milroy to Sidney Herbert, February 13, 1855, CO 28/184, no. 1467, 195, NA. See also Milroy, "Observations on Dr. Gavin's Report," CO 28/184, no. 4283, CO no. 1470, May 1855, 136, NA.

99. There is some debate about the numbers of those killed. Carter considers 20,000 to be the minimum number of deaths in Barbados; see Carter, "1854 Cholera Epidemic," 412, 413, 417. Roberts argues that this figure was probably incorrect and, without "a system of death registration," little "more than a guess"; see Roberts, "Emigration from the Island of Barbados," 273. He takes issue with the Jamaican numbers for the same reasons but acknowledges that cholera was "one of the greatest catastrophes ever experienced in the island"; see Roberts, *Population of Jamaica*, 177, 256. More recent scholars have pointed to similar problems in identifying the number of dead, although Higgins and Kiple have concluded that 40,000 to 50,000 is a reasonable estimate; see Kiple, "Cholera and Race," 166, 167, and Kiple and Higgins, "Cholera in Mid-Nineteenth Century Jamaica," 42, 44. See also Sheridan, *Doctors and Slaves*, 337, 338; Wilkins, "Medical Services in Jamaica," 51–53; Senior, "Asiatic Cholera in Jamaica," 25, 26; and Fryer, "Moral Politics of Cholera," 598, 613 n. 1. However, there is little debate about the devastating nature of the epidemics. Some forty years later, the *Daily Gleaner* estimated the number of dead in Jamaica at 23,000, a third of the overall population, with "misery and loss of life" and an impact on the "industrial welfare of the colony" worse than in other parts of the empire; see "The Black Cloud," DG, August 1, 1892, 4.

100. Grey to the Governors of the West India Islands, January 1, 1851, no. 2, in *Correspondence Relating to Cholera*, 48.

101. C. Macaulay, assistant secretary of the General Board of Health, to Benjamin Hawes, January 1, 1851, encl. 2 in no. 4, in Correspondence Relating to Cholera, 25, 26.

102. Grey, Circular Despatch to the Governors of the West India Islands, January 1, 1851, no. 2, in Correspondence Relating to Cholera, 48.

103. English General Board of Health, "Precautions against the Cholera—Extracted from the Notifications of the General Board of Health in England," in Correspondence Relating to Cholera, 49. For more on the discussion about the contagiousness of cholera and the "futility" of quarantine, see Earl Grey to Governor Sir Charles Grey, November 27, 1850, no. 1, in Correspondence Relating to Cholera, 22, and Earl Grey to Governor Sir C. Grey, February 15, 1851, encl. 7, in Correspondence Relating to Cholera, 26, 27, 30.

104. "Salubrity of Kingston," 312, New York Academy of Medicine.

105. Milroy, "Report on Cholera," 14, 15, 35, 38–41; Gavin Milroy, "Observations on Dr. Gavin's Report," May 1855, CO 28/184, CO no. 1470, Barbados no. 4283, 128, 129, NA; Green, British Slave Emancipation, 313, 314. On this point, see also Pemberton, "Dirt, Disease, and Death," 51.

106. Levy, Emancipation, Sugar, and Federalism, 115, 116; Carter, "1854 Cholera Epidemic," 401. Pemberton has detailed some of the responses by various Caribbean governments; see Pemberton, "Dirt, Disease, and Death," 54. On the impact of poor nutrition in Jamaica, see Senior, "Asiatic Cholera in Jamaica," 27.

107. James Laidlaw to Benjamin Hawes, January 31, 1851, CO 318/194, no. 1720, NA.

108. "An Act to Establish a Central Board of Health and for the other Purposes," in Correspondence Relating to Cholera, 130; CO 111/301, no. 35, NA; CO 111/304, no. 1186, NA; Senior, "Asiatic Cholera in Jamaica," 36; Beckles, History of Barbados, 106, 107. On some of the public health measures introduced in Barbados, including piped water for Bridgetown, see Carter, "1854 Cholera Epidemic," 414, 415.

109. See De Barros, Order and Place; Richardson, Panama Money, esp. chap. 2; Moore and Johnson, "Squalid Kingston"; and Beckles, History of Barbados, 106, 107.

110. The widely cited figure of 200 physicians in 1833 is probably based on a calculation derived by a survey undertaken by the College of Physicians and Surgeons of Jamaica in 1833. See "College of Physicians and Surgeons of Jamaica," 377, 378, New York Academy of Medicine. However, the 1861 census notes a total of 67 "medical doctors and surgeons," "medical men," and "physicians and surgeons." See Higman, Jamaican Censuses of 1844 and 1861, 57. See also Bryan, Jamaican People, 166; Sheridan, Doctors and Slaves, 338, 339; Green, British Slave Emancipation, 310, 311; and Wilkins, "Medical Profession in Jamaica," 30.

111. See Milroy, "Report on Cholera," 15–19, 21, 23, 35, 76, 92, 93.

112. Gavin Milroy, "Report on the Measures of Prevention Necessary for Securing the Colony against the Ravages of Cholera," August 25, 1851, appendix C, CO 111/283, CO no. 8072/61, BG no. 122, 3, NA.

113. Hector Gavin, "Appendix C to Dr. Gavin's Report," rpt. in [British Guiana] Royal Gazette, Thursday, August 14, 1851, encl. in Gavin to Benjamin Hawes, undersecretary of state for the colonies, August 27, 1851, CO 318/194, no. 8134, NA.

114. These numbers refer to physicians, surgeons, and apothecaries. Barbados had 60 "'apothecaries' or 'apothecarized doctors'" in 1820, but the number of physicians

and surgeons is unknown. The number of medical practitioners in Barbados at the time of the epidemic is uncertain, but numbers available for the 1860s suggest that there were at least seventeen. The 1865 almanac notes twenty-three medical practitioners in total, six of whom had arrived after 1854. Higman's figures on the number of medical practitioners in the British Caribbean during the late slave period seem to be the most complete of all the secondary sources on the subject; see Higman, *Slave Populations*, 261, 262. And on Barbados, see *Barbados Almanac and Directory for the Year 1882*, 35, and *Barbados Almanac for the Year 1865*, 39.

115. Earl Grey to Governor Sir C. Grey, February 15, 1851, encl. 7, in Correspondence Relating to Cholera, 26, 27, 30.

116. On Grey's views about the necessity for taxes as inducement to labor, see Holt, *Problem of Freedom*, 47–49.

117. Earl Grey to Governor Sir C. Grey, February 15, 1851, encl. 7, in Correspondence Relating to Cholera, 26, 27, 30.

118. Ibid., 31.

119. Gavin Milroy, "Observations on Dr. Gavin's Report," May 1855, CO 28/184, CO no. 1470, Barbados no. 4283, 129–31, NA.

120. Milroy, "Report on Cholera," 93.

121. Ibid., 19.

122. Ibid., 93.

123. Ibid., 94. And see "Petition of the Kingston Board of Health, to the House of Assembly," December 13, 1850, in Correspondence Relating to Cholera, 18, 19.

124. Gavin Milroy, "Observations on Dr. Gavin's Report," May 1855, CO 28/184, CO no. 1470, Barbados no. 4283, 135, NA.

125. Watson, "Cholera in Jamaica," 567; Milroy, "Report on Cholera," 14. Milroy recognized that the behavior of former slaves may have been caused by fear and acknowledged that some acted in a "praiseworthy" fashion; see Milroy, "Report on Cholera," 94.

126. In making this point, Roberts was discussing late nineteenth- and early twentieth-century representations of African Americans' purported susceptibility to tuberculosis, but his general argument is applicable to views held of former slaves in the British Caribbean during the cholera epidemics. Roberts notes that one U.S. medical doctor who helped develop these ideas, Frederick Hoffman, used the example of "disappearing" populations in the Philippines and Hawaii as evidence. As Roberts observed, "African Americans were in the good company of an entire roster of peoples whose demise at the hands of their own biological inferiority was imminent and preordained" (Roberts, *Infectious Fear*, 49, 50; also see 243 n. 33). Brantlinger has explored "extinctionist" discourse in areas of European imperial control in the nineteenth and early twentieth centuries and noted that many scholars believed that "primitive race and cultures" were "doomed," not only "by the inexorable laws of nature but also as meriting their pending extinctions" (Brantlinger, *Dark Vanishings*, 164, 165). And see Levine, "Anthropology, Colonialism, and Eugenics."

127. Pim, *Negro and Jamaica*, 22. On Pim's paper, see Rainger, "Race, Politics, and Science," 51. On McHenry, see Bonner, "Slavery, Confederate Diplomacy, and the Racialist Mission of Henry Hotze," 301.

128. On the use of taxation policy in the postslavery period, see Bolland, "Systems of Domination," 594, and Marshall, "Emergence and Survival of the Peasantry," 186, 187.

129. Wilkins, "Medical Services in Jamaica," 29–31.

130. Ibid., 34, 35. One shilling seemed to have been the standard amount charged, a sum that the Jamaican planter Alexander Geddes described as "moderate." See United Kingdom, House of Commons, "Report from the Select Committee on West India Colonies," 348, 350, 351.

131. Barkly to Grey, August 25, 1851, CO 111/283, CO no. 8072/61, BG no. 122, NA. See also Gavin Milroy, "Report on the Measures of Prevention Necessary for Securing the Colony against the Ravages of Cholera," August 25, 1851, appendix C, CO 111/283, CO no. 8072/61, BG no. 122, 2, NA. It is not clear whether similar arrangements were in effect in Barbados during this period.

132. Milroy, "Report on Cholera," 114, 115. See also Senior, "Asiatic Cholera in Jamaica," 37.

133. Wodehouse to Bart, July 21, 1854, CO 111/301, CO no. 7216, BG no. 40, NA. See also Barkly to Grey, August 25, 1851, CO 111/283, CO no. 8072/61, BG no. 122, NA.

134. Gavin Milroy, "Report on the Measures of Prevention Necessary for Securing the Colony against the Ravages of Cholera," August 25, 1851, appendix C, CO 111/283, CO no. 8072/61, BG no. 122, 2, NA.

135. Milroy, "Report on Cholera," 90, 112–14; Gavin Milroy, "Report on the Measures of Prevention Necessary for Securing the Colony against the Ravages of Cholera," August 25, 1851, appendix C, CO 111/283, CO no. 8072/61, BG no. 122, 3, NA.

136. Milroy, "Report on Cholera," 113, 114.

137. Ibid., 112–14; Gavin Milroy, "Report on the Measures of Prevention Necessary for Securing the Colony against the Ravages of Cholera," August 25, 1851, appendix C, CO 111/288, CO no. 8072/51, BG no. 122, 3, NA.

138. Wodehouse to Bart, July 21, 1854, CO 111/301, CO no. 7216, BG no. 40, NA.

139. Bell, Obeah, 6.

140. Milroy, "Report on Cholera," 93.

141. Ibid., 93, 112.

142. Ibid., 89.

143. Banton, Administering the Empire, 122.

144. Christopher, "Quest for a Census," 269; Bashford and Levine, "Introduction," 11.

145. Jamaica Archives and Record Department.

146. Christopher, "Quest for a Census," 275, 278.

147. Ibid., 278.

148. Sewell, Ordeal of Free Labor, 60, 245.

149. Drescher, Mighty Experiment, 215. Clayton wrongly identifies Sewell as an "American." He was born in what would become Canada; see Clayton, "Managing the Transition to a Free Labor Society," 92–94. Sewell's articles were subsequently collected in a book that was published in 1861 as The Ordeal of Free Labor in the West Indies.

150. Governor to the Duke of Buckingham, March 23, 1868, in CO 137/432, CO no. 62, Jamaica no. 3840, 312, 316, 317, NA.

151. Jamaica, "Registrar General's Returns, 1880–1," CO 140/185, 1, NA.

152. Rawson, Report upon the Population of Barbados, 8.

153. Sewell, *Ordeal of Free Labor*, 154, 155, 161–64, 245.

154. Ibid., 245, 246.

155. Ibid., 154, 155.

156. One of the governor's informants, the planter and local magistrate, or custos, for St. Thomas parish, Peter Espeut, noted in his response that the secretary of state had asked whether Jamaica's population was shrinking just as Antigua's was and as Sewell had maintained. See Espeut to Irving, August 20, 1867, in CO 137/432, CO no. 62, Jamaica no. 3840, 320, NA. Holt has identified Espeut as a "brown St. Thomas planter and assemblyman." I have used Holt's account for identifying information about the other respondents. See Holt, *Problem of Freedom*, 460 n. 88, 337, 99.

157. In CO 137/432, CO no. 62, Jamaica no. 3840, NA, see the following: Espeut to Irving, August 20, 1867, 320; Whitelocke to Irving, July 11, 1867, 328, 329; Westmoreland to Irving, July 12, 1867, 321–24; and Hosack to Irving, August 10, 1867, 324. See also Holt, *Problem of Freedom*, 460 n. 88.

158. Governor to Secretary of State, March 23, 1868, in CO 137/432, CO no. 62, Jamaica no. 3840, 316, 317, NA.

159. Governor to the Duke of Buckingham, March 23, 1868, in CO 137/432, CO no. 62, Jamaica no. 3840, 312–15, NA.

160. Roberts, "Some Observations on the Population of British Guiana," 192; Roberts, "Note on Mortality in Jamaica," 64; Roberts, *Population of Jamaica*, 15–17.

161. *Report of Commission on Poor Relief, Bridgetown, 1875–77*, 15, DABB.

162. W. L. Haynes, registrar, to the Colonial Secretary, January 24, 1905, CO 28/264, Barbados no. 28510, 94, 95, NA.

163. HRC to Mr. Lucas, 17/11, CO 28/264, CO no. 169, Barbados no. 39746, NA.

164. *Proceedings of the First West Indian Intercolonial Tuberculosis Conference*, 66, 67, LSTM.

Chapter Two

1. Packard, *Making of a Tropical Disease*, 115.

2. Ibid., 115, 116.

3. Wilkinson and Hardy, *Prevention and Cure*, 51.

4. Farley, *Bilharzia*, 1, 3.

5. Worboys, "Colonial World as Mission and Mandate," 211.

6. Power, "Calcutta School of Tropical Medicine," 180.

7. Dumett, "Campaign against Malaria," 163.

8. Haynes, *Imperial Medicine*, 2; Johnson, "West African Medical Staff," 422, 423.

9. MacLeod, "Introduction," 8.

10. Jones, *Outcast London*, 128, 286–88; Himmelfarb, *Poverty and Compassion*, bks. 1 and 2.

11. Jones, *Outcast London*, 286, 287.

12. Dwork, "Milk Option," 53; Porter, "'Enemies of the Race,'" 160, 161.

13. "Interdepartmental Committee on Physical Deterioration," 296, 297. On the report, see Soloway, *Demography and Degeneration*, 42–46; Dwork, "Milk Option," 54, 54 n. 9; Fulton, "Infantile Mortality," 1514, 1515; and Brunton, "Report of the Inter-Departmental Committee," 275, 278, 279.

14. Green, "Emancipation to Indenture," 117; Beckles, *History of Barbados*, 128.

15. The 1883 prices were not seen again until World War I, but the 1902 decision of European governments to remove the bounties on their beet sugar and increasing U.S. and Canadian purchases of British Caribbean sugar in the late nineteenth and early twentieth centuries had an impact on sugar prices. See Richardson, "Depression Riots," 172. The information in this paragraph is drawn from the following: Rodney, *History of the Guyanese Working People*, 19–22, 28, 29; Beckles, *History of Barbados*, 131 132, 141; Drescher, *Mighty Experiment*, 179, 180; Levy, *Emancipation, Sugar, and Federalism*, 108, 109; Richardson, *Economy and Environment in the Caribbean*, 2; Bulmer-Thomas, *Economic History of the Caribbean*, chaps. 5 and 9; and San Miguel, "Economic Activities Other Than Sugar," 121, 127. Levy and Bulmer-Thomas have drawn on figures from Noel Deerr's work; see Deerr, *History of Sugar*.

16. San Miguel, "Economic Activities other than Sugar," 121–23, 126, 127.

17. Ibid., 124; Holt, *Problem of Freedom*, 124, 347–65.

18. Richardson, "Depression Riots," 172, 173; Rodney, *History of the Guyanese Working People*, 23–25.

19. No. 16 (no. 50), Metcalfe to Russell, March 30, 1840, in United Kingdom, House of Commons, "Papers Relative to the West Indies," 90, 91.

20. Northrup, *Indentured Labor*, 156, 157, 159. Smaller numbers were also imported into other British Caribbean colonies. See Look Lai, *Indentured Labor*, 276. Look Lai and Northrup cite Roberts and Bryne, "Summary Statistics on Indenture," 127, for some of their numbers. See also Laurence, "Importation of Labour," 195. On postslavery African migration to the Caribbean, see Schuler, *Alas, Alas, Kongo*; Adderley, "New Negroes from Africa," chaps. 1 and 2; and Northrup, *Indentured Labor*, 23, 24.

21. Northrup, *Indentured Labor*, 159.

22. Look Lai, *Indentured Labor*, 107, 108, 118, 185, 175, 185–87, 276. In Jamaica, the dramatic spike in the death rate following the devastating earthquake in 1907 may have convinced planters to make the case for more imports from South Asia. Look Lai's figures for Indian migration to Jamaica show a notable increase after 1906. On the earthquake, see *Annual Report on the Public Health and Sanitation of the City of Kingston, Jamaica, for the Year Ending 31st December 1908*, 11, LSTM. On the role of indentured Indians on Jamaica's sugar estates, see also Holt, *Problem of Freedom*, 366.

23. Look Lai, *Indentured Labor*, 136.

24. Brown, "Experiments in Indenture," 34; Beckles, *History of Barbados*, 128, 129.

25. This estimate of net emigration from Barbados is from Roberts. The governor of the Windward Islands and Barbados, Rawson W. Rawson, estimated a higher figure, 31,787, for the years between 1861 and 1871 and noted that this number was around 11,000 fewer than had been killed by cholera in 1854. See Roberts, "Emigration from the Island of Barbados," 272, 274, 275, and Rawson, *Report upon the Population of Barbados*, 7. On Barbadian emigration to Guyana, see Brown, "Experiments in Indenture," 48, and Rodney, "Barbadian Immigration," 4. Thanks to Laurence Brown for providing me a copy of this article.

26. Richardson, "Freedom and Migration"; Brown, "Experiments in Indenture," 34.

27. Between 1904 and 1913, approximately 19,900 contract workers left Barbados for the Canal Zone. See Richardson, "Caribbean Migrants," 206, and Richardson, *Panama Money*, 123–25.

28. Approximately 146,000 Jamaicans emigrated between 1881 and 1921. See Roberts, *Population of Jamaica*, 139, 140. On Caribbean migration to Central America, see Harpelle, *West Indians of Costa Rica*, pt. 1; Chomsky, "Afro-Jamaican Traditions," 837; Putnam, *Company They Kept*; and Opie, *Black Labor Migration*.

29. Roberts, *Population of Jamaica*, 47, 48.

30. British Guiana, "Report of the Surgeon General for the Year 1892–93," CO 114/57, 9–11, NA.

31. *Barbados Mercury*, March 30, 1833, qtd. in Higman, "Slavery and the Development of Demographic Theory," 190.

32. Fletcher, "Evolution of Poor Relief," 173; Millington, "Maternal Health Care," 5. See also *Report of the Poor Law Inspector for the Half-Year Ending June 30th, 1902*, 2117, and *Half-Yearly Report of the Poor Law Inspector, January–June 1903*, 1849, DABB.

33. Lawance, *Census of Barbados*, 11.

34. Brown, "Experiments in Indenture," 32, 34–36; Roberts, "Emigration from the Island of Barbados," 252–55; Fletcher, "Evolution of Poor Relief," 177.

35. Rawson, *Report upon the Population of Barbados*, 3, 4.

36. Roberts, "Emigration from the Island of Barbados," 262; Lambert and Howell, "John Pope Hennessy"; Craton, "Continuity Not Change"; Belle, "Abortive Revolution of 1876."

37. *Report of Commission on Poor Relief, Bridgetown, 1875–1877*, 4, 6, DABB; Roberts, "Emigration from the Island of Barbados," 263.

38. Lawance, *Census of Barbados*, 11.

39. Ralph Williams, "Barbados. Report for 1899," May 7, 1900, CO 28/252, CO no. 16457, Barbados no. 100, 33, NA.

40. Ibid.; Lawance, *Census of Barbados*, 11.

41. Roberts, "Emigration from the Island of Barbados," 250, 251; Rawson, *Report upon the Population of Barbados*, 8; Watson, "'Walk and Nyam Buckras.'" In the late nineteenth century, though, some poor whites managed to improve their economic and class standing. See Beckles, *History of Barbados*, 133, 134.

42. Roberts, "Emigration from the Island of Barbados," 250, 251; Watson, "'Walk and Nyam Buckras.'" On poor whites in colonial contexts, see Stoler, "Rethinking Colonial Categories," 150, 152.

43. Rawson, *Report upon the Population of Barbados*, 8.

44. Ibid.

45. Lawance, *Census of Barbados*, 13–15; Lofty, *Report on the Census of Barbados*, 7, 21.

46. Lawance, *Census of Barbados*, 13–15. Perceptions that whites were unable to cope with the rigors of tropical life were not limited to the Caribbean, of course. Anderson, for example, has discussed similar views directed at white U.S. men in the Philippines who were believed to suffer from "'tropical neurasthenia.'" See Anderson, "Trespass Speaks," 1344, 1345.

47. Jamaica, "Report of the Registrar General, 1880–1," CO 140/185, 4, NA.

48. *Third Annual Report of the Central Poor Law Board* (1883), 19, DABB.

49. On Grieve, see "Obituary Notice, Robert Grieve"; "Obituary, Robert Grieve, MD, CMG," 1749; Nehaul, "History of the British Guiana Branch," 31, 36, 37; Wise, "Presidential Address," 117; and Gramaglia, "Introduction," xiii–xxviii. The *British*

Guiana Medical Annual evolved out of the *British Guiana Medical Annual and Hospital Report*, the first of which appeared in 1889. K. S. Wise claimed that it was the first such publication regularly written, published, and produced in the tropics; see Wise, "Presidential Address," 117. Other local branches also published journals. See *Leeward Islands Medical Journal, being the proceedings of the British Medical Association and the Jamaica Physical Journal* (Kingston), 1834–36.

50. Grieve, "Infant Mortality," 242, 243, rpt. from the *Asylum Journal for 1882*.

51. Ibid.

52. Grieve, "Infant Hygiene," 253, rpt. from the *Asylum Journal for 1882*.

53. Grieve, "Prolongation of Human Life," 361, rpt. from the *Asylum Journal for 1883*.

54. Sheridan, *Doctors and Slaves*.

55. Walford, *Walford's County Families*, 540. Godfrey was the acting surgeon general in 1898–99 and 1901–2 and was appointed to the position permanently in 1903 with the approaching retirement of the current surgeon general, David Palmer Ross. See Crichton-Browne, "Obituary, Sir David Palmer Ross," and Swettenham to Lyttleton, March 9, 1904, CO 111/540, CO no. 10568, BG no. 63, NA.

56. A photograph of Wishart included with *Stabroek News*'s obituary of his daughter suggests he was of European origin. See "Obituary, Winfred [Wishart] Hunter." And thanks to M'lilwana Osanku for his information about the photograph.

57. Godfrey, "Presidential Address," viii; "British Guiana Medical Annual and Hospital Reports."

58. Wishart, untitled talk, xxiii.

59. Godfrey, "Presidential Address," v.

60. Dwork, "Milk Option"; Ferguson et al., "Glasgow Corporation Milk Depot"; Atkins, "White Poison?"; Lewis, "Milk, Mothers, and Infant Welfare"; De Barros, "'To Milk or Not to Milk.'" And see British Guiana, "Report of the Surgeon General for the Year 1903–4," CO 114/103, 465, NA.

61. Dwork, "Milk Option," 57–59; Grieve, "Infant Hygiene," 254, 255; Wishart, "The High Mortality Rate of Georgetown," xxiii; *Annual Report on the Health and Sanitation of the City [Kingston], for the Year Ending 30th December 1905*, 7, LSTM.

62. British Guiana, "Report of the Surgeon General for the Year 1898–99," CO 114/82, 11, NA.

63. Godfrey, "Presidential Address," vi, v. On South Asians in the Guyanese milk industry, see De Barros, *Order and Place*, and De Barros, "'To Milk or Not to Milk.'"

64. United Kingdom, House of Commons, "Report of the West India Royal Commission" [C8655], 28, 37, 38, 229. On Hogg, see Rodney, *History of the Guyanese Working People*, 26, 124, and Woods and Stern, "Hogg, Quintin." The surgeon general for St. Lucia, C. Denneby, was unusual in concluding that parents generally took "fair care of the children" (United Kingdom, House of Commons, "Report of the West India Royal Commission" [1898], 65).

65. United Kingdom, House of Commons, "Report of the West India Royal Commission, Appendix C, Vol. II," 268. For more examples of these comments, see United Kingdom, House of Commons, "Report of the West India Royal Commission, Appendix C, Vol. III, Containing Parts VI to XIII," 219, 220. Whereas some colonial officials such as Charles Mosse argued that laziness was behind the inability of

Caribbean people to find adequate food, the West Indians themselves who testified pointed to the impact of the economic crisis. See United Kingdom, House of Commons, "Report of the West India Royal Commission, Appendix C, Vol. III, Containing Parts VI to XIII," 206, 274, 275. United Kingdom, House of Commons, "Report of the West India Royal Commission, Appendix C, Vol. II," 262.

66. United Kingdom, House of Commons, "Report of the West India Royal Commission" [C8655], 229, 38.

67. Pearson, "Negro in the West Indies," 243–45.

68. Ibid., 246, 250.

69. Pearson, "Life History of an East Indian."

70. British Guiana, "Report of the Surgeon General for the Year 1898–99," CO 114/82, 57, 58, NA.

71. Wise and Minett, "Review of the Milk Question," 79.

72. Godfrey, "Presidential Address," vi, v.

73. Swettenham arrived in 1901 after stints in Ceylon, Cyprus, and Singapore. See Rashidi Pakri, "An Imperial or a Personal Legacy?," 7.

74. Swettenham to Chamberlain, January 5, 1903, CO 111/536, no. 3798, BG no. 4, NA.

75. A.A.P. to Lucas, 8/2, CO 111/536, no. 3798, BG no. 4, NA; see also Will, Constitutional Change, 78, 241, 243.

76. Pearson to Lucas, 8/2, CO 111/536, no. 3798, BG no. 4, NA.

77. Ibid.

78. Will's discussion of the Colonial Office discussions in this period about trusteeship has helped shape some of my thinking about this. See Will, Constitutional Change, 242, 243.

79. Guyanese officials collected these statistics from the early 1880s, and Jamaica's registrar general did so from the 1870s. Official sources in Barbados noted them intermittently in the late nineteenth century but did not seem to have tabulated them regularly until after the Swettenham dispatch. This was also the case for Trinidad.

80. On late nineteenth- and early twentieth-century imperial concerns about population decline in Britain's Pacific colonies, see Jolly, "Other Mothers," 182, 183.

81. Christopher, "Quest for a Census," 268–85.

82. See British Guiana, "Report of the Surgeon General for the Year 1903–4," CO 114/103, 465, NA, and British Guiana, "Report of the Surgeon General for the Year 1904–5," CO 114/107, 12, NA.

83. Hodgson to Lyttleton, February 14, 1905, CO 111/541, no. 34724, BG no. 358, NA; Hodgson to Lyttelton, July 29, 1905, CO 111/546, no. 30483, BG no. 219, NA.

84. CPL to Mr. Lucas, July 7, 1906, CO 111/551, no. 29159, NA.

85. Report of the British Guiana Mortality Commission, 8; De Barros, Order and Place, 88.

86. The occurrence of a massive riot in Georgetown while the commission was sitting that resulted in a number of deaths, significant property damage, and the arrival of imperial troops was a further example of the effects of poverty. See De Barros, Order and Place, chaps. 3 and 7.

87. Report of the British Guiana Mortality Commission, 14, 15.

88. Wallbridge, "Some Remarks on the Mortality Commission Report," 47, 48.

89. *Report of the British Guiana Mortality Commission*, 8, 13.

90. "Mortality Commission," *Daily Chronicle*, October 19, 1905, 4.

91. On concerns in France and its empire about the perceived social and health costs of illegitimacy and the introduction of "paternity suits" as a solution, see Pedersen, "'Special Customs,'" 46, 47. On a similar discourse in the Dutch imperial context, see Pattynama, "Secrets and Danger," 99. And see Stoler, "Making Empire Respectable," 365.

92. Levine, "Sexuality, Gender, and Empire," 135, 136.

93. Clark, *Struggle for the Breeches*, 42–44.

94. Turner, *Slaves and Missionaries*, 73, 75; Green, "'Civil Inconvenience'?"; Ryden, *West Indian Slavery*, 198–201.

95. Higman, *Slave Populations*, 351, 352; Higman, *Slave Population and Economy*, 156, 168, 173–75; Bush, "Hard Labor," 87. And see Hinton, *Memoir of William Knibb*, 45, 48.

96. Green, "'Civil Inconvenience'?," 3, 39, 40.

97. Turner, *Slaves and Missionaries*, 73, 75. See also Green, "'Civil Inconvenience'?," 1, 2.

98. Higman, *Slave Population and Economy*, 156, 168, 173–75; Higman, "Slave Family," 284.

99. Altink, "'To Wed or Not to Wed?,'" 1, 2, 5.

100. Premium, *Eight Years in British Guiana*, 137.

101. Barrow, "'Living in Sin,'" 51; Moore, *Cultural Power*, 102–4, 173–74; Chamberlain, "Small Worlds," 189–92.

102. A. Musgrave, "Report of the Jamaica Blue Book, 1882," CO 140/186, xxiv, NA.

103. Smith, "Caribbean Family," 506, 507, 509, 512; Higman, "Slave Family," 261; Smith, "Culture and Social Structure in the Caribbean."

104. Barrow, "'Living in Sin,'" 56, 57, 58.

105. Trotman, *Crime in Trinidad*, 239; Laurence, *Question of Labour*, 243–50.

106. In 1868, the governments of India and the Colonial Office established a quota of 40 women for every 100 men. See Mohapatra, "'Restoring the Family,'" 231.

107. Trotman, "Women and Crime," 253.

108. Mohapatra, "'Restoring the Family,'" 231–36. See also Kale's discussion of this in Kale, "Projecting Identities," 81–83.

109. Longden to Earl of Carnarvon, February 1, 1877, CO 111/410, no. 22, NA.

110. Jamaica, "Registrar General's Report, 1879," CO 140/181, 3, 4, NA.

111. *Report of Commission on Poor Relief, Bridgetown, 1875–1877*, 6, 7, DABB.

112. *Report of the Poor Law Inspector for the Half-Year January–June 1905*, 40, DABB.

113. United Kingdom, House of Commons, "Report of the West India Royal Commission, Documents Relating to the Windward Islands, the Leeward Islands, and Jamaica" (1898), 377.

114. Jamaica, "Registrar General's Report, 1879," CO 140/181, 4, NA.

115. *Report of the British Guiana Mortality Commission*, 14.

116. Jamaica, "Report on the Registrar-General's Department for the Year Ended 31st March, 1900," CO 140/224, 213; Jamaica, "Report on the Registrar-General's Department for the Year Ended 31st March, 1901," CO 140/224, 296, 297; Jamaica, "Report by the Registrar-General for the Year Ended 31st March, 1903," CO 140/228,

335; Jamaica, "Report by the Registrar-General for the Year Ended 31st March, 1905," CO 140/231, 354; Jamaica, "Report by the Registrar General for the Year Ended 31st March, 1907," CO 140/234, 388; Jamaica, "Report for the Year Ended 31st March, 1909," CO 140/237, 361, all in NA.

117. Jamaica, "Report for the Year Ended 31st March, 1909," CO 140/237, 361, NA.

118. Grieve, "Infant Mortality," 242, 243.

119. Kirke, "Our Criminal Classes," 9.

120. Jamaica, "Annual Report of the Island Medical Department for the Financial Year 1882–3," CO 140/186, 102, NA.

121. Jamaica, "Annual Report of the Island Medical Department for the Year Ended 31st March, 1892," CO 140/209, 11, NA.

122. Altink, "'I Did Not Want to Face the Shame of Exposure,'" 355, 356, 361.

123. "The Massacre of the Babes," DG, September 16, 1897, 4.

124. United Kingdom, House of Commons, "Report of the West India Royal Commission, Documents Relating to the Windward Islands, the Leeward Islands, and Jamaica" (1898), 65, 180, 377.

125. Ibid., 180.

126. Report of the British Guiana Mortality Commission, 14.

127. Ibid., iii, iv.

128. Ibid., vi, viii, ix.

129. Jamaica, "Report by the Registrar-General for the Year Ended 31st March, 1903," CO 140/228, 335, NA; Jamaica, "Annual Report for the Registrar General for the Year Ended 30th September, 1886," CO 140/191, 2, NA.

130. Jamaica, "Report by the Registrar-General for the Year Ended 31st March, 1903," CO 140/228, 335, NA; Moore and Johnson, Neither Led nor Driven, 114, 115, 375 n. 69, chap. 4.

131. Will, Constitutional Change, 322. A more limited investigation was held in Trinidad in the same period. In 1903–4, the assistant medical officer of health, J. R. Dickson, investigated infant mortality for Port of Spain, Trinidad. He identified many of the same causes as those noted in the Guyanese inquiry, namely "congenital defects," "maternal ignorance," and "improper and careless feeding" (Annual Report of the Surgeon General for 1903–4, 13, 14, NATT).

132. "Report on the Social Conditions Prevailing," DG, July 29, 1904, 10; Moore and Johnson, Neither Led nor Driven, 114–15, 375 n. 69.

133. "Report on the Social Conditions Prevailing," DG, July 29, 1904, 10.

134. Ibid., 12.

135. Ibid., 10.

136. "To Improve Our Social Conditions," DG, July 30, 1904, 12.

137. On the poor law system in Barbados and Jamaica, see Fletcher, "Evolution of Poor Relief in Barbados," and Jones, Public Health in Jamaica, chap. 3.

138. Report of the Poor Law Inspector for the Half-Year January–June 1905, 40, 52, 64, DABB.

139. Ibid., 59.

140. Hutson was the poor law inspector from 1901 to 1924 and took the post of public health inspector in 1905. See Hutson, Memories of a Long Life, 35, 36, 42, 43, DABB.

141. Hutson was also one of the founding members of the Barbados branch of the British Medical Association in 1888. See "Association Intelligence."

142. See *Half-Yearly Report of the Poor Law Inspector, July–December 1903*, 801, DABB.

143. *Half-Yearly Report of the Poor Law Inspector, July–December 1904*, 787, 788, DABB. Hutson continued to make similar points in the 1910s and later.

144. Ibid., 788. This data seems to have been collected since 1891. See "An Abstract of Births Registered during the year 1891 by the various Police Registrars of Births," CO 28/231, no. 6188, Barbados no. 69, 299, NA.

145. Carter to Lyttleton, May 30, 1905, CO 28/264, no. 20513, Barbados no. 77, 543, NA; Carter to Lyttelton, July 27, 1905, CO 28/264, no. 28510, Barbados no. 124, 92, NA; Knaggs to Secretary of State for the Colonies, August 21, 1905, no. 132, in *Barbados Infant Mortality Report, 1905*, LSTM.

146. Richardson, *Panama Money*, 57.

147. *Half-Yearly Report of the Poor Law Inspector, July–December 1904*, 787, DABB.

148. Carter to Lyttleton, May 30, 1905, no. 77, CO 28/264, no. 543, Barbados no. 20513, NA.

149. *Report of Commission on Poor Relief, Bridgetown, 1875–1877*, 35, DABB.

150. Greaves to Carter, January 19, 1905, CO 28/264, no. 28510, 94, NA; "Sir W. H. Greaves Dead," *Montreal Gazette*, December 19, 1936.

151. Greaves to Carter, January 19, 1905, and Haynes to Knaggs, January 24, 1905, CO 28/264, no. 28510, 94, NA.

152. Knaggs to Carter, January 25, 1905, CO 28/264, no. 25810, 93, 94, NA.

153. Lyttleton to Carter, June 30, 1905, CO 28/264, no. 20513, 543, NA; Lyttleton to Carter, August 15, 1905, CO 28/264, no. 28510, 97, NA.

154. Knaggs to Elgin, August 21, 1906, in *Barbados Infant Mortality Report, 1905*, LSTM.

155. Ibid.; Richardson, *Panama Money*, 57.

156. Greaves, "Copy of Minute," January 25, 1906, in *Barbados Infant Mortality Report, 1905*, LSTM.

157. Circular from Colonial Secretary S. W. Knaggs to the Boards of Poor Law Guardians, February 8, 1906, and Knaggs to Elgin, August 21, 1906, in *Barbados Infant Mortality Report, 1905*, LSTM.

158. Circular from Colonial Secretary S. W. Knaggs to the Boards of Poor Law Guardians, February 8, 1906, and Knaggs to Elgin, August 21, 1906, in *Barbados Infant Mortality Report, 1905*, LSTM.

159. Carter to Knaggs, January 26, 1905, CO 28/264, no. 28510, 96, NA.

160. Knaggs to Elgin, August 21, 1906, in *Barbados Infant Mortality Report, 1905*, LSTM.

161. Greaves to the Governor, January 25, 1905, in *Barbados Infant Mortality Report, 1905*, LSTM.

162. TCM to Lucas, August 11, 1905, CO 28/264, no. 28510, 89, NA.

Chapter Three

1. IWMLBG, *Eleventh Annual Report, 1924*, 11, LSTM.

2. Dance, *Chapters from a Guianese Log-Book*, 76. See also Kirke, *Twenty-Five Years in British Guiana*, 269.

3. Deacon, "Midwives and Medical Men," 275.

4. For a summary of these debates, see Marland and Rafferty, "Introduction"; Deacon, "Midwives and Medical Men," 273; and Leavitt, *Brought to Bed*.

5. For example, see Hattori, "'The Cry of the Little People of Guam'"; Forbes, "Managing Midwifery"; and Nguyen, "French-Educated Midwives."

6. Gewin, "Careless and Unscientific Midwifery with Special Reference to Some Features of the Work of Midwives," *Alabama Medical Journal* 18 (1906): 629–35, and F. Underwood, "Development of Midwifery in Mississippi," *Southern Medical Journal* 19 (1926): 683–85, both qtd. in Devitt, "Statistical Case for the Elimination of the Midwife," 89; Loudon, "Midwives and the Quality of Maternal Care," 180, 181.

7. Fett, *Working Cures*, 45; Ladd-Taylor, "'Grannies' and 'Spinsters'"; Craven and Glatzel, "Downplaying Difference."

8. Leavitt, "'Science' Enters the Birthing Room."

9. Loudon, "Midwives and the Quality of Maternal Care," 190, 196; De Brouwere, "Comparative Study of Maternal Mortality."

10. Lang, "Drop the Demon Dai," 367, 368.

11. Ibid., 366; Arnold, *Colonizing the Body*, 257.

12. Arnold, *Colonizing the Body*, 257.

13. McIntosh, "Profession, Skill, or Domestic Duty?"

14. Mottram, "State Control in Local Context," 134; Fox, "Honourable Calling," 237.

15. McIntosh, "Profession, Skill, or Domestic Duty?," 408, 411.

16. Lang, "Drop the Demon Dai," 368. See also Jones, "Infant and Maternal Health Services." For the Cape Colony, see Deacon, "Midwives and Medical Men."

17. Arnold, *Colonizing the Body*, 258, 259–61; Harrison, *Public Health in British India*, fn. 214, 269.

18. Deacon, "Midwives and Medical Men," 277, 278.

19. Bell, "Midwifery Training," 293, 296, 298, 299, 302.

20. Trotman, *Crime in Trinidad*, 223, 229, qtd. in De Barros, "Dispensers, Obeah, and Quackery," 253. See Bryan, *Jamaican People*, 39, and esp. the Paton and Forde collection, *Obeah and Other Powers*.

21. Handler, "Slave Medicine and Obeah," 84.

22. Sewell, *Ordeal of Free Labor*, 257; Madden, *Twelvemonth's Residence*, 65–67; Bell, *Obeah*, 147–49.

23. Thornton, "'Obeah' in Jamaica"; Cruickshank, *Black Talk*, 8; Hardy, *Life and Adventure*, 98; Bronkhurst, *Colony of British Guyana*, 382, 383, 306, 307.

24. Beckwith, *Notes on Jamaican Ethnobotany*, 8, 9.

25. Inniss, "'Any Elderly, Sensible, Prudent Woman.'"

26. See Sheridan, *Doctors and Slaves*, 92–94, 310; Higman, *Slave Populations*, 266, 576; Mair, *Historical Study of Women in Jamaica*, 136, 203–5; Inniss, "'Any Elderly, Sensible, Prudent Woman'"; and Williamson, *Medical and Miscellaneous Observations*, 2:207.

27. Long, *History of Jamaica*, 436; Morgan, "Slave Women and Reproduction," 44.

28. Williamson, *Medical and Miscellaneous Observations*, 2:202 and 1:vii, viii, 63.

29. Renny, *History of Jamaica*, 207, also qtd in Mair, *Historical Study of Slave Women*, 214.

30. Frank Cundall, ed., *Lady Nugent's Journal: Jamaica One Hundred Years Ago* (London: Adam and Charles Black, 1907), 164, qtd. in Inniss, "'Any Elderly, Sensible, Prudent Woman,'" 46.

31. Jamaica, "Annual Report of the Island Medical Department for the Year Ending 30th September, 1885," CO 140/194, 35, NA; United Kingdom, House of Commons, "Report of the West India Royal Commission, Appendix C, Vol. III, parts VI to XIII," 219, 220.

32. Charles Hutson was Barbados's poor law inspector in the late nineteenth century; he was replaced in 1901 by John Hutson. See *Thirty-Fourth Report of the Poor Law Inspector, January–June 1897*, 21, DABB.

33. *Seventeenth Half-Yearly Report on Poor Relief, July–December 1888*, 7, DABB.

34. Loudon, "Deaths in Childbirth," 22, 23.

35. Loudon, "Measurement of Maternal Mortality," 314.

36. *Report of the British Guiana Mortality Commission*, 23, vi.

37. Mary Sutphen's argument about the acceptance of the germ theory in explaining plague due to its confirmation of "long-held views on the etiology of disease" can be applied here. See Sutphen, "Not What but Where," 83, 84.

38. *Half-Yearly Report of Poor Law Inspector, January to June, 1905*, 51, DABB; British Guiana, "Report of the Surgeon General for the Year 1904–5," CO 114/107, 521, NA. For Jamaica, see Jones, *Public Health in Jamaica*, 59.

39. Jamaica, "Annual Report of the Island Medical Department for the Year Ending 30th September, 1885," 35, NA; *Third Annual Report of the Central Poor Law Board, 1883*, 20, DABB.

40. *Annual Report on the Health and Sanitation of Kingston, 1905*, 7, and *Annual Report on the Public Health and Sanitation of Kingston, 1908*, 11, both in LSTM.

41. Jamaica, "Annual Report of the Island Medical Department for the Year Ending 30th September, 1885," CO 140/194, 35, NA; Jamaica, "Annual Report of the Island Medical Department, 1886–7," CO 140/195, 157, NA.

42. Jamaica, "Report on the Island Medical Department for Eighteen Months, from 1st October, 1889 to 31st March, 1891," CO 140/205, 9, NA.

43. "Report on the VJLH, for the Year Ending 31st March, 1902," CO 140/224, 31, NA; "Report on the VJLH for the Year Ending 31st March, 1904," CO 140/228, 58, NA; "Annual Report of the VJLH for the Year Ended 31st March, 1899," CO 140/220, 107, NA.

44. "Annual Report of the VJLH for the Year Ended 31st March, 1899," CO 140/220, 107, NA.

45. "Report on the VJLH for the Year Ended 31st March, 1897," CO 140/217, 92, NA.

46. "Report on the VJLH for the Year Ended 31st March, 1901," CO 140/224, 183, NA.

47. Legislation providing for midwifery training was passed in 1886. See British Guiana, "Report of the Surgeon General for the Year 1888," CO 114/44, 16, NA, and British Guiana, "Report of the Surgeon General for the Year 1894–95," CO 114/64, 6, NA.

48. *Seventeenth Half-Yearly Report on Poor Relief, July–December 1888*, 7, DABB. See also *Fourteenth Half-Yearly Report of the Poor Law Inspector, January–July 1887*, 12; *Twenty-Sixth Half-Yearly Report of the Poor Law Inspector* [1893], 46; *Barbados Poor Law Report, January–December 1901*, 1901, 1918; *Half-Yearly Report of the Poor Law Inspector, July–December 1903*, 315; and *Second Annual Report of the Public Health Inspector, 1914*, 21, 22, all in DABB.

49. *Sixth Half-Yearly Report of the Poor Law Inspector, January–June 1883*, 1, DABB. His successor also kept track of these cases. See, for example, *Half-Yearly Report of the Poor Law Inspector, July–December 1903*, 819, 820, 825, and *Half-Yearly Report of the Poor Law Inspector, July–December 1904*, 806, DABB.

50. *Sixth Half-Yearly Report of the Poor Law Inspector, January–June 1883*, 1, DABB.

51. *Twenty-Sixth Half-Yearly Report of the Poor Law Inspector* [1893], 58, DABB.

52. Historians have argued that Barbados's elites supported the creation of the Colonial Hospital in 1844 as a response to the economic and social changes following the end of slavery. It was to provide health care for poor black Barbadians as well as for whites. However, Fletcher has suggested that concern for the latter may have been a key motivating factor. See Fletcher, "Evolution of Poor Relief," 173, 174, 200, 203 n. 22; Millington, "Creation of the General Hospital," 172; and Levy, *Emancipation, Sugar, and Federalism*, 93. And see Jones, "Mapping Racial Boundaries."

53. Stoler, "Rethinking Colonial Categories," 150, 152.

54. Hutson expressed the same moral qualms as Gaskin but argued that these women should not be abandoned and that all impoverished parturient women should be helped. See *Half-Yearly Report of the Poor Law Inspector, July–December 1908*, 1914, 1915, DABB.

55. Jamaica, "Annual Report of the Island Medical Department, 1886–7," CO 140/194, 157, NA; "Annual Report of the VJLH for the Year Ended 31st March, 1899," CO 140/218, 107, NA. And see "Maternity Hospital, Kingston, Jamaica," CO 137/702, CO no. 74, Jamaica no. 11323, NA. As Jones notes, some almshouses in Jamaica also had maternity facilities; see Jones, *Public Health in Jamaica*, 59. For Guyana, see Craigen, "Practice of Midwifery," 25.

56. Hart, "West Indies as a Health Resort."

57. See De Barros, "'Spreading Sanitary Enlightenment.'"

58. British Guiana, "Report of the Surgeon General for the Year 1906–7," CO 114/116, 13, 15, NA.

59. With the exception of the sections on East Indians, the early twentieth-century British Caribbean census reports did not correlate ethnicity and occupation. The Jamaican and Trinidadian census reports indicate the number of South Asian midwives, whereas the Guyanese ones include midwives in a larger "medical" category. However, most of the South Asian women in this group were probably midwives, as men dominated the other two professions. In 1911, they totaled 33; in 1921, 24. In Jamaica, only a few South Asian women were listed as midwives in the census reports, 3 in 1911 and 1 in 1921. The numbers for Trinidad were similar. The census report for 1911, for example, shows that 21 East Indian women worked as midwives. See Balfour, *Census of Jamaica and Its Dependencies*, 1911, 80, and Balfour, *Census of Jamaica and Its Dependencies*, 1921, 62. See also *Report on the Results of the Census of the Population*, 1911 [British Guiana], 71; *Report on the Results of the Census of the Population*, 1921 [British Guiana], 72, 74, 75; and *Census of the Colony of Trinidad and Tobago*, 1911, 72, NATT.

60. "British Guiana's Nurses," NDC, June 1, 1926, 7.

61. On this point for Sudan, see Bell, "Midwifery Training," 294, 301.

62. The training courses varied in length. Guyana's started at six months but was lengthened to eight months by 1915 and to two years by the early 1920s. Jamaica's

course was around six months in length and Barbados's was three. See British Guiana, "Report of the Surgeon General for the Year 1895–96," CO 114/68, 7, 8, NA; Craigen, "Hospitals of British Guiana," 17; De Freitas, "Retrospect of Medical Practice," 151; British Guiana, "Report of the Surgeon General, for the Nine Months, April to December, 1915," CO 114/154, 4, NA; and Half-Yearly Report of the Poor Law Inspector, July–December 1903, 815, DABB.

63. Craigen, "Practice of Midwifery," 25.

64. The following discuss the training of midwives: "Annual Report of the VJLH for the Year Ended 31st March, 1895," CO 140/214, 253, NA; British Guiana, "Report of the Surgeon General for the Year 1896–97," CO 114/74, 6, NA; British Guiana, "Report of the Surgeon General for the Year 1906–7," CO 114/116, 550, NA; Half-Yearly Report of the Poor Law Inspector, July–December 1903, 815, 823, DABB; Twenty-Sixth Half-Yearly Report of the Poor Law Inspector, 46, DABB; and Half-Yearly Report of the Poor Law Inspector, July–December 1904, 802, 803, DABB.

65. Wishart, untitled talk, vii, viii.

66. Mosse to Brown, January 20, 1896, encl. 4, CO 854/33, 5–6, NA.

67. "Report on the VJLH for the Year Ending 31st March, 1904," CO 140/230, 58, NA.

68. "Annual Report of the VJLH for the Year Ended 31st March, 1895," CO 140/214, 253, NA; "Report on the VJLH for the Year Ending 31st March, 1904," CO 140/230, 58, NA; "Report on the VJLH for the Year Ending 31st March, 1905," CO 140/232, 40, NA.

69. "Report on the VJLH for the Year Ending 31st March, 1905," CO 140/232, 40, NA; "Report on the VJLH for the Year Ending 31st March, 1904," CO 140/230, 58, NA.

70. "Medical Aid to the People," DG, October 28, 1901, 4.

71. Godfrey, "Presidential Address," v, vii; British Guiana, "Report of the Surgeon General for the Year 1897–98," CO 114/78, 6, NA.

72. British Guiana, "Report of the Surgeon General for the Year 1897–98," CO 114/78, 6, NA; British Guiana, "Report of the Surgeon General for the Year 1903–4," CO 114/103, 468–69, NA. From the late nineteenth century, both British pounds sterling and British Guiana dollars were used as currency. According to Bulmer-Thomas, in the early twentieth century, the exchange was BG$4.80 to £1. See Bulmer-Thomas, Economic History of the Caribbean, 497, 565, 566.

73. British Guiana, "Report of the Surgeon General for the Year 1903–4," CO 114/103, 468–69, NA.

74. Ibid.

75. British Guiana, "Report of the Surgeon General for the Year 1907–08," CO 114/121, 499; British Guiana, "Report of the Surgeon General for the Year 1911–12," CO 114/139, 5; British Guiana, "Report of the Surgeon General for the Year 1912–13," CO 114/143, 489; British Guiana, "Report of the Surgeon General for the Year 1916," CO 114/158, 5; British Guiana, "Report of the Surgeon General for the Year 1917," CO 114/162, 5, all in NA.

76. British Guiana, "Report of the Surgeon General for the Year 1904–5," CO 114/107, 526, NA; Report of the British Guiana Mortality Commission, 23.

77. See British Guiana, "Report of the Surgeon General for the Year 1908–9," CO 114/126, 543, NA; British Guiana, "Report of the Surgeon General for the Year

1905–6," CO 114/112, 519, NA; British Guiana, "Report of the Surgeon General for the Year 1913–14," CO 114/148, 565, NA.

78. While on leave in England in 1903, Hutson met with Colonial Office officials to discuss the infant mortality problem. He learned about the actions of the Guyanese government in supporting midwifery training and its inquiry into infant mortality. See minutes in CO 28/264, no. 20513, 541, esp. Pearson to Lucas, June 27, 1905, NA.

79. *Barbados Poor Law Report, January–December 1902*, 2111; *Fifth Annual Report of the Public Health Inspector, 1917*, 23–24; *Second Annual Report of the Public Health Inspector, 1914*, 21, 22, all in DABB.

80. *Barbados Poor Law Report, January–December 1902*, 2111, 2115, 2116, DABB; *Half-Yearly Report of the Poor Law Inspector, July-December 1903*, 822–25, 832, DABB.

81. *Half-Yearly Report of the Poor Law Inspector, July–December 1903*, 815, DABB.

82. *Half-Yearly Report of the Poor Law Inspector, July–December 1914*, 18, DABB.

83. *Fifth Annual Report of the Public Health Inspector, 1917*, 22–24, DABB.

84. Boyce, *Census of Barbados, 1911*, 69; Lofty, *Report on the Census of Barbados*, 81.

85. Balfour, *Census of Jamaica and Its Dependencies, 1921*, 4, 13, 14, 30–31; Balfour, *Census of Jamaica and Its Dependencies, 1911*, 4, 13, 14, 29–32.

86. "Report on the VJLH for the Year Ending 31st March, 1905," CO 140/232, 40, NA.

87. "Medical Aid to the People," DG, October 28, 1901, 4.

88. See "Report on the VJLH for the Year Ending 31st March, 1904," CO 140/230, 58, NA; British Guiana, "Report of the Surgeon General for the Year 1917," CO 114/162, 5, NA.

89. "Annual Report of the VJLH for the Year Ended 31st March, 1899," CO 140/220, 107, NA; "Annual Report of the VJLH for the Year Ended 31st March, 1895," CO 140/214, 253, NA.

90. "Annual Report of the VJLH for the Year Ended 31st March, 1899," CO 140/220, 107, NA.

91. "Report on the VJLH for the Year Ended 31st March, 1897," CO 140/217, 92, NA.

92. "Annual Report of the VJLH for the Year Ended 31st March, 1899," CO 140/220, 107, 108, NA.

93. "The Massacre of the Babes," DG, September 16, 1897, 4.

94. "Report on the VJLH for the Year Ended 31st March, 1897," CO 140/217, 92, NA.

95. "Report on the VJLH for the Year Ending 31st March, 1905," CO 140/232, 40, NA.

96. *Half-Yearly Report of the Poor Law Inspector, July–December 1897*, 31, DABB.

97. Ibid.

98. "Annual Report of the VJLH for the Year Ended 31st March, 1895," CO 140/214, 253, NA.

99. "Report on the VJLH for the Year Ending 31st March, 1905," CO 140/232, 40, NA.

100. Ibid.

101. Balfour, *Census of Jamaica and Its Dependencies, 1911*, 17. See also Moore and Johnson, "Squalid Kingston."

102. "Report on the VJLH for the Year Ending 31st March, 1908," CO 140/236, 263, NA.

103. Hart, "West Indies as a Health Resort," 1097.

104. *Second Annual Report of the Public Health Inspector, 1914*, 21, 22, DABB.

105. *Fifth Annual Report of the Public Health Inspector, 1917*, 24, DABB.

106. "Report on the VJLH for the Year Ending 31st March, 1905," CO 140/232, 40, NA.

107. BSLBG, *Second Annual Report, 1915*, 5, LSTM.

108. "General Regulations with Regard to Nurse-Midwives Registered, Subsidized and Appointed under Section II of the Medical Ordinance, 1886, Amendment Ordinance 1890," in British Guiana, "Report of the Surgeon General for the Year 1903–4," CO 114/103, 24, 25, NA.

109. Craigen, "Practice of Midwifery," 25; Hart, "West Indies as a Health Resort," 1097. The number of beds in the maternity ward in the Kingston and St. Andrew Union Poor House in Jamaica is uncertain. See Jones, *Public Health in Jamaica*, 59.

110. See reports of the poor law inspector, Barbados, between 1902 and 1916, DABB; Boyce, *Census of Barbados, 1911*, 4; and Lofty, *Report on the Census of Barbados*, 8.

111. *Second Annual Report of the Public Health Inspector, 1914*, 21, 22, DABB.

112. "Report on the VJLH," 1892–1924; see also "Report on the VJLH for the Year Ending 31st March, 1902," 31, CO 140/227, NA. The numbers do not include 1920–22, as data for those years could not be located. For Guyana, see British Guiana, "Report of the Surgeon General for the Year 1920," CO 114/117, 11, NA.

113. See Brereton, "Society and Culture in the Caribbean," 91, 92.

114. Balfour, *Census of Jamaica and Its Dependencies, 1911*, 10; Balfour, *Census of Jamaica and Its Dependencies, 1921*, 9; *Report on the Results of the Census of the Population, 1921* [British Guiana], xxxiv.

115. Seecharan, *"Tiger in the Stars,"* 262, notes that over 75 percent of South Asians in this colony were not literate in English by the late 1920s.

116. *Fifth Annual Report of the Public Health Inspector, 1917*, 22–24, DABB; British Guiana, "Report of the Surgeon General for the Year 1906–7," CO 114/116, 13, 15, 494, NA; British Guiana, "Report of the Surgeon General for the Year 1909–10," CO 114/130, 452, NA.

117. Minett, "Infant Mortality," 58.

118. Lang, "Drop the Demon Dai," 367.

119. British Guiana, "Report of the Surgeon General for the Year 1913–14," CO 114/148, 559, NA.

120. Jamaica, "Report for the Year Ended 31st December 1926," CO 140/264, 371, NA.

121. Minett, "Infant Mortality," 58. These points were repeated in a report of the Baby Saving League when Minett was league medical officer. See BSLBG, *Eighth Annual Report, 1921*, 7, LSTM.

122. IWMLBG, *Eleventh Annual Report, 1924*, 11, LSTM.

123. British Guiana, "Report of the Surgeon General for the Year 1895–96," CO 114/68, 7 (emphasis in original), 8, NA.

124. See, for example, *Annual Report of the Acting Poor Law Inspector, 1926*, 1225, and *Half-Yearly Report of the Poor Law Inspector, July–December 1903*, 807, DABB. District medical officers were responsible for seeing to midwifery cases among indentured South Asians. For Jamaica, see, for example, letter from Kerr, November 19, 1912, CO 137/699, no. 345, NA.

125. *Half-Yearly Report of Poor Law Inspector, January to June 1905*, 71, DABB. See also *Half-Yearly Report of the Poor Law Inspector, July–December 1904*, 815, DABB.

126. Millington, "Maternal Health Care," 7.

127. "Scheme for Reorganization of Medical Service," DG, August 9, 1926. By 1930, regulations stipulated that district medical officers in Jamaica could charge £2 2s for midwifery cases, and significantly less for "families of European Sub-Officers of the Constabulary, £1 1." See no. 102, Jamaica, "Revised Rules and Regulations for the Government Medical Service of Jamaica," in "Colonial Advisory and Sanitary Committee, Meetings Held during 1930, Part 1," CO 885/32/1, 191, NA.

128. "General Regulations with Regard to Nurse-Midwives Registered, Subsidized and Appointed under Section II of the Medical Ordinance, 1886, Amendment Ordinance 1890," and "Memorandum for the Guidance of Nurse-Midwives," both in British Guiana, "Report of the Surgeon General for the Year 1903–4," CO 114/103, 24, 25, NA. See also British Guiana, "Report of the Surgeon General for the Year 1897–98," CO 114/78, 6, 7, NA.

129. "General Regulations with Regard to Nurse-Midwives Registered, Subsidized and Appointed under Section II of the Medical Ordinance, 1886, Amendment Ordinance 1890," in British Guiana, "Report of the Surgeon General for the Year 1903–4," CO 114/103, 24, 25, NA.

130. British Guiana, "Report of the Surgeon General for the Year 1907–8," CO 114/121, 546, NA; British Guiana, "Report of the Surgeon General for the Year 1906–7," CO 114/116, 563, NA.

131. Craigen, untitled talk, 138–40.

132. IWMLBG, *Eleventh Annual Report*, 1924, 9, LSTM.

133. British Guiana, "Report of the Surgeon General for the Year 1903–4," CO 114/103, 468, NA; British Guiana, "No. 5 of 1886. An Ordinance to Establish a Government Medical Service, and to enforce the Registration of Practitioners in Medicine or Surgery," in Nunan, *Laws of British Guiana*, ss 40, 41, 43, 44. This is the (1900) amended version of this ordinance.

134. British Guiana, "Report of the Surgeon General for the Year 1903–4," CO 114/103, 468–69, NA.

135. Draft response to Cavenish Boyle, December 22, 1900, CO 111/522, no. 39724, BG no. 429, NA.

136. Roth, *Report of the Pomeroon District*, 5.

137. BSLBG, *Ninth Annual Report*, 1922, 6, LSTM.

138. BSLBG, *First Annual Report*, 1914, 7, LSTM; BSLBG, *Second Annual Report*, 1915, 5, LSTM.

139. British Guiana, "Report of the Inspector General of Police for the Year 1918," CO 114/167, 517, NA; British Guiana, "Report of the Inspector General of Police for the Year 1919," CO 114/172, 545, 548, NA.

140. Enclosure in no. 158, Wishart to the surgeon general, "Minute by the Medical Officer of Health for Georgetown," CO 885/27/4, 357, NA.

141. Jamaica, "[Central Board of Health] Report for the Year Ended 31st March, 1915," CO 140/249, 370, NA; Jamaica, "[Central Board of Health] Report for the Year Ending 31st March 1919," CO 140/256, 236, NA.

142. "Protest. Pursuant to the Notice of Protest given in Council on the Passing of the Third Reading of the Bill entitled, 'A Law to Further Amend the Midwifery Law 1919,'" CO 137/839/2, Jamaica no. 512, NA; Cundall, *Handbook of Jamaica for 1920*, 139.

143. "Enquiry into Work of Medical Department," DG, August 19, 1920, 3; "Inquiry into the State of the Medical Services of the Colony," DG, September 3, 1920, 4.

144. See Minett, "Infant Mortality."

145. *Second Annual Report of the Public Health Inspector, 1914*, 22, DABB; *Fifth Annual Report of the Public Health Inspector, 1917*, 22–24, DABB.

146. *Tenth Annual Report of the Public Health Inspector, 1922*, 11, 13, DABB; *Report of the Chief Medical Officer for the Period 1st January 1932 to 31st March 1933*, 5, DABB.

147. British Guiana, "Report of the Surgeon General for the Year 1917," CO 114/162, 5, NA; IWMLBG, *Eleventh Annual Report*, 1924, 9, LSTM. Unfortunately, the Guianese census reports did not list midwives or, indeed, health care workers at all as separate categories in 1911 and 1921.

148. Jamaica, "[Registrar General] Report for the Year Ended 31st December, 1923," CO 140/260, 362, NA. The absence (until the early 1930s) of a regulatory framework for certifying informally trained midwives in Barbados means that a similar comparison cannot be undertaken for this colony.

Chapter Four

1. Colonial governments invariably expressed a preference for "English" women, a term that had racial and imperial connotations; it referred to white women born and educated in Great Britain, the center of the empire.

2. Davin, "Imperialism and Motherhood," 28.

3. Rafferty and Solano, "Rise and Demise of the Colonial Nursing Service," 147.

4. Chamberlain to All Crown Colonies, Circular Despatch, June 27, 1896, M.O. 11087, CO 854/33, 2472, 6907/96, NA; CNA, "The Colonial Nursing Association," in ibid., 1–2.

5. CNA, "Terms and Regulations for the Engagement of Trained Private Nurses for the Colonies," CO 854/33, 1–3, NA; see also "Particulars Under Circular Letter from the Secretary of State, February 15, 1904, with Regard to the Selection of Nurses for Colonial Appointments from the CNA," encl. II, CO 111/542, no. 1067, no. 473, 3, NA.

6. Birkett, "'White Woman's Burden,'" 177.

7. Nestel, "(Ad)ministering Angels," 259; Jones, "Heroines of Lonely Outposts," 150; Birkett, "'White Woman's Burden,'" 178, 179.

8. Birkett, "'White Woman's Burden,'" 177–79.

9. Nestel, "(Ad)ministering Angels," 259.

10. Birkett, "'White Woman's Burden,'" 178.

11. Ibid., 182; Rafferty and Solano, "Rise and Demise of the Colonial Nursing Service," 249–50.

12. Birkett, "'White Woman's Burden,'" 180–82.

13. See Dr. Gage Brown and others to the Colonial Office, n.d., CO 854/33, 1–2, NA.

14. Seheult, "Review of the Evolution of Health Services," 9, NATT.

15. Mosse to Brown, January 20, 1896, encl. 4, CO 854/33, 5–6, NA.

16. Snell to Brown, January 16, 1896, encl. 1, CO 854/33, 2, NA; British Guiana, "Report of the Surgeon General's Office for the Year 1898–99," CO 114/82, 17, NA.

17. Hodgson to Lyttelton, December 28, 1904, CO 111/542, no. 1067, no. 473, NA.

18. Godfrey to the Government Secretary, December 27, 1904, in CO 111/542, no. 1067, no. 473, NA. See also "Obituary, J. H. Conyers" and "Government Medical Officers in 1921 Classified According to Race," in Collett to Churchill, April 6, 1921, CO 111/638, no. 74076, NA.

19. Victoria A. Hickes Beach, honorary secretary of the CNA, to the Undersecretary of State, October 23, 1912, CO 137/696, no. 33608, NA.

20. Governor to Secretary of State, August 8, 1911, CO 137/692, no. 291, Jamaica no. 27422, NA.

21. H. J. Read to Miss Thompson, November 5, 1912, CO 137/696, no. 33608, NA; "Application for Employment at Matron in the Colonies," CO 137/696, no. 33608, NA.

22. British Guiana, "Report of the Surgeon General's Office for the Year 1904–5," CO 114/107, 13, NA.

23. Sir Charles A. Cameron, CO 111/542, no. 1067, NA.

24. Lambert H. Ormsby, CO 111/542, no. 1067, NA.

25. Edith M. Mowbay, Honorary Secretary, CNA, to the Undersecretary of State, April 8, 1910, CO 111/575, no. 10413, NA.

26. "Application for Employment of Matron in the Colonies," in ibid.

27. Cox to Harcourt, December 7, 1911; Godfrey to Government Secretary, December 6, 1911; "Medical History of Miss Drummond's Illness," December 5, 1911, all in CO 111/580, no. 4120, BG no. 402, NA. And see British Guiana, "Report of the Surgeon General for the Year 1911–12," CO 114/139, 39, NA.

28. Craigen, "Hospitals of British Guiana," 17.

29. Mowbay to the Undersecretary of State, April 12, 1910, CO 111/575, no. 10900, NA; application for employment as nurse in the colonies from Janet Wilkie Anderson and Undersecretary of State for the Colonies to Anderson, April 22, 1910, both in CO 111/575, no. 14126, NA; Hodgson to Lord Crewe, March 3, 1910, CO 111/570, no. 8438, no. 62, NA.

30. Mowbay to the Undersecretary of State, May 10, 1910; "Application for Employment as Nurse in the Colonies"; and Undersecretary of State to Miss A. A. Brown, May 19, 1910, all in CO 111/575, no. 14126, NA.

31. Godfrey to Cox, December 14, 1911, encl. in Cox to Harcourt, CO 111/580, no. 412, no. 1042, NA.

32. Acting Honorary Secretary of the Overseas Nursing Association to the Undersecretary of State, September 16, 1920, and "Application for Employment as Divisional Nurse in the Colonies," both in CO 111/634, no. 42072/1920, no. 46195, NA.

33. "Application for Employment as Matron or Nurse in the Colonies," encl. in Mowbay to the Undersecretary of State, November 12, 1910, CO 111/575, no. 34817, NA. And see Mowbay to the Undersecretary of State, November 12, 1910, in ibid.

34. "Record of Miss L. B. Thorpe's Services, CNA Imperial Institution," October 21, 1910, encl. in ibid.

35. Mowbay to Undersecretary of State, November 12, 1910, CO 111/575, no. 34817, NA; Godfrey to Cox, December 14, 1911, CO 111/580, no. 412, no. 1042, NA.

36. Godfrey to Cox, December 14, 1911, CO 111/580, no. 1042, BG no. 412, NA.

37. Ibid.

38. Ibid.

39. Memo to Cox, January 26, 1912, CO 111/580, no. 1042, NA; British Guiana, "Report of the Surgeon General for the Year 1912–13," CO 114/143, 4, NA.

40. "Report on the VJLH for the Year Ending 31st March, 1902," CO 140/227, 31, NA.

41. "Annual Report of the VJLH for the Year Ended 31st March, 1899," CO 140/220, 107, NA; "Report on the VJLH for the Year Ended 31st March, 1897," CO 140/217, 92, NA; "Report on the VJLH for the Year Ending 31st March, 1905," CO 140/232, 41, NA.

42. Godfrey to Cox, December 14, 1911, CO 111/580, no. 1042, BG no. 412, NA.

43. British Guiana, "Report of the Surgeon General for the Year 1910–11," CO 140/135 475, NA; "Government Medical Officers in 1921 Classified According to Race," CO 111/638, no. 20586, NA.

44. British Guiana, "Report of the Surgeon General for the Year 1912–13," CO 114/143, 43, NA; "Government Medical Officers in 1921 Classified According to Race," CO 111/638, no. 20586, NA.

45. Byatt to Amery, December 17, 1926, CO 318/389/4, no. 35244, Trinidad no. 431, NA.

46. Edith M. Antrobus (honorary secretary of the Overseas Nursing Association) to Undersecretary of State, CO 318/389/4, no. 35244, NA.

47. Ibid.; "Memorandum to Nurses," Antrobus, to Undersecretary of State, CO 318/389/4, no. 35244, NA.

48. Grindle to the Honorary Secretary of the Overseas Nursing Association, March 21, 1927, CO 318/389/4, no. 35244, NA.

49. Memorandum by Grindle, 17/3/27, CO 318/389/4, no. 35244, NA.

50. Smith, "Illustrations from the Wellcome Institute Library," 359; "Government Medical Officers of 1912," CO 111/638, no. 74076, NA.

51. *Annual Report on the Health of and Sanitation of Kingston, 1908*, 11, LSTM.

52. Wishart, untitled talk, xxi, xxii, xxiii.

53. *Annual Report of the Surgeon General for 1903–4*, 13–14, NATT.

54. *Annual Report of the Surgeon General for 1906–7*, 8, NATT.

55. Craigen, untitled talk, 138–40.

56. *Administrative Report of the Acting Surgeon-General for Year 1912–13*, 26, NATT. In 1916, district nurses were appointed for smaller towns. See *Administration Reports of the Medical Inspector of Health, 1919*, 11–12, NATT, and *Administrative Report of the Acting Surgeon-General for Year 1918*, 13, NATT.

57. *Annual Report on the Health of and Sanitation of Kingston, 1909*, 6, LSTM. On Crosswell, see "Dr. Crosswell Passed Away Yesterday," DG, September 19, 1923, 19.

58. *Annual Report on the Health of and Sanitation of Kingston, 1909*, 6, LSTM; Crosswell, "Infantile Mortality," 49, 50, LSTM.

59. Ford and Cundall, *Handbook of Jamaica for 1919*, 514; Bryan, *Jamaican People*, 234.

60. "Child Welfare Department," DG, May 1, 1922, 10.

61. *Twelfth Annual Report of the Public Health Inspector, 1924*, DABB.

62. *Half-Yearly Report of the Poor Law Inspector, January–June 1912*, 2, 3, DABB. On Chandler, see Sinckler, *Barbados Handbook* (1914), 74, 85.

63. See De Barros, "'Laudable Experiment.'" And see *Second Annual Report of the Public Health Inspector, 1914*, 3; *Half-Yearly Report of the Poor Law Inspector, January–June 1912*, 2, 3, 16, 17, 25; "Vestry Minutes, April 1, 1912," *St. George Vestry Minute Books, 1892–1929*; and "Minutes of St. George Vestry Sanitary Commissioners, April 1, 1912," *St. George Vestry Sanitary Commissioners Minute Books, 1907–1959*, all in DABB; and Richardson, *Panama Money*, 79.

64. *Half-Yearly Report of the Poor Law Inspector, January–June 1912*, 16, DABB.

65. "Minutes of St. George Vestry Sanitary Commissioners, July 8, 1912," *St. George Vestry Sanitary Commissioners Minute Books, 1907–1959*; *Half-Yearly Report of the Poor Law Inspector, January–June, 1912*, 25, both in DABB.

66. "Vestry Minutes, March 3, 1913," *St. George Vestry Minute Books, 1892–1929*; "Minutes of St. George Vestry Sanitary Commissioners, April 14, 1913," and "Minutes of St. George Vestry Sanitary Commissioners, October 14, 1912," both in *St. George Vestry Sanitary Commissioners Minute Books, 1907–1959*; *Half-Yearly Report of the Poor Law Inspector, January–June 1912*, 17, all in DABB.

67. *Second Annual Report of the Public Health Inspector, 1914*, 3, DABB.

68. Colonial Office minutes, CO 111/546, no. 37072, NA; "Government Medical Officers in 1921 Classified According to Race," CO 111/638, CO no. 20586, NA. Craigen may have been the son of William Craigen, a justice of the peace in Guyana and member of the Court of Policy. See *Minutes of Court of Policy, January–December 1887–1888*, 58, National Archives of Guyana, Georgetown, and "Obituary Notice of Dr. A. J. Craigen," 231.

69. Colonial Office minutes, CO 111/546, CO no. 37072, NA; "Government Medical Officers in 1921 Classified According to Race," CO 111/638, no. 20586, NA.

70. Craigen, untitled talk, 140, 141.

71. British Guiana, "Report of the Surgeon General for the Year 1908–9," CO 114/125, 568, NA; British Guiana, "Report of the Surgeon General for the Year 1909–10," CO 114/130, 452, 490–91, NA.

72. Craigen, untitled talk, 138.

73. British Guiana, "Report of the Surgeon General for the Year 1912–13," CO 114/143, 48, NA.

74. British Guiana, "Report of the Surgeon General for the Year 1908–9," CO 114/125, 543, 567, NA.

75. The annual reports did not identify who authored them until 1922, when medical officer Fitzherbert Johnson inaugurated the practice of signing his name. Ethel Minett, who was the league's medical officer between 1920 and mid-1922, probably wrote the reports for this period. The unattributed reports produced between 1914 and 1921 doubtless reflected the views of the league's presidents. From 1914 to 1918, the surgeon general, K. S. Wise, held that position. In 1918, F. G. Rose, the government bacteriologist, was the league's president, a position he held until Conyers took over in 1920; Rose likely wrote the reports while president. The names of the presidents and medical officers are indicated in the reports themselves. See the reports of the BSLBG for 1914–22, LSTM.

76. Johnson replaced Minett as the league medical officer. See BSLBG, *Tenth Annual Report, 1923*, 6, LSTM.

77. BSLBG, *First Annual Report, 1914*, 6; BSLBG, *Second Annual Report, 1915*, 8; BSLBG, *Seventh Annual Report, 1919*, 8, all in LSTM. The subsidy was temporary, until the midwives had established their practices, much like the government system of subsidies discussed in Chapter 3. Mothers had to pay the midwives' fee, but "recognised paupers" received free treatment. See BSLBG, *Third Annual Report, 1916*, 8, 9, LSTM.

78. BSLBG, *Fourth Annual Report, 1917*, 9, LSTM.

79. Porter, *Health, Civilization, and the State*, 179, 180; Davies, "Health Visitor."

80. Davis, "Stillbirth Registration," 635.

81. Porter, *Health, Civilization, and the State*, 179.

82. See *Proceedings of the First West Indian Intercolonial Tuberculosis Conference*, 8, 88, 90, LSTM.

83. Joseph Nunan, "The Early Notification of Births Bill. Explanatory Memorandum," October 25, 1912, CO 111/585, no. 35790, no. 329, NA. In contrast, the act came into effect in Trinidad in 1918. See *Administration Reports of the Medical Inspector of Health for the Year 1918*, 11–12, NATT.

84. Wishart, "Infant Welfare Work," 53; *Daily Chronicle*, July 7, 1921, 7.

85. In 1933, the number of health visitors was increased from five to seven. See Department of Maternity and Child Welfare, *Annual Report of the Public Health Department of the City of Georgetown for the Year 1933*, 42, LSTM, and Wishart, "Infant Welfare Work," 53.

86. "Minutes," November 13, 1928, MTC, 593.

87. Wishart, "Infant Welfare Work," 53; see also *Daily Chronicle*, July 7, 1921, 7.

88. "Annual Report of the Public Health Department of the City of Georgetown for the Year 1914," MTC, 8. On the nature of the health visitors' reports, see the report by M. Garratt, health visitor, May 1916, in MTC, 622, and "Annual Report of the Public Health Department of the City of Georgetown for the Year 1924," MTC, 633–37. See also health visitor reports by J. Legall, J. Selman, and A. Lawrence, July–December 1921, MTC, 467–70.

89. Wishart, "Infant Welfare Work," 53; health visitor report by M. Garratt, April 1916, in MTC, 622.

90. "Annual Report of the Public Health Department of the City of Georgetown for the Year 1924," MTC, 633–37; "Annual Report of the Public Health Department of the City of Georgetown for the Year 1920," MTC, 508, 509; Wishart, "Infant Welfare Work," 53, 54.

91. See, for example, health visitor report by M. Garratt, April 1916, in MTC, 622.

92. BSLBG, *First Annual Report, 1914*, 5, LSTM.

93. BSLBG, *Second Annual Report, 1915*, 10, 13, LSTM.

94. BSLBG, *Eleventh Annual Report, 1924*, 8, LSTM.

95. Ibid., 9.

96. BSLBG, *Sixth Annual Report, 1919*, 8, 9, LSTM.

97. BSLBG, *Seventh Annual Report, 1920*, 8, LSTM.

98. Minett, "New School."

99. BSLBG, *Seventh Annual Report, 1920*, 8, 9, LSTM.

100. Ibid., 9, 10.

101. BSLBG, *Eighth Annual Report, 1921*, 7, LSTM.

102. Balfour, "Tropical Field for Medical Women," 12, 13. This piece was published in 1928, some years after Minett had left Guyana, but it referred to her experiences in that colony.

103. "Annual Report of the Public Health Department of the City of Georgetown for the Year 1913," MTC, 15.

104. Wishart repeated this in his report that was relayed to the members of the Colonial Advisory Medical and Sanitary Committee in 1923. See enclosure in no. 158, Wishart to the surgeon general, "Minute by the Medical Officer of Health for Georgetown," CO 885/27/4, 357, NA.

105. Josephine Legall, "Report for May, 1916," 626; E. Fennens, "Report on January, 1916," both in MTC.

106. Davin, "Imperialism and Motherhood," 37; Porter, *Health, Civilization, and the State*, 179.

107. BSLBG, *Second Annual Report*, 1915, 11.

108. "Annual Report of the Public Health Department of the City of Georgetown for the Year 1924," MTC, 633–39; "Annual Report of the Public Health Department of the City of Georgetown for the Year 1933," MTC, 13. See also Charlton, "National Health Society Almanack," 56, 57.

109. "Annual Report of the Public Health Department of the City of Georgetown for the Year 1933," MTC, 13.

110. "Meetings Held. Examinations," *Journal Supplement of the Royal Sanitary Institute* 42 (1921–22): 83, CPP; "Meetings Held. Examinations," *Journal Supplement of the Royal Sanitary Institute* 43 (1922–23): 109, CPP; E. P. Minett, "Discussion," in *Report of the Proceedings of the West Indian Medical Conference, 1921*, 4, ICS. And see Smith, "Illustrations from the Wellcome Institute Library," 359. On Minett's role in establishing the Royal Sanitary Institute in Guyana, see "Government Medical Officers of 1912," CO 111/638, no. 74076, NA. The institute's board of examiners in the Caribbean was to be comprised of physicians from all three colonies, but as of 1926, Barbados had not appointed a representative.

111. *Twelfth Annual Report of the Public Health Inspector, 1924*, 4, 5, DABB; *Annual Report of the Chief Medical Officer for the Year 1934–35*, 13, 14, DABB.

112. "Royal Sanitary Institute," 171; "Meetings Held. Examinations," *Journal Supplement of the Royal Sanitary Institute* 43 (1922–23): 109, CPP.

113. See applications for position as health visitor, in MTC, January–March 1923, 260–95; see also Public Health Committee, "The Report of the Public Health Committee," in MTC, January–March 1923, 256.

114. "The Report of the Public Health Committee," in MTC, January–March 1923, 256.

115. See applications for position as health visitor, in MTC, January–March 1923, 260–95; "Meetings Held. Examinations," *Journal Supplement of the Royal Sanitary Institute* 42 (1921–22): 39, CPP.

116. See applications for position as health visitor, in MTC, January–March 1923, 260–95; "Meetings Held. Examinations," *Journal Supplement of the Royal Sanitary Institute* 42 (1921–22): 39, CPP.

117. Rodney, *History of the Guyanese Working People*, 170, 171; De Barros, "Congregationalism and Afro-Guianese Autonomy"; "Berbice News," *Daily Chronicle*, May 4, 1911.

118. Rodney has described Moore as a "black Anglican priest." See "Application from Johanna Duggin," MTC, January–March 1923, 269; Rodney, *History of the Guyanese Working People*, 115.

119. "Application from Johanna Duggin," MTC, January–March 1923; see also letter from Fr. Louis Quick, December 1, 1922, 269, encl. in Duggin's application.

120. Public Health Committee, "The Report of the Public Health Committee," MTC, January–March 1923, 256.

121. Few South Asian women were involved in health visiting. Very few Indo-Guyanese girls attended secondary school until after World War II, so they lacked the educational background needed to qualify for these positions. See Brereton, "Society and Culture," and Seecharan, *"Tiger in the Stars,"* chaps. 17 and 18.

122. Moore and Johnson, *Neither Led nor Driven*, 8, 9; Macpherson, *From Colony to Nation*; Reddock, *Women, Labour, and Politics*, chap. 6. Brereton has noted that in nineteenth-century Trinidad, few white women worked outside the home for pay unless they were impoverished, but that this changed by the late 1910s. See Brereton, "White Elite of Trinidad," 45.

123. "Minutes, Monday, July 9, 1928," MTC, 399, 400. Health visitors received a small travel and clothing allowance. See "Minutes, November 6, 1917," 781, 806; "Minutes, February 28, 1923," 562; and Wishart to town clerk, February 14, 1923, 562, all in MTC.

124. Sinclair and Fyfe, *Handbook of Jamaica*, 412, 413; Moore and Johnson, *Neither Led nor Driven*, 188–90; Bryan, *Philanthropy and Social Welfare*, chap. 3.

125. Newton, *Children of Africa in the Caribbean*, 110, 182; Millington, "Creation of the General Hospital," 159.

126. Fraser, *Barbados Diamond Jubilee Directory*, 142.

127. Sinclair and Fyfe, *Handbook of Jamaica*, 414, 415. Rosenberg, "New Woman," 47, notes that the Jamaican organization was directed toward "white and elite women." On Guyana, see Peake, "Development and Role of Women's Political Organizations in Guyana," 111; Trotz and Peake, "Work, Family, and Organizing," 214; and Bayley, *Handbook of British Guiana*, 569. In Trinidad, the Afro-Trinidadian Audrey Jeffers founded the Coterie of Social Workers in the early 1920s, an organization that, among other things, included poor women and children in its mandate. See Reddock, "Diversity, Difference, and Caribbean Feminism," 10.

128. "Acting Governor and Child Welfare Work," DG, April 17, 1926, 14. DeCordova's name is spelled variously, but I have opted to use what seems the most common spelling.

129. "Official List of Members of the Conference," in *Report of the Proceedings of the English-Speaking Conference on Infant Mortality*.

130. BSLBG, *First Annual Report, 1914*, 3, 4.

131. Secretary of the Child Saving League, "Annual Report of the Child Saving League, for Year Ending November 16, 1917," in Earle and Crosswell, *Jamaica Public Health Bulletin*, 1917, 197, 198, LSTM; "Public Bodies are Moving to Save Infant Life in

the City," DG, August 2, 1916, 6. Two years later, Trinidad's governor, Lord Chancellor, also cited Guyana's influence on the establishment of a baby-saving league in this island. See ERD, 27/4/18, CO 111/616, no. 19767, NA; Chancellor to Long, May 2, 1918, CO 295/516, no. 143, p. 445, NA; and *Administration Reports of the Medical Inspector of Health for the Year 1918*, 11–12, NATT.

132. Minute by Grindle, June 11, 1914, CO 323/649, no. 20820, pp. 78–80, NA. For Belize, see Macpherson, "Colonial Matriarchs," 514, 515, and Macpherson, "Citizens v. Clients," 294, 295. For St. Kitts, see Edith G. Floissac, *Ninth Annual Report of the Child Welfare Association, St. Lucia*, 1938, CO 950/417, 1, 2, NA. For Jamaica, see Manning Carley, *Medical Services in Jamaica*, 17. For Trinidad, see Seheult, *Survey of the Trinidad Medical Service*, 50–53, NATT.

133. Colonial Office minutes, in CO 111/600, no. 27782; CPL to Mr. Lucas, 7/7/06, CO 111/551, no. 29159; minute, 11/16/15, CO 111/600, no. 259, BG no. 27782; draft minute from Bonar Law, September 24, 1915, CO 111/601, no. 39937, no. 285, all in NA.

134. Wise to Egerton, July 31, 1915, CO 111/601, no. 285, NA.

135. Ford and Cundall, *Handbook of Jamaica for 1919*, 514; Bryan, *Jamaican People*, 234.

136. *Tenth Annual Report of the Public Health Inspector*, 1922, 2; *Fifteenth Annual Report of the Public Health Inspector (Acting)*, 1927, 8; *Report of the Chief Medical Officer for the Period 1st January 1932 to 31st March 1933*, 5, all in DABB. The donation from St. Michael's parish rose to £100 by the late 1920s and £150 by the early 1930s.

137. *Eleventh Annual Report of the Public Health Inspector*, 1923, 4, DABB.

138. *Twelfth Annual Report of the Public Health Inspector*, 1924, 4, DABB.

139. Secretary of the Child Saving League, "Annual Report of the Child Saving League, for the Year Ending November 16, 1917," in Earle and Crosswell, *Jamaica Public Health Bulletin*, 1917, 199–203, LSTM; Cundall, *Handbook of Jamaica for 1920*, 513; "Annual Meeting of the Child Welfare Association," DG, May 20, 1927, 3; Jamaica, "Report for the Year Ended 31st December, 1925," CO 140/264, 283, NA.

140. BSLBG, *First Annual Report*, 1914, 7, LSTM; BSLBG, *Fourth Annual Report*, 1917, 10, LSTM.

141. Wishart, "Infant Welfare Work," 54; IWMLBG, *Eleventh Annual Report*, 1924, 7, 8, LSTM; "Annual Report of the Public Health Department of the City of Georgetown for the Year 1924," MTC, 633–36. And see enclosure in no. 158, Wishart to the surgeon general, "Minute by the Medical Officer of Health for Georgetown," CO 885/27/4, 357, NA.

142. BSLBG, *First Annual Report*, 1914, 7; BSLBG, *Fourth Annual Report*, 1917, 16–18; BSLBG, *Tenth Annual Report*, 1923, 19; BSLBG, *Thirteenth Annual Report*, 1926, 23, all in LSTM.

143. BSLBG, *Thirteenth Annual Report*, 1926, 23, LSTM.

144. BSLBG, *Fourth Annual Report*, 1917, 8, LSTM.

145. BSLBG, *Eighth Annual Report*, 1921, 7, LSTM.

146. De Freitas, "Review of the Salient Stages in the Medical History of the Colony," 63; Watkins, *Handbook of the Leeward Islands*, 286.

147. Stubbs to Passfield, January 16, 1931, Jamaica no. 12, CO 137/791/10, 5, NA.

148. "Successful Nabaclis-Bachelors' Adventure Baby Show," NDC, September 8, 1927, 7.

149. Bryan, *Jamaican People*, 70–72. For the names of the committee members of the Jamaican Child Welfare Association, see "The Saving of Child Life Here," DG, August 10, 1920, 4; "For the Babies," DG, October 26, 1918, 3; "The Annual Meeting of the Child Welfare Society," DG, May 20, 1927, 3; "Acting Governor and Child Work," DG, April 17, 1926, 14. For the names of physicians based in Jamaica, see Cundall, *Handbook of Jamaica for 1931*, 139–51.

150. August, "Historical Profile," 303, 304, 307, 308.

151. Vassell, "Introduction," 1, 2. For a list of the members in 1930, see Child Welfare Association, Ltd., *Fourteenth Annual Report for the Year Ending 31st March, 1930*, CO 137/791/10, 2, 3, 25, NA.

152. Ford and Cundall, *Handbook of Jamaica for 1919*, 516, 517. Marie Cassidy was a white Jamaican woman and a medical doctor. See "Wedding Bells," DG, November 28, 1913, 6.

153. *Report of the Acting Chief Medical Officer Showing the Sanitary Condition of Barbados up to the 31st December 1929*, 9, 10; *Annual Report of the Acting Chief Medical Officer for the Year 1936–7*, 6, both in DABB.

154. Sinckler, *Barbados Handbook* (1914), 83, 84.

155. "Sixteenth Session Held at Jamaica on November 17, 1938" (witness: JPL), in WIRC, "JPL, Memorandum of Evidence," CO 950/111, 35, NA.

156. Ibid., 33.

157. Ibid., 34, 35.

158. JPL, "Memorandum of the Jamaica Deputation Committee under the Auspices of the JPL," in WIRC, "JPL, Memorandum of Evidence," CO 950/111, 5, NA.

159. "Mrs. Knibb Defends Her Evidence before Commission Admonishes Mrs. DeCordova," Plain Talk, November 26, 1938, 7, qtd. in Vassell, *Voices of Women*, 42.

160. "Reply of Child Welfare Association to Mrs. Knibb" (by Judith DeCordova), DG, November 19, 1938, 12, qtd. in Vassell, *Voices of Women*, 42.

161. "Annual Meeting of the Child Welfare Association," DG, May 20, 1927, 3.

162. See the reports of BSLBG, LSTM, for the years between 1916 and 1924. For information about Glasgow, see A. W. Wilson to Rev. George Cousins, LMS Joint Foreign Secretary, May 24, 1907, in LMS Incoming Letters—West Indies, 4, 5, School of Oriental and African Studies, London; see also De Barros, "Congregationalism and Afro-Guianese Autonomy," 89–103. For information about Browne, see Clementi to Long, confidential, March 26, 1917, confidential, CO 111/611, no. 21957, NA.

163. "West Bank Baby Show," NDC, August 20, 1926, 7.

164. *Twelfth Annual Report of the Public Health Inspector, 1924*, 4, DABB; *Report of the Chief Medical Officer for the Period 1st January 1932 to 31st March 1933*, 5, DABB.

165. Secretary of the Child Saving League, "Annual Report of the Child Saving League, for the Year Ending November 16, 1917," in Earle and Crosswell, *Jamaica Public Health Bulletin*, 1917, 199–203, LSTM; Cundall, *Handbook of Jamaica for 1920*, 513; "Annual Meeting of the Child Welfare Association," DG, May 20, 1927, 3.

166. See IWMLBG, *Eleventh Report*, 1924, 9, 11, LSTM.

167. *Twelfth Annual Report of the Public Health Inspector, 1924*, 4, DABB; *Report of the Chief Medical Officer for the Period 1st January 1932 to 31st March 1933*, 5, DABB; Jamaica, "[Medical Department] Report for the Year Ended 31st December, 1923," CO 140/261, 487, NA.

168. Child Welfare Association Ltd., *Fourteenth Annual Report for the Year Ending 31st March, 1930*, CO 137/791/10, 13, NA.

169. Ibid.; see enclosure in no. 158, Wishart to the surgeon general, "Minute by the Medical Officer of Health for Georgetown," CO 885/27/4, 356, NA.

170. "Acting Governor and Child Work," DG, April 17, 1926, 14; BSLBG, *Second Annual Report*, 1915, 9, LSTM.

171. *Report on the Health of Kingston, Jamaica, February, 1918*, 2, LSTM; see also reports for the rest of 1918, 1919, and 1920.

172. "For the Babies," DG, October 26, 1918, 3.

173. Minett, "Infantile Mortality," 149, 150.

174. Secretary of the Child Saving League, "Annual Report of the Child Saving League, for the Year Ending November 16, 1917," in Earle and Crosswell, *Jamaica Public Health Bulletin*, 1917, 199–203, LSTM; Cundall, *Handbook of Jamaica for 1920*, 513; "Annual Meeting of the Child Welfare Association," DG, May 20, 1927, 3.

175. "Successful Nabaclis-Bachelors' Adventure Baby Show," NDC, September 8, 1927, 7.

176. "Berbice News. Annual Baby Show," NDC, November 30, 1927, 5.

177. "Successful Nabaclis-Bachelors' Adventure Baby Show," NDC, September 8, 1927, 7. Individuals such as Rose and others in attendance provided the prizes, which were probably monetary.

178. Ibid.

179. "Baby Show on West Coast," NDC, March 29, 1927, 7.

180. Brereton, *History of Modern Trinidad*, 127, 128, 129; Brereton, "Society and Culture"; Seecharan, *"Tiger in the Stars,"* chaps. 17 and 18. And see Smith, *British Guiana*, 116.

181. Some middle-class Indo-Guyanese organized the East Indian Association around the same time, but it is not clear whether this provided an organizational vehicle for middle-class Indo-Guyanese women.

182. Boris, "Power of Motherhood," 225, 226; Macpherson, "Colonial Matriarchs," 511; Gordon, "Black and White Visions of Welfare," 570.

183. The historical commentaries in the Caribbean volume of Robert Hill's Universal Negro Improvement Association papers note the dates when the branches were established. On Guyana, see Westmaas and De Barros, "Historical Commentaries," clxviii; on Barbados, see Johnson and Brown, "Historical Commentaries," clii. For a list of branches in 1926, see Martin, *Race First*, 369.

184. Glen Richards, "Historical Commentaries," ccxxix, notes the class background of Garveyite supporters in the Leeward Islands, but a similar pattern existed in other colonies.

185. Macpherson, "Colonial Matriarchs," 509.

186. Lewis, *Marcus Garvey*, 68, 69. On Belize, see Macpherson, "Colonial Matriarchs," 514, and *From Colony to Nation*, 74–76. With the exception of Belize, details about the activities of the Black Cross Nurses in individual colonies are scarce. On Guyana, for example, see Martin, "Marcus Garvey," 19. (Thanks to Nigel Westmaas for giving me a copy of the article.) Honor Ford-Smith, "Unruly Virtues," 24, has noted their presence in Jamaica.

187. Macpherson, *From Colony to Nation*, 74–76; Macpherson, "Colonial Matriarchs," 511. See also Assad Shoman, *Thirteen Chapters of a History of Belize* (Belize City: Angelus Press, 1994), 184, qtd. in Bolland, "Historical Commentaries," clxxviii. And see Bolland, "Historical Commentaries," clxxvi, clxxviii, on the nurses and the Universal Negro Improvement Association in Belize.

188. "Memorandum on the Need for Agricultural and Industrial Education Submitted to the Commission on the West Indies by the Negro Progress Convention of British Guiana," in British Guiana, *Negro Progress Convention Memorandum of Evidence*, CO 950/667, NA.

189. Cudjoe, *Caribbean Visionary*, 109, 110. Also see annotations to "Article in the *Daily Argosy*," in Hill, *Marcus Garvey and Universal Negro Improvement Association Papers*, 279 n. 1, 279 n. 2, 280.

190. Graeme Thompson to the secretary of state for the colonies, April 9, 1924, CO 111/652, no. 20595, NA.

191. *Daily Argosy*, May 11, 1924, 4. See also *Daily Argosy*, April 4, 1924. A member of the Georgetown town council also blamed the organization for the violence in 1924 and argued that its "founders had come to the colony with their pernicious doctrine; it was 'Garveyism' . . . and [they] were doing harm" and "sowing race-hatred" (*Daily Argosy*, June 24, 1924).

192. "Negro Progress Convention," NDC, August 6, 1926.

Chapter Five

1. Roberts, *Population of Jamaica*, 47. On Roberts's place in this early generation of Caribbean social scientists, see Carnegie, "Fate of Ethnography," 8.

2. Bulmer-Thomas, *Economic History of the Caribbean*, 230–232, 236, and esp. Table 9.2, 237. See also Monteith, *Depression to Decolonization*, 36, 37, 283 n. 14, 285 n. 15, 82, 88–90; Brereton, *History of Modern Trinidad*, 205, 206; and Holt, *Problem of Freedom*, 365, 366.

3. United Kingdom, House of Commons, "Report by the Honourable E. F. L. Wood," 46–49. Bulmer-Thomas notes that during World War I, the British government moved away from its earlier free trade policies, and that after the war concluded, it took steps "towards imperial preference," a change that affected its Caribbean colonies. In 1924 and again in 1928, additional protections were offered for imperial producers, including those in the Caribbean. See Bulmer-Thomas, *Economic History of the Caribbean*, 215, 216.

4. United Kingdom, House of Commons, "Report by the Honourable E. F. L. Wood," 49, 50.

5. Jamaica, "[Registrar General], Report for the Year Ended 31st December, 1918," CO 140/251, 8, 11, NA.

6. Lofty, *Report on the Census of Barbados*, 5, 9; Beckles, *History of Barbados*, 135.

7. Lofty, *Report on the Census of Barbados*, 10, 11.

8. Ibid., 5, 9.

9. United Kingdom, House of Commons, "Report by the Honourable E. F. L. Wood," 84, 85.

10. Laurence, *Question of Labour*, chap. 13. On opposition to indentureship, see Look Lai, *Indentured Labor*, chap. 6, and Seecharan, *Bechu*.

11. Mangru, *Indenture and Abolition*, 123–26. And see minutes in CO 111/623, no. 31087, BG no. 182, NA.

12. "Colonisation or Decline," *Daily Chronicle*, January 28, 1919, CO 111/425, no. 68160, BG no. 477, NA. And see correspondence in CO 111/623, no. 31087, BG no. 182, NA. R. V. (Robert Victor) Evan Wong was the son of J. H. Evan Wong (Wong Yan-Sau) and by the 1930s was an elected member of the government. On Wong, see Rodney, *History of the Guyanese Working People*, 109, and Hall, "Trial and Error," 168. On Dias, see Dias, "Our Place in Guiana." See also Bayley, *Handbook of British Guiana*, 561–64.

13. Collet to Churchill, April 28, 1922, in Government Secretary's Despatches to the Secretary of State, January–June 1922, 164, National Archives of Guyana, Georgetown.

14. Mangru, *Indenture and Abolition*, 128–33. In 1930, the governor referred to the "drastic economy which [had] had to be exercised throughout the Public Service" for the past few years. See no. 97, Denham to the Secretary of State, October 10, 1930, CO 885/32/1, 185, NA.

15. British Guiana, "Report of the Surgeon General for the Year 1927," CO 114/205, 12, NA.

16. Martin, "Marcus Garvey," 17–19; Martin, "African and Indian Consciousness," 279.

17. "Memorandum of 'Reasoned Statement,' Submitted by The Negro Progress Convention," CO 111/652, no. 20595, 6, 7, 9, NA.

18. Graeme Thompson to the secretary of state for the colonies, April 9, 1924, CO 111/652, no. 20595, NA; in this file, see also encl. Joseph J. Nunan to Sir Graeme Thompson, November 23, 1923.

19. Graeme Thompson to the secretary of state, April 9, 1924, CO 111/652, no. 20595, NA; in this file, see also encl. 5, telegrams to governors of Sierra Leone, Gold Coast, and Nigeria, November 19, 1923; and see encl. 7, Government Notice.

20. "Colonisation or Decline," *Daily Chronicle*, January 28, 1919, CO 111/425, no. 68160, BG no. 477, NA.

21. "Colonisation Scheme, Report," March 6, 1920, CO 111/629, no. 17614, BG no. 119, NA.

22. "Paper Recently Read before Medical Association by Dr. Oliver Cross," *DG*, October 1, 1919, 4.

23. Taylor, *To Hell with Paradise*, 30–36; Jones, *Public Health in Jamaica*, 94.

24. "Mosquitos and Malaria," *DG*, January 28, 1902, 4; "Some Diseases of the Tropics," *DG*, January 26, 1906, 5.

25. As Rush notes, the *Gleaner* was the only daily newspaper in Jamaica for much of this period and a key information source in the colony. It espoused "conservative" views but seemed politically ecumenical. De Lisser as editor was also known for his fiction and nonfiction writings. He was also secretary of the Jamaica Imperial Association, which advocated for a number of issues, including improved labor relations, increasing productivity, and reducing health problems in the colony. On de Lisser, see Rush, "Bonds of Empire," 26 n. 44, 191 n. 16, and Birbalsingh, "H. G. de Lisser," 141–49. On the Imperial Association, see "First Year's Record of Jamaica's Imperial Association: Report to be Presented Today," *DG*, February 18, 1919, 13.

26. "Our Mad Methods," *DG*, August 5, 1909, 8.

27. United Kingdom, House of Commons, "Report by the Honourable E. F. L. Wood," 57, 58.

28. Balfour and Scott, *Health Problems of the Empire*, chap. 6.

29. McNeill, *Mosquito Empires*, 52–53.

30. Crosswell and Earle, "Preface," LSTM. According to E. D. Gideon, a district medical officer in Jamaica, in 1921, that colony's branch was "dormant." See "Transactions of the Meeting of the BGBBMA, April 16, 1920," 134.

31. Wise suggested "exhaustion" following the recent "exceptional birth-rate" or poor economic conditions were also possible factors. See British Guiana, "Report of the Surgeon General for the Year 1916," CO 114/158, 11, NA, and British Guiana "Report of the Surgeon General, for the Nine Months, April to December, 1915," CO 114/154, 11, 12, NA.

32. Minett, "Mosquito Prophylaxis," 173.

33. Wise, "Malaria," 5–7, 13–14, 15.

34. Minett, "Mosquito Prophylaxis," 174.

35. Arnold, "'Ancient Race Outworn,'" 124, 125, 127.

36. Levine's use of the phrase "racial poison" to describe perceptions of venereal diseases is useful in this context. See Levine, *Prostitution, Race, and Politics*, 195, 196, and Wise, "Malaria," 5–7, 13–14, 15.

37. The London School of Tropical Medicine sent expeditions to the British Caribbean, Fiji, South Africa, and several other places from 1900 to 1912. See Dumett, "Campaign against Malaria," 163 n. 56.

38. "Transactions of the Meeting of the BGBBMA, August 28, 1901," xvi; Knaggs to Elgin, July 18, 1906, in Ross/147/01/08, Ross Archives, File 35, LSTM; Wilkinson and Hardy, *Prevention and Cure*, 51, 52. On Low's research in the Caribbean, see Cook, *Caribbean Diseases*.

39. Sendall to Chamberlain, June 17, 1901, CO 111/527, no. 22807, BG no. 211, NA; "Measures to be Taken for the Prevention of Malaria, by Sir Michael Foster, K.C.B., F.R.S., M.P., and approved by Lord Lister, President of the Royal Society, 28th July, 1900," CO 854/36, no. 15089/99, NA. Chamberlain tended to support Manson's recommendation for protective measures rather than Ross's call to eradicate mosquito-breeding areas, an approach that reflected the latter's admiration of the results obtained by the Americans in Panama and Cuba. See Dumett, "Campaign against Malaria," 165. See also Carrillo and Birn, "Neighbours on Notice," 241.

40. Sendall to Chamberlain, June 17, 1901, CO 111/527, no. 22807, BG no. 211, NA; Sendall to Chamberlain, March 29, 1899, CO 111/512, no. 9275, BG no. 81, NA.

41. See the following: Boyce, *Health Progress and Administration*, 232–41; British Guiana, "Report of the Surgeon General for the Year 1912–13," CO 114/143, 16, NA; John Hutson, "Return of Malarial Fever, Black Water Fever, Yellow Fever, Filariasis, and Dengue, during the Year from the 1st January to the 31st December, 1910," CO 111/579, no. 32055, no. 308, NA; correspondence in no. 5, Egerton to the Secretary of State, January 2, 1913, in "West Indies. Correspondence Relating to the Measures for the Elimination of Mosquitos," CO 884/12, WI no. 195, NA. In the same source, see no. 8, Probyn to the Secretary of State, February 4, 1913, 23, 24. And see Minett,

"Mosquito Prophylaxis"; Wise, "Examination of the City of Georgetown"; Jones, *Public Health in Jamaica*, 88, 89; Packard, *Making of a Tropical Disease*, 118–26; and Webb, *Humanity's Burden*, chap. 5.

42. Hodgson to Lyttleton, January 23, 1904, CO 28/262, no. 4912, Barbados no. 18, NA. From Barbados he moved to Guyana, where he would remain until 1911. On Hodgson, see Wasserman, "Ashanti War."

43. Manson to Lucas, February 2, 1909, CO 28/272, no. 3211, NA. Boyce attributed the relatively small size of the epidemic to the "conscientiousness and vigilance" of John Hutson and other physicians and criticized the hostility expressed in some newspapers against early notification. See Boyce, "Interim Report to the Governor Barbados," March 26, 1909, 8, and Boyce, "Interim Report to the Administrator of the Government of British Guiana," May 1, 1909, 13, both in CO 884/10, WI no. 175, NA.

44. Hopwood to Ross, December 11, 1908, Ross Archives, File 35, LSTM.

45. Boyce, "Interim Report to the Governor Barbados," March 26, 1909, CO 884/10, WI no 175, 9, NA; Boyce, *Health Progress and Administration*, 145. See also McNeill, *Mosquito Empires*, 28, 29.

46. John Hutson, "Return of Malarial Fever, Black Water Fever, Yellow Fever, Filariasis, and Dengue, during the Year from the 1st January to the 31st December, 1910," CO 111/579, no. 32055, no. 308, NA; Probyn to Ross, November 13, 1911 (Barbados no. 234), Ross/147/17/24, Ross Archives, LSTM.

47. Probyn to Ross, November 13, 1911 (Barbados no. 234), Ross/147/17/24, Ross Archives, LSTM.

48. Prout, "Malaria in Jamaica," 377. Prout's comment about segregation is from F02-890: 1903, qtd. in Frenkel and Western, "Pretext or Prophylaxis?," 211.

49. Prout, "Malaria in Jamaica," 376, 377, 379.

50. Ibid., 377–79; "Malarial Work in Jamaica," 353, 354. For a more detailed report by Prout on the Jamaican expedition, see Prout, "Reports of the Twenty-First Expedition of the Liverpool School of Tropical Medicine, Jamaica, 1908–1909," 471–551, LSTM. On the Jamaican malaria commission, see P. C. Cork and E. Jamaica, "Appendix No. IX. Preliminary Report of the Commissioners on Malarial Fever," February 1910, in Jamaica, "Departmental Reports for 1911–1912," CO 140/241, 1–3, NA.

51. Prout, "Malaria in Jamaica," 377–79. The Jamaican antimosquito measures are detailed in the Superintending Medical Officer to the Secretary of State for the Colonies, November 4, 1911, CO 137/686, CP no. 40263, Jamaica no. 430, NA. And see Jamaica, "Report for the Year Ended 31st March, 1911," CO 140/241, 247, NA.

52. The authors of the Jamaica Imperial Association's first report urged the government to restart the antimalaria campaign. See "First Year's Record of Jamaica's Imperial Association: Report to be Presented Today," DG, February 18, 1919, 13. On Prout's visit, see Jones, *Public Health in Jamaica*, 95–101.

53. BSLBG, *Second Annual Report*, 1915, 7, LSTM.

54. Henry Tillman to the Superintending Medical Officer, September 18, 1911, CO 137/686, no. 430, NA.

55. BSLBG, *Third Annual Report*, 1916, 8, LSTM.

56. BSLBG, *Second Annual Report*, 1915, 7, LSTM.

57. "Annual Report of the Public Health Department of the City of Georgetown for the Year 1921," MTC, 7, 8.

58. See Wise, "Malaria," and see British Guiana, "Report of the Surgeon General for the Year 1913–14," CO 114/148, 558, 559, NA.

59. Balfour and Scott, *Health Problems of the Empire*, 323–27. Andrew Balfour and Henry Scott were influential tropical medicine researchers. Balfour had worked in Khartoum as the director of the Wellcome Research Laboratories, and Scott was a bacteriologist in Jamaica in the mid-1910s. By the early 1920s, they were based at the London School of Hygiene and Tropical Medicine, of which Balfour was the director. Balfour was also a member of the Colonial Advisory Medical and Sanitary Committee. See Jones, *Health Policy in Britain's Model Colony*, 3 n. 8, and Palmer, *Launching Global Health*, 56.

60. Balfour and Scott, *Health Problems of the Empire*, 327–30.

61. Ibid., 64.

62. Ibid., 331.

63. Ibid., 331, 332.

64. Ibid. (emphasis in original).

65. "The First Step," DG, March 30, 1916, 8.

66. Soloway, "Counting the Degenerates," 154, 155.

67. Levine, *Prostitution, Race, and Politics*, 195, 196.

68. Ibid., 38, 40–43; Challenger, "Benign Place of Healing?"

69. Brunton, "Report of the Inter-Departmental Committee," 275.

70. Balfour and Scott, *Health Problems of the Empire*, 323–27.

71. Levine, *Prostitution, Race, and Politics*, 122–23; Tomkins, "Palmitate or Permanganate," 382.

72. Tomkins, "Palmitate or Permanganate," 386; Towers, "Health Education and Policy," 77–79; Walther, "Sex, Public Health and Colonial Control," 198. Thanks to Deb Neill for her help with this section of the chapter.

73. Tomkins, "Palmitate or Permanganate," 384–86.

74. British Guiana, "British Guiana Report of the Surgeon General for the Year 1916," CO 114/158, 23, NA.

75. "Message from His Excellency the Governor the Honourable the Legislative Council," in Earle and Crosswell, *Jamaica Public Health Bulletin*, 1917, 146–49, 153, LSTM.

76. "Abstract from the Blue Book for the Year 1916–17," in Earle and Crosswell, *Jamaica Public Health Bulletin*, 1917, 139, 140, LSTM; "Paper Recently Read before Medical Association by Dr. Oliver Crosswell," DG, October 1, 1919, 4. Jones notes that around the same time, the colonial government canceled the £2,000 previously approved to tackle malaria. See Jones, *Public Health in Jamaica*, 101.

77. "Message from His Excellency the Governor the Honourable the Legislative Council," in Earle and Crosswell, *Jamaica Public Health Bulletin*, 1917, 146, 147, LSTM.

78. *Report of the Proceedings of the West Indian Medical Conference*, 1921, 111, 112, ICS; "Memorandum by the [Barbados] Attorney General," Barbados, *Venereal Disease Report*, 1, 2.

79. Encl. in no. 58, "Report on Work Performed under the Venereal Diseases Act for the Half-Year Ended 31st December, 1922," 113, and no. 58, G. B. Haddon-Smith to Secretary of State for the Colonies, March 29, 1923, 109, both in CO 885/27/4, NA.

80. Paterson, "Discussion," in *Report of the Proceedings of the West Indian Medical Conference, 1921*, 117, 118, ICS.

81. Letter from Colonial Secretary, January 1917, in *Venereal Disease Report*, 1, DABB.

82. Greaves to the Colonial Secretary, ibid., 2.

83. Hutson to the Colonial Secretary, ibid. And see Phillips to the Colonial Secretary, ibid., 3, 4.

84. "Obituary, Dr. Edward Howard Bannister"; Bannister to the Colonial Secretary, in *Venereal Disease Report*, 5, DABB.

85. Boxill to the Colonial Secretary, in *Venereal Disease Report*, 3, DABB.

86. *Report of the Proceedings of the West Indian Medical Conference, 1921*, 111, 112, 116–18, ICS.

87. Tomkins, "Palmitate or Permanganate," 385, 386.

88. Levine, "Battle Colors," 7, 8.

89. On the enlistment of Afro-Caribbean men to fight in the war, see Howe, *Race, War, and Nationalism*, 29–31, 41, 206, and Downes, "From Boys to Men," 14, 15.

90. Levine, "Battle Colors," 8. For a discussion about this in the British Caribbean during World War I, see Howe, "Military Selection," 42.

91. United Kingdom, House of Commons, "Report by the Honourable E. F. L. Wood," 58.

92. Balfour and Scott, *Health Problems of the Empire*, 315.

93. Fairfield, "Venereal Diseases," 321, 322. The visit seemed to have prompted the Jamaican legislative council to provide money (£1,000) to establish a venereal disease clinic in Kingston. See Devonshire to the governor of Jamaica, July 25, 1923, no. 120, CO 885/27/4, 249, NA. On Wright, see "Obituary, A. F. Wright."

94. Howe, "Military Selection," 40. See also Fairfield, "Venereal Diseases," 321, 322; Letitia D. Fairfield, "Blood Diseases in Colonies in the West Indies," DG, August 24, 1921, 3; "Abstract from the Blue Book for the Year 1916–17," in Earle and Crosswell, *Jamaica Public Health Bulletin*, 1917, 139, LSTM; and L. S. Blackden, Brigadier General, January 21, 1918, confidential minute, CO 137/725, no. 10173, 138, NA.

95. Fairfield, "Venereal Diseases," 321, 322; United Kingdom, House of Commons, "Report by the Honourable E. F. L. Wood," 58.

96. "Blood Diseases Widespread Here," DG, October 20, 1920, 11. Wright made this appeal in a talk a few days later. See "The Combatting of Blood Diseases in This Island," DG, October 25, 1920, 3.

97. "The Combatting of Blood Diseases in This Island," DG, October 25, 1920, 3.

98. "Blood Diseases Widespread Here," DG, October 20, 1920, 11.

99. "Women's Social Services Club Deals with Sanitation of City," DG, October 30, 1920, 6.

100. *Report of the British Guiana Mortality Commission*, xi; Knaggs to the secretary of state for the colonies, August 21, 1905, in *Barbados Infant Mortality Report*, 1905, LSTM.

101. Edward G. W. Deane to the chairman, Poor Law Guardians, St. Michael, February 24, 1906, in *Barbados Infant Mortality Report*, 1905, LSTM.

102. *Report of the Medical Officer, St. Vincent, for the Year 1912–13*, LSTM.

103. "Enquiry into Work of Medical Department," DG, August 19, 1920, 3; "Inquiry into the State of the Medical Services of the Colony," DG, September 3, 1920, 4.

104. Minett, "Infant Mortality," 59.

105. Ninth Annual Report of the Public Health Inspector, 1921, 7, DABB.

106. Ibid.

107. Eighth Annual Report of the Public Health Inspector, 1920, 9, DABB.

108. "Obituary, Dr. Edward Howard Bannister"; Barbados Women's Social Welfare League, "Report of the Work of the Barbados' Social Welfare League and Affiliated Societies for the Year 1937–38," DABB. On Fellowes, see Sinckler, Barbados Handbook (1912), 84.

109. On the work of the Barbados Women's Social Welfare League, see Barbados Women's Social Welfare League, "Report of the Work of the Barbados' Social Welfare League and Affiliated Societies for the Year 1937–38"; Fifteenth Annual Report of the Public Health Inspector (Acting), 1927, 8; and Report of the Acting Chief Medical Officer Showing the Sanitary Condition of Barbados up to the 31st December 1929, 9, 10, all in DABB.

110. Eighth Annual Report of the Public Health Inspector, 1920, 8, 9, DABB.

111. Wright and Fairfield, "Extract from Confidential Report of West Indies Commission to the NCCVD (British), 1921," in CO 28/302, no. 29973, 302, 303, NA.

112. Ibid., 303.

113. Ibid., 299.

114. Elston, "Fairfield, (Josephine) Letitia Denny."

115. Memorandum by John Hutson, "Barbados. Medical and Sanitary Services," no. 97, January 17, 1922, CO 885/27/4, 198, 199, NA.

116. Ibid., 199; Devonshire to the Governor of Barbados, September 14, 1923, no. 138, in CO 885/27/4, 307, NA. Wood read Hutson's report on Barbados in preparation for his visit. See CRD to Acheson, 1/6/23, CO 28/302, no. 29973, NA.

117. Clover, "West Indian Club Ltd.," 4, 6, 7.

118. See Testimony of G. B. Mason, "Minutes of Evidence," 1921, CO 885/26/13, 54–56, NA.

119. G. B. Mason, "Medical Conference," DG, September 10, 1921, 6.

120. Wright and Fairfield, "Extract from Confidential Report of West Indies Commission to the NCCVD (British), 1921," in CO 28/302, no. 29973, 297, NA. The 1921 census report put the number at 6.7 percent.

121. Ibid.

122. Devonshire to the Governor of Barbados, September 14, 1923, no. 138, CO 885/27/4, 307, NA.

123. Draft letter, Devonshire to governor of Barbados, September 14, 1923, in CO 28/302, no. 29973, 318–20, NA. This letter was reprinted in CO 885/27/4.

124. Initially, Hutson was on the committee, but he was eventually replaced by his cousin and member of the Hutson medical clan, Lionel Hutson. See Barbados, Report of the Public Health Commission, Barbados, 1925–6, in CO 28/306/6, no. 37510, 3, 4, NA. On Hawkins, see Sinckler, Barbados Handbook (1912), 81.

125. Barbados, Report of the Public Health Commission, Barbados, 1925–6, in CO 28/306/6, no. 37510, 6, 13, 14, NA.

126. J. W. Hawkins and A. J. Hanschell, "Minority Report B," encl. in ibid., iii.

127. Ibid., iii, iv, 27, 14.

128. "Paper Recently Read before Medical Association by Dr. Oliver Crosswell," DG, October 1, 1919, 4.

129. Palmer, *Launching Global Health*, 59; Stern, *Eugenic Nation*, 39–41; Renda, *Taking Haiti*; Stepan, "Interplay between Socioeconomic Factors and Medical Science"; Lord, "'Imperial Obligation.'"

130. See no. 1, Lewis Harcourt to various colonial governors, October 8, 1912, in "West Indies. Correspondence Relating to Measures for the Elimination of Mosquitos," no. 195, CO 884/10, WI no. 175, 9, NA.

131. Palmer, *Launching Global Health*, 25–27, 59; Pemberton, "Different Intervention," 90.

132. Guyana was chosen first as a "demonstration colony," its early work on hookworm and other public health problems making it a useful example. One Colonial Office official described it as a "model colony" unlike "other colonies, [where] in spite of our constant reminders, sanitary work [was] apt to lag" (HRD to Mr. Read, 18/4/16, CO no. 17332, CO 111/609, NA). See Pemberton, "Different Intervention," 90.

133. Harcourt to the Governors in British Guiana Correspondence, 1915 and earlier, RAC.

134. Palmer, *Launching Global Health*, 8, 42, 43, 69; Riley, *Poverty and Life Expectancy*, 82–91; Pemberton, "Different Intervention." On treatments in Guyana, see correspondence in CO 111/505, no. 22991, BG no. 315, NA.

135. Palmer, *Launching Global Health*, 43, 44.

136. Boyce, "Report on Ankylostomiasis Amongst the Indentured Labourers," May 1, 1909, CO 884/10, WI no. 175, 7, NA. See also Palmer, *Launching Global Health*, 44.

137. Palmer, *Launching Global Health*, 69.

138. Boyce, "Interim Report to His Excellency the Administrator of the Government of British Guiana upon certain health protective measures," May 1, 1909, CO 884/10, WI no. 175, 14, NA.

139. Ibid.; BSLBG, *Second Annual Report*, 1915, 6, LSTM.

140. Anderson, *Colonial Pathologies*, 183; Jones, *Public Health in Jamaica*, 116.

141. Palmer, *Launching Global Health*, 263 n. 6. See also "Extract from Report of Proposals and Finance Sub-Committee" [of "Proceedings of a Meeting of the Sanitation Sub-Committee of the General Colonisation Scheme"], folder 253, box 42, series 423, subseries 2, record group 5, RAC.

142. "The Petition on Jamaica's Constitution," *DG*, November 27, 1917, 14.

143. "First Year's Record of Jamaica's Imperial Association: Report to be Presented Today," *DG*, February 18, 1919, 13.

144. Jones, *Public Health in Jamaica*, 118.

145. Washburn, "Report of the Co-operative Public Health Work in Jamaica," in "Medical and Sanitary Conditions in Jamaica," CO 137/784/35833, 20, NA; Washburn, "Economic Value of a Hookworm Campaign," 613. See also Pemberton, "Different Intervention," 96, 99, and Riley, *Poverty and Life Expectancy*, 112. For a summary of the extensive public health activities of the Rockefeller Foundation in Jamaica, see "Cooperative Health Work in Jamaica," *DG*, June 7, 1929, 19.

146. "Health Problems and Activities," *DG*, March 15, 1928, 10; "Public Health 'Rainbow' in This Island," *DG*, May 27, 1925, 15.

147. Washburn, *Supplement to the Jamaica Gazette*, 70, no. 3 (May 1, 1927): 27, 34, in CO 137/785/4, NA. See also "Annual Report of Bureau of Health Education Here," *DG*,

April 27, 1928, 6, and Riley, *Poverty and Life Expectancy*, 62, 112. And see Jones, *Public Health in Jamaica*, 126.

148. "Meeting of Child Welfare Association," DG, April 23, 1928, 29.

149. "Annual Meeting of the Child Welfare Association," DG, May 20, 1927, 3.

150. "Meeting of Child Welfare Association," DG, April 23, 1928, 29.

151. "Physical Health Is the First Thing Needed," DG, October 5, 1928, 10; "Mrs. Passingham Speaks on the Care of Children," DG, July 3, 1929, 17.

152. "Meeting of Child Welfare Association," DG, April 23, 1928, 29.

153. Palmer, *Launching Global Health*, 80, 81.

154. Briggs posed a similar argument about the utility of British imperial concepts and approaches for the United States. See Briggs, *Reproducing Empire*, 45.

155. See Stern, *Eugenic Nation*, esp. chap. 1, on ideas about race, whiteness, and U.S. tropical medicine in the Americas.

156. Rose, "Progress of Sanitation in British Guiana," 62; DG, August 20, 1927, 1.

157. W. C. F. Robertson to Lord Passfield, October 3, 1929, CO 28/308/12, 5, NA.

158. "Health Week to be Observed in the Empire," DG, August 20, 1927, 1.

159. Ibid. And see "Annual Report of the Public Health Department of the City of Georgetown for the Year 1933," MTC.

160. "The Special Feature of Health Week," DG, September 3, 1924, 3.

161. "Health Week Meeting in Ward Theatre," DG, October 6,1927, 6.

162. "Annual Report of Bureau of Health Education Here," DG, April 27, 1928, 6; Riley, *Poverty and Life Expectancy*, 112; "Preparations for Health Week in Parish of St. Ann," DG, October 3, 1927, 23; "Health Week Preparations in Town and Country," DG, August 30, 1927, 5.

163. "Preparations for Health Week in Parish of St. Ann," DG, October 3, 1927, 23.

164. G. Grindle to P. J. Michelli, March 3, 1921; A. Alcock to the undersecretary of state, March 11, 1921; Grindle to the secretary, January 18, 1921, all in GB0809 Leiper/01, Leiper Archive, LSTM.

165. Milner to the governors, August 4, 1920, GB0809 Leiper/01, Leiper Archive, LSTM.

166. G. B. Mason, "Medical Conference," DG, September 10, 1921, 6.

167. Milner to the governors, August 4, 1920, GB0809 Leiper/01, Leiper Archive, LSTM.

168. Hutson, "Response to Discussion," in *Report of the Proceedings of the West Indian Medical Conference, 1921*, 44, 45, ICS.

169. Gideon, "Response to Discussion," in *Report of the Proceedings of the West Indian Medical Conference, 1921*, 44, ICS.

170. *Report of the Proceedings of the West Indian Medical Conference, 1921*, 42, ICS.

171. Turda, "Race, Science, and Eugenics," 66; Anderson, "Immunities of Empire," 110, 111. See also Anderson, "Going through the Motions," 697.

172. Anderson, "Response to Discussion," in *Report of the Proceedings of the West Indian Medical Conference, 1921*, 43, ICS.

173. Hutson, "Response to Discussion," in *Report of the Proceedings of the West Indian Medical Conference, 1921*, 43, ICS.

174. Ibid. On Paterson, see *Grenada Handbook*, 49.

175. Gideon, "Response to Discussion," in *Report of the Proceedings of the West Indian Medical Conference, 1921,* 42, ICS.

176. "Resolutions to be Forwarded to the Secretary of State for the Colonies," in *Report of the Proceedings of the West Indian Medical Conference, 1921,* 147, ICS.

177. Ibid., 147–49. These are also listed in the following: G. B. Haddon-Smith, governor of Windward Islands, to Winston Churchill, secretary of state, no. 29, February 5, 1923, CO 885/27/4, 39, NA.

178. See correspondence in CO 885/27/4, NA, especially the following: Thompson to the Secretary of State for the Colonies, April 28, 1923, no. 86, CO 885/27/4, 181. See also Devonshire to the Governor of Guyana, October 3, 1923, no. 146, 325; "Resolutions to be Forwarded to the Secretary of State for the Colonies," encl. in no. 123, in Probyn to the Secretary of State for the Colonies, July 13, 1923, no. 123, CO 885/27/4, 251–55; and O'Brien to the Secretary of State for the Colonies, June 6, 1923, no. 105, CO 885/27/4, 221, 222.

179. H. E. Sutherland Richards, "Response to Presentations," in *Report of the Proceedings of the West Indian Medical Conference, 1921,* 61, ICS.

180. G. B. Mason, "Medical Conference," DG, September 10, 1921, 6.

181. Balfour, "Why Hygiene Pays," 929, 930.

182. Ibid., 930.

183. "Health and Hygiene" resolution, January 31, 1929, CO 318/395/3, NA.

184. Stanton, 4/4, 1929, CO 318/395/3, NA.

185. Webber was also the secretary of the Colonization Committee. It is not clear whether this influenced the *Chronicle*'s emphasis on the 1921 medical conference, although Cudjoe argues that Webber used these newspapers to influence popular views on current social and political issues. The *Daily Argosy* also covered the conference, but at least by the late 1920s, it was edited by Sam Lumpton. Cudjoe describes him as a "displaced Englishman living in British Guiana who used the *Daily Argosy* to promote his brand of reactionary politics." On Webber, see Cudjoe, *Caribbean Visionary,* 6, 38, 39, 41, and on Lumpton, see 86.

186. *Daily Argosy,* June 30 to July 7, 1921, in GB0809 Leiper/01, Leiper Archive, LSTM; see also "The Medical Conference of the West Indies," DG, July 29, 1921, 4.

187. G. B. Mason, "Medical Conference," DG, September 10, 1921, 6; Mason, "British West Indies Medical Services," 693, 695; G. B. Mason, "The British West Indian Medical Services," DG, November 25, 1922, 6; G. B. Mason, "Medical Services in the West Indies," DG, July 21, 1924, 17; Balfour and Scott, *Health Problems of the Empire,* 64–66.

188. "The Medical Conference of the West Indies," DG, July 29, 1921, 4.

189. I am grateful to Henrice Altink for giving me a copy of her forthcoming article "A True Maverick," which addresses Anderson.

190. Beckles, *Great House Rules,* 186, 187.

Conclusion

1. See Knight's summary, "Caribbean in the 1930s." See also Bolland, *On the March*; Bolland, *Politics of Labour*; and Fraser, "Twilight of Colonial Rule," 2. For Guadeloupe, see Jennings, *Vichy in the Tropics,* 82, 83.

2. For this paragraph I have drawn on the following: Johnson, "Political Uses of Commissions," 257, 258, 262; Bolland, *On the March*, pt. 2; Seekings, "'Pa's Pension,'" 541; and Browne, "1937 Disturbances." With the exception of Browne, most of the historians whose work I have consulted about the protests seemed to have relied on Lewis's *Labour in the West Indies* for their estimates of the numbers killed and injured during the unrest. See Lewis, *Labour in the West Indies*, 13, 16, 21, 28.

3. Knight, "Caribbean in the 1930s," 42, 43; Bolland, *Politics of Labour*, 357, 358.

4. Bolland, *Politics of Labour*, 358, 359. In a number of colonies, the franchise was extended to some women in this period. For example, women over age twenty-five who met a property qualification were enfranchised in Jamaica in 1919. See Altink, "'We Are Equal to Men in Ability to Do Anything!,'" 79.

5. See, for example, Bolland, *Politics of Labour*, 360, 358; Fryer, *Staying Power*, 343, 344; and Price, "Cleave to the Black," 43.

6. Price, "Cleave to the Black," 36; Martin, "African and Indian Consciousness," 248–50.

7. See Rush, "Imperial Identity"; Killingray, "'To Do Something for the Race'"; Whittal, "Creolising London"; James, *Holding Aloft the Banner of Ethiopia*; Holt, *Problem of Freedom*, epilogue.

8. Holt, *Problem of Freedom*, 392.

9. Gregg, *Caribbean Women*, 74, 75. See also Rosenberg, "New Woman," 51, and Reddock, "Diversity, Difference, and Caribbean Feminism," 9.

10. Vassell, "Introduction," 1, 2; James, *Holding Aloft the Banner of Ethiopia*, 3, 4, 270, 271.

11. French, "Women and Colonial Policy," 129; Bryan, *Philanthropy and Social Welfare*, 40, 41. On Bailey, see Altink, "'Misfortune of Being Black and Female.'"

12. Brodber, "Pioneering Miss Bailey," 9, 10.

13. Bryan, *Philanthropy and Social Welfare*, 41; Vassell, "Introduction," 1–4.

14. Gregg, "'How with This Rage,'" 32; Amy Bailey, "Lack of Civic Pride," DG, May 27, 1935, 12, qtd. in ibid., 31.

15. Eulalie Domingo, "Women's Clubs of Jamaica," *Public Opinion*, May 1, 1937, 10, rpt. in Vassell, *Voices of Women*, 35.

16. *Handbook of Jamaica*, 1948, 660, qtd. in Bryan, *Philanthropy and Social Welfare*, 40.

17. Gregg, *Caribbean Women*, 74; Rosenberg, "New Woman," 51.

18. Cooper, "African Workers and Imperial Designs," 301, 302. See also Holt, *Problem of Freedom*, 382, and Johnson, "Political Uses of Commissions," 266, 267.

19. Holt, *Problem of Freedom*, 388.

20. Johnson, "Political Uses of Commissions," 267, 268.

21. BPP, "WIRC Report," xvii.

22. On Crowdy, see Pedersen, "Maternalist Moment," 188.

23. Johnson, "Political Uses of Commissions," 271–73.

24. Fraser, "Twilight of Colonial Rule," 16; Holt, *Problem of Freedom*, 397.

25. For a summary of the health recommendations, see BPP, "WIRC Report," 155–73, 227, chap. 25.

26. Ibid., 355; Constantine, *Making of British Colonial Development Policy*, 222–24; Johnson, "Political Uses of Commissions," 268; Fraser, "Twilight of Colonial Rule," 16.

27. Tignor, *W. Arthur Lewis*, 67.

28. BPP, "WIRC Report," 427–29.

29. Ibid., 357–59.

30. "Resolution passed by Sixth Meeting of the First West Indies Conference held on the 31st January, 1929, at Barbados," CO 318/395/3, no. 66637, NA.

31. "Minutes of the Three Hundred and Sixtieth Meeting," May 21, 1935, in "Part I, Colonial Advisory Medical Committee, Minutes of Meetings Held During 1935," CO 885/44, no. 449, 18, NA.

32. For example, see no. 65, Robertson to the Secretary of State, February 11, 1932, 152, 153, and no. 69, Denham to the Secretary of State, November 17, 1931, 156, 157, both in "Part II, Correspondence, 1931, Relating to Medical and Health Matters," CO 885/33/4, no. 420, NA.

33. For example, see "Minutes of the Three Hundred and Sixty-third Meeting," October 15, 1935, in "Part I, Colonial Advisory Medical Committee, Minutes of Meetings Held During 1935," CO 885/44, no. 449, 31, NA.

34. On Blacklock, see Manderson, "Women and the State," 154, and Allen, *Managing Motherhood*, 19, 20, 21–25. And see Blacklock, "Co-operation in Health Education."

35. "[O'Brien] Obituary." Ittmann has described O'Brien as "play[ing] a critical role in the discussion of population issues, especially in the West Indies" ("Demography as Policy Science," 438, 439).

36. British Medical Association, "Medical Services in the West Indies," in WIRC, "BMA. Memorandum of Evidence," CO 950/888, 2, 17, NA. In the same report, see also WIRC, "Ninth Session Held in London on Friday the 12th May 1939," 1. In the 1930s, J. L. Gilks and D. G. Anderson visited the British Caribbean, where they had toured medical institutions and met government and medical officials. On Gilks, see Pedersen, "National Bodies," 657.

37. Malcolm MacDonald, "Note by the Colonial Secretary," in WIRC, "Dr. John Hutson, Memorandum of Evidence," CO 950/571, NA.

38. John Hutson, "Additional Memorandum to the West Indies Royal Commission, January 1939," in WIRC, "Dr. John Hutson, Memorandum of Evidence," 3, CO 950/571, NA.

39. British Medical Association, "Medical Services in the West Indies," in WIRC, "BMA. Memorandum of Evidence," CO 950/888, 2, 17, NA. In the same report, see also WIRC, "Ninth Session Held in London on Friday the 12th May 1939," 1.

40. BPP, "WIRC Report," 12, 136, 139, 154, 156, 434.

41. Ibid., 155–71.

42. A. J. R. Rushton, "Medical Services," in WIRC, "Medical Services. Colonial Office Memorandum," CO 950/47, 1, 2, 14, NA.

43. Ibid., 14–17, 39–43; see also "Witness: Dr. O'Brien," in WIRC, "Medical Services. Colonial Office Memorandum," CO 950/47, 56, NA.

44. Holt, *Problem of Freedom*, 392; La Guerre, "Moyne Commission," 62.

45. Stevens, 16/11/38, 11; Emmens, 16/11/38, 11, 12; Stevens memo, 15/12/38, 13; Richards to MacDonald, November 16, 1938, confidential, 22, all in CO 318/435/2, NA. See also Whittal, "Creolising London," 320.

46. Lloyd, September 16, 1938; Crowdy to Lloyd, September 17, 1938; Lloyd to Moody, September 20, 1938, all in League of Coloured Peoples, "Memorandum of Evidence," CO 950/30, n.p., NA.

47. Whittal, "Creolising London," 24, 22; Wahab, "Padmore, George," 358.

48. Killingray, "Blackman, Peter."

49. Sherwood, "Blackman, Peter McFarren."

50. Killingray, "'To Do Something for the Race,'" 51, 52. See also Rush, "Imperial Identity," on some of these points. See the International African Service Bureau, the League of Coloured Peoples, and the Negro Welfare Association, "Memorandum on the Economic, Political, and Social Conditions in the West Indies and British Guiana," CO 950/30, 19–21, 23, 26–28, NA.

51. Holt has noted that their recommendations "anticipated some aspects of development policy that the Colonial Office would initiate in later years by linking welfare services to economic development," notably in the area of medicine and health. See Holt, *Problem of Freedom*, 393.

52. "Recommendations of the Unemployment Committee of Bermuda," in "Bermuda. Birth Control," CO 37/282/9, no. 67544, NA. See also Ittmann, "Colonial Office and the Population Question," 66.

53. Waddington to Parkinson, September 12, 1935, in "Bermuda. Birth Control," CO 37/282/9, no. 67544, 10, NA. On Waddington, see Rotberg, *Black Heart*, 234.

54. MacDonald, August 1, 1935, in "Bermuda. Birth Control," CO 37/282/9, no. 67544, 15, NA.

55. MacDonald to Lady Astor, July 26, 1935, in "Bermuda. Birth Control," CO 37/282/9, no. 67544, 16, NA.

56. "British Governor Raises Storm by Declaration in Favour of Birth Control," December 18, 1936, in "Bermuda. Birth Control," CO 37/285/5, no. 67544, 36, NA. See also Ittmann, "Colonial Office and the Population Question," 66.

57. No. 106, draft telegram to the Governor of Bermuda, December 3, 1937, 36, 11, and telegram from the Governor of Bermuda, December 3, 1937, 36, 10, both in "Bermuda. Birth Control," CO 37/285/5, no. 67544, NA.

58. Alexander, "Bermuda Government to Sterilize Negroes." See "Editorial Board" in this issue as well as "For the Members." This publication was originally the *International Negro Worker's Review* before a name change in 1931. On the *Negro Worker*, see Campbell, "'Black Bolsheviks,'" 7. On Charles Alexander, see Solomon, *Cry Was Unity*, 109, 186.

59. The International African Service Bureau, the League of Coloured Peoples, and the Negro Welfare Association, "Memorandum on the Economic, Political, and Social Conditions in the West Indies and British Guiana," September 9, 1938, in League of Coloured Peoples, "Memorandum of Evidence," CO 950/30, 23, NA.

60. See Briggs, *Reproducing Empire*, 18, 110, 115. For a useful summary of some of this scholarship, see Bashford, "Nation, Empire, Globe," esp. 170–73.

61. Ittmann, "Colonial Office and the Population Question," 63. But see also BPP, "WIRC Report," 9–12.

62. BPP, "WIRC Report," 243.

63. Ibid., 244, 245.

64. P. Granville Edge, "Estimated Population in Certain British West Indian Colonies for the Years 1938 and 1950," in WIRC, "Medical Services. Population," CO 950/48, 1, NA. See Edge's 1937 article on this subject, "Demography of British Colonial Possessions."

65. P. Granville Edge, "Estimated Population in Certain British West Indian Colonies for the Years 1938 and 1950," 1, 2, and Edge to Lloyd, September 27, 1938, both in WIRC, "Medical Services. Population," CO 950/48, NA.

66. Edge to Lloyd, September 27, 1938, in WIRC, "Medical Services. Population," CO 950/48, NA.

67. O'Brien, "Medical Services," in WIRC, "Medical Services. Colonial Office Memorandum," CO 950/47, 55, 56, NA; BPP, "WIRC Report," 9, 389.

68. Wase-Bailey to the Colonial Secretary, March 23, 1940, encl. 2, in "Royal Commission Report, Medical and Public Health, Barbados," secret, CO 318/444/18, esp. 1–3, NA, but the whole report details the effects of overpopulation. On Wase-Bailey's background, see British Guiana, "Report of the Surgeon-General for the Year 1936," CO 114/223, 3, NA, and "Dr. Wase-Bailey Dies."

69. Waddington, "Extract from a Memorandum on the West India Royal Commission 1938–39," in "Royal Commission Report, Medical and Public Health, Barbados," secret, CO 318/444/18, 6, 7, NA.

70. Ibid., 6.

71. Ibid.

72. Ibid., 7.

73. Ittmann, "Colonial Office and the Population Question," 65.

74. Report of the Chief Medical Officer for the Year 1st April 1933 to 31st March 1934, 6, DABB.

75. BPP, "WIRC Report," 9–12.

76. Ibid., 220, 221.

77. Ibid.

78. Ibid., 220.

79. Ibid.

80. WIRC, "Eighth Session Held in Jamaica, 10th November, 1938, witness, Edith Clark," in WIRC, 1938–1939. Oral Evidence, Jamaica, CO 950/925, 2:66, NA.

81. Clarke, My Mother Who Fathered Me, 12. According to Pat McDonnough, "Biographical Note," 230, this book originated in Clarke's written submission to the Moyne Commission.

82. BPP, "WIRC Report," 220.

83. Amy Bailey, "The Illegitimacy Question: From the Top Down (1938–1939)," in Gregg, Caribbean Women, 148, excerpted from Amy Bailey, "Are We Satisfied?," pt. 3, Public Opinion, February 5, 1938.

84. Bailey, "This Illegitimacy Problem."

85. Ibid.

86. The commissioners noted that some witnesses argued that the legacy of slavery was a factor behind illegitimacy, something which they tended to dismiss. See BPP, "WIRC Report," 221. Bailey proposed slavery's legacy as an explanation in one of her publications; see Bailey, "This Illegitimacy Problem."

87. See BPP, "WIRC Report," 221, and Bailey, "This Illegitimacy Problem."

88. BPP, "WIRC Report," 245, 246.

89. Ibid., 244; Ittmann, "Colonial Office and the Population Question," 65, 66. The extent to which ideas about biological race colored some views is suggested by the recommendations offered by some Barbadians. Some of Hutson's "friends" told him to suggest to the commissions that "surplus" Barbadians should be sent to Liberia or the "'West Coast of Africa,'" a plan that he found "fantastic" and prohibitive. See Hutson, "Additional Memorandum," in WIRC, "Dr. John Hutson, Memorandum of Evidence," CO 950/571, 6, NA.

90. BPP, "WIRC Report," 245.

91. Ibid., 12.

92. Ibid., 246.

93. Ittmann, "Colonial Office and the Population Question," 64.

94. "Women Workers' Conference," NDC, June 24, 1927, 8.

95. "Transactions of the B. G. Branch of the British Medical Association for the Years 1925 to 1932," 133.

96. Ittmann, "Colonial Office and the Population Question," 66, 67.

97. See Bourbonnais's very interesting discussion of the Gleaner's role in discussions about birth control in Jamaica in this period, in "'Dangerously Large,'" 43, 44.

98. Amy Bailey, "Amy Bailey with Yvonne Grinam," DG, February 8, 15, 1990, from Gregg, Amy Bailey.

99. Bailey, "This Illegitimacy Problem."

100. Brodber, "Pioneering Miss Bailey," 10, 11. See also Ittmann, "Colonial Office and the Population Question," 58, 59, 66, 67.

Bibliography

Archival Sources

BARBADOS

Department of Archives, Bridgetown

Hutson, John. *Memories of a Long Life*. Barbados, 1948. Pam A 463.

Report of Commission on Poor Relief, Bridgetown, 1875–77. Pam C 72.

Report of the Women's Social Welfare League. 1937–38. Srl 258.

Reports of the Central Poor Law Board. 1883, 1888.

Reports of the Chief Medical Officer. 1929–37.

Reports of the Poor Law Inspector. 1883–1926.

Reports of the Public Health Inspector. 1914–28.

St. George Vestry Minute Books. 1892–1929. BS 82.

St. George Vestry Sanitary Commissioners Minute Books. 1907–59. BS 99.

GUYANA

National Archives of Guyana, Georgetown

Government Secretary's Despatches to the Secretary of State, January–June 1922

Minutes of Court of Policy

Minutes of Georgetown Town Council. 1916, 1917, 1921, 1923, 1925, 1928.

TRINIDAD AND TOBAGO

National Archives of Trinidad and Tobago, Port of Spain

Census of the Colony of Trinidad and Tobago, 1911. Trinidad, 1913.

Reports of the Surgeon General. 1903–4, 1906–7, 1912–13, 1918.

Reports of Medical Inspector of Health. 1918, 1919.

Seheult, R. "A Review of the Evolution of Health Services in Trinidad." February 1936.

———. *A Survey of the Trinidad Medical Service, 1814–1944*. Trinidad, 1948.

UNITED KINGDOM

Institute of Commonwealth Studies, London

Minutes of the British Guiana Combined Court. No. 344. *Report of the Commission Appointed to Enquire into and Report upon the General and Infantile Mortality*. 1906.

Report of the Proceedings of the West Indian Medical Conference, 1921. Georgetown: "The Argosy" Co., 1921.

London School of Hygiene and Tropical Medicine

Annual Reports on the Public Health and Sanitation of the City of Kingston, Jamaica. 1905, 1908, 1909, 1911, 1918, 1919, 1920.

Barbados Infant Mortality Report, 1905. Barbados 132. EL 755.

Crosswell, L. Oliver. "Infantile Mortality." In Earle and Crosswell, Jamaica Public Health Bulletin, 1917, 46–50.

Crosswell, L. Oliver, and E. R. C. Earle. "Preface." In Earle and Crosswell, Jamaica Public Health Bulletin, 1917.

Earle, Edward R. "Mortality Amongst Infants and Children in Jamaica." In Earle and Crosswell, Jamaica Public Health Bulletin, 1917, 107–18.

Earle, Edward R., and L. Oliver Crosswell, eds. The Jamaica Public Health Bulletin, 1917. Kingston: Times Printery, 1918.

Howard, H. H. "Pre-Natal Hookworm Infection." In Earle and Crosswell, Jamaica Public Health Bulletin, 1917, 21–24.

Leiper Archive

Medical Reports for St. Vincent. 1912–13.

Proceedings of the First West Indian Intercolonial Tuberculosis Conference Held in Trinidad, March 1913. Trinidad, 1913. P21950.

Public Health Reports for Georgetown, British Guiana (Guyana). 1913–35.

Report of the Medical Officer, St. Vincent, for the Year 1912–13.

Reports of Infant Welfare and Maternity League of British Guiana.

Reports of the British Guiana Baby Saving League.

Ross Archives

National Archives, London

CO 28, CO 111, CO 114, CO 137, CO 140, CO 295, CO 318, CO 854, CO 884, CO 885, CO 950, CO 1069

School of Oriental and African Studies, London

LMS Incoming Letters—West Indies (with British Guiana). 1900–1908. Box 2, folder West Indies 1907.

UNITED STATES

College of Physicians of Philadelphia, The Historical Library and Wood Institute, Philadelphia, Pa.

Journal Supplement of the Royal Sanitary Institute 42 (1921–22), FCWI.

Journal Supplement of the Royal Sanitary Institute 43 (1922–23), FCWI.

New York Academy of Medicine, New York, N.Y.

"College of Physicians and Surgeons of Jamaica." Jamaica Physical Journal, June 7, 1834, 377–84.

Milroy, Gavin. Report on the Cholera in Jamaica. 1853.

"The Salubrity of Kingston." Jamaica Physical Journal, May 3, 1834, 312–13.

Rockefeller Foundation Archives, Tarrytown, N.Y.

British Guiana Correspondence, 1915 & earlier. Folder 168, box 11, series 431, record group 5, ss 2, RF-RAC.

Printed/Digital Government Reports

Balfour, David, comp. *Census of Jamaica and Its Dependencies, 1921.* Jamaica: Government Printing Office, 1922.

———. *Census of Jamaica and Its Dependencies Taken on the 3rd April, 1911.* Jamaica: Government Printing Office, 1912.

Boyce, E. P., comp. *The Census of Barbados, 1911.* Barbados: T. K. King & Co., n.d.

Clark, Henry James, comp. *Census of the Colony of Trinidad, 1891.* Trinidad: Port-of-Spain, 1892.

Jamaica Archives and Record Department, Ministry of Youth, Sports, and Culture. Island Records Office-I.R.O. (1B/11), http://archives.jard.gov.jm/our-collections/historical-collections/public-central-records/administrative.html. Accessed June 20, 2011.

Lawance, C. J. *The Census of Barbados (1881–91).* Barbados: T. E. King & Co., n.d.

Leeward Islands. *Census 1891. With Tabular Statements and Report.* 1892. Trinidad: Central Statistical Office, 1964.

Lofty, Henry W., comp. *Report on the Census of Barbados, 1921.* Barbados: Advocate Co., n.d.

Nunan, Joseph. *The Laws of British Guiana (1803 to 1921).* Vol. 3. London: Waterlow & Sons Limited, 1923.

Report on the Results of the Census of the Population, 1911 [British Guiana]. Georgetown: Argosy Co., 1912.

Report on the Results of the Census of the Population, 1921 [British Guiana]. Georgetown: Argosy Co., 1921.

United Kingdom. *Hansard Parliamentary Debates* (online). "Slave Trade Abolition Bill." February 5, 1807, vol. 8, cc657–72, http://hansard.millbanksystems.com/lords/1807/feb/05/slave-trade-abolition-bill. Accessed June 8, 2012.

———. *Hansard Parliamentary Debates* (online). "Slave Trade Abolition Bill." February 23, 1807, vol. 8, cc945–95, http://hansard.millbanksystems.com/lords/1807/feb/05/slave-trade-abolition-bill. Accessed June 8, 2012.

United Kingdom. House of Commons. "Copies of the Last Census of the Population taken in each of the British West India Islands and in British Guiana." 1845 (426) XXXI.329. *British Parliamentary Papers.* House of Commons Parliamentary Papers Online, 2005.

———. "Papers Relative to the West Indies, 1841. British Guiana." 1841. Session 1 [321] (1). *British Parliamentary Papers.* House of Commons Parliamentary Papers Online, 2005.

———. "Report by the Honourable E. F. L. Wood on his Visit to the West Indies and British Guiana. December, 1921–February, 1922." *British Parliamentary Papers.* 1922. Cmd. 1679 xvi: 355.

———. "Report from the Select Committee on Negro Apprenticeship in the Colonies; Together with the Minutes of Evidence." 1836 (560). *British Parliamentary Papers.* House of Commons Parliamentary Papers Online, 2008.

———. "Report from the Select Committee on West India Colonies Together with the Minutes of Evidence, Appendix and Index." 1842 (479). *British Parliamentary Papers.* House of Commons Parliamentary Papers Online, 2005.

———. "Report of the West India Royal Commission." *British Parliamentary Papers.* 1898 [C8655]. House of Commons Parliamentary Papers Online, 2006.

———. "Report of the West India Royal Commission, Appendix C, Vol. II, containing Parts II, III, IV, and V, Proceedings, Evidence, and Documents Relating to British Guiana, Barbados, Trinidad, and Tobago." *British Parliamentary Papers.* 1898 [C8657]. House of Commons Parliamentary Papers Online, 2006.

———. "Report of the West India Royal Commission, Appendix C, Vol. III, Containing Parts VI to XIII, Proceedings, Evidence, and Documents Relating to the Windward Islands, the Leeward Islands, and Jamaica." *British Parliamentary Papers.* 1898 [C8669]. House of Commons Parliamentary Papers Online, 2006.

———. "Report of the West India Royal Commission, Appendix C, Vol. III, parts VI to XIII." *British Parliamentary Papers.* 1897 [C8656]. House of Commons Parliamentary Papers Online, 2006.

———. "Sugar Growing Colonies. Copies or Extracts of any Recent Correspondence between the Secretary of State and the Governors of the Sugar Growing Colonies, as to the Distress now existing in those Colonies, not already laid before the House." *British Parliamentary Papers.* 1847–48 (749). House of Commons Parliamentary Papers Online, 2005.

———. "West India Royal Commission Report, 1944–45." *British Parliamentary Papers.* [Cmd. 6607]. House of Commons Parliamentary Papers Online, 2006.

Newspapers

Daily Argosy
Daily Chronicle
Daily Gleaner

Books, Articles, Dissertations, Theses, and Manuscripts

Adamson, Alan. *Sugar without Slaves: The Political Economy of British Guiana, 1838–1904.* New Haven: Yale University Press, 1972.

Adderley, Rosanne Marion. *"New Negroes from Africa": Slave Trade, Abolition, and Free African Settlement in the Nineteenth-Century Caribbean.* Bloomington: Indiana University Press, 2006.

Alexander, Charles. "Bermuda Government to Sterilize Negroes." *Negro Worker* 7, no. 2 (February 1937): 7, 10.

Allen, Denise Roth. *Managing Motherhood, Managing Risk: Fertility and Danger in West Central Tanzania.* Ann Arbor: University of Michigan Press, 2002.

Allman, Jean. "Making Mothers: Missionaries, Medical Officers and Women's Work in Colonial Asante, 1924–1945." *History Workshop Journal* 38 (Autumn 1994): 23–47.

Altink, Henrice. "'I Did Not Want to Face the Shame of Exposure': Gender Ideologies and Child Murder in Post-Emancipation Jamaica." *Journal of Social History* 41, no. 2 (Winter 2007): 355–87.

———. "'The Misfortune of Being Black and Female': Black Feminist Thought in Interwar Jamaica." *Thirdspace: A Journal of Feminist Theory and Culture* 5, no. 2 (Winter 2006): n.p. http://www.thirdspace.ca/journal/article/view/altink. Accessed February 9, 2013.

———. "'To Wed or Not to Wed?': The Struggle to Define Afro-Jamaican Relationships, 1834–1838." *Journal of Social History* 38, no. 1 (Fall 2004): 81–111.

———. "A True Maverick: The Political Career of Dr. Oswald E. Anderson, 1914–1944." *New West Indian Guide* 87, nos. 3 & 4 (2013), forthcoming.

———. "'We Are Equal to Men in Ability to Do Anything!' African Jamaican Women and Citizenship in the Interwar Years." In *Women's Activism: Global Perspectives from the 1890s to the Present*, edited by Francisca de Haan, Margaret Allen, June Purvis, and Krassimira Daskolova, 77–89. New York: Routledge, 2013.

Anderson, Benedict. *Imagined Communities: Reflections on the Origin and Spread of Nationalism*. London: Verso, 2003.

Anderson, Warwick. *Colonial Pathologies: American Tropical Medicine, Race, and Hygiene in the Philippines*. Durham: Duke University Press, 2006.

———. "Going through the Motions: American Public Health and Colonial 'Mimicry.'" *American Literary History* 14, no. 4 (2002): 686–719.

———. "Immunities of Empire: Race, Disease, and the New Tropical Medicine, 1900–1920." *Bulletin of the History of Medicine* 70, no. 1 (1996): 94–118.

———. "The Trespass Speaks: White Masculinity and Colonial Breakdown." *American Historical Review* 102, no. 5 (December 1997): 1343–70.

Arnold, David. "'An Ancient Race Outworn': Malaria and Race in Colonial India, 1860–1930." In *Race, Science, and Medicine, 1900–1960*, edited by Waltraud Ernst and Bernard Harris, 123–43. London: Routledge, 1999.

———. *Colonizing the Body: State Medicine and Epidemic Disease in Nineteenth-Century India*. Berkeley: University of California Press, 1993.

———, ed. *Imperial Medicine and Indigenous Societies*. Manchester: Manchester University Press, 1988.

———. *Warm Climates and Western Medicine: The Emergence of Tropical Medicine, 1500–1900*. Amsterdam: Rodopi, 1996.

"Association Intelligence." *British Medical Journal* 1, no. 1466 (February 2, 1889): 261–66.

Atkins, P. J. "White Poison? The Social Consequences of Milk Consumption, 1850–1930." *Social History of Medicine* 5, no. 2 (1992): 207–27.

August, Thomas G. "An Historical Profile of the Jewish Community of Jamaica." *Jewish Social Studies* 49, no. 3/4 (Summer/Autumn 1987): 303–16.

Bailey, Amy. "This Illegitimacy Problem." *Public Opinion*, July 9, 1938, 10–11. Reprinted in *Amy Bailey JamaicaWriting*, by Veronica M. Gregg. https://sites.google.com/site/amybaileyjamaicawriting/home. Accessed February 13, 2013.

Balfour, Andrew. "The Tropical Field for Medical Women: Its Possibilities for Medical Women." *Journal of Tropical Medicine and Hygiene* 31, no. 21 (November 1, 1928): 1–21.

———. "Why Hygiene Pays." *British Medical Journal* 1, no. 3413 (June 5, 1926): 929–32.

Balfour, Andrew, and Henry Scott. *Health Problems of the Empire*. New York: Henry Holt, 1924.

Banton, Mandy. *Administering the Empire, 1801–1968: A Guide to the Records of the Colonial Office in the National Archives of the UK*. London: Institute of Historical Research, 2008.

The Barbados Almanac and Directory for the Year 1882. Bridgetown: Bowen and Sons, 1882.

The Barbados Almanac for the Year 1865. Barbados, 1865.

Barrow, Christine. "'Living in Sin': Church and Common-Law Union in Barbados." *Journal of Caribbean History* 29, no. 2 (1995): 47–70.

Bashford, Alison. "Nation, Empire, Globe: The Spaces of Population Debate in the Interwar Years." *Comparative Studies in Society and History* 49, no. 1 (January 2007): 170–201.

Bashford, Alison, and Philippa Levine. "Introduction." In *The Oxford Handbook of the History of Eugenics*, edited by Alison Bashford and Philippa Levine, 3–24. Oxford: Oxford University Press, 2010.

Bayley, George D., ed. and comp. *The Handbook of British Guiana, 1909*. London: Dulau & Co., 1909.

Beckles, Hilary. *Centering Woman: Gender Discourses in Caribbean Slave Society*. Kingston: Ian Randle, 1999.

———. *Great House Rules: Landless Emancipation and Workers' Protest in Barbados, 1838–1938*. Kingston: Ian Randle, 2004.

———. *A History of Barbados*. Cambridge: Cambridge University Press, 1990.

Beckwith, Martha. *Jamaican Folklore*. 1928. Reprint, New York: American Folklore Society, 1966.

———. *Notes on Jamaican Ethnobotany*. New York: Vassar College, 1927.

Bell, Heather. "Midwifery Training and Female Circumcision in the Inter-War Anglo-Egyptian Sudan." *Journal of African History* 39 (1998): 293–312.

Bell, Hesketh J. *Obeah: Witchcraft in the West Indies*. 1889. Reprint, Westport: Negro Universities Press, 1970.

Belle, George. "The Abortive Revolution of 1876 in Barbados." In *Caribbean Freedom: Economy and Society from Emancipation to the Present*, edited by Hilary Beckles and Verene Shepherd, 181–91. Kingston: Ian Randle, 1993.

Besson, Jean. *Martha Brae's Two Histories: European Expansion and Caribbean Culture-Building in Jamaica*. Chapel Hill: University of North Carolina Press, 2002.

———. "Reputation and Respectability Reconsidered: A New Perspective on Afro-Caribbean Peasant Women." In *Women and Change in the Caribbean: A Pan-Caribbean Perspective*, edited by Janet Momsen, 15–37. Kingston: Ian Randle, 1993.

Birbalsingh, Frank M. "H. G. de Lisser." In *Dictionary of Literary Biography*. Vol. 117, *Twentieth-Century Caribbean and Black African Writers*, edited by B. Lindfors and R. Sander, 141–49. Detroit: Gale Research International, 1992.

Birkett, Dea. "The 'White Woman's Burden' in the 'White Man's Grave': The Introduction of British Nurses in Colonial West Africa." In *Western Women and Imperialism: Complicity and Resistance*, edited by Nupur Chaudhuri and Margaret Strobel, 177–88. Bloomington: Indiana University Press, 1992.

Birn, Anne-Emanuelle. "Child Health in Latin America: Historiographic Perspectives and Challenges." *História, Ciências, Saúde* 14, no. 3 (July–September 2007): 677–708.

———. "Historiography of Infant and Child Health in Latin America." In *Healing the World's Children: Interdisciplinary Perspectives on Child Health in the Twentieth Century*, edited by Cynthia Comacchio, Janet Golden, and George Weisz, 74–108. Montreal-Kingston: McGill-Queen's University Press, 2008.

———. "'No More Surprising Than a Broken Pitcher?' Maternal and Child Health in the Early Years of the Pan American Sanitary Health." *Canadian Bulletin of Medical History* 19, no. 1 (2002): 17–46.

Blacklock, Mary. "Certain Aspect of the Welfare of Women and Children in the Colonies." *Tropical Medicine and Parasitology* 30 (1936): 221–64.

———. "Co-operation in Health Education." *Africa: Journal of the International African Institute* 4, no. 2 (April 1931): 202–8.

Boa, Sheen. "Experiences of Women Estate Workers during the Apprenticeship Period in St. Vincent, 1834–38." *Women's History Review* 10, no. 3 (2001): 381–408.

Bolland, O. Nigel. "Historical Commentaries: British Honduras (Belize)." In *The Marcus Garvey and Universal Negro Improvement Association Papers*. Vol. 11, *The Caribbean Diaspora, 1910–1920*, edited by Robert Hill, clxxv–clxxx. Durham: Duke University Press, 2011.

———. *On the March: Labour Rebellions in the British Caribbean, 1934–39*. Kingston: Ian Randle, 1995.

———. *The Politics of Labour in the British Caribbean: The Social Origins of Authoritarianism and Democracy in the Labour Movement*. Kingston: Ian Randle, 2001.

———. "Reply to William A. Green's 'The Perils of Comparative History.'" *Comparative Studies in Society and History* 26, no. 1 (January 1984): 120–25.

———. "Systems of Domination after Slavery: The Control of Land and Labor in the British West Indies after 1838." *Comparative Studies in Society and History* 23, no. 4 (October 1981): 591–619.

Bolt, Christine. *Victorian Attitudes towards Race*. London: Routledge & Kegan Paul, 1971.

Bonner, Robert E. "Slavery, Confederate Diplomacy, and the Racialist Mission of Henry Hotze." *Civil War History* 51, no. 3 (September 2005): 288–316.

Boris, Eileen. "The Power of Motherhood: Black and White Activist Women Redefine the 'Political.'" In *Mothers of a New World: Maternalist Politics and the Origins of Welfare States*, edited by Seth Koven and Sonya Michel, 213–45. New York: Routledge, 1993.

Bourbonnais, Nicole. "'Dangerously Large': The 1938 Labor Rebellion and the Debate over Birth Control in Jamaica." *New West Indian Guide/Nieuwe West-Indische Gids* 38, nos. 1 & 2 (2009): 37–68.

Boyce, Rupert W. *Health Progress and Administration in the West Indies*. New York: E. P. Dutton, 1910.

Bradley, James, Anne Crowther, and Marguerite Dupree. "Mobility and Selection in Scottish University Education, 1858–1886." *Medical History* 40 (1996): 1–24.

Brantlinger, Patrick. *Dark Vanishings: Discourse on the Extinction of Primitive Races, 1800–1930*. Ithaca: Cornell University Press, 2003.

Brereton, Bridget. "Family Strategies, Gender, and the Shift to Wage Labor in the British Caribbean." In *Gender and Slave Emancipation in the Atlantic World*, edited by Pamela Scully and Diana Paton, 143–61. Durham: Duke University Press, 2005.

———. "General Problems and Issues in Studying the History of Women." In *Gender in Caribbean Development*, edited by Patricia Mohammed and Catherine Shepherd, 123–41. Kingston: Canoe Press, 1999.

———. *A History of Modern Trinidad, 1783–1962*. Kingston: Heinemann Educational (Caribbean) Books, 1981.

———. *Race Relations in Colonial Trinidad, 1870–1900*. 1979. Reprint, Cambridge: Cambridge University Press, 2002.

———. "Society and Culture in the Caribbean: The British and French West Indies, 1870–1980." In *The Modern Caribbean*, edited by Franklin W. Knight and Colin A. Palmer, 81–110. Chapel Hill: University of North Carolina Press, 1989.

———. "The White Elite of Trinidad, 1838–1950." In *The White Minority in the Caribbean*, edited by Howard Johnson and Karl Watson, 32–70. Kingston: Ian Randle, 1980.

Brereton, Bridget, and Terecita Martinez-Vergne, eds. *General History of the Caribbean*. Vol. 5, *The Caribbean in the Twentieth Century*. London: Macmillan Education/ UNESCO, 2004.

Briggs, Charles L., with Clara Mantini-Briggs. *Stories in the Time of Cholera: Racial Profiling during a Medical Nightmare*. Berkeley: University of California Press, 2003.

Briggs, Laura. *Reproducing Empire: Race, Sex, Science, and U.S. Imperialism in Puerto Rico*. Berkeley: University of California Press, 2002.

"The British Guiana Medical and Hospital Reports." *British Medical Journal* 2, no. 1565 (December 27, 1890): 1483.

"The British Guiana Medical Annual and Hospital Reports." *British Medical Journal* 2, no. 1715 (November 11, 1893): 1054.

Brodber, Erna. "The Pioneering Miss Bailey." *Jamaican Journal* 19, no. 2 (1986): 9–14.

Bronkhurst, H. V. P. *The Colony of British Guyana and Its Labouring Population*. London, 1883.

Brown, Laurence. "Experiments in Indenture: Barbados and the Segmentation of Migrant Labor in the Caribbean, 1863–1865." *New West Indian Guide/Nieuwe West Indische Gids* 79, nos. 1 & 2 (2006): 31–54.

Brown, Laurence, and Tara Inniss. "Family Strategies and the Transition to Freedom in Barbados." In *Women and Slavery: The Modern Atlantic*, vol. 2, edited by Gwyn Campbell, Suzanne Miers, and Joseph C. Miller, 172–85. Athens: Ohio University Press, 2008.

Brown, Vincent. "Spiritual Terror and Sacred Authority in Jamaican Slave Society." *Slavery and Abolition* 24, no. 1 (April 2003): 24–53.

Browne, David V. C. "The 1937 Disturbances and Barbadian Nationalism." In *The Empowering Impulse: The Nationalist Tradition of Barbados*, edited by Glenford D. Howe and Don D. Marshall, 149–64. Kingston: Canoe Press, University of the West Indies, 2001.

Brunton, Lauder. "The Report of the Inter-Departmental Committee on Physical Degeneration." *Public Health* 17 (1904): 274–92.

Bryan, Patrick. *The Jamaican People, 1880–1902*. London: Macmillan, 1991.

———. *Philanthropy and Social Welfare in Jamaica: A Historical Survey*. Mona: Institute of Social and Economic Research, University of the West Indies, 1990.

Bulmer-Thomas, Victor. *The Economic History of the Caribbean since the Napoleonic Wars*. Cambridge: Cambridge University Press, 2012.

Burton, Antoinette. *Burdens of History: British Feminists, Indian Women, and Imperial Culture, 1865–1915*. Chapel Hill: University of North Carolina Press, 1994.

———. "The White Woman's Burden: British Feminists and the Indian Woman, 1865–1915." *Women's Studies International Forum* 13, no. 4 (1990): 295–308.

Bush, Barbara. "Hard Labor: Women, Childbirth, and Resistance in British Caribbean Slave Societies." In *More Than Chattel: Black Women and Slavery in the Americas*, edited by David Barry Gaspar and Darlene Clark Hine, 193–217. Bloomington: Indiana University Press, 1996.

———. "Hard Labor: Women, Childbirth, and Resistance in Caribbean Slave Societies." *History Workshop Journal* 36 (Autumn 1993): 83–99.

Buxton, Charles. *Slavery and Freedom in the British West Indies*. London: Green, Longman and Roberts, 1860.

Campbell, Susan. "'Black Bolsheviks' and Recognition of African-America's Right to Self-Determination by the Communist Party, USA." *Science and Society* 58, no. 4 (Winter 1994): 1–18.

Capadose, Henry. *Sixteen Years in the West Indies*. Vol. 2. London: T. C. Newby, 1845.

Carlyle, Thomas. "Occasional Discourses on the Negro Question." *Fraser's Magazine*, December 1849, 670–79.

Carnegie, Charles V. "The Fate of Ethnography: Native Social Science in the English-Speaking Caribbean." *New West Indian Guide/Nieuwe West-Indische Gids* 66, nos. 1 & 2 (1992): 5–25.

Carrillo, Ana María, and Anne-Emanuelle Birn. "Neighbours on Notice: National and Imperialist Interests in the American Public Health Association, 1872–1921." *Canadian Bulletin of Medical History* 25, no. 1 (2008): 225–54.

Carter, Alvin. "The 1854 Cholera Epidemic." *Journal of the Barbados Museum and Historical Society* 38, no. 4 (1990): 376–421.

Cassedy, James H. "Hygeia: A Mid-Victorian Dream of a City of Health." *Journal of the History of Medicine and Allied Sciences* 17, no. 2 (1962): 217–28.

Cateau, Heather. "The Crisis of the Plantation." Pt. 2, "The Years after Emancipation." In *General History of the Caribbean*. Vol. 4, *The Long Nineteenth Century: Nineteenth-Century Transformations*, edited by K. O. Laurence, 85–103. London: Macmillan Education/UNESCO, 2011.

Chace, Russell. "Protest in Post-Emancipation Dominica: The 'Guerre Negre' of 1844." *Journal of Caribbean History* 23, no. 2 (1989): 118–41.

Challenger, Denise. "A Benign Place of Healing? The Contagious Hospital and Medical Discipline in Post-Slavery Barbados." In *Health and Medicine in the Circum-Caribbean, 1800–1968*, edited by Juanita De Barros, Steven Palmer, and David Wright, 98–120. New York: Routledge, 2009.

Chamberlain, Mary. "Small Worlds: Childhood and Empire." *Journal of Family History* 27, no. 2 (April 2002): 189–92.

Charlton, Christopher. "The National Health Society Almanack, 1883." *Local Population Studies* 32 (Spring 1984): 268–85.

Chomsky, Avi. "Afro-Jamaican Traditions and Labor Organizing on United Fruit Company Plantations in Costa Rica, 1910." *Journal of Social History* 29, no. 4 (Summer 1995): 837–55.

Christopher, A. J. "The Quest for a Census of the British Empire." *Journal of Historical Geography* 34, no. 2 (2008): 54–57.

Clark, Anna. *The Struggle for the Breeches: Gender and the Making of the British Working Class.* Berkeley: University of California Press, 1995.

Clarke, Edith. *My Mother Who Fathered Me: A Study of the Families in Three Selected Communities of Jamaica.* 1957. Reprint, Kingston: University of the West Indies Press, 1999.

Clayton, Nichola. "Managing the Transition to a Free Labor Society: American Interpretations of the British West Indies during the Civil War and Reconstruction." *American Nineteenth Century History* 7, no. 1 (2006): 89–108.

Clover, David. "The West Indian Club Ltd.: An Early 20th Century West Indian Interest in London." In *The Society for Caribbean Studies Annual Conference Papers* 8 (2007), edited by Sandra Courtman, 1–10. http://www.caribbeanstudies.org.uk/papers/vo18.htm. Accessed May 15, 2013.

Conklin, Alice L. *A Mission to Civilize: The Republican Idea of Empire in France and West Africa, 1895–1930.* Stanford: Stanford University Press, 1997.

Constantine, Stephen. *The Making of British Colonial Development Policy, 1914–1940.* London: Frank Cass, 1984.

Cook, Gordon C. *Caribbean Diseases: Doctor George Low's Expedition in 1901–02.* Oxon: Radcliffe Publishing, 2009.

Cooper, Frederick. "African Workers and Imperial Designs." In *Black Experience and the Empire,* edited by Philip D. Morgan and Sean Hawkins, 286–316. Oxford: Oxford University Press, 2004.

Cordell, Dennis D., Karl Ittmann, and Gregory H. Maddox. "Counting Subjects: Demography and Empire." In *The Demographics of Empire: The Colonial Order and the Creation of Knowledge,* edited by Karl Ittmann, Dennis D. Cordell, and Gregory H. Maddox, 1–21. Athens: Ohio University Press, 2010.

Craigen, A. J. "The Hospitals of British Guiana and Their Administration." In *Report of the Proceedings of the West Indian Medical Conference, 1921,* 16–18. Georgetown: "The Argosy" Co., 1921.

———. "Practice of Midwifery at the Public Hospital, Georgetown." *British Guiana Medical Annual* 17 (1910): 25–33.

———. Untitled talk in "Transactions of the British Guiana Branch of the British Medical Association, for 1913 and 1914." *British Guiana Medical Annual for 1913* 20 (1913): 131–41.

Craton, Michael. "Continuity Not Change: The Incidence of Unrest among Ex-slaves in the British West Indies, 1838–1876." In *Caribbean Freedom: Economy and Society from Emancipation to the Present,* edited by Hilary Beckles and Verene Shepherd, 192–206. Kingston: Ian Randle, 1993.

———. "Death, Disease and Medicine on the Jamaican Slave Plantations: The Example of Worthy Park, 1767–1838." In *Caribbean Slave Society and Economy,* edited by Hilary Beckles and Verene Shepherd, 183–96. Kingston: Ian Randle, 1991.

Craven, Christa, and Mara Glatzel. "Downplaying Difference: Historical Accounts of African American Midwives and Contemporary Struggles for Midwifery." *Feminist Studies* 36, no. 2 (Summer 2010): 330–58.

Crichton-Browne, James. "Obituary, Sir David Palmer Ross." *British Medical Journal* 1, no. 2269 (June 25, 1904): 1519.

Crozier, Anna. *Practising Colonial Medicine: The Colonial Medical Service in British East Africa.* London: I. B. Tauris & Co., 2007.

Cruickshank, J. Graham. *Black Talk; Being Notes on Negro Dialect in British Guiana with (Inevitably) a Chapter on the Vernacular of Barbados.* Demerara: "The Argosy" Co., 1916.

Cudjoe, Selwyn R. *Caribbean Visionary: A. R. F. Webber and the Making of the Guyanese Nation.* Jackson: University of Mississippi Press, 2009.

Cundall, Frank. *The Handbook of Jamaica for 1920.* Kingston: Government Printing Office, 1920.

———. *The Handbook of Jamaica for 1931.* Kingston: Government Printing Office, 1931.

Curtin, Philip D. *Death by Migration: Europe's Encounter with the Tropical World in the Nineteenth Century.* Cambridge: Cambridge University Press, 1989.

Dabydeen, David, John Gilmore, and Cecily Jones, eds. *The Oxford Companion to Black British History.* Oxford: Oxford University Press, 2007.

Dance, Charles Daniel. *Chapters from a Guianese Log-Book.* Georgetown, 1881.

Daniels, C. W. "Correspondence. The Malaria Parasite." *British Medical Journal* 2, no. 1817 (October 26, 1895): 1062–63.

———. "Notes on Malaria and Other Tropical Diseases." *British Guiana Medical Annual* 12 (1902): 40–46.

Davies, Celia, "The Health Visitor as Mother's Friend: A Woman's Place in Public Health, 1900–14." *Social History of Medicine* 1, no. 1 (1988): 39–59.

Davin, Anna. "Imperialism and Motherhood." *History Workshop Journal* 5 (Spring 1978): 9–65.

Davis, David Brion. *The Problem of Slavery in the Age of Revolution, 1770–1823.* 1975. Reprint, Oxford: Oxford University Press, 1999.

Davis, Gayle. "Stillbirth Registration and Perceptions of Infant Death, 1900–60: The Scottish Case in National Context." *Economic History Review* 62, no. 3 (2009): 629–54.

Davis, Kingsley. "Introduction." In *The Population of Jamaica,* by G. W. Roberts, xvii–xxii. Cambridge: Conservation Foundation at the University Press, 1957.

Dayton, Cornelia H., and Lisa Levenstein. "The Big Tent of U.S. Women's and Gender History: A State of the Field." *Journal of American History* 99, no. 3 (December 2012): 793–817.

Deacon, Harriet. "Midwives and Medical Men in the Cape Colony before 1860." *Journal of African History* 39 (1998): 271–92.

De Barros, Juanita. "Congregationalism and Afro-Guianese Autonomy." In *Nation Dance: Religion, Identity, and Cultural Difference in the Caribbean,* edited by Patrick Taylor, 89–103. Bloomington: Indiana University Press, 2001.

———. "Dispensers, Obeah, and Quackery: Medical Rivalries in Post-Slavery British Guiana." *Social History of Medicine* 20, no. 2 (2007): 243–61.

———. "'A Laudable Experiment': Infant Welfare Work and Medical Intermediaries in Early Twentieth-Century Barbados." In *Public Health in the British Empire: Intermediaries, Subordinates, and the Practice of Public Health, 1850–1960,* edited by Ryan Johnson and Amna Khalid, 100–117. New York: Routledge, 2012.

———. *Order and Place in a Colonial City: Patterns of Struggle and Resistance in Georgetown, British Guiana, 1889–1924.* Montreal-Kingston: McGill-Queen's University Press, 2002.

———. "Sanitation and Civilization in Georgetown, British Guiana." *Caribbean Quarterly* 49, no. 4 (December 2003): 65–86.

———. "'Setting Things Right': Medicine and Magic in British Guiana, 1803–1834." *Slavery and Abolition* 25, no. 1 (April 2004): 28–50.

———. "'Spreading Sanitary Enlightenment': Race, Identity, and the Emergence of a Creole Medical Profession in British Guiana." *Journal of British Studies* 42, no. 4 (October 2003): 483–504.

———. "'To Milk or Not to Milk': Regulation of the Milk Industry in Colonial Georgetown." *Journal of Caribbean History* 31, nos. 1 & 2 (1997): 36–53.

De Barros, Juanita, Steven Palmer, and David Wright, eds. *Health and Medicine in the Circum-Caribbean, 1800–1968.* New York: Routledge, 2009.

De Brouwere, Vincent. "The Comparative Study of Maternal Mortality over Time: The Role of the Professionalisation of Childbirth." *Social History of Medicine* 20, no. 3 (2007): 541–62.

Deerr, Noel. *The History of Sugar.* 2 vols. London: Chapman, 1949.

De Freitas, Q. B. "A Retrospect of Medical Practice in British Guiana, 1900–1935." *British Guiana Medical Annual* (1936): 148–52.

———. "Review of the Salient Stages in the Medical History of the Colony from 1900 to 1944." *Timehri* 26 (1944): 61–65.

Devitt, Neal. "The Statistical Case for the Elimination of the Midwife: Fact versus Prejudice, 1890–1935." Pt. 1. *Women and Health* 4 (1979): 81–96.

Dias, Francis. "Our Place in Guiana: The Portuguese." In *The British Guiana Centenary Year Book, Commemorating the Union of the Three Colonies of Demerara, Berbice, and Essequibo into the Constitution of British Guiana, 1831–1931,* edited by E. Sievewright Stoby. Georgetown: *Daily Chronicle,* 1931. Reprinted in "Glimpses of Guyanese History," *Stabroek News,* December 10, 2008. http://www.stabroeknews. com/2008/guyana-review/12/10/glimpses-of-guyanese-history-2/. Accessed April 7, 2013.

Downes, Aviston D. "From Boys to Men: Colonial Education, Cricket and Masculinity in the Caribbean, 1870–c. 1920." *International Journal of the History of Sport* 22, no. 1 (January 2005): 3–21.

"Dr. Wase-Bailey Dies." *Barbados Advocate,* August 4, 1951, 5. http://ufdc.ufl.edu/ UF00098964/02649.

Drescher, Seymour. *Capitalism and Antislavery: British Mobilization in Comparative Perspective.* 1986. Reprint, New York: Oxford University Press, 1987.

———. *Econocide: British Slavery in the Era of Abolition.* Pittsburgh: University of Pittsburgh Press, 1977.

———. *The Mighty Experiment: Free Labor versus Slavery in British Emancipation.* Oxford: Oxford University Press, 2002.

Dumett, Raymond E. "The Campaign against Malaria and the Expansion of Scientific Medical and Sanitary Services in British West Africa, 1898–1910." *African Historical Studies* 1, no. 2 (1968): 153–97.

Dumont, Jacques. "Health in the French Antilles: The Impact of the First World War." In *Health and Medicine in the Circum-Caribbean, 1800–1968,* edited by Juanita De Barros, Steven Palmer, and David Wright, 195–210. New York: Routledge, 2009.

Dwork, Debòrah. "Childhood." In *Companion Encyclopaedia of the History of Medicine*, vol. 2, edited by W. F. Bynum and Roy Porter, 1072–91. London: Routledge, 1993.

———. "The Milk Option: An Aspect of the History of the Infant Welfare Movement in England, 1898–1908." *Medical History* 31 (1987): 51–69.

———. *War Is Good for Babies and Other Young Children: A History of the Infant and Child Welfare Movement in England, 1898–1918*. London: Tavistock, 1987.

Edge, P. Granville. "The Demography of British Colonial Possessions: A Note on the Assembly and Interpretation of Data." *Journal of the Royal Statistical Society* C, pt. 2 (1937): 182–231.

Elston, M. A. "Fairfield, (Josephine) Letitia Denny." In *Oxford Dictionary of National Biography*. Oxford: Oxford University Press, 2004. http://www.oxforddnb.com. libaccess.lib.mcmaster.ca/view/article/54196. Accessed April 23, 2013.

Eltis, David. "Abolitionist Perceptions of Society after Slavery." In *Slavery and British Society, 1776–1846*, edited by James Walvin, 195–213. Baton Rouge: Louisiana State University Press, 1982.

Ernst, Waltraud. "Introduction. Historical and Contemporary Perspectives on Race, Science, and Medicine." In *Race, Science, and Medicine, 1900–1960*, edited by Waltraud Ernst and Bernard Harris, 1–28. London: Routledge, 1999.

Ettling, John. *The Germ of Laziness: Rockefeller Philanthropy and Public Health in the New South*. Cambridge: Harvard University Press, 1981.

Fairfield, Letitia D. "Venereal Diseases: The West Indian Commission." *West India Committee Circular*, August 4, 1921, 321–22.

Farley, John. *Bilharzia: A History of Imperial Tropical Medicine*. Cambridge: Cambridge University Press, 1991.

———. *To Cast Out Disease: A History of the International Health Division of the Rockefeller Foundation (1913–1951)*. Oxford: Oxford University Press, 2004.

Ferguson, Angus H., et al. "The Glasgow Corporation Milk Depot, 1904–1910, and Its Role in Infant Welfare: An End or a Means?" *Social History of Medicine* 19, no. 3 (2006): 443–60.

Fett, Sharla M. *Working Cures: Healing, Health, and Power on Southern Slave Plantations*. Chapel Hill: University of North Carolina Press, 2002.

Findlay, Eileen. *Imposing Decency: The Politics of Sexuality and Race in Puerto Rico, 1870–1902*. Durham: Duke University Press, 1999.

Fletcher, Leonard P. "The Evolution of Poor Relief in Barbados, 1838–1900." *Journal of Caribbean History* 26, no. 2 (1992): 171–209.

Forbes, Geraldine. "Managing Midwifery in India." In *Contesting Colonial Hegemony: State and Society in Africa and India*, edited by Dagmar Engels and Shula Marks, 152–72. London: British Academic Press, 1994.

Ford, Joseph C., and Frank Cundall. *The Handbook of Jamaica for 1919, Comprising Historical, Statistical and General Information Concerning the Island, Compiled from Official and Other Reliable Records*. Kingston: Government Printing Office, 1919.

Ford-Smith, Honor. "Unruly Virtues of the Spectacular: Performing Engendered Nationalism in the UNIA in Jamaica." *Interventions: International Journal of Postcolonial Studies* 6, no. 1 (2004): 18–44.

Fox, Enid. "An Honourable Calling or a Despised Occupation: Licensed Midwifery and Its Relationship to District Nursing in England and Wales before 1948." *Social History of Medicine* 6, no. 2 (1993): 237–59.

Fraser, Cary. "The Twilight of Colonial Rule in the British West Indies: Nationalist Assertion vs Imperial Hubris in the 1930s." *Journal of Caribbean History* 30, nos. 1 & 2 (1996): 1–27.

Fraser, S. J., ed. *The Barbados Diamond Jubilee Directory, 1907–08.*

French, Joan. "Colonial Policy towards Women after the 1938 Uprising: The Case of Jamaica." *Caribbean Quarterly* 34, nos. 3 & 4 (September & December 1988): 38–61.

———. "Women and Colonial Policy in Jamaica after the 1938 Uprising." In *Subversive Women: Women's Movements in Africa, Asia, Latin America and the Caribbean,* edited by Saskia Wieringa, 121–46. London: Zed Books, 1997.

Frenkel, Stephen, and John Western. "Pretext or Prophylaxis? Racial Segregation and Malaria Mosquitos in a British Tropical Colony: Sierra Leone." *Annals of the Association of American Geographers* 78, no. 2 (1988): 211–28.

Froude, James Anthony. *The English in the West Indies; Or, The Bow of Ulysses.* London: Longmans, Green, 1888.

Fryer, Christina. "The Moral Politics of Cholera in Postemancipation Jamaica." *Slavery and Abolition* 34, no. 4 (2013): 598–618.

Fryer, Peter. *Staying Power: The History of Black People in Britain.* 1984. Reprint, New York: Pluto Press, 2010.

Fulton, George C. H. "Infantile Mortality: Its Causes and Prevention." *British Medical Journal* 2, no. 2292 (December 3, 1904): 1513–15.

Gibbs, Bentley. "The Establishment of the Tenantry System in Barbados." In *Emancipation II: Aspects of the Post-Slavery Experiment in Barbados,* edited by Woodville Marshall, 23–45. Bridgetown: National Cultural Foundation/Department of History, University of the West Indies, 1987.

Gilmore, Glenda Elizabeth. *Gender and Jim Crow: Women and the Politics of White Supremacy in North Carolina, 1896–1920.* Chapel Hill: University of North Carolina Press, 1996.

Godfrey, J. E. "The Presidential Address, February 10, 1898, Branch Meeting." *British Guiana Medical Annual* 10 (1898): ii–viii.

Gordon, Linda. "Black and White Visions of Welfare: Women's Welfare Activism, 1890–1945." In *"We Specialize in the Wholly Impossible": A Reader in Black Women's History,* edited by Darlene Clark Hine, Wilma King, and Linda Reed, 449–86. Brooklyn: Carlson, 1995.

Gramaglia, Letizia. "Introduction. Dr. Robert Grieve (1839–1906): An 'Apostle of Science.'" In *The Asylum Journal,* vol. 1., by Robert Grieve, xiii–xxviii. 1882. Reprint, Guyana: Caribbean Press, 2010.

Green, Cecilia A. "'The Abandoned Lower Class of Females': Class, Gender, and Penal Discipline in Barbados, 1875–1929." *Comparative Studies in Society and History* 53, no. 1 (January 2011): 144–79.

———. "'A Civil Inconvenience'? The Vexed Question of Slave Marriage in the British West Indies." *Law and History Review* 25, no. 1 (Spring 2007): 1–59.

Green, William A. *British Slave Emancipation: The Sugar Colonies and the Great Experiment,* *1830–1865.* Oxford: Oxford University Press, 1976.

———. "Emancipation to Indenture: A Question of Imperial Morality." *Journal of* *British Studies* 22, no. 2 (Spring 1983): 98–121.

———. "Perils of Comparative History: Belize and the British Sugar Colonies after Slavery." *Comparative Studies in Society and History* 26, no. 1 (January 1984): 112–19.

———. "The West Indies and Indentured Labour Migration—The Jamaican Experience." In *Indentured Labour in the British Empire, 1834–1920,* edited by Kay Saunders, 1–41. London: Croom Helm, 1984.

Gregg, Veronica M. "'How with This Rage Shall Beauty Hold a Plea': The Writings of Miss Amy Beckford Bailey as Moral Education in the Era of Jamaican Nation Building." *Small Axe* 11, no. 2 (June 2007): 16–33.

———, ed. *Amy Bailey: JamaicaWriting.* https://sites.google.com/site/ amybaileyjamaicawriting/home.

———. *Caribbean Women: An Anthology of Non-Fiction Writing.* Notre Dame: University of Notre Dame Press, 2005.

The Grenada Handbook, Directory and Almanac for the Year 1901–1902. London: Sampson, Low, Marston & Co., 1901.

Grieve, Robert. "Infant Hygiene." In *The Asylum Journal,* vol. 1, by Robert Grieve, 253–56. 1882. Reprint, Guyana: Caribbean Press, 2010.

———. "Infant Mortality." In *The Asylum Journal,* vol. 1, by Robert Grieve, 241–45. 1882. Reprint, Guyana: Caribbean Press, 2010.

———. "The Prolongation of Human Life by Sanitary Progress." In *The Asylum Journal,* vol. 2, 1883–1886, by Robert Grieve, 359–62. 1883. Reprint, Guyana: Caribbean Press, 2010.

Guy, Donna. *Women Build the Welfare State: Performing Charity and Creating Rights in* *Argentina, 1880–1955.* Durham: Duke University Press, 2009.

Hall, Catherine. *Civilising Subjects: Metropole and Colony in the English Imagination,* *1830–1867.* Chicago: University of Chicago Press, 2002.

Hall, Douglas. *Free Jamaica, 1838–1865: An Economic History.* New Haven: Yale University Press, 1959.

Hall, Laura. "Trial and Error: Representations of a Recent Past." In *Encounters: People* *of Asian Descent in the Americas,* edited by Roshni Rustomji-Kernas, 163–76. Lanham, Md.: Rowman & Littlefield, 1999.

The Handbook of Jamaica for 1929. Kingston: Government Printing Office, 1929.

Handler, Jerome. "Slave Medicine and Obeah in Barbados, circa 1650 to 1834." *New* *West Indian Guide* 74, nos. 1 & 2 (2000): 57–90.

Hardy, Alfred. *Life and Adventure in the "Land of Mud."* London, 1913.

Harpelle, Ronald N. *The West Indians of Costa Rica: Race, Class, and the Integration of an* *Ethnic Minority.* Montreal-Kingston: McGill-Queen's University Press, 2001.

Harris, Bernard. "Pro-Alienism, Anti-Alienism, and the Medical Profession in Late Victoria and Edwardian Britain." In *Race, Science, and Medicine, 1900–1960,* edited by Waltraud Ernst and Bernard Harris, 189–217. London: Routledge, 1999.

Harrison, Mark. *Public Health in British India: Anglo-Indian Preventive Medicine, 1859–1914.* Cambridge: Cambridge University Press, 1994.

Hart, Ernest. "The West Indies as a Health Resort." *British Medical Journal* 2, no. 1920 (October 16, 1897): 1097–99.

Hattori, Anne Perez. "'The Cry of the Little People of Guam': American Colonisation, Medical Philanthropy, and the Susan Hospital for Chamorro Women, 1889–1941." *Health and History* 8, no. 1 (2006): 4–26.

Havinden, Michael A., and David Meredith. *Colonialism and Development in Britain and Its Tropical Colonies, 1850–1950.* New York: Routledge, 1993.

Haynes, Douglas. *Imperial Medicine: Patrick Manson and the Conquest of Tropical Disease.* Philadelphia: University of Pennsylvania Press, 2001.

Headrick, Daniel R. *Tools of Empire: Technology and European Imperialism in the Nineteenth Century.* Oxford: Oxford University Press, 1981.

Heuman, Gad. "'Is This What You Call Free?' Riots and Resistance in the Anglophone Caribbean." In *Contesting Freedom: Control and Resistance in the Post-Emancipation Caribbean*, edited by Gad Heuman and David Trotman, 104–17. Oxford: Macmillan Caribbean, 2005.

———. *"The Killing Time": The Morant Bay Rebellion in Jamaica.* Knoxville: University of Tennessee Press, 1984.

Higman, B. W. "The Slave Family and Household in the British West Indies, 1800–1834." *Journal of Interdisciplinary History* 6, no. 2 (Autumn 1975): 261–87.

———. *Slave Population and Economy in Jamaica, 1807–1834.* Cambridge: Cambridge University Press, 1976.

———. *Slave Populations of the British Caribbean, 1807–1834.* Kingston: University of the West Indies Press, 1995.

———. "Slavery and the Development of Demographic Theory in the Age of the Industrial Revolution." In *Slavery and British Society, 1776–1846*, edited by James Walvin, 164–94. Baton Rouge: Louisiana State University Press, 1982.

———, ed. *The Jamaican Censuses of 1844 and 1861.* Kingston: Social History Project, Department of History, University of the West Indies, Mona, 1980.

Hill, Robert, ed. *The Marcus Garvey and Universal Negro Improvement Association Papers.* Vol. 11, *The Caribbean Diaspora, 1910–1920.* Durham: Duke University Press, 2011.

Himmelfarb, Gertrude. *Poverty and Compassion: The Moral Imagination of the Late Victorians.* New York: Vintage, 1991.

Hinton, John Howard. *Memoir of William Knibb: Missionary in Jamaica.* London: Houlston and Stoneman, 1849.

Hoefte, Rosemarijn. *In Place of Slavery: A Social History of British Indian and Javanese Laborers in Suriname.* Gainesville: University Press of Florida, 1998.

Holt, Thomas. *The Problem of Freedom: Race, Labor, and Politics in Jamaica and Britain, 1832–1938.* Baltimore: Johns Hopkins University Press, 1992.

Howe, Glenford. "Military Selection and Civilian Health: Recruiting West Indians for World War." *Caribbean Quarterly* 44, nos. 3 & 4 (September & December 1998): 35–49.

———. *Race, War, and Nationalism: A Social History of West Indians in the First World War.* Kingston: Ian Randle, 2002.

Hunt, Nancy Rose. "'Le bébé en brousse': European Women, African Birth Spacing, and Colonial Intervention in Breast Feeding in the Belgian Congo." In *Tensions of*

Empire: Colonial Cultures in a Bourgeois World, edited by Frederick Cooper and Ann Laura Stoler, 287–321. Berkeley: University of California Press, 1997.

Inniss, Tara A. "'Any Elderly, Sensible, Prudent Woman': The Practice and Practitioners of Midwifery during Slavery in the British Caribbean." In *Health and Medicine in the Circum-Caribbean, 1800–1968*, edited by Juanita De Barros, Steven Palmer, and David Wright, 40–52. New York: Routledge, 2009.

———. "From Slavery to Freedom: Children's Health in Barbados, 1823–1838." *Slavery and Abolition* 23, no. 31 (August 2006): 251–60.

"Interdepartmental Committee on Physical Deterioration." *British Medical Journal* 2, no. 2275 (August 6, 1904): 296–97.

Ittmann, Karl. "The Colonial Office and the Population Question in the British Empire, 1918–62." *Journal of Imperial and Commonwealth History* 27, no. 3 (1999): 55–81.

———. "Demography as Policy Science in the British Empire, 1918–69." *Journal of Policy History* 15, no. 4 (2003): 417–48.

———. "'Where Nature Dominates Man': Demographic Ideas and Policy in British Colonial Africa, 1890–1970." In *The Demographics of Empire: The Colonial Order and the Creation of Knowledge*, edited by Karl Ittmann, Dennis D. Cordell, and Gregory H. Maddox, 59–88. Athens: Ohio University Press, 2010.

Jacklin, Laurie. "British Colonial Healthcare in a Post-Emancipation Plantation Society: Creolising Public Health and Medicine in Trinidad to 1916." Ph.D. diss., McMaster University, 2009.

James, Winston. *Holding Aloft the Banner of Ethiopia: Caribbean Radicalism in Early Twentieth Century America*. London: Verso, 1998.

Jennings, Eric T. *Vichy in the Tropics: Petain's National Revolution in Madagascar, Guadeloupe, and Indochina, 1940–1944*. Stanford: Stanford University Press, 2001.

Johnson, Alana, and David Browne. "Historical Commentaries: Barbados." In *The Marcus Garvey and Universal Negro Improvement Association Papers*. Vol. 11, *The Caribbean Diaspora, 1910–1920*, edited by Robert Hill, cli–cliii. Durham: Duke University Press, 2011.

Johnson, Howard. "The Political Uses of Commissions of Enquiry (1): The Imperial-Colonial West Indies Context. The Forster and Moyne Commissions." *Social and Economic Studies* (Jamaica) 27, no. 3 (1978): 256–83.

Johnson, Ryan. "The West African Medical Staff and the Administration of Imperial Tropical Medicine, 1902–14." *Journal of Imperial and Commonwealth History* 38, no. 3 (September 2010): 419–39.

Jolly, Margaret. "Introduction. Colonial and Postcolonial Plots in Histories of Maternities and Modernities." In *Maternities and Modernities: Colonial and Postcolonial Experiences in Asia and the Pacific*, edited by Kalpana Ram and Margaret Jolly, 1–25. Cambridge: Cambridge University Press, 1998.

———. "Other Mothers: Maternal 'Insouciance' and the Depopulation Debate in Fiji and Vanuatu, 1890–1930." In *Maternities and Modernities: Colonial and Postcolonial Experiences in Asia and the Pacific*, edited by Kalpana Ram and Margaret Jolly, 177–212. Cambridge: Cambridge University Press, 1998.

Jones, Cecily. "Contesting the Boundaries of Gender, Race, and Sexuality in Barbados Plantation Society." *Women's History Review* 12, no. 2 (2003): 195–231.

Jones, Gareth Stedman. *Outcast London: A Study in the Relationship between Classes in Victorian Society.* 1971. Reprint, Harmondsworth: Penguin, 1976.

Jones, Margaret. *Health Policy in Britain's Model Colony (1900–1948).* Hyderabad: Orient Longman Private Limited, 2004.

———. "Heroines of Lonely Outposts or Tools of the Empire? British Nurses in Britain's Model Colony: Ceylon, 1878–1948." *Nursing Inquiry* 11, no. 3 (2004): 148–60.

———. "Infant and Maternal Health Services in Ceylon, 1900–1948: Imperialism or Welfare?" *Social History of Medicine* 15, no. 2 (2002): 263–89.

———. *Public Health in Jamaica, 1850–1940: Neglect, Philanthropy and Development.* Kingston: University of the West Indies Press, 2013.

Kale, Madhavi. "'Capital Spectacles in British Frames': Capital, Empire and Indian Indentured Migration to the British Caribbean." *International Review of Social History* 41 (1996): 109–33.

———. "Projecting Identities: Empire and Indentured Labor Migration from India to Trinidad and British Guiana, 1836–1885." In *Nation and Migration: The Politics of Space in the South Asian Diaspora,* edited by Peter van der Veer, 73–92. Philadelphia: University of Pennsylvania Press, 1995.

Killingray, David. "Blackman, Peter." In *The Oxford Companion to Black British History,* edited by David Dabydeen, John Gilmore, and Cecily Jones, 58. Oxford: Oxford University Press, 2007.

———. "The Influenza Pandemic of 1918–1919 in the British Caribbean." *Social History of Medicine* 7, no. 1 (1994): 59–87.

———. "'A New Imperial Disease': The Influenza Pandemic of 1918–1919 and Its Impact on the British Empire." *Caribbean Quarterly* 49, no. 4 (December 2003): 30–49.

———. "'To Do Something for the Race': Harold Moody and the League of Coloured Peoples." In *West Indian Intellectuals in Britain,* edited by Bill Schwarz, 51–70. Manchester: Manchester University Press, 2003.

King, Wilma. "'Suffer with Them Till Death': Slave Women and Their Children in Nineteenth Century America." In *More Than Chattel: Black Women and Slavery in the Americas,* edited by David Barry Gaspar and Darlene Clark Hine, 147–68. Bloomington: Indiana University Press, 1996.

Kiple, Kenneth. *The Caribbean Slave: A Biological History.* Cambridge: Cambridge University Press, 1984.

———. "Cholera and Race in the Caribbean." *Journal of Latin American Studies* 17 (May 1985): 157–77.

Kiple, Kenneth, and Brian T. Higgins. "Cholera in Mid-Nineteenth Century Jamaica." *Jamaican Historical Review* 17 (1991): 31–47.

Kirke, Henry. "Our Criminal Classes." *Timehri: The Journal of the Royal Agricultural and Commercial Society of British Guiana* 2 (1888): 1–16.

———. *Twenty-Five Years in British Guiana.* London: S. Low, Marston, 1898.

Klaus, Alisa. "Depopulation and Race Suicide: Maternalism and Pronatalist Ideologies in France and the United States." In *Mothers of a New World: Maternalist Politics and the Origins of Welfare States,* edited by Seth Koven and Sonya Michel, 188–212. New York: Routledge, 1993.

Klausen, Susanne. "'For the Sake of the Race': Eugenic Discourses of Feeblemindedness and Motherhood in the South African Medical Record, 1903–1926." *Journal of Southern African Studies* 23, no. 1 (March 1997): 27–50.

Knight, Franklin W. "The Caribbean in the 1930s." In *General History of the Caribbean.* Vol. 5, *The Caribbean in the Twentieth Century,* edited by Bridget Brereton and Terecita Martinez-Vergne, 42–81. London: Macmillan Education/UNESCO, 2004.

Koven, Seth, and Sonya Michel. "Introduction. 'Mother Worlds.'" In *Mothers of a New World: Maternalist Politics and the Origins of Welfare States,* edited by Seth Koven and Sonya Michel, 1–42. New York: Routledge, 1993.

Ladd-Taylor, Molly. "'Grannies' and 'Spinsters': Midwife Education under the Shepperd-Towner Act." *Journal of Social History* 22, no. 2 (Winter 1988): 255–74.

———. "Toward Defining Maternalism in U.S. History." *Journal of Women's History* 5, no. 2 (Fall 1993): 110–13.

La Guerre, John. "The Moyne Commission and the Jamaican Left." *Social and Economic Studies* 31, no. 3 (1982): 59–94.

Lambert, David, and Philip Howell. "John Pope Hennessy and the Translation of 'Slavery' between Late Nineteenth-Century Barbados and Hong Kong." *History Workshop Journal* 55 (Spring 2003): 1–24.

Lang, Sean. "Drop the Demon Dai: Maternal Mortality and the State in Colonial Madras, 1840–1875." *Social History of Medicine* 18, no. 3 (2005): 357–78.

Laurence, K. O. "The Importation of Labour Contract Systems." In *General History of the Caribbean, Vol. 4, The Long Nineteenth Century: Nineteenth-Century Transformations,* edited by K. O. Laurence, 191–222. London: Macmillan Education/UNESCO, 2011.

———. *A Question of Labour: Indentured Immigration into Trinidad and British Guiana, 1875–1917.* Kingston: Ian Randle, 1994.

———, ed. *General History of the Caribbean.* Vol. 4, *The Long Nineteenth Century: Nineteenth-Century Transformations.* London: Macmillan Education/UNESCO, 2011.

Law, W. F. "President's Address." *British Guiana Medical Annual for 1906* 15 (1906): iv–ix.

Leavitt, Judith W. *Brought to Bed: Childbearing in America, 1750–1950.* Oxford: Oxford University Press, 1997.

———. "'Science' Enters the Birthing Room: Obstetrics in America since the Eighteenth Century." *Journal of American History* 70, no. 2 (September 1983): 281–304.

Levine, Philippa. "Anthropology, Colonialism, and Eugenics." In *The Oxford Handbook of the History of Eugenics,* edited by Alison Bashford and Philippa Levine, 43–61. Oxford: Oxford University Press, 2010.

———. "Battle Colors: Race, Sex, and Colonial Soldiery in World War I." *Journal of Women's History* 9, no. 4 (Winter 1998): 104–30.

———. *Prostitution, Race and Politics: Policing Venereal Disease in the British Empire.* London: Routledge, 2003.

———. "Sexuality, Gender, and Empire." In *Gender and Empire,* edited by Philippa Levine, 134–55. New York: Oxford University Press, 2004.

Levy, Claude. *Emancipation, Sugar, and Federalism: Barbados and the West Indies, 1833–1876.* Gainesville: University Press of Florida, 1980.

Lewis, Gordon K. *Growth of the Modern West Indies*. New York: Modern Reader Paperbacks, 1968.

————. *Main Currents in Caribbean Thought: The Historical Evolution of Caribbean Society in Its Ideological Aspects, 1492–1900*. Baltimore: Johns Hopkins University Press, 1983.

Lewis, Milton. "Milk, Mothers, and Infant Welfare." In *Twentieth Century Sydney: Studies in Urban and Social History*, edited by Jill Roe, 194–207. Sydney: Sydney History Group, 1980.

Lewis, Rupert. *Marcus Garvey: Anti-Colonial Champion*. Trenton: Africa World Press, 1988.

Lewis, W. Arthur. *Labour in the West Indies: The Birth of a Workers' Movement*. London: Fabian Society, 1939.

Long, Edward. *The History of Jamaica*. 1774. Reprint, Montreal-Kingston: McGill-Queen's University Press, 2003.

Look Lai, Walton. *Indentured Labor, Caribbean Sugar: Chinese and Indian Migrants to the British West Indies, 1838–1918*. Baltimore: Johns Hopkins University Press, 1993.

Lord, Rebecca. "'An Imperial Obligation': Public Health and the United States Military Occupation of the Dominican Republic, 1916–1924." Ph.D. diss., University of Maryland, 2003.

————. "Quarantine in the Fort Ozama Dungeon: The Control of Prostitution and Venereal Disease in the Dominican Republic." *Caribbean Quarterly* 49, no. 4 (December 2003): 12–29.

Loudon, Irvine. *Death in Childbirth: An International Study of Maternal Care and Maternal Mortality, 1800–1950*. Oxford: Clarendon Press, 1992.

————. "Deaths in Childbirth from the Eighteenth Century to 1935." *Medical History* 30 (January 1986): 1–41.

————. "The Measurement of Maternal Mortality." *Journal of the History of Medicine* 54 (April 1999): 312–29.

————. "Midwives and the Quality of Maternal Care." In *Midwives, Society, and Childbirth: Debates and Controversies in the Modern Period*, edited by Hilary Marland and Anne Marie Rafferty, 180–200. London: Routledge, 1997.

MacLeod, Roy. "Introduction." In *Disease, Medicine, and Empire: Perspectives on Western Medicine and the Experience of European Expansion*, edited by Roy MacLeod and Milton Lewis, 1–18. London: Routledge, 1988.

MacLeod, Roy, and Milton Lewis. *Disease, Medicine, and Empire: Perspectives on Western Medicine and the Experience of European Expansion*. London: Routledge, 1988.

Macpherson, Anne. "Citizens v. Clients: Working Women and Colonial Reform in Puerto Rico and Belize, 1932–45." *Journal of Latin American Studies* 35 (2003): 279–310.

————. "Colonial Matriarchs: Garveyism, Maternalism, and Belize's Black Cross Nurses, 1920–1952." *Gender and History* 15, no. 3 (November 2003): 507–27.

————. *From Colony to Nation: Women Activists and the Gendering of Politics in Belize, 1912–1982*. Lincoln: University of Nebraska Press, 2007.

————. *Women Activists and the Gendering of Politics in Belize, 1912–1982*. Lincoln: University of Nebraska Press, 2007.

Madden, Robert Richard. *A Twelvemonth's Residence in the West Indies, During the Transition from Slavery to Apprenticeship*. 1835. Reprint, Westport: Negro Universities Press, 1970.

Mair, Lucille Mathurin. *A Historical Study of Women in Jamaica, 1655–1844*, edited by Verene Shepherd and Hilary Beckles. 1974. Reprint, Kingston: University of the West Indies Press, 2006.

"Malarial Work in Jamaica." *British Medical Journal* 1, no. 2625 (April 22, 1911): 353–54.

Manderson, Lenore. "Shaping Reproduction: Maternity in Early Twentieth-Century Malaya." In *Maternities and Modernities: Colonial and Postcolonial Experiences in Asia and the Pacific*, edited by Kalpana Ram and Margaret Jolly, 26–49. Cambridge: Cambridge University Press, 1998.

———. *Sickness and the State: Health and Illness in Colonial Malaya, 1870–1940*. Cambridge: Cambridge University Press, 1996.

———. "Women and the State: Maternal and Child Welfare in Colonial Malaya, 1900–1940." In *Women and Children First: International Maternal and Infant Welfare, 1870–1945*, edited by Valerie Fildes, Lara Marks, and Hilary Marland, 154–77. London: Routledge, 1992.

Mangru, Basdeo. *Indenture and Abolition: Sacrifice and Survival on the Guyanese Plantations*. Toronto: TSAR, 1993.

Manning Carley, Mary. *Medical Services in Jamaica*. Jamaica: Institute of Jamaica, 1943.

Marks, Shula. "What Is Colonial about Colonial Medicine? And What Has Happened to Imperialism and Health?" *Social History of Medicine* 10, no. 2 (1997): 206–19.

Marland, Hilary, and Anne Marie Rafferty. "Introduction. Midwives, Society, and Childbirth: Debates and Controversies." In *Midwives, Society, and Childbirth: Debates and Controversies in the Modern Period*, edited by Hilary Marland and Anne Marie Rafferty, 1–13. London: Routledge, 1997.

Marshall, Woodville K. "The Emergence and Survival of the Peasantry." In *General History of the Caribbean*. Vol. 4, *The Long Nineteenth Century: Nineteenth-Century Transformations*, edited by K. O. Laurence, 149–90. London: Macmillan Education/UNESCO, 2011.

———. "Metayage in the Sugar Industry of the British Windward Islands, 1838–1865." In *Caribbean Freedom: Economy and Society from Emancipation to the Present*, edited by Hilary Beckles and Verene Shepherd, 64–79. Kingston: Ian Randle, 1993.

———. "The Post-Slavery Labour Problem Revisited." In *Slavery, Freedom, and Gender: The Dynamics of Caribbean Society*, edited by Brian L. Moore, B. W. Higman, Carl Campbell, and Patrick Bryan, 115–32. Kingston: University of the West Indies Press, 2001.

———. "The Termination of the Apprenticeship in Barbados and the Windward Islands: An Essay in Colonial Administration and Politics." *Journal of Caribbean History* 2, no. 1 (1971): 1–45.

———. "'We Be Wise to Many More Tings': Blacks' Hopes and Expectations of Freedom." In *Caribbean Freedom: Economy and Society from Emancipation to the Present*, edited by Hilary Beckles and Verene Shepherd, 12–20. Kingston: Ian Randle, 1993.

Martin, Tony. "African and Indian Consciousness." In *General History of the Caribbean*. Vol. 5, *The Caribbean in the Twentieth Century*, edited by Bridget Brereton and Terecita Martinez-Vergne, 224–81. London: Macmillan Education/UNESCO, 2004.

———. "Marcus Garvey the Great Emancipator: Notes on His Universal Negro Improvement Association in Guyana." Unpublished conference paper, "Genesis of a Nation II," 1–23. Georgetown, Guyana, 1994.

———. *Race First: The Ideological and Organizational Struggles of Marcus Garvey and the Universal Negro Improvement Association*. Westport: Greenwood Press, 1976.

Mason, G. B. "British West Indies Medical Services." *United Empire: The Royal Colonial Institute Journal* 13, no. 11 (November 1922). Rpt. in *United Empire: The Royal Colonial Institute Journal*, vol. 12 (new series, 1922), edited by Edward Salmon, 692–98. London: Sir Isaac Pitman and Sons, 1922.

McDonnough, Pat. "A Biographical Note on Edith Clarke." In *My Mother Who Fathered Me: A Study of the Families in Three Selected Communities of Jamaica*, by Edith Clarke, 229–32. 1957. Reprint, Kingston: University of the West Indies Press, 1999.

McIntosh, Tania. "Profession, Skill, or Domestic Duty? Midwifery in Sheffield, 1881–1936." *Social History of Medicine* 11, no. 3 (1998): 403–20.

McNeill, J. R. *Mosquito Empires: Ecology and War in the Greater Caribbean, 1620–1914*. New York: Cambridge University Press, 2010.

Mead, Karen. "Beneficient Maternalism: Argentine Motherhood in Comparative Perspective, 1880–1920." *Journal of Women's History* 12, no. 3 (Autumn 2000): 120–45.

Meik, Kindon T. "Disease and Hygiene in the Construction of a Nation: The Public Sphere, Public Space, and the Private Domain in Buenos Aires, 1871–1910." Ph.D. diss., Florida International University, Miami, 2010.

Michel, Sonya. "Maternalism and Beyond." In *Maternalism Reconsidered: Motherhood, Welfare and Social Policy in the Twentieth Century*, edited by Marian van der Klein, Rebecca Jo Plant, Nichole Sanders, and Lori R. Weintrob, 22–37. New York: Berghahn Books, 2012.

Millington, Claire. "The Creation of the General Hospital: Examining Philanthropy in 19th Century Barbados." *Journal of the Barbados Museum and Historical Society* 3 (2006): 155–76.

———. "Maternal Health Care in Barbados, 1880–1940." History Forum seminar paper, University of the West Indies, 1995.

Minett, E. P. "Mosquito Prophylaxis." *Timehri: The Journal of the Royal Agricultural and Commercial Society of British Guiana*, 3rd ser., 2 (1912): 172–78.

Minett, Ethel M. "Infantile Mortality." *British Guiana Medical Annual for 1923* (1923): 148–50.

———. "Infant Mortality." In *Report of the Proceedings of the West Indian Medical Conference, 1921*, 58–60. Georgetown: "The Argosy" Co., 1921.

———. "A New School." *Timehri: The Journal of the Royal Agricultural and Commercial Society of British Guiana*, 3rd ser., 3 (1913): 73–77.

Mintz, Sidney W. *Caribbean Transformations*. New York: Columbia University Press, 1974.

Mintz, Sidney W., and Douglas Hall. "The Origins of the Jamaican Internal Marketing System." In *Caribbean Slavery in the Atlantic World*, edited by Hilary Beckles and Verene Shepherd, 758–73. Kingston: Ian Randle, 2000.

Mohapatra, Prabhu C. "'Restoring the Family': Wife Murders and the Making of a Sexual Contract for Indian Immigrant Labour in the British Caribbean Colonies." *Studies in History*, n. s., 11, no. 2 (1995): 227–60.

Moitt, Bernard. "Slave Women and Resistance in the French Caribbean." In *More Than Chattel: Black Women and Slavery in the Americas*, edited by David Barry Gaspar and Darlene Clark Hine, 239–58. Bloomington: Indiana University Press, 1996.

Monteith, Kathleen E. A. *Depression to Decolonization: Barclays Bank (DCO) in the West Indies, 1926–1962*. Kingston: University of the West Indies Press, 2008.

Moore, Brian L. *Cultural Power, Resistance and Pluralism: Colonial Guyana, 1838 -1900*. Montreal-Kingston: McGill-Queen's University Press, 1995.

Moore, Brian L., and Michele A. Johnson. *Neither Led nor Driven: Contesting British Cultural Imperialism in Jamaica, 1865–1920*. Kingston: University of the West Indies Press, 2004.

———, eds. *"Squalid Kingston," 1890–1920: How the Poor Lived, Moved and Had Their Being*. Social History Project. Kingston: University of the West Indies Press, 2000.

Morgan, Kenneth. "Slave Women and Reproduction in Jamaica, ca. 1776–1834." In *Women and Slavery: The Modern Atlantic*, vol. 2, edited by Gwyn Campbell, Suzanne Miers, and Joseph C. Miller, 27–53. Athens: Ohio University Press, 2008.

Mottram, Joan. "State Control in Local Context: Public Health and Midwife Regulation in Manchester, 1900–1914." In *Midwives, Society and Childbirth: Debates and Controversies in the Modern Period*, edited by Hilary Marland and Anne Marie Rafferty, 134–52. London: Routledge, 1997.

Nehaul, B. B. G. "History of the British Guiana Branch of the British Medical Association." *Caribbean Medical Journal* 17, nos. 1–2 (1955): 31–38.

Nestel, Sheryl. "(Ad)ministering Angels: Colonial Nursing and the Extension of Empire in Africa." *Journal of Medical Humanities* 19, no. 4 (1998): 257–77.

Newton, Melanie. *The Children of Africa in the Caribbean: Free People of Color in Barbados in the Age of Emancipation*. Baton Rouge: Louisiana State University Press, 2008.

Nguyen, Thuy Linh. "French-Educated Midwives and the Medicalization of Childbirth in Colonial Vietnam." *Journal of Vietnamese Studies* 5, no. 2 (Summer 2010): 132–82.

Northrup, David. *Indentured Labor in the Age of Imperialism, 1834–1922*. Cambridge: Cambridge University Press, 1995.

"Obituary, A. F. Wright." *British Medical Journal* 1, no. 4961 (February 4, 1956): 296.

"Obituary, C. W. Daniels, M.B., F.R.C.P." *British Medical Journal* 2, no. 3475 (August 13, 1927): 287.

"Obituary, Dr. Edward Howard Bannister." *British Medical Journal* 1, no. 4182 (February 17, 1940): 280.

"Obituary, J. H. Conyers." *British Medical Journal* 1, no. 4129 (February 24, 1940): 325.

"Obituary, Robert Grieve, MD, CMG." *British Medical Journal* 2, no. 2398 (December 15, 1906): 1749.

"Obituary, Winfred [Wishart] Hunter." *Stabroek News*, December 2, 2007. http://www.stabroeknews.com/2007/features/sunday/12/02/obituary-4/. Accessed November 27, 2013.

"Obituary Notice, Robert Grieve." *British Guiana Medical Annual for 1906* 15 (1906), n.p.

"Obituary Notice of Dr. A. J. Craigen." *British Guiana Medical Annual* 28 (1947): 230–31.

"[O'Brien] Obituary." *British Medical Journal* 1, no. 4133 (March 23, 1940): 508–9.

Offen, Karen. "Depopulation, Nationalism, and Feminism in Fin-de-Siècle France." *American Historical Review* 89, no. 3 (June 1984): 648–76.

Opie, Frederick Douglass. *Black Labor Migration in Caribbean Guatemala, 1882–1923*. Gainesville: University Press of Florida, 2009.

Packard, Randall M. *The Making of a Tropical Disease: A Short History of Malaria*. Baltimore: Johns Hopkins University Press, 2007.

Palmer, Steven. *Launching Global Health: The Caribbean Odyssey of the Rockefeller Foundation*. Ann Arbor: University of Michigan Press, 2010.

Paton, Diana. "Decency, Dependence and the Lash: Gender and the British Debate over Slave Emancipation, 1830–34." *Slavery and Abolition* 17, no. 3 (December 1996): 163–84.

———. *No Bond but the Law: Punishment, Race, and Gender in Jamaican State Formation, 1780–1870*. Durham: Duke University Press, 2004.

Paton, Diana, and Maarit Forde, eds. *Obeah and Other Powers: The Politics of Caribbean Religion and Healing*. Durham: Duke University Press, 2012.

Pattynama, Pamela. "Secrets and Danger: Interracial Sexuality in Louis Couperus's *The Hidden Force* and Dutch Colonial Culture around 1900." In *Domesticating the Empire: Race, Gender, and Family Life in French and Dutch Colonialism*, edited by Julia Clancy-Smith and Frances Gouda, 84–107. Charlottesville: University Press of Virginia, 1998.

Paul, Diane B., and James Moore. "The Darwinian Context: Evolution and Inheritance." In *The Oxford Handbook of the History of Eugenics*, edited by Alison Bashford and Philippa Levine, 27–42. Oxford: Oxford University Press, 2010.

Peake, Linda. "The Development and Role of Women's Political Organizations in Guyana." In *Women and Change in the Caribbean: A Pan-Caribbean Perspective*, edited by Janet Momsen, 109–31. Kingston: Ian Randle, 1993.

Peard, Julian G. *Race, Place, and Medicine: The Idea of the Tropics in Nineteenth-Century Brazilian Medicine*. Durham: Duke University Press, 1999.

Pearson, J. G. "The Life History of an East Indian in British Guiana." *Timehri: The Journal of the Royal Agricultural and Commercial Society of British Guiana*, n.s., 11 (1897): 136–46.

———. "The Negro in the West Indies." *Timehri: The Journal of the Royal Agricultural and Commercial Society of British Guiana*, n.s., 8 (1894): 244–50.

Peckman, Robert. "Infective Economies: Empire, Panic, and the Business of Disease." *Journal of Imperial and Commonwealth History* 41, no. 2 (2013): 211–37.

Pedersen, Jean Elisabeth. "'Special Customs': Paternity Suits and Citizenship in France and the Colonies, 1870–1912." In *Domesticating the Empire: Race, Gender, and Family Life in French and Dutch Colonialism*, edited by Julia Clancy-Smith and Frances Gouda, 43–64. Charlottesville: University Press of Virginia, 1998.

Pedersen, Susan. "The Maternalist Moment in British Colonial Policy: The Controversy over 'Child Slavery' in Hong Kong, 1917–1941." *Past & Present* 171 (2001): 161–202.

———. "National Bodies, Unspeakable Acts: The Sexual Politics of Colonial Policy-Making." *Journal of Modern History* 63, no. 4 (December 1991): 647–80.

Pemberton, Rita. "A Different Intervention: The International Health Commission/ Board, Health, Sanitation in the British Caribbean, 1914–1930." *Caribbean Quarterly* 49, no. 4 (December 2003): 87–103.

———. "Dirt, Disease, and Death: Control, Resistance, and Change in the Post-Emancipation Caribbean." *História, Ciências, Saúde—Manguinhos* 19, supl. dez. (2012): 47–58.

Phillippo, James M. *Jamaica: Its Past and Present State*. Philadelphia, 1843.

Pim, Bedford. *The Negro and Jamaica*. London: Trubner and Co., 1866.

Plant, Rebecca Jo, and Marian van der Klein. "Introduction. A New Generation of Scholars on Maternalism." In *Maternalism Reconsidered: Motherhood, Welfare and Social Policy in the Twentieth Century*, edited by Marian van der Klein, Rebecca Jo Plant, Nichole Sanders, and Lori R. Weintrob, 1–21. New York: Berghahn Books, 2012.

Porter, Dorothy. "'Enemies of the Race': Biologism, Environmentalism, and the Public Health in Edwardian England." *Victorian Studies* 34, no. 2 (Winter 1991): 159–78.

———. *Health, Civilization and the State: A History of Public Health from Ancient to Modern Times*. London: Routledge, 1999.

Power, Helen. "The Calcutta School of Tropical Medicine: Institutionalizing Medical Research in the Periphery." *Medical History* 40 (1996): 197–214.

Premium, Barton. *Eight Years in British Guiana*. London, 1850.

Price, Charles Reavis. "Cleave to the Black: Expressions of Ethiopianism in Jamaica." *New West Indian Guide/Nieuwe West-Indische Gids* 77, nos. 1 & 2 (2003): 31–64.

Prout, W. T. "Malaria in Jamaica." In *The Prevention of Malaria*, edited by Ronald Ross, 376–81. New York: E. P. Dutton, 1910.

Putnam, Lara. *The Company They Kept: Migrants and the Politics of Gender in Caribbean Costa Rica, 1870–1960*. Chapel Hill: University of North Carolina Press, 2002.

———. "To Study the Fragments/Whole: Microhistory and the Atlantic World." *Journal of Social History* 39, no. 3 (Spring 2006): 615–30.

Rafferty, Anne Marie, and Diana Solano. "The Rise and Demise of the Colonial Nursing Service: British Nurses in the Colonies, 1896–1966." *Nursing History Review* 15 (2007): 147–54.

Rainger, Ronald. "Race, Politics, and Science: The Anthropological Society of London in the 1860s." *Victorian Studies* 22, no 1 (Autumn 1978): 51–70.

Ramusack, Barbara N. "Cultural Missionaries, Maternal Imperialists, Feminist Allies: British Women Activists in India, 1865–1945." *Women's Studies International Forum* 13, no. 4 (1990): 309–21.

Rashidi Pakri, Mohamad. "An Imperial or a Personal Legacy? The Rivalry of W. E. Maxwell and F. A. Swettenham in British Malaya." *Journal of the Malaysian Branch of the Royal Asiatic Society* 84, no. 2 (September 2011): 33–44.

Rawson, Rawson W. *Report upon the Population of Barbados*. Barbados, 1871.

Reddock, Rhoda. "Diversity, Difference, and Caribbean Feminism: The Challenge of Anti-Racism." *Caribbean Review of Gender Studies* 1 (April 2007): 1–24.

———. *Women, Labour, and Politics in Trinidad and Tobago: A History*. Kingston: Ian Randle, 1994.

Renda, Mary A. *Taking Haiti: Military Occupation and the Culture of U.S. Imperialism, 1915–1940*. Chapel Hill: University of North Carolina Press, 2001.

Renny, Robert. *An History of Jamaica*. London, 1807.

Report of the Proceedings of the English-Speaking Conference on Infant Mortality, held at Caxton Hall, Westminster, on August 4th and 5th, 1913. London, 1913.

Rich, Paul B. *Race and Empire in British Politics*. Cambridge: Cambridge University Press, 1986.

Richards, Glen. "Historical Commentaries: Leeward Islands." In *The Marcus Garvey and Universal Negro Improvement Association Papers*. Vol. 11, *The Caribbean Diaspora, 1910–1920*, edited by Robert Hill, ccxxix–ccxl. Durham: Duke University Press, 2011.

Richardson, Bonham C. *Caribbean Migrants: Environment and Human Survival on St. Kitts and Nevis*. Knoxville: University of Tennessee Press, 1983.

———. "Caribbean Migrants." In *The Modern Caribbean*, edited by Franklin W. Knight and Colin A. Palmer, 203–28. Chapel Hill: University of North Carolina Press, 1989.

———. "Depression Riots and the Calling of the 1897 West India Royal Commission." *New West Indian Guide* 66, nos. 3 & 4 (1992): 169–91.

———. *Economy and Environment in the Caribbean: Barbados and the Windwards in the Late 1800s*. Barbados: Press University of the West Indies, 1997.

———. "Freedom and Migration in the Leeward Caribbean, 1838–48." *Journal of Historical Geography* 6, no. 4 (1980): 391–408.

———. *Panama Money in Barbados, 1900–1920*. Knoxville: University of Tennessee Press, 1985.

Riley, James C. *Poverty and Life Expectancy: The Jamaica Paradox*. Cambridge: Cambridge University Press, 2005.

Roberts, G. W. "Emigration from the Island of Barbados." *Social and Economic Studies* 4, no. 3 (September 1955): 245–88.

———. "A Note on Mortality in Jamaica." *Population Studies* 4, no. 1 (June 1950): 64–85.

———. *The Population of Jamaica*. Cambridge: Conservation Foundation at the University Press, 1957.

———. "Some Observations on the Population of British Guiana." *Population Studies* 2, no. 2 (September 1948): 185–218.

Roberts, G. W., and Joycelyn Bryne. "Summary Statistics on Indenture and Associated Migration Affecting the West Indies, 1834–1918." *Population Studies* 20, no. 1 (June 1966): 125–34.

Roberts, Samuel Kelton, Jr. *Infectious Fear: Politics, Disease, and the Health Effects of Segregation*. Chapel Hill: University of North Carolina Press, 2009.

Rodney, Walter. "Barbadian Immigration into British Guiana 1863–1924." Unpublished paper. Conference of the Association of Caribbean Historians, Barbados, 1977.

———. *A History of the Guyanese Working People, 1881–1905*. Baltimore: Johns Hopkins University Press, 1981.

Rooke, Patricia T., and Rudy L. Schnell. "'Uncramping Child Life': International Children's Organisations, 1914–1939." In *International Health Organisations and Movements, 1918–1939*, edited by Paul Weindling, 176–202. Cambridge: Cambridge University Press, 1995.

Rose, F. G. "The Progress of Sanitation in British Guiana." *Timehri: The Journal of the Royal Agricultural and Commercial Society of British Guiana*, 3rd ser., 7, no. 24 (1921): 61–64.

Rosenberg, Charles E. *The Cholera Years: The United States in 1832, 1849, and 1866*. 1962. Reprint, Chicago: University of Chicago Press, 1987.

———. "Introduction. Framing Disease: Illness, Society, and History." In *Framing Disease: Studies in Cultural History*, edited by Charles E. Rosenberg, xiii–xxvi. New Brunswick: Rutgers University Press, 1997.

Rosenberg, Leah. "The New Woman and 'The Dusky Strand': The Place of Feminism and Women's Literature in Early Jamaican Nationalism." *Feminist Review* 95 (2010): 45–63.

Rotberg, Robert I. *Black Heart: Gore-Browne and the Politics of Multiracial Zambia*. Berkeley: University of California Press, 1977.

Roth, Walter E. *Report of the Pomeroon District, for the Year 1915*. Georgetown: "The Argosy" Co., 1916.

"The Royal Sanitary Institute: Women Health Workers and Child Welfare Workers." *British Journal of Nursing*, September 9, 1922.

Rush, Anne Spry. "The Bonds of Empire: West Indians and Britishness, 1900–1970." Ph.D. diss., American University, 2004.

———. "Imperial Identity in Colonial Minds: Harold Moody and the League of Coloured Peoples, 1931–50." *Twentieth-Century British History* 13, no. 4 (November 2002): 356–83.

Ryden, David Beck. *West Indian Slavery and British Abolition, 1783–1807*. New York: Cambridge University Press, 2009.

Sanders, Nichole. "Protecting Mothers in Order to Protect Children: Maternalism and the 1935 Pan-American Child Congress." In *Maternalism Reconsidered: Motherhood, Welfare and Social Policy in the Twentieth Century*, edited by Marian van der Klein, Rebecca Jo Plant, Nichole Sanders, and Lori R. Weintrob, 148–67. New York: Berghahn Books, 2012.

San Miguel, Pedro L. "Economic Activities Other Than Sugar." In *General History of the Caribbean*. Vol. 4, *The Long Nineteenth Century: Nineteenth-Century Transformations*, edited by K. O. Laurence, 104–48. London: Macmillan Education/UNESCO, 2011.

Schuler, Monica. *Alas, Alas, Kongo: A Social History of Indentured African Immigration into Jamaica, 1841–1865*. Baltimore: Johns Hopkins University Press, 1980.

Scully, Pamela. "Narratives of Infanticide in the Aftermath of Slave Emancipation in the Nineteenth-Century Cape Colony, South Africa." *Canadian Journal of African Studies* 30, no. 1 (1996): 88–105.

———. "Rape, Race, and Colonial Culture: The Sexual Politics of Identity in the Nineteenth-Century Cape Colony, South Africa." *American Historical Review* 100, no. 2 (April 1995): 335–59.

Seecharan, Clem. *Bechu: "Bound Coolie" Radical in British Guiana, 1894–1901*. Kingston: University of the West Indies Press, 1999.

———. *"Tiger in the Stars": The Anatomy of Indian Achievement in British Guiana, 1919–29*. London: Macmillan Caribbean, 1997.

Seekings, Jeremy. "'Pa's Pension': The Origins of Non-Contributory Old-Age Pensions in Late Colonial Barbados." *Journal of Imperial and Commonwealth History* 35, no. 4 (December 2007): 529–47.

Senior, C. H. "Asiatic Cholera in Jamaica (1850–1855)." *Jamaica Journal* 26, no. 2 (1994): 25–42.

Sewell, William G. *The Ordeal of Free Labor in the British West Indies.* New York, 1861.

Shepherd, Verene, Bridget Brereton, and Barbara Bailey, eds. *Engendering History: Caribbean Women in Historical Perspective.* Kingston: Ian Randle, 1999.

Sheridan, Richard. *Doctors and Slaves: A Medical and Demographic History of Slavery in the British West Indies, 1680–1834.* Cambridge: Cambridge University Press, 1985.

Sherwood, Monica. "Blackman, Peter McFarren." In *Oxford Dictionary of National Biography Online.* http://www.oxforddnb.com. Accessed January 11, 2013.

Sinckler, E. Goulburn, comp. *The Barbados Handbook.* London: Duckworth and Co., 1912.

———. *The Barbados Handbook.* London: Duckworth and Co., 1914.

Sinclair, A. C., and Laurence R. Fyfe. *The Handbook of Jamaica for 1887–88, Comprising Historical, Statistical and General Information Concerning the Island.* London: Edward Standford, 1887.

Smith, Jennifer. "Illustrations from the Wellcome Institute Library: The Archive of the Health Visitors' Association in the Contemporary Medical Archives Centre." *Medical History* 39 (1995): 358–67.

Smith, Raymond T. *British Guiana.* Oxford: Oxford University Press, 1962.

———. "The Caribbean Family: Continuity and Transformation." In *General History of the Caribbean.* Vol. 5, *The Caribbean in the Twentieth Century,* edited by Bridget Brereton and Terecita Martinez-Vergne, 506–36. London: Macmillan Education/UNESCO, 2004.

———. "Culture and Social Structure in the Caribbean: Some Recent Work on Family and Kinship Studies." *Comparative Studies in Society and History* 6, no. 1 (October 1963): 24–46.

Solomon, Mark. *The Cry Was Unity: Communists and African Americans, 1917–1936.* Jackson: University Press of Mississippi, 1998.

Soloway, Richard. "Counting the Degenerates: The Statistics of Race Deterioration in Edwardian England." *Journal of Contemporary History* 17, no. 1 (January 1982): 137–64.

———. *Demography and Degeneration: Eugenics and the Declining Birthrate in Twentieth-Century Britain.* Chapel Hill: University of North Carolina Press, 1990.

Steckel, Richard. "Women, Work, and Health under Plantation Slavery in the United States." In *More Than Chattel: Black Women and Slavery in the Americas,* edited by David Barry Gaspar and Darlene Clark Hine, 43–60. Bloomington: Indiana University Press, 1996.

Stepan, Nancy Leys. *"The Hour of Eugenics": Race, Gender, and Nation in Latin America.* Ithaca: Cornell University Press, 1991.

———. "The Interplay between Socioeconomic Factors and Medical Science: Yellow Fever Research, Cuba, and the United States." *Social Studies of Science* 8, no. 4 (1978): 397–423.

Stephen, James. *The Slavery of the British West India Colonies Delineated.* Vol. 2. London: Saunders and Benning, 1830.

Stern, Alexandra Minna. *Eugenic Nation: Faults and Frontiers of Better Breeding in Modern America.* Berkeley: University of California Press, 2005.

—————. "Responsible Mothers and Normal Children: Eugenics, Nationalism, and Welfare in Post-Revolutionary Mexico, 1920–1940." *Journal of Historical Sociology* 12, no. 4 (December 1999): 369–97.

Steven, G. H., and A. G. Coia, eds. *British Guiana Medical Annual for 1932: The Twenty-Fifth Year of Issue.* British Guiana: "The Daily Chronicle" Office, 1933.

Stoler, Ann Laura. "Intimidations of Empire: Predicaments of the Tactile and Unseen." In *Haunted by Empire: Geographies of Intimacy in North American History,* edited by Ann Laura Stoler, 1–23. Durham: Duke University Press, 2006.

—————. "Making Empire Respectable: The Politics of Race and Sex in Twentieth-Century Colonial Cultures." *American Ethnologist* 16, no. 4 (1989): 634–60.

—————. "Rethinking Colonial Categories: European Communities and the Boundaries of Rule." *Society for Comparative Studies in Society and History* 31, no. 1 (January 1989): 134–61.

Stoler, Ann Laura, and Frederick Cooper. "Between Metropole and Colony: Rethinking a Research Agenda." In *Tensions of Empire: Colonial Cultures in a Bourgeois World,* edited by Frederick Cooper and Ann Laura Stoler, 1–6. Berkeley: University of California Press, 1997.

Sturge, Joseph, and Thomas Harvey. *The West Indies in 1837.* 1838. Reprint, London: Dawson of Pall Mall, 1968.

Sutphen, Mary P. "Not What but Where: Bubonic Plague and the Reception of Germ Theories in Hong Kong and Calcutta, 1894–1897." *Journal of the History of Medicine and Allied Sciences* 52, no. 1 (January 1997): 81–113.

Tadman, Michael. "The Demographic Cost of Sugar: Debates on Slave Societies and Natural Increase in the Americas." *American Historical Review* 105, no. 5 (December 2000): 1534–75.

Taylor, Frank Fonda. *To Hell with Paradise: A History of the Jamaican Tourist Industry.* Pittsburgh: University of Pittsburgh Press, 1993.

Thome, James A., and J. Horace Kimball. *Emancipation in the West Indies: A Six Months' Tour in Antigua, Barbados and James, in the Year 1837.* New York: American Anti-Slavery Society, 1838.

Thornton, Leslie S. "'Obeah' in Jamaica." *Journal of the Society of Comparative Legislation* 5 (1903): 262–70.

Tignor, Robert L. *W. Arthur Lewis and the Birth of Development Economics.* Princeton: Princeton University Press, 2006.

Titus, Noel. *The Amelioration and Abolition of Slavery in Trinidad, 1812–1834.* Bloomington, Ind.: Authorhouse, 2009.

Tomkins, S. M. "Palmitate or Permanganate: The Venereal Prophylaxis Debate in Britain, 1916–1926." *Medical History* 37 (1993): 382–98.

Towers, Bridget A. "Health Education and Policy, 1916–1926: Venereal Disease and the Prophylaxis Dilemma." *Medical History* 24 (1984): 70–87.

"Transactions of the B.G. Branch of the British Medical Association for the Years 1925 to 1932." In *The British Guiana Medical Annual for 1932, the Twenty-Fifth Year of Issue,* edited by G. H. Steven and A. G. Coia, 125–47. British Guiana: "The Daily Chronicle" Office, 1933.

"Transactions of the Meeting of the British Guiana Branch of the British Medical Association, August 28, 1901." *The British Guiana Medical Annual for 1901.*

"Transactions of the Meeting of the British Guiana Branch of the British Medical Association, April 16, 1920." *The British Guiana Medical Annual for 1923.*

Trotman, David V. *Crime in Trinidad: Conflict and Control in a Plantation Society, 1838–1900.* Knoxville: University of Tennessee Press, 1986.

———. "Women and Crime in Late Nineteenth Century Trinidad." In *Caribbean Freedom: Economy and Society from Emancipation to the Present,* edited by Hilary Beckles and Verene Shepherd, 251–59. Kingston: Ian Randle, 1993.

Trotz, D. Alissa, and Linda Peake. "Work, Family, and Organizing: An Overview of the Emergence of the Economic, Social, and Political Roles of Women in British Guiana." *Social and Economic Studies* 49, no. 4 (December 2000): 189–222.

Turda, Marius. "Race, Science, and Eugenics in the Twentieth Century." In *The Oxford Handbook of the History of Eugenics,* edited by Alison Bashford and Philippa Levine, 62–79. Oxford: Oxford University Press, 2010.

Turner, Mary. *Slaves and Missionaries: The Disintegration of Jamaican Slave Society, 1787–1834.* Kingston: University of the West Indies Press, 1982.

van Beusekom, Monica M. "From Underpopulation to Overpopulation: French Perceptions of Population, Environment, and Agricultural Development in French Soudan (Mali), 1900–1960." *Environmental History* 4, no. 2 (April 1999): 198–219.

van der Klein, Marian, Rebecca Jo Plant, Nichole Sanders, and Lori R. Weintrob, eds. *Maternalism Reconsidered: Motherhood, Welfare and Social Policy in the Twentieth Century.* New York: Berghahn Books, 2012.

Vassell, Linette. "Introduction." In *Voices of Women in Jamaica, 1898–1939,* edited by Linette Vassell, 1–4. Kingston: Department of History, University of the West Indies, 1993.

———, ed. *Voices of Women in Jamaica, 1898–1939.* Kingston: Department of History, University of the West Indies, 1993.

Wahab, Amar. "Padmore, George." In *The Oxford Companion to Black British History,* edited by David Dabydeen, John Gilmore, and Cecily Jones, 358–59. Oxford: Oxford University Press, 2007.

Walford, Edward. *Walford's County Families of the United Kingdom.* Vol. 59. London: Spottiswoode, Ballantyne & Co., 1919.

Wallbridge, J. S. "Some Remarks on the Mortality Commission Report." *British Guiana Medical Annual for 1906* 15 (1906): 43–50.

Walther, Daniel J. "Sex, Public Health and Colonial Control: The Campaign against Venereal Diseases in Germany's Overseas Possessions, 1884–1914." *Social History of Medicine* 26, no. 2 (2013): 182–203.

Ward, J. R. *British West Indian Slavery, 1750–1834.* Oxford: Oxford University Press, 1988.

Washburn, B. E. "The Economic Value of a Hookworm Campaign." In *Proceedings of the International Conference on Health Problems in Tropical America. Held at Kingston, Jamaica, B.W.I., July 22 to August 1, 1924, by Invitation of the Medical Department, United Fruit Company,* 613–23. Boston: United Fruit Company, 1924.

Wasserman, B. "The Ashanti War: A Study in Cultural Conflict." *Africa* 31, no. 2 (April 1961): 167–79.

Watkins, Frederick Henry. *Handbook of the Leeward Islands*. London: West India Company, 1924.

Watson, John. "Cholera in Jamaica: An Account of the First Outbreak of the Disease in That Island in 1850." *Lancet* 1 (1850): 567.

Watson, Karl. "'Walk and Nyam Buckras': Poor-White Emigration from Barbados, 1834–1900." *Journal of Caribbean History* 34, nos. 1 & 2 (2000): 130–56.

Webb, James L. A., Jr. *Humanity's Burden: A Global History of Malaria*. Cambridge: Cambridge University Press, 2009.

"West Indian Medical Conference." *British Medical Journal* 2, no. 3169 (September 24, 1921): 493–94.

Westmaas, Nigel, and Juanita De Barros. "Historical Commentaries: British Guiana (Guyana)." In *The Marcus Garvey and Universal Negro Improvement Association Papers*. Vol. 11, *The Caribbean Diaspora, 1910–1920*, edited by Robert Hill, clxvii–clxxvi. Durham: Duke University Press, 2011.

Whittal, Daniel. "Creolising London: Black West Indian Activism and the Politics of Race and Empire in Britain, 1931–1948." Ph.D. diss., University of London, 2012.

Wilkins, Nadine Joy. "The Medical Profession in Jamaica in the Post-Emancipation Period." *Jamaica Journal* 21, no. 4 (1988–89): 27–32.

———. "Medical Services in Jamaica, 1834–1850." Unpublished M.A. research paper. Department of History, University of the West Indies, Mona, 1987.

Wilkinson, Lise. "Burgeoning Visions of Global Public Health: The Rockefeller Foundation, the London School of Hygiene and Tropical Medicine, and the 'Hookworm Connection.'" *Studies in History and Philosophy of Science. Part C: Biological and Biomedical Sciences* 31, no. 3 (2000): 397–407.

Wilkinson, Lise, and Anne Hardy. *Prevention and Cure: The London School of Hygiene and Tropical Medicine: A Twentieth-Century Quest for Global Public Health*. London: Kegan Paul, 2001.

Will, H. A. *Constitutional Change in the British West Indies, 1880–1903: With Special Reference to Jamaica, British Guiana, and Trinidad*. Oxford: Clarendon Press, 1970.

———. "Problems of Constitutional Reform in Jamaica, Mauritius and Trinidad, 1880–1895." *English Historical Review* 81 (1996): 693–716.

Williams, Eric. *Capitalism and Slavery*. Chapel Hill: University of North Carolina Press, 1944; new ed., 1994.

Williamson, John. *Medical and Miscellaneous Observations, Relative to the West India Islands*. Vols. 1 & 2. Edinburgh, 1817.

Wise, K. S. "An Examination of the City of Georgetown, British Guiana, for the Breeding Places of Mosquitos." *Annals of Tropical Medicine and Parasitology* 5 (1911): 435–41.

———. "Malaria: The Problem of British Guiana." *British Guiana Medical Annual for 1919* 22 (1919): 1–28.

———. "Presidential Address." *British Guiana Medical Annual for 1913* 20 (1913): 117–22.

Wise, K. S., and E. P. Minett. "Review of the Milk Question in British Guiana." *Journal of the Royal Sanitary Institute, Colonial Supplement* 33 (October 1911): 75–84.

Wishart, William de Weaver. "Infant Welfare Work in Georgetown—Past, Present, and Future." In *Report of the Proceedings of the West Indian Medical Conference, 1921*. Georgetown: "The Argosy" Co., 1921.

————. Untitled talk in "The Transactions of the British Guiana Branch of the British Medical Association for 1898." *British Guiana Medical Annual* 10 (1898): xxi–xxv.

Woods, G. S., and Roger T. Stern. "Hogg, Quintin." In *Oxford Dictionary of National Biography*. Oxford: Oxford University Press, 2004. http://www.oxforddnb.com.libaccess.lib.mcmaster.ca/view/article/33926?docPos=1.

Worboys, Michael. "The Colonial World as Mission and Mandate: Leprosy and Empire, 1900–1940." *Osiris* 15 (2000): 207–18.

Index

British, use and meaning of term, 105, 178 (n. 2), 179 (n. 13). *See also* White British women

British Caribbean: colonial administration of, 3; commonalities in approaches to population crisis in, 1–2, 4–7; forms of government in, 3; mainland territories of, 6, 178 (n. 9); voting rights in, 3, 161, 225 (n. 4). *See also specific colonies*

British Guiana, use of term, 178 (n. 9). *See also* Guyana

British Guiana Labour Union, 124, 130

British Guiana Medical Annual (journal), 49, 192 (n. 49)

British Guiana Medical Annual and Hospital Report (journal), 193 (n. 49)

British Honduras. *See* Belize

British Medical Association, 48, 49, 134, 164, 165, 173, 197 (n. 141), 217 (n. 30)

British Medical Journal, 76

British women. *See* White British women

Browne, Florence Sinclair, role of in infant welfare, 118

BSLBG. *See* Baby Saving League of British Guiana

Bureau of Health Education (Jamaica), 152

Bush medicine, 67, 71–72

Buxton, Charles, 16, 17, 18

Buxton, Thomas Fowell, 16

Cane sugar. *See* Sugar production

Caribbean, British. *See* British Caribbean; *and specific colonies*

Carlyle, Thomas, "Occasional Discourse," 28, 185 (n. 86)

Censuses, 36–38; in Barbados, 37, 46–47, 48; barriers to reliable counts in, 26, 169; critics of, 26, 37; decennial timing of, 37; establishment of, 37; ethnicity and occupation correlations in, 200 (n. 59); in Guyana, 45, 46–47; in imperial policy, importance of, 13; in Jamaica, 26, 37, 45, 46–47, 187 (n. 110);

midwives in, 83, 200 (n. 59), 205 (n. 147); physicians in, 187 (n. 110); results of, 1841–1931, 46–47; uniformity of, 37; in wake of emancipation, 26

Central Midwives' Board, 70

Chamberlain, Joseph, 40, 42, 52, 53, 135, 217 (n. 39)

Childbirth, 74–80; dangers of, 69–70; at home, 74; in India, 69–70; male physicians' role in, 68, 72, 73, 90; outdoors, 77–78. *See also* Maternity wards; Midwives

Child-rearing practices, teaching of. *See* Maternal education

Children: born outside of marriage (*See* Illegitimacy); economic cost of death of, 126, 137–38; free, mistreatment of, 20; malaria in, 133, 134, 137–38; slave, emancipation of, 19

Children's Protection Society (Guyana), 115

Child Saving Association (Jamaica), 116. *See also* Child Welfare Association

Child Welfare Association (Jamaica), 103, 114, 116, 117–19, 120, 152

Chinese, use and meaning of term, 178 (n. 2)

Cholera, 29–36; British response to, 30–36; fear in response to, 33–34, 188 (n. 125); former slaves blamed for, 29, 32–34, 50; history of outbreaks of, 29–30; labor shortages caused by, 32; malnourishment and, 31; mechanisms of spread of, 30; medical taxes and, 34–36; memories of outbreaks of, 186 (n. 96); mortality from, 29, 30, 33–34, 186 (nn. 93, 99); as sign of failure of emancipation, 9, 29; symptoms of, 29; treatment of, 29, 30–34; whites affected by, 47

Civilizing mission, British: anti-hookworm campaigns in, 151; emancipation in, 21, 23; International Health Board in, 10; marriage in, 13; Moyne Commission and, 163, 164;

DeCordova, Michael, 133
DeCordova family, 132
De Lisser, Herbert George, 133, 216
  (n. 25)
Democratic League, 158
Disease(s), 133–37; as barrier to immigration, 132; as barrier to population growth, 126, 129, 133–37, 151;
  definitions of, 179 (n. 26); discovery
  of causes of, 41; germ theory of, 41,
  74; home visitors and, 107; in infant
  mortality, 54; miasmas, 30, 41, 50, 64;
  race in, as topic at medical conference of 1921, 155–56; as sign of failure
  of emancipation, 9–10; U.S. involvement in eradication of, 149–54. See also
  specific types
Dispensary systems, 34–36, 189 (n. 130)
Doctors. See Physicians
Domingo, Eulalie, 159, 160, 161–62
Dominica, censuses of, 26, 46–47

Early Notification of Births Ordinance of
  1907, 107
East Indian Association, 214 (n. 181)
East Indians, use and meaning of term,
  178 (n. 2). See also South Asians
Economic crises: censuses during, 37;
  after emancipation, 27–28; global
  depression of 1930s, 160, 163, 164;
  government investigation of (1896),
  50–51, 193 (n. 65); and infant mortality, 57, 59; and sugar production, 43
Economic health: infant mortality's
  impact on, 126; shrinking populations
  and, 126–33; sugar production in,
  127–28
Edge, P. Granville, 169
Education: of midwives (See Midwives,
  trained); of mothers (See Maternal
  education); of nonwhite middle class,
  122
Elites: maternal education supported by,
  105; in philanthropic organizations,
  114, 117

Emancipation, 16–39; abolitionists'
  arguments for, 16, 17–18; apprenticeship system in transition to, 19–20; in
  civilizing mission, 21, 23; economic
  crisis after, 27–28; as failure, perception of, 9–10, 16, 27–28, 29; former
  slaves' goals for, 16–17, 21–23; imperial
  goals for, 16–17, 19, 20–21; legislation
  enacting (1834), 19; parliamentary
  committee on results of, 23–24, 34;
  population growth after, estimates of,
  24–26; population growth as goal of,
  1, 2, 9, 16, 17–18, 24–26; slave owners
  compensated for, 19
Emigration. See Immigration
Empire-building, tropical medicine in,
  10, 42, 180 (n. 29)
Empire Health Week, 153–54
Employment opportunities, for Caribbean women, 113, 211 (n. 122)
England. See Britain
English, use and meaning of term, 179
  (n. 13), 205 (n. 1). See also White British
  women
English General Board of Health, 30
Environmental factors, in infant mortal-
  ity, 49–50
Epidemics. See Disease(s)
Equality, racial, white views on, 28
Estates. See Plantations
Ethnic diversity: of Baby Saving League
  members, 119; of Georgetown Public
  Hospital staff, 79
Ethnicity: of home visitors, 111; and
  occupation, censuses on, 200 (n. 59);
  of trained midwives, 79, 200 (n. 59);
  use and meaning of terms denoting,
  178 (n. 2)
Eugenics, 8, 138, 144, 179 (n. 20)
Eyre, Edward, 29, 38

Fairfield, Letitia, 143, 145–48
Fathers. See Black Caribbean men; Paren-
  tal care
Food shortages: and cholera, 31; and

102–10; at maternity wards, 76–77, 79, 80, 87; number of, 93; poor women's use of, 88; South Asian, 79, 200 (n. 59); traditional, criticism of, 68, 74, 88–89, 92, 106–7; traditional, regulation of, 91–93

Guyanese population: in 1891, vs. Barbados, 7; approaches to crisis in, 1–2, 6; blacks as minority in, 130–31; censuses of, 45, 46–47; concerns about decline of, 40, 129, 130–32; immigration in growth of, 45, 130–31; midwives in, 200 (n. 59); physicians in, 31–32; reproduction in growth of, 48–49; slaves in, 18; South Asian immigrants in, 6, 44, 130–31, 200 (n. 59); in wake of emancipation, 25, 26–27; whites as percentage of, 7

Hall, Catherine, 9, 28, 183 (n. 28)
Health care. See Medical care
Health missionaries, midwives as, 102
Health visitors: certification of, 111–12; creolization of, 110; in disease prevention, 107; income of, 113, 211 (n. 123); in maternal education, 107–8, 110–13; midwives as, 109, 112; midwives replaced by, 107; training of, 111–12
Health weeks, 153–54
Higman, B. W., 55, 188 (n. 114)
Hodgson, Frederick, 52, 53, 105, 135, 218 (n. 42)
Holt, Thomas, 9, 28, 161, 162, 190 (n. 156), 227 (n. 51)
Home Industries and Self-Help Society, 114
Home visitors, 110–13; Duggin, Johanna, 112–13; legislation on, 107, 209 (n. 83); maternal education by, 103, 104, 107–8, 110–13, 120; from philanthropic organizations, 107, 120; race and class of, 110, 111; Tennet, E., 111, 113; training of, 111–12; Wilson, Kathleen Eloise, 112
Hookworm: as barrier to population

growth, 133, 151; campaigns against, 146, 150–53; mechanisms of spread of, 150
Hospitals: medical care at, 74–75; preference for white administrators in, 97; public vs. private, 75. See also Maternity wards
How-Martyn, Edith, 173–74
Hutson, Charles: on medical care for poor women, 77; on midwifery training, 74, 77; as poor law inspector until 1901, 199 (n. 32); on poor women's use of maternity wards, 84–85; on traditional midwives in infant mortality, 73–74
Hutson, John: on baby-saving leagues, 116; in British Medical Association, 197 (n. 141); on distribution of trained midwives, 86; on illegitimacy in infant mortality, 62–63, 64; on maternal education, 104; at medical conference of 1921, 155, 156; on midwifery training, 77, 82, 83, 202 (n. 78); at Moyne Commission, 164–65, 229 (n. 89); as poor law inspector from 1901 to 1924, 196 (n. 140), 199 (n. 32); on poor women's use of maternity wards, 79, 200 (n. 54); on public health policies of Barbados, 145–49; on registration of deaths, 39; on regulation of midwives, 93; and tropical diseases, 136, 218 (n. 43); on venereal diseases, 142, 145; wife of, in philanthropic organizations, 114
Hutson, Lionel, 221 (n. 124)

Illegitimacy: and compulsory sterilization, 167–68; definition of, 58; in infant mortality, 54–63, 171; Moyne Commission on, 170–72, 228 (n. 86); and poverty, 57
Immigration: from Barbados, 44–48, 63–64, 129, 191 (nn. 25, 27); legislation on, 45; and marriage rates, 56; in population growth, 45, 126, 129–32; restrictions on, in 1930s, 168; as solution to

population surpluses, 172, 229 (n. 89); of South Asians, 6, 44, 129–31; of South Asian women, 56–57, 195 (n. 106); for sugar production, 44–45; as topic at medical conference of 1921, 155; of whites out of islands, 47–48

Immorality: of black people, white views on, 2, 8, 12–13, 17; and cholera, 31; and infant mortality, 54–63; of slavery, abolitionist views on, 16, 17

Imperialism, maternal, 12

Indentureship system, South Asians in, 44, 129–30

India: childbirth practices in, 69–70; opposition to immigration in, 129–30. See also South Asians

Infant mortality, 48–66; in Britain, 49, 55, 63, 165; as criminal matter, 59, 64; dispensary systems and, 35; as economic and social crisis vs. personal tragedy, 4, 137; economic cost of, 126, 137–38; environmental factors in, 49–50; hookworm in, 151; illegitimacy and, 54–63, 171; malaria in, 54, 137–38; maternal education as solution to, 50, 75–76, 80, 95; midwives blamed for, 73, 76, 89; midwives in reduction of, 80, 95; Moyne Commission on, 165; origins of concerns about, 48–49; parents blamed for, 4, 8, 41, 49–50, 54, 59, 95; poverty in, 8, 41, 53–54, 58, 64–65; rates of, 1900–1921, 128, 129; as regional trend, recognition of, 52; among South Asians, 50, 51; systematic collection of data on, 48, 49, 52–54, 194 (n. 79); utility of, 65; venereal diseases in, 54, 140, 144–45

Infant welfare: key role of women in programs for, 4–5, 11–12, 94–95; Moyne Commission on, 164–66. See also Infant mortality; Maternal education

Infant Welfare and Maternity League of British Guiana, 116

Influenza, 128

Interdepartmental Committee on

Physical Deterioration, 42, 53, 140

International Health Board (Commission), 150–54; anti-hookworm campaign of, 146, 150–53; arrival of in British Caribbean, 4, 150, 151; change to name of, 180 (n. 33); in civilizing mission, 10

Jamaica: apprenticeship system in, 20; birth control in, 173; cholera in, 30–31, 32–33, 186 (nn. 96, 99); dispensary system in, 34–35, 189 (n. 130); earthquake of 1907 in, 86, 191 (n. 22); emancipation in (See Emancipation); emigration of workers from, 192 (n. 28); Empire Health Week in, 153–54; English nurses in, 97–98, 100 (See also Nurses, English); food production in, 44; former slaves as smallholders in, 22, 23; forms of government in, 3, 18, 29; hookworm in, 150–53; illegitimacy in, 56–62; importance of as colony, 5; infant mortality in, 53, 76, 128, 129, 194 (n. 79); land availability in, 22; literacy rates in, 88; malaria in, 134, 136–37, 218 (n. 52), 219 (n. 76); marriage rates in, 24, 56; maternal education in, 102–3, 115–20; in medical conference of 1921, 154–58; Morant Bay uprising in, 28–29, 38; philanthropic organizations in, 114–20, 211 (n. 127); physician shortage in, 31, 187 (n. 110); protests of 1930s in, 160; public health in, U.S. involvement in, 149–54; sanitation in, lack of, 30–31, 132; size of island, 5; social mobility in, 122; sugar production in, 44; UNIA in, 123; venereal diseases in, 141, 143–44, 145, 220 (n. 93); voting rights in, 3, 225 (n. 4)

Jamaica Imperial Association, 151, 218 (n. 52)

Jamaican midwives, 67–93; duration of training of, 200 (n. 62); geographic distribution of, 83; maternal education by, 103; at maternity wards, 75,

76, 79, 81, 84–86, 87; number of, 93; poor women's use of, 87, 88; South Asian, 79, 200 (n. 59); traditional, criticism of, 72–73, 75–76; traditional, regulation of, 91, 92, 93

Jamaican population: in 1891, vs. Barbados, 6; approaches to crisis in, 1–2, 5–6; censuses of, 26, 37, 45, 46–47, 187 (n. 110); concerns about decline in, 36, 37, 38, 128, 132, 190 (n. 156); after emancipation, 26, 36; immigrants in growth of, 45; Jewish Jamaicans, 117; midwives in, 200 (n. 59); mortality rates and, 36, 128; physicians in, 31, 187 (n. 110); slaves in, 18; South Asian immigrants in, 6, 44, 191 (n. 22), 200 (n. 59); whites as percentage of, 7

Jamaica Physical Journal, 30

Jamaica Progressive League, 118

Jamaica Public Health (monthly), 152, 154

Jeffers, Audrey, 211 (n. 127)

Journal of Public Health and Sanitary Review, 8

Kerr, John Errington, 84–85, 87, 97–98

Kingston (Jamaica): earthquake of 1907 in, 86; maternity wards in, 75, 86, 203 (n. 109); midwives in, 83, 103; sanitation in, 30–31; venereal diseases in, 141, 220 (n. 93)

Labor: apprenticeship system in, 19–20; indentureship system in, 44, 129–30; slave (*See* Slavery)

Labor control laws, 22

Labor movement, rise of, 161

Labor protests: of 1934–38, 2, 159–62, 225 (n. 2); UNIA and, 123

Labor shortages: cholera and, 32; emigration from Barbados and, 44–48, 63–64, 129, 191 (nn. 25, 27); in Guyana, regularity of, 6; immigration of South Asians and, 44, 129–31; in sugar production, 44–46, 128; in wake of emancipation, 22, 24, 129

Land: availability of to former slaves, 22, 32; taxes on, 32

Laws. *See* Legislation; *and specific laws*

League of Colored Peoples, 161, 166

Legislation: amelioration, 19, 55; "bastardy," 45, 62–63; on birth and death registration, 38–39; compulsory sterilization, 167; emancipation, 19; on emigration from islands, 45, 46; on home visiting, 107, 209 (n. 83); labor control, 22; marriage, 60–61; on midwives, 91–93, 199 (n. 47); poor, 62–63; on venereal diseases, 141–42. *See also specific laws*

Levine, Philippa, 140, 217 (n. 36)

Light, Henry, 26–27, 28

Lofty, Henry, 128–29, 155

London School of Tropical Medicine, 134–35, 154, 155, 217 (n. 37), 219 (n. 59)

Lying-in facilities. *See* Maternity wards

MacDonald, Malcolm, 163, 167

Macpherson, Anne, 123, 181 (n. 42)

Malaria: as barrier to population growth, 133–37; campaigns against, 133–37, 219 (n. 76); and infant mortality, 54, 137–38; mechanisms of spread of, 133; outbreaks of in 1930s, 164

Manson, Patrick, 42, 97, 135–36, 154, 217 (n. 39)

Marriage: barriers to, 56; British views on need for, 13, 55–57; children born outside of (*See* Illegitimacy); in civilizing mission, 13; cost of, 56, 61; after emancipation, rise of, 24, 55; by English nurses, restrictions on, 99–100; vs. faithful concubinage, 171–72; by health visitors, restrictions on, 113; laws regulating, 60–61; during slavery, 55

Marson, Una, 162

Mason, G. B., 126, 137, 147, 148, 154–55, 157

Maternal care. *See* Parental care

Maternal education, 94–125; English

nurses in, 95–102, 103, 106; health missionaries in, 102; home visitors in, 103, 104, 107–8, 110–13, 120; midwives in, 75, 80, 94, 95, 102–10; pamphlets in, 102–3; philanthropic organizations in, 107, 113–21; political barriers to, 104; racial uplift and, 121–25; as solution to infant mortality, 50, 75–76, 80, 95

Maternal imperialism, 12

Maternalist initiatives, 11–12, 123, 162, 181 (n. 39)

Maternal mortality, midwives and, 69–70, 89

Maternal welfare, key role of women in programs for, 4–5, 11–12, 94–95

Maternity wards, 74–80; emergence of, 74–77; layout of, 75; limited space for patients in, 85, 87–88; midwifery training in, 70, 74–77, 79–80, 85; poor women's use of, 68, 77–79, 83–86

Medical Act of 1886, 92

Medical care: African-derived religious practices and, 36; in cholera outbreaks, 30–36; through dispensary systems, 34–36, 189 (n. 130); before vs. after emancipation, 25, 31; for former slaves, gaps in, 25, 31–33; germ theory of disease and, 41; at hospitals, 74–75; nineteenth-century revolution in, 41–42; physician shortage and, 31–32, 38, 187 (nn. 110, 114); on plantations, 25, 31, 35; in population declines, 38; for pregnant women (See Maternity wards); taxes for, 34–36. See also Physicians

Medical conferences: of 1903 and 1913, 154; of 1921, 154–58; of 1929, 157; media coverage of medical conference of 1921, 157, 224 (n. 185)

Medical education, at hospitals, 74–75. See also Midwives, trained

Medical facilities. See Hospitals; Maternity wards

Medicine: bush, 67, 71–72; tropical (See Tropical medicine)

Men, black. See Black Caribbean men

Merivale, Herman, 21–22

Metcalfe, C. T., 24, 26, 44, 45

Middle class, nonwhite: educational opportunities for, 122; emergence of, 3, 122; employment opportunities for women of, 113, 211 (n. 122); as home visitors, 110, 112–13; in oppositional organizations, 123–24; in philanthropic organizations, 121, 122; and racial uplift, 121–25

Midwives, traditional, 67–93; certification of, 82, 91; cost of using, 87; criticism of, 67–76, 89, 91; incorporation of into regulatory system, 91–93; infant mortality blamed on, 73, 76, 89; legislation on, 91–93; maternal mortality blamed on, 69–70, 89; number of, 93; poor women's continued use of, 86–93; slaves as, 72–73; South Asians as, 79, 89, 200 (n. 59); superstitions of, 69, 89; trained midwives and physicians as rivals to, 82, 86–93; trained midwives as replacement for, 67–68, 80, 91

Midwives, trained, 67–93; in Africa, 70–71; in Britain, 70; certification of, 67, 70, 74, 88, 89–90; cost of using, 80–81, 87, 107, 209 (n. 77); duration of training of, 200 (n. 62); English nurses in education of, 96, 106; equipment of, 87, 88, 89; establishment of programs for, 67, 70, 71, 76–77; ethnicity of, 79, 200 (n. 59); geographic distribution of, 80–83, 86–88; goals of, vs. colonial goals, 80–83; as health missionaries, 102; as health visitors, 109, 112; health visitors as replacement for, 107; in India, 69–70; in infant mortality reduction, 80, 95; legislation on, 199 (n. 47); limitations on access to, 85, 87–88; maternal education by, 75, 80, 94, 95, 102–10; at maternity wards, education of, 70, 74–77, 79–80, 85;

number of, 88, 93; outdoor, 103, 106; physicians as rivals to, 89–90; poor women's use of, 68, 83–87; problems with system of, 80–83; reorganization of programs for, 82; social class of, 79, 88; subsidies for, 81, 82, 106, 209 (n. 77); supervision of, 90–91, 108–10; traditional midwives as rivals to, 82, 86–93; Western vs. indigenous ideas in education of, 80

Midwives Act of 1902, 70, 93

Midwives and Nurses Registration Act of 1932, 93

Milk, for infants, 50, 51–52, 104, 109

Milk depots, 109

Milroy, Gavin, 30–36, 41, 188 (n. 125)

Minett, Edward Pigott (E. P.), 51, 102, 111, 134

Minett, Ethel: arrival of in Guyana, 102; in Baby Saving League, 89, 102, 109–10, 208 (n. 75); career of, 102; departure of from Guyana, 109; on superstitions of traditional midwives, 89; supervision of midwives by, 109–10; on venereal diseases, 144

Missionaries: cultural, 12; health, midwives as, 102; on population growth after emancipation, 25; on results of emancipation, 23–24

Montserrat: censuses of, 46–47; population growth after emancipation in, 26

Moody, Harold, 161, 166

Moore, J. R., 112, 211 (n. 118)

Morality. See Immorality

Morant Bay uprising (1865), 28–29, 38

Morris-Knibb, Mary, 118–19, 162

Mortality rates: from cholera, 29, 30, 33–34, 186 (nn. 93, 99); infant (See Infant mortality); maternal, 69–70, 89; and population size, 36, 128; and sugar production, 128; in wake of emancipation, 25, 36

Mosse, Charles: on causes of infant mortality, 59, 62, 193 (n. 65); on English nurses, 96–97, 100, 108; on maternity

wards, 84; on midwives, 73, 76

Mothercraft movement, 107–8

Mothers: "bad," discourse of, 8–9, 95; slavery's impact on health of, 19, 20. See also Maternal entries; Parental care

Moyne (West India Royal) Commission, 14, 162–76; audience listening to, 175, 175–76; Caribbean perspective in, 14, 163, 166; establishment of, 162–63; hearings of, 163–71, 175–76; mandate of, 162–63; members of, 162–63, 164; on population surpluses, 160, 168–73; recommendations and report of, 13–14, 163–65, 170–74; "triumphant empiricism" of, 13–14

Myalism, 36

National Council for Combating Venereal Diseases, 142–43

Nationalist movements, emergence of, 2

Nationality, use of terms denoting, 178 (n. 2)

Negro Progress Convention, 123, 124, 131, 158, 215 (n. 191)

Negro Worker (publication), 167

Nevis: infant mortality in, 129; sugar production in, 43

Newsholme, Arthur, 152

Nichols, Theodore Theophilus (T. T.), 124, 158

Nurses, English, 12, 95–102; Brown, Ada Agnes Baird, 99–100; career paths of, 99; CNA guidelines and criteria for, 96–98; Cowie, Isabella M., 98, 106; Cumming, Miss, 108, 110–11; Davis, Jessica, 100, 108–9; district, 75; divisional, 98–99; Drummond, Kate, 98, 99, 100–101; goals of, vs. colonial goals, 96; in maternal education, 95–102, 103, 106; midwife education by, 96, 106; midwife supervision by, 108–9 Nurse, Violet, 67, 72, 89, 109; Parkinson, Florence, 99; patient education by, 75; race and class of, 94, 95–98; in racial hierarchies, 100–102; salaries

and travel costs of, 96; sexuality of, 96, 99–100; Thompson, Edith, 97–98; Thorpe, Lydia Beatrice, 99; training of, 96, 97; Westwood, Mary, 97
Nurses Union, 103

Obeah, 71–72; bush medicine and, 67, 71–72; definition of, 36, 71; midwives and, 67, 71–72; physician-based medicine replacing, 36
O'Brien, Arthur John Rushton (A. J. R.), 164, 165, 169, 173, 226 (n. 35)
Ogilvie, James, 76, 102, 103
Oliver, Sydney, 52
O'Neale, Charles Duncan, 158
Overseas Nursing Association, 95, 101–2. See also Colonial Nursing Association

Padmore, George, 161, 166, 168
Palmer, Steven, 11, 150, 153
Pan-Africanism, 101, 161, 167
Parental care: fathers' neglect in, 60, 62–63; infant mortality blamed on, 4, 8, 41, 49–50, 54, 59, 95; population declines blamed on, 38
Parliamentary committee of 1842, 23–24, 34
Philanthropic organizations, 113–21; elites in, 114, 117; examples of, 114; government support for, 115–17; home visits by, 107, 120; in maternal education, 107, 113–21; middle-class participation in, 121, 122; missions of, 114; race and class restrictions on membership in, 118–19
Phillippo, James, 24
Physical deterioration, 42, 53, 54
Physicians: in childbirth, role of, 68, 72, 73, 90; in CNA guidelines for nurses, 96–97; Deane, Edward, 144; Dickson, J. R., 103, 196 (n. 131); Eakin, J. W., 103; fees for midwifery services by, 90, 204 (n. 127); Gideon, E. D., 92–93, 155, 156, 217 (n. 30); on infant mortality, 48–49, 63; MacDonald, Angus,

39; on maternal education, 102–3; in maternity wards, 79; at medical conference of 1921, 154–58; Nedd, J. S., 101; nonwhite, 79, 101, 105; Paterson, P. W., 141, 156; Ramdeholl, J. E., 101; Richards, H. E. Sutherland, 157; Rowland, Ernest Daniel (E. D.), 103; shortage of, 31–32, 38, 90–91, 105, 187 (nn. 110, 114); Tillman, Henry, 137–38; traditional midwives as rivals to, 86–93; traditional midwives criticized by, 68–69, 71, 72, 89, 91; trained midwives as rivals to, 89–90; trained midwives supervised by, 90–91. See also Anderson, D. G.; Anderson, Oswald; Boxill, Norman Laurence; Conyers, J. H.; Craigen, Allen James; Crosswell, L. Oliver; Godfrey, Joseph Edward; Grabham, Michael; Grieve, Robert; Hutson, Charles; Kerr, John Errington; Mason, G. B.; Mosse, Charles; Ogilvie, James; O'Neale, Charles Duncan; Rose, Frederick Gardner; Ross, David Palmer; Wise, K. S.; Wishart, William de Weever
Plantations: in civilizing mission, 21; former slaves residing on, 21, 23, 184 (n. 46); former slaves' resistance to working on, 21–23, 32, 34; hookworm on, 150, 151; medical care provided on, 25, 31, 35
Planters: amelioration laws on slave treatment by, 19; bankruptcies among, 27; former slaves criticized by, 25; land shortages created by, 22; reports on slave populations from, 18; on results of emancipation, 25, 27; treatment of pregnant slaves by, 19, 20
Poor Law Commission (1874–75), 57
Poor laws, 62–63
Population counts. See Censuses
Population growth: commonalities in approaches to crisis in, 1–2, 4–7; concerns about declines in, in 1920s, 127–33; disease as barrier to, 126, 129,

34; as plantation residents, 21, 23, 184 (n. 46); plantation work by, resistance to, 21–23, 32, 34; population declines blamed on, 37–38; as settlers, 131; as smallholders, 22–23; white views on laziness of, 25, 28. *See also* Black(s)

Social class: biases regarding, in approaches to population health, 42–43; of home visitors, 110, 111; of nurses, 95–98; in philanthropic organizations, 119; in respectability, 79, 94, 111; and skin color, link between, 78; of trained midwives, 79, 88. *See also* Elites; Middle class

Social mobility, for nonwhites, 122

Society for the Promotion of Social Purity, 60

Society for the Protection of Children, 114

Society of Medical Officers of Health, 134

South Asians: hookworm and, 151; immigration of to British Caribbean, 6, 44, 129–31; infant mortality among, 50, 51; literacy rates of, 88, 203 (n. 115); marriage among, 56–57; milk production by, 50, 51–52; as percentage of population in Guyana, 6; use and meaning of term, 178 (n. 2)

South Asian women: as health visitors, 211 (n. 121); immigration by, 56–57, 195 (n. 106); maternity wards used by, 79; as midwives, 79, 89, 200 (n. 59)

Sterilization, compulsory, 166–68

Sturge, Joseph, 20, 24, 183 (n. 28)

Subsidies, for trained midwives, 81, 82, 106, 209 (n. 77)

Sugar production, 43–52; economic significance of, 127–28; after emancipation, decline of, 27, 44; fall of sugar prices and duties, 27, 43, 191 (n. 15); vs. food production, 44, 184 (n. 61); immigrant labor in, 44; labor shortage in, 44–46, 128; migration of workers in, 44–45

Swettenham, James, 40, 52, 53, 61, 194 (n. 73)

Syphilis, 139–41; and infant mortality, 54, 140, 144; treatment of, 140–41

Taxes: on land, 32; medical, 34–36; poor relief funded by, 62

Tourism, in Jamaica, 132

Trinidad and Tobago: censuses of, 46–47; employment for women in, 211 (n. 122); English nurses in, 97, 101–2; former slaves as smallholders in, 22, 23; forms of government in, 18; home visitors in, 107, 112, 209 (n. 83); hookworm in, 150–51; immigration of neighboring islanders to, 45; infant mortality in, 51, 129, 194 (n. 79), 196 (n. 131); land availability in, 22; maternal education in, 103, 107, 112; in medical conference of 1921, 154; philanthropic organizations in, 114, 115, 211 (n. 127), 212 (n. 131); population in 1891, vs. Barbados, 6; protests of 1930s in, 160; slave population in, 18; South Asian immigrants in, 6, 44, 200 (n. 59); South Asian midwives in, 79, 200 (n. 59); sugar production in, 43; UNIA in, 123; venereal diseases in, 143; voting rights in, 3

Tropical climates: Europeans on unhealthiness of, 10; whites' ability to cope with, 48, 192 (n. 46)

Tropical diseases. *See* Disease(s)

Tropical medicine: in civilizing mission, 10; education about diseases in, 134–35; emergence of, 10, 42; in empire-building, 10, 42, 180 (n. 29); institutionalization of, 42. *See also* Disease(s)

Tuberculosis, 107, 156

UNIA. *See* Universal Negro Improvement Association

United Home Industries and Self-Help Association, 114

United States: immigration from British Caribbean to, 45; public health